Human Rights of Persons with Disabilities: Laws and Policies

Human Rights of Persons with Disabilities: Laws and Policies

Edited by Louis Harrison

CLANRYE INTERNATIONAL
www.clanryeinternational.com

Clanrye International,
750 Third Avenue, 9th Floor,
New York, NY 10017, USA

ISBN: 978-1-64726-674-5

Cataloging-in-Publication Data

Human rights of persons with disabilities : laws and policies / edited by Louis Harrison.
p. cm.
Includes bibliographical references and index.
ISBN 978-1-64726-674-5
1. People with disabilities--Legal status, laws, etc. 2. Human rights. 3. People with disabilities--Government policy.
4. People with disabilities--Civil rights. I. Harrison, Louis.
K637 .H86 2023
342.087--dc23

For information on all Clanrye International publications visit our website at www.clanryeinternational.com

CLANRYE INTERNATIONAL

Contents

Preface

Every book is a source of knowledge and this one is no exception. The idea that led to the conceptualization of this book was the fact that the world is advancing rapidly; which makes it crucial to document the progress in every field. I am aware that a lot of data is already available, yet, there is a lot more to learn. Hence, I accepted the responsibility of editing this book and contributing my knowledge to the community.

Persons with disability include those people who have long-term physical, mental, intellectual or sensory impairments. Social and environmental barriers along with the disabilities in such persons may impede their participation in the society. A disabled person's inability to access any public place or institution can be considered as the society's inability to ensure the well-being and progress for all the people of the society, including the disabled. These people constitute a sizable portion of the world population but they remain a vulnerable and marginalized section of the society. They encounter human rights abuses such as stigma and discrimination, isolation, lack of access to education, health and employment opportunities, and institutionalization. Laws and policies with respect to disability human rights seek to protect and promote the rights of persons with disability. It aims to adopt and implement policies, laws and programs that remove barriers and ensure that the disabled are able to exercise their civil, cultural, economic, political and social rights. This book outlines the human rights laws and policies with respect to disabled people in detail. It will prove to be immensely beneficial to students and researchers in this field.

While editing this book, I had multiple visions for it. Then I finally narrowed down to make every chapter a sole standing text explaining a particular topic, so that they can be used independently. However, the umbrella subject sinews them into a common theme. This makes the book a unique platform of knowledge.

I would like to give the major credit of this book to the experts from every corner of the world, who took the time to share their expertise with us. Also, I owe the completion of this book to the never-ending support of my family, who supported me throughout the project.

Editor

1

From Disability Rights to the Rights of the Dying (and Back Again)

Harold Braswell

Albert Gnaegi Center for Health Care Ethics, Saint Louis University, St. Louis, MO 63104, USA; harold.braswell@slu.edu

Abstract: This article argues for civil rights for dying people. The creation of such rights should be understood as complementary to, but distinct from, existing initiatives to provide dying people with social benefits. A basis for rights for terminally ill people can be found in the disability rights movement. Through an ethnographic case study of two dying individuals, I argue that terminally ill people can be subjected to disability discrimination as it is understood within the dominant theoretical framework of disability rights: the social model of disability. Nevertheless, while disability rights provides a theoretical basis for understanding discrimination against people who are dying, existing U.S. disability rights legislation largely does not recognize, nor address this discrimination. For this reason, it is necessary to develop a separate set of rights of the dying. I conclude by arguing that such "dying rights" are a logical extension of disability rights, and will bring ancillary benefits to both disabled people and the disability rights movement itself. There is thus a strong foundation for a legal and political alliance between disability rights advocates and advocates for people who are dying.

Keywords: disability rights; terminal illness; death and dying; ethnography; civil rights; bioethics; physician-assisted suicide

---

1. Introduction

This article argues for civil rights for dying people. By "dying people", I mean people who have been given a medical prognosis of six months or less to live. Though contestable, this definition is standard in the health policy and law of the United States, the country in which my argument is set (Lynn et al. 1996). This argument builds on Bruce Jennings' recent call for a "public" approach to end-of-life care (Jennings 2013, p. 272). Such an approach would not understand "inadequate" care as an issue that is primarily "personal" or "familial." It would be considered a product of a "failing civic system of health care and communal provision" (Jennings 2013, p. 273). Ameliorating it requires the development of what Jennings calls "civic palliative care". Such care creates "a social and cultural lifeworld" for terminally ill people (Jennings 2013, p. 275). This "public" framing is, according to Jennings, better suited to identify the resources needed by the dying, and to articulate ethical justifications for their provision.

The present article extends Jennings' vision. In it, I argue that law can play a central role in the development of such "public" end-of-life care. It can do so through the articulation of civil rights for the dying. Such rights would understand "terminally ill" people to be a protected class that can be subjected to discrimination. These rights would also enjoin the state to provide dying people with resources, not based on welfare, but because they are entitled to them as citizens. Such rights are not a substitute for the rich communal networks that Jennings prescribes. However, they can provide an essential context for such networks to exist. Indeed, the lack of such rights can, I argue, be a central cause of "inadequacies" of the sort that Jennings identifies.

I make this argument through a study of end-of-life care in the United States. First, I will show how the lack of a civil rights movement has facilitated the creation of a U.S. hospice system that is both underfunded and inadequate in its provision of care. Though a civil rights approach will not be a panacea, it allows for the articulation of stronger claims regarding the obligation of the state to provide resources for dying people. However, though U.S. end-of-life care might suffer for the lack of a civil rights movement for dying people, this in itself is not sufficient grounds to examine whether such a movement should exist. To do so, it is necessary to consider what kind of specific civil rights laws might apply to the dying.

A good model for such laws is, I argue, disability rights. Disability rights, through their basis in the "social model of disability", provide a potential theoretical framework through which we might understand dying people as vulnerable to discrimination. To explore whether this framework can be applied to the dying, I present an ethnographic case study of two patients dying in U.S. hospice care. I argue that both of these patients can, and should, be understood as victims of discrimination as defined by the social model of disability and, more specifically, well-established disability rights. A disability rights framework thus provides a feasible starting point for the elaboration of a "rights of the dying".

The same cannot be said, however, of most existing U.S. disability rights legislation. Although terminally ill people can be subjected to discrimination, as understood within a "social model", the particular form that this discrimination takes can be very different than discrimination leveled at disabled people. For this reason, existing U.S. disability rights legislation is of limited use in addressing the needs of the dying. I show this through an analysis of the applicability of the Americans with Disabilities Act (ADA) to terminally ill people. The limits of the ADA in addressing discrimination against the dying provides a justification for the creation of a distinct piece of civil rights legislation on their behalf.

I conclude, rather, by arguing that such "rights of the dying" are consonant with the goals of the disability rights movement, and, as such, they should be supported by disability rights advocates. Such support should not solely be based on shared philosophical premises. Though primarily targeted at terminally ill people, rights for the dying will likely have significant ancillary benefits for disabled people. Furthermore, an alliance between disability rights advocates and advocates for the dying will help garner the political capital necessary to advance causes that benefit both dying people and disabled people. In this sense, the rights of the dying represent a more complete realization of the project of disability rights itself.

Though the case studies in this article are set in the U.S., my theoretical framework and, more broadly, the political alliance I recommend would apply across national borders. Before I can articulate the rationale for such an alliance, I must begin by addressing the issue that, more than any other, has halted its emergence: physician-assisted suicide (PAS).

2. Why This Article Is Not about Physician-Assisted Suicide

PAS has dominated interaction between disability rights advocates and advocates for dying people (for recent examples of this interaction see (Davis 2013; Gill 2010; Neumann 2016)). To an extent, this domination is understandable: PAS is an important issue both in general and, specifically, for disabled people, even in a country such as the U.S., where the practice is limited only to the terminally ill. However, it is also unfortunate.

Discussions of the relationship between disability rights advocates and advocates for PAS generally center on the conflict between these two groups. There is a substantial conflict—as has been argued forcefully by scholars such as Carol Gill and Paul Longmore—and it is worth discussing (Gill 1998; Longmore 2005). However, this conflict is not the only way to imagine the relationship between the two constituencies putatively represented by "disability rights" and PAS: the long-term disabled and the terminally ill. As I hope to show here, there are substantial intersections between dying people and disabled people that have nothing to do with PAS. Such intersections represent points of alliance, and productive opportunities to rethink the relationship between these two groups. Yet, such opportunities are lost if the focus is limited to PAS.

PAS would not, in theory, have to be the "focus" of an article exploring the relationship between disability rights and the rights of the dying. However, in practice, it almost certainly would be. In part, this is because the enormous amount of attention the issue has received over the past two decades has likely conditioned readers to ascribe to it an importance that—as Ira Byock has recently argued—it may not deserve (Byock 2012, pp. 272–96). But it is also because, even after these two decades, there are still significant disagreements on whether PAS should be considered a legitimate right at all. These disagreements are worthwhile, and I address them elsewhere (Braswell 2018). But, however one resolves them, it is likely to alienate a substantial group of people who, except for PAS, might agree with the framework for conceptualizing the relationship between terminal illness and disability that I develop here.

This framework is, I believe, of greater importance than the issue of PAS itself. Even if one supports PAS, that does not mean that it should be considered the primary, much less the only, right of the dying. In this respect, advocates for the dying can learn a great deal from advocates for disability rights. There are disability rights advocates who support legalizing PAS (Batavia 1997; Behuniak 2011; Davis 2013). Such advocates argue that PAS is a logical extension of disability rights. They do not argue, however, that PAS could conceivably replace disability rights.

And yet, this is where we are with regard to the "rights of the dying." For (at least) the past two decades, there have been repeated debates about PAS for terminally ill people (Dowbiggin 2007). However, these debates have come prior to the establishment of significant laws to protect the dying from discrimination. There are valid justifications for why PAS might be given greater prominence in discussions of terminal illness than it is in long-term disability: the increased severity of medical conditions, the significantly heightened proximity to death. However, these reasons cannot justify the almost complete opposition between how the issue has been framed in these two populations.

Dying people and disabled people are different. However, they are not opposed in every fashion. They do, as I will show here, have shared interests, and shared enemies. PAS can figure into conversations about such communalities, but it need not do so, and cannot be the primary point of entry. By setting it aside—for the time being—I hope to create an opening for something new. I will now explain why that "something" is necessary in the United States.

3. The Limits of a Social Benefits Approach

In the United States, federal legislation for dying people has generally not taken the form of civil rights. Instead, federal legislation for the dying has generally adhered to a "social benefits" model (on social benefits in the U.S., see (Hacker 2002)). Such benefits are not considered to be legal obligations essential to the freedom of their recipients from discrimination. Rather, they are understood through the lens of charitable beneficence and, in a kind of paradox, efficient economic management. To understand this paradox—and its effect on terminally people—it is necessary to consider the signature piece of federal legislation for people who are dying: the Medicare Hospice Benefit (MHB).

Prior to the Medicare Hospice Benefit, "hospice" in the U.S. was a grassroots movement that lacked a uniform structure outside of its general meaning of "care for the dying" (Paradis and Cummings 1986). The very meaning of "hospice" varied from state to state, even hospice to hospice, as did the kinds of care that would be included under the "hospice" label. This decentralized structure was itself a product of the lack of any standardized reimbursement mechanism for hospice services. Different hospices had to work within different reimbursement mechanisms, and these mechanisms influenced their own local conception of hospice care (Hoyer 1998; Paradis and Cummings 1986). It is thus debatable whether there was a uniform U.S. definition of hospice prior to the MHB's passage in 1982.

The MHB changed this situation by providing a reimbursement mechanism at the federal level. This reimbursement mechanism would pay for hospice. However, it would also define the very meaning of "hospice" itself. To receive Medicare reimbursement, hospices would have to comply with Medicare regulations. These regulations would require them to change their conceptions of care, in some ways dramatically (as I will explain further below). Thus, by creating a federal reimbursement structure, the MHB created a uniform national definition of "hospice". Decisions about what would be included—or excluded—from this definition were shaped by the priorities of the congressional legislators who supported the benefit. These legislators were motivated by two principal justifications: one clinical, one economic.

Clinically, there was a growing recognition of the inappropriate and even harmful nature of much U.S. care for the dying (Abel 2013, 2017). Dying Americans were either treated as if they were curable, in hospitals; or they were treated as if they were chronically disabled, and sent to nursing homes. Neither institution was appropriate to their needs.

This clinical justification was accompanied by an economic one. Hospital and nursing home care of the dying were extremely expensive. The government carried much of the cost of this care through Medicare and Medicaid. U.S. hospice leaders argued that hospice would reduce the cost of care relative to these other treatment modalities. These claims were, to a degree, confirmed by a number of studies (Kidder 1992; Mor and Kidder 1985). It thus seemed that funding hospice would both save the government money and provide the dying with better care.

In theory, it is possible such an arrangement could work. However, it does pose a potential conflict: at what point does the need to save money endanger the proposed clinical benefits? There is strong evidence that, at the time of the MHB's passage, U.S. hospice leaders were aware of such a possibility, and indeed believed that it was inherent to the MHB itself. As Emily Abel has found, U.S. hospice leaders at the time believed the MHB's reimbursement rate to be "far too low" (Abel 2017, p. 126). The result would set up a structure in which individual hospices would have to choose between providing appropriate care, from a clinical perspective, and remaining financially solvent, not to mention profitable. There is ample evidence that this conflict between cost and care remains present—and has even worsened—in hospice today (Halabi 2014; Perry and Stone 2011).

This conflict shaped not only how much the Benefit paid for its services; it also influenced what services were included in it at all. The Medicare Hospice Benefit does not include comprehensive long-term care. Such long-term care includes assistance with activities of daily living, such as feeding, clothing, and basic hygiene. As long-term care is expensive (Institute of Medicine 2014, p. 296), this lack of long-term care coverage significantly reduced the benefit's cost on the government. However, it created a clinical gap: terminally ill patients are highly disabled and, as such, have significant long-term health needs.

This raises a question: who provides dying Americans with long-term care? The U.S. hospice system is designed for such care to be provided by the patient's primary caregiver, a person who, in hospice literature, is frequently considered to be a member of their "family" (a term that in this case does not require biological relation) (Rabow et al. 2004). Such familial caregivers are not reimbursed, by Medicare, for their services. As such, the Medicare Hospice Benefit, while providing some support for the dying, itself gives a significant amount of the burden of end-of-life care to the family (Institute of Medicine 2014, p. 297). This dependence on the family is largely a result of the Benefit's cost-savings function. However, it creates clinical problems for the dying.

Dying patients have extremely significant medical conditions, indeed, arguably the most significant medical conditions imaginable. However, the MHB's structure is premised on care being provided to these individuals by family members who often lack basic knowledge in medication management (Institute of Medicine 2014, p. 311). In addition, a number of sociological factors—lowering birth rates, rising divorce—have made it so that many Americans do not have family members available to care for them (Levitsky 2014). Even when a person does have family, the lack of paid familial leave in the U.S. makes it extremely difficult for family members to obtain leave from work sufficiently to care for their kin (Levitsky 2014, p. 26). Even when a person has the financial resources to provide care, there are other barriers, including caregiver disabilities, interpersonal conflict, and negative "neighborhood effects" that can impede family caregivers from providing appropriate care (Levitsky 2014; Sampson 2012). The result is a significant gap between the abilities of caregivers and the requirements of the MHB. This gap can lead dying patients, in the home context, to suffer significant neglect, and even abuse, and, more generally, can lead to dramatic instability in care delivery (Institute of Medicine 2014, p. 281).

When a suitable familial caregiver is not available, dying individuals are generally sent to nursing homes. Nursing homes are institutions that provide long-term care. They do so, in general, for a population that is long-term disabled. However, they also provide long-term care to dying patients who cannot remain at home. Such patients continue to receive hospice, which is provided on an outpatient basis. But though, under Medicare rules, hospice patients cannot receive "skilled" nursing care—complex medical interventions designed for disabled people—they may be housed in facilities that provide it. These facilities have a financial incentive to "skill" patients, and they may also believe it to be clinically necessary, since dying people can benefit from skilled care. However, because of the way the MHB is structured, providing them with such care requires removing them from hospice. The result generates an inherent tension between hospice and nursing home providers that can lead to the unnecessary discharge of dying patients from hospice (Aragon et al. 2012; Institute of Medicine 2014, p. 297). Finally, the high rate of turnover in nursing home staff itself presents a barrier to care in general and the delivery of hospice in particular (Stevenson and Bramson 2009). As a result, there are significant—and perhaps systemic—difficulties in coordinating hospice and nursing home care (Aragon et al. 2012).

The lack of long-term care in the Medicare Hospice Benefit thus creates a barrier to the delivery of care both at home and in the nursing home context. At the time the MHB was passed, hospice advocates knew about this problem and testified to Congress on the need for significantly more inpatient, long-term end-of-life care (The Connecticut Hospice 1982). Their protests went unheeded then and the problem has arguably gotten worse over the following 30 years.

The conflict between the MHB's economic rationale and its clinical one has significantly hampered the efficiency of hospice care. This inefficiency has been noted by the recent Institute of Medicine report on the state of U.S. end-of-life care, which recommends that a "major reorientation of Medicare and Medicaid is needed ... to address the central needs of nearly all Americans nearing the end-of-life" (Institute of Medicine 2014, p. 266). Given the cost of such reorientation, it is unlikely to happen in a legislative context that remains focused on reducing the cost of government expenditures in general and, more particularly, at the end-of-life (often exaggerating the cost of end-of-life care in the process) (Aldridge and Kelley 2015). Ameliorating this problem requires finding a new way to approach the care of the dying that is not predicated on a tradeoff between clinical care and cost-savings. Such an approach can be found in civil rights.

4. The Benefits of a Civil Rights Approach

Discussing the disability rights movement, Andrew Batavia and Kay Schriner articulate the benefits of taking a "civil rights" approach to improving the well-being of disabled people:

> [C]ivil rights laws have not been subject to the strict budgetary and regulatory restraints of other types of legislation for people with disabilities. There is a recognition that, because civil rights are fundamental to justice, once they are recognized they must be provided largely irrespective of cost. Congress and the implementing agencies may determine and impose the most cost-effective means of ensuring the right, but cannot deny the right due exclusively to the costs (Batavia and Schriner 2001, p. 696).

A civil rights model thus provides a different framework for understanding government expenditures than a social benefits approach. Within hospice, essential services were arguably denied, to a great extent, solely on the grounds of cost. Reframing the provision of such services as a right would obviate this argument.

It is important not to overstate the importance of this contrast: as the history of the ADA shows, civil rights can be significantly curbed, if not outright denied, on the basis of costs (Krieger 2003). Additionally, a civil rights approach can be limiting in manners that a social benefits approach is not; indeed, many current disability advocates are now arguing in favor of adopting social benefits approaches much like the MHB (Bagenstos 2009, pp. 131–50; Schriner and Scotch 2003, pp. 183–84). My argument here is not that a civil rights approach to the dying is inherently superior to a social benefits approach. However, it does open up new ways of recognizing and remedying the significant problems facing the dying in America.

Writing about civil rights for the elderly, Nina Kohn has eloquently expressed the power of reframing as rights issues that were previously largely discussed in terms of charity or social benefits:

> [A] focus on rights is of significant value where the rights in question have not yet been recognized as such. In the context of elder rights, there has yet to emerge any meaningful, broad-based political agitation, and none is likely to emerge unless these political actors are aware of these problems and consider them to be important ones. By labeling and describing these problems as ones that threaten rights, and especially ones that threaten constitutional rights, a rights-based approach can both bring needed attention to them and elevate their perceived importance. As such, it is not an alternative to a political strategy, but potentially a prerequisite for one (Kohn 2010, p. 76).

The same is true of rights for the dying, a group that, like the elderly, has not generally had their concerns (aside from physician-assisted suicide) framed in legal or even political terms. Through such a reframing, the "rights of the dying" will provide additional leverage to resolve some of the major problems that we already know exist in U.S. end-of-life care, and perhaps an additional ability to identify some problems that are, for now, not even recognized at all.

But beyond even its instrumental value with regard to particular issues, a rights-based reframing can create a powerful political network that extends from dying individuals to those that care about them throughout American society. The creation of such a network can be valuable in itself, cultivating what Jennings, in his essay on civic palliative care, refers to as "solidarity", which is based in the "discernment of connections among human beings that are obscured by structures of wealth, power, and privilege" (Jennings 2013, p. 280). Such solidarity can be a source of immense comfort, particularly in cases where individuals experience extreme isolation, as is, unfortunately, the case with a significant portion of the dying.

While intrinsically valuable, solidarity can in turn also have instrumental value beyond the ambit of rights. Networks of solidarity created, in part, by civil rights can be mobilized in the service of organizing for more social benefits, even if those benefits themselves do not depend on civil rights. In this sense, while it is important to recognize the limits of rights in general, and anti-discrimination law in particular, rights have immense power both within the law and beyond it. A civil rights approach to the dying will not solve all our problems. However, when joined with the existing social benefits approach, it will provide a much more promising starting place.

But however useful a civil rights approach might be, it cannot solely be justified by the inefficiencies in U.S. hospice care delivery that I have outlined above. Such inefficiencies need to be reframed and identified as violations of fundamental rights. Here we come to a problem: how can we identify that the rights of the dying are being violated if there has not yet been a movement to establish such rights?

It is here that the disability rights movement can be of such help. Terminally ill people are highly disabled (Lunney et al. 2003). As such, they may be subject to disability rights. However, that is not necessarily the case. To establish whether or not a particular population might be protected under disability rights, it is not enough to show that they are disabled. It is necessary to demonstrate that they experience disability discrimination. And it is not necessarily true that terminally ill individuals experience such discrimination. Indeed, the assumption of disability rights advocates, in discussing terminally ill people, has often been that they do not.

This assumption has underpinned both opposition to and support for physician-assisted suicide among the disability rights community. Disability rights opponents of PAS have worried that legalizing the practice will lead to the conflation of terminal illness and disability (Heyer 2011). Disability rights supporters of PAS have supported it, in part, on the grounds that terminally ill people have more significant medical conditions, which create a stronger argument for making PAS available to them (Batavia 1997; Davis 2013). Though some disability rights commentators have identified instances of disability discrimination against terminally ill people (Gill 2010), there has not been a sustained scholarly argument to that effect, nor any argument that extends beyond the highly limited context of the PAS.

Prior to any attempt to apply existing disability rights law to terminally ill people, it is first necessary to examine whether terminally ill people can be subjected to disability discrimination. I will now consider this question via an analysis of the situation of two terminally ill individuals who I studied as part of a larger ethnography of U.S. hospice care. I will refer to them as "Simon" and "Mary", and, in the interest of de-identification, I have changed several details of their identities.

5. Simon and Mary

Simon had lived the last twenty years of his life in California, largely by himself. However, when he was diagnosed with lung cancer, he realized that he would need help. So he moved: first to Florida to be with his ex-wife, then to Atlanta, Georgia to live with his brother. Simon began hospice service while at his brother's house, and at first it went well. But then his brother got a job as a flight attendant that required him to be out of town for long stretches of time. As a result, Simon was left home alone. Though he continued to receive hospice care, he spent most of his time unaccompanied.

In these circumstances, Simon became extremely isolated. He was too debilitated to drive, and his sprawling Atlanta suburb lacked access to public transportation, and was not readily walkable. His hospice providers came regularly, but still he dealt with untreated pain. His brother's house was inaccessible, and he fell several times. Due to these factors, he became depressed. He began sleeping for as much as twelve hours at a time, and stopped eating. This depression was in part caused by a general feeling that he described as "uselessness", and of being a burden on his already struggling brother.

Simon did not want to go to a nursing home. Having been in nursing homes before, he preferred to stay in his brother's house, even with the adverse and potentially life-threatening consequences. Ultimately, an alternative presented itself: Simon was able to move to a charitable Catholic facility that was up to his standards. In this home, he achieved a higher degree of social integration than had been available to him in his brother's house. His depression lifted and he outlived his prognosis by several months. However, this "solution" to Simon's isolation at home did not come from within the US hospice system. It came from escaping it.

Mary Bonner, in contrast to Simon, did pursue the "solution" that would have been available to Simon had he stayed within hospice. She was eighty-two years old, and had been admitted to hospice with Parkinson's disease and advanced dementia. This combination of dementia with Parkinson's had made it impossible for her husband—who was also in his early eighties—to care for her. As a result, she had been placed in an Atlanta-area nursing home that I will refer to as "Sunny Day Nursing Home".

Though living in Sunny Day, Mary had family members that, though unable to care for her personally, were very supportive. The home was only five miles from her house, and her husband would visit her almost every evening. She also had several grandchildren living in the area, who would visit her two or three times a month. Most importantly, Mary had her son, who lived nearby, and who visited her several times a week. During these visits, Mary's son not only kept Mary company—serving as an invaluable connection between her life inside the nursing home and her life outside of it—but also advocated for her with both hospice and nursing home staff. Nevertheless, even this advocacy was insufficient to assure Mary the delivery of either adequate long-term or end-of-life care.

Mary encountered repeated difficulties in receiving not only her pain medication, but also her dementia care. Over the coming weeks, the nursing home staff failed several times to provide her with her medications at regularly scheduled hours. This failure persisted despite the presence of Mary's son as a strong patient advocate. However, he was in a hard position. He had to hunt down nursing home personnel who seemed to change every other day, and who—even when consistent—were so busy that they did not have time to talk; at the same time, he had to talk by phone with hospice personnel who only visited his mother at Sunny Day around twice a week. The result was a process at once exhausting and futile. Mary endured untreated pain, and her son's final months with his mother were lost in bureaucracy.

While Mary was at Sunny Day, the nursing home had an outbreak of pneumonia. As a result of this outbreak, Mary became sick, as did several other patients in the home. Though she recovered from the pneumonia, the experience was traumatizing for both her and her son. In addition, she fell several times at the home. Though these falls only bruised her, these bruises were painful and—when coupled with her dementia and the nursing home's lack of skill with pain medication—they left Mary in a state of both pain and persistent confusion. In addition to this, she endured inadvertent, and likely unintentional, abuse from nursing home staff, who bruised her arms repeatedly while moving her. These questions of inadequate and abusive treatment were not resolved prior to Mary's eventual death.

Having the presented the cases of Simon and Mary, I will now analyze the extent to which they might justify a "disability rights" approach to terminal illness.

6. The Applicability of a "Disability Rights" Approach to the Terminally Ill

As I described above, the fundamental theoretical question, in determining whether a disability rights approach might be applied to terminally ill people, is whether or not terminally ill individuals experience disability discrimination. Such discrimination would be understood through the lens of the "social model" of disability. The social model of disability is best understood in contrast to what is referred to, in disability studies, as the "medical model" of disability (Shakespeare 2013). The social model and the medical model are distinct ways of understanding existing inequalities between disabled and non-disabled people. The medical model attributes these inequalities largely to the biological nature of disability; it argues that disability is an inherently negative condition, and that this negativity in large part accounts for the limited access that disabled people have to shared social resources. The social model, in contrast, argues that the negative aspects of disability are not, in general, inherent to its biology. They are products of a discriminatory society. This discrimination, not disability itself, is the reason for existing inequalities between disabled and non-disabled people and, moreover, for much of the suffering experienced by disabled people in general. The social model of disability thus reframes disabled people as a political group that can be—and frequently is—subject to discrimination.

From the perspective of the social model of disability, Simon and Mary both experienced disability discrimination. To be sure, both had extremely significant and limiting medical conditions. Simon's cancer was painful, and it limited his mobility significantly; Mary's Parkinson's and dementia were similarly limiting. But both individuals, in addition to these medical limitations, experienced significant social limitations as well. These social limitations are significant enough to justify a formulation of what might be called a "social model of terminal illness".

Simon was living in a house that was extremely inaccessible, and had in fact become physically, mentally, and emotionally dangerous to his well-being. This house, in turn, formed part of a local community that was itself largely inaccessible. As a result, he was effectively trapped within it. The result was physical injury, and an environmentally induced depression that significantly shortened his life expectancy. Very little of this situation can be described as "inherent" to his terminal illness. Social isolation is not a medical condition, and many of Simon's "medical" problems can in fact be attributed to a hospice system that repeatedly failed to provide him with appropriate medical and long-term care. The result was the effective segregation of him within his home.

Simon's alternative to such home-based segregation was Mary's fate: segregation within an institution. Mary was living in—and died within—a nursing home. Such nursing homes have long been considered segregationist institutions from a disability rights perspective (Johnson 2003). If such a perspective can be applied to disabled people, it can also be applied to people who are terminally ill. Indeed, the argument against nursing homes, from the perspective of the dying, is arguably stronger. Nursing homes, however segregationist, are institutions designed for disabled people. They are not institutions for dying people. Dying individuals require significantly more medical care than would be provided in an "unskilled" nursing home, and significantly different care than would be provided in a "skilled" facility. Indeed, Mary's nursing home lacked the means to provide her with appropriate pain medication, dementia care, or even basic long-term care. Its workers were largely untrained in caring for a patient as sick as her, resulting in routine injuries and service failures. The result was a denial of care that significantly worsened her condition in a manner that was not "inherent" to her medical trajectory.

Thus, for both Simon and Mary, the only options available to them in the U.S. hospice system were segregated. This segregation occurred informally, in the home context, in the case of Simon. It occurred formally in Mary's placement in a nursing home. In both cases, neither individual had the basic resources to be integrated into society. This lack of integration, in turn, was both a product of, and a cause of, the harms that they suffered in each site. Though some of these harms might be attributable to their terminal diseases, a significant portion of them were due to the current arrangement of U.S. hospice care: specifically, in these cases, to the lack of long-term care in hospice.

In the preceding section of this article, I argued that this lack of long-term care is attributable, in part, to the lack of civil rights for dying people in America. The Medicare Hospice Benefit's character as social welfare, not civil rights, led to a conflict between clinical care and cost efficiency. This conflict led to the exclusion, from the very definition of "hospice", of features that U.S. hospice leaders deemed—and continue to deem—essential, such as long-term care. This section builds on that argument: the MHB's lack of long-term care was not only a creation of the lack of "rights" for the dying; it creates a situation—in the cases of Simon and Mary—where the dying can be housed in segregated environments that deprive them of what are, and should be considered, disability rights.

Ruth Colker's recent book *When is Separate Unequal?* provides a window into the extent of this problem. Colker argues that, at times, segregated institutions for disabled people may be justified from a disability rights perspective, as more integrated institutions may overlook the needs of those who are most disabled (Colker 2008). I am sympathetic to this argument. Indeed, to a degree, Simon's case might illustrate it. Simon was living in the "integrated" environment of the home. However, this home environment was so inadequate to his needs that it effectively resulted in his implicit segregation and neglect.

Compared to this home environment, the Catholic charitable facility that he spent his final months in was superior. Indeed, I would argue that this facility, though "segregated" in that it was designed for terminally ill people, was less segregated than Simon's home. The stability that he enjoyed there allowed him to have routine visitors, and arguably more fulfilling contact with these visitors than had previously been possible to him in his desperate situation. This is not to say that, even in Simon's case, such a separate facility should necessarily have been the first option. Better long-term care, better fall prevention: these are interventions that might have made it possible for Simon to remain at home.

My point here, rather, is that, in the U.S. hospice system, both the "segregated" and the "integrated" options available to Simon were effectively the same. It is thus telling that the only escape from such segregation, for Simon, was by leaving the hospice system altogether. The nursing home where Simon would have otherwise ended up would not likely have been a "separate but equal" facility for dying people. Indeed, the housing of dying people in nursing homes, if anything, illustrates Colker's critique of integration. By integrating dying people within a larger long-term disabled population, their needs are subsumed.

The problem is that no such "separate but equal" institutions for dying people exist in the U.S. hospice system. There are isolated examples of them in U.S. society: homes run by religious charities, the "hospice home" movement (Wyatt 2015). But these examples are not systemic, and they in general operate through either private pay or charitable donations. The institutions that do exist within the U.S. hospice system are short-term: generally only for respite care or for patients with a few days to live. In addition, they are growing fewer and fewer, with only one in five U.S. hospices having such a facility (National Hospice and Palliative Care Organization 2012).

Thus, in both Simon and Mary's cases, there is evidence of disability discrimination against terminally ill people. Such discrimination is, in some ways, different than the disability discrimination experienced by long-term disabled people. Mary and Simon had more significant medical conditions than most long-term disabled individuals, and the resources they needed might be different than those that would be supplied under a standard "disability rights" framework. However, this difference is one of degree. It is possible to understand the state of terminally ill individuals from a disability rights perspective.

This raises another question: while, in theory, a disability rights framework can be applied to terminally ill people, how well might existing disability rights legislation work to provide them with civil rights? I will now examine this question, in the American context, by looking at the Americans with Disabilities Act.

7. The ADA and Dying People

The ADA is the landmark piece of civil rights legislation for disabled people in the United States. The Act identifies disabled people as victims of discrimination who needed specific state protection. To this extent, it was modeled on earlier civil rights legislation, particularly the Civil Rights Act of 1964 (Colker 2005, p. 17). However, the ADA goes beyond this legislation by postulating a state obligation to not only remove barriers to access, but also to provide the goods and services necessary for access to be achieved (though the extent of this divergence between the ADA and earlier civil rights legislation is debated) (Bagenstos 2009, pp. 10, 55–75). Though cost was a justification for the ADA—and certainly one that has figured prominently in the Act's interpretation—it was not the primary justification, and the Act has been at times interpreted in ways that establish a state obligation to go beyond what is strictly cost-effective (Batavia and Schriner 2001).

Similarly, though the Act provides benefits to disabled people, such benefits are not justified in terms of welfare or charity. In fact, the ADA is an explicit rejection of such charitable and welfarist models of disability (Scotch 2001). Rather, the justification of the ADA is the freedom of disabled people from discrimination. Though this justification has been limited by both concerns of cost, as well as those of what constitutes appropriate care, the ADA's fundamental basis in freedom makes such limitations legible and identifiable in a way that would not otherwise be possible (Batavia and Schriner 2001).

This freedom is interpreted, in the ADA, through the lens of the Act's three main titles. Title I establishes a right to "reasonable accommodation" in employment for disabled people (Americans with Disabilities Act 1991). This right is not proactive—employers do not have to design their businesses according to a model of universal design—but rather reactive, to be reinforced retroactively in response to successful litigation on behalf of disabled plaintiffs. In general, such litigation has not fared well (Colker 2005). The 2008 ADA Amendments Act was largely designed to create a statutory basis to reverse this trend, and it has had some success in doing so (Befort 2013).

Title II prohibits discrimination against disabled people by any entity receiving federal financial assistance. This title can be used to ensure that disabled people have equal access "nearly any program or activity conducted by a public entity ranging from higher education to prisons to public health care" (Colker 2005, p. 20). Indeed, as disabled people utilize such services in a disproportionately higher amount than the general population, they have benefited greatly from this part of the Act (Colker 2005, p. 126). A particularly significant court ruling regarding this title is *Olmstead v. L.C.*, 527 U.S. 581 (1999), which found that "unjustified isolation is discrimination on the basis of disability under ADA Title II" (Colker 2005, p. 127). *Olmstead* established a precedent for justifying the removal of disabled people from segregated institutions and their integration into appropriate community settings.

Title III prohibits discrimination against disabled people in places of public accommodation. Such discrimination includes "outright exclusion, discriminatory policies and eligibility criteria, as well as broad physical barriers that impede accessibility" (Colker 2005, p. 21). The title's coverage is "broad", including entities that individuals visit on a frequent basis to enhance the quality of their lives, such as restaurants, hotels, and places of amusement and recreation (Colker 2005, p. 21). Though this Title has had a positive effect, particularly with the construction of new facilities, its effectiveness has been significantly limited by its only allowing plaintiffs injunctive relief, not monetary damages (Bagenstos 2009; Colker 2005).

These three titles make up the core of the ADA. This core has been (in general) expanded on by the ADA Amendments Act of 2008, which attempts to broaden the Act's definition of disability, with specific reference to the range of people who can qualify for reasonable accommodation in the workplace (Emens 2012). The UN Convention on the Rights of Persons with Disabilities (UNCRPD) is even more ambitious, but it has not been adopted in the U.S., though sections of it may be incorporated into future disability rights legislation (Harpur 2012).

Having outlined the basic framework of the ADA, I will now examine how this framework might apply to dying people.

8. The Relevance of the ADA to Dying People

As I argued above, there is little question that dying people would qualify as disabled under the ADA. The problem, however, is that while they would qualify under the ADA, the Act's key provisions have not in general been applied to them and in many cases cannot be applied to them.

This is particularly the case with Title I. Title I pertains only to employment. Though in theory dying people could experience employment discrimination, in practice that would be almost impossible to prove. The reasoning why is the opposite of why so many ADA cases have failed. The question is not whether dying people are disabled. The reality is that dying people are generally too disabled to work, regardless of any reasonable accommodation. As a result of this, Title I of the ADA would not, in general, apply to them.

Title II of the ADA is more promising. Dying people are extremely dependent on public services. Indeed, the U.S. hospice system is a public one. Medicare pays for 85.5% of hospice care (National Hospice and Palliative Care Organization 2015). Medicaid pays for the majority of nursing home care (Harrington et al. 2015). Beyond that, many dying receive Social Security, veterans benefits, and other forms of governmental assistance. There are thus many potential areas in which dying people may be discriminated against under Title II.

The *Olmstead* decision provides a particularly compelling precedent. Nursing homes have long been decried by the disability rights community as segregationist institutions, a description that *Olmstead*, to a degree, upholds. If the isolation of disabled people in nursing homes can be considered "unjustified", that would seem doubly true for terminally ill people. Nursing homes are at the very least designed for disabled people. They are not facilities for people who are terminally ill. And yet, in the U.S., they are considered the appropriate facilities for when homecare fails. Given both the segregationist bent of nursing homes, as well as their well-documented failures to provide dying people with requisite services, their continued usage might, in certain cases, be considered an abrogation of the rights of the dying as protected under the Title II of the ADA.

There is an opposite problem as well. Some dying individuals may prefer to live in the segregated environment of the nursing home, but may not be allowed entry. Such a preference should be understood in the context of the limited options available to them in U.S. society. As I have argued above, the lack of long-term care within the U.S. hospice system can make the home into an environment that is every bit as dangerous—and isolating—as the nursing home. Additionally, many dying individuals do not want to "burden" their families. The result can be that, in some cases, dying individuals might prefer to receive care in the nursing home, however "segregated". *Olmstead* would be of limited usage in such cases, as it does not create a mandate for "segregation", even if that is the individual's preference (Chambers 2009).

Title III of the ADA forces places of public accommodation to make themselves accessible. This could be immensely helpful to the dying. Due to the U.S. hospice system's basis in the home environment, terminally ill individuals depend on access to many of the kinds of businesses covered under the title. Ensuring the accessibility of these locations would be of great service to terminally ill people. The problem is that the impact of Title III has been significantly limited by its enforcement scheme. As I noted above, this scheme only allows for injunctive relief—not monetary reward—and has thus strongly disincentivized plaintiffs from seeking legal recourse (Colker 2005, p. 166). But even with a monetary reward, it would be extremely difficult for dying people to bring lawsuits due to their significant physical limitations and shortened lifespans.

Indeed, the very nature of ADA litigation arguably precludes dying people from benefitting under it. In the ADA, individuals must bring lawsuits retroactively, after a putative violation has occurred. Such an approach works against the dying. Dying individuals may themselves be too sick to pursue such lawsuits, and they are likely to die before their consummation. However, though this is to a degree true, it does not have to be an absolute barrier to reward under the ADA. A cause lawyering approach—as advocated by Nina Cohn with regard to the civil rights of elderly people—might make it possible to raise and clarify the status of the civil rights of dying people under the ADA (Kohn 2010, p. 75). As I have shown here, there may be cases in which such rights apply. Unfortunately, there will also be many in which they do not, and the retroactive nature of ADA claims will disincentivize much action on behalf of dying people.

Due to the limits of the ADA, it is necessary to develop a separate piece of legislation to protect the rights of dying people.

9. The Need for the Rights of the Dying

The limited applicability of the ADA to the dying can be illustrated by the decision that, above, I argued might be most promising: *Olmstead v. L.C.* Under the ADA, an individual may be moved from a nursing home if a more communally integrated setting exists. The problem for dying people is that, in the U.S., a dying person would not have likely arrived in a nursing home if there were a more communally integrated setting. The U.S. hospice system is based in the home. If a person is in a nursing home, it means that home care options have failed.

This does not make the segregation of the dying in nursing homes any less abominable from a disability rights perspective. However, it does limit the extent to which the ADA can end this segregation. Without an equivalent, but more integrated setting for care available, then *Olmstead* would not apply. Such a setting will not likely be available without dramatically changing the U.S. hospice system to include outpatient long-term care. The ADA has not proven an effective vehicle for extending such long-term care in general (Batavia and Schriner 2001; Bagenstos 2009), and it might be a particularly poor vehicle for doing so on behalf of the dying. Their long-term care needs are likely to be even more costly than those of a long-term disabled person, and courts have typically interpreted the ADA in a manner that takes such cost into account (Colker 2005).

There is other disability rights legislation that is better suited than the ADA to advance the interests of the dying. For example, the Fair Housing Act could be marshaled—in a manner similar to what Eric Carlson has argued—to make it difficult for nursing homes to reject dying patients on account of their medical needs (Carlson 2007); it might also be used to make it more difficult for assisted living facilities to involuntarily discharge dying patients when their medical needs become too extensive (Kohn 2010, p. 54).

Alternatively, recent attempts by disability advocates to legally challenge the institutional bias of Medicaid could be of assistance to dying people (Bagenstos 2009, pp. 145–48). Indeed, this institutional bias is even stronger at the end of life. Dying people do not just need Medicaid funding for personal assistance services; they may also need to coordinate this funding with Medicare funding for hospice. Such "dual eligibility" is theoretically possible. However, in practice, it generally only applies to Medicaid funding for nursing homes. Recently, in 2016, the State of North Carolina amended their Clinical Coverage Policy 3D to allow concurrent hospice and personal care services to be made available to dual eligible state residents (North Carolina Division of Medical Assistance 2016). Such legislation, if implemented more broadly, would be of tremendous assistance in advancing the civil rights of the dying. However, by itself, it can only be implemented on a state-by-state basis.

As an alternative to the ADA, the Rehabilitation Act of 1973 might provide a better vehicle for advancing the rights of dying people. Unlike the ADA, the Rehabilitation Act focuses on federally funded programs. Specifically, it prohibits discrimination against disabled people by programs that receive federal funding (Chamusco 2017). As such, it applies to both Medicare and Medicaid. The Rehabilitation Act could be used to impose requirements on state Medicaid programs as a condition of the receipt of federal funding. These requirements could be expanded to include a prohibition against discrimination on the basis of terminal illness. If such discrimination were defined to include, for example, access to personal care services, the Rehabilitation Act could provide a means of dramatically expanding access to long-term care amongst dying people in a manner much more efficient than a state-by-state approach.

Such an intervention could be thwarted by the way that courts have interpreted civil rights laws for disabled people. As Leslie Francis and Anita Silvers argue in an article published in this special issue of *Laws*, the courts have interpreted *Alexander v. Choate*—the dominant case regarding the definition of "access" in civil rights legislation for the disabled—in a manner that does not ensure that disabled people receive adequate care (Francis and Silvers 2017). On the contrary, this interpretation has argued that inadequate care in publicly funded programs is non-discriminatory so long as it is universally applied. This interpretation would likely provide a barrier to an argument that the lack of available personal care assistants is discriminatory against the dying, since this lack is relatively widespread. However, it might provide some foundation for a claim of discrimination, in circumstances in which dying people are uniquely hindered from access to such care because they are already receiving the Medicare Hospice Benefit. Regardless, Francis and Silvers have themselves reinterpreted *Alexander v. Choate* in a manner that collapses this access/content distinction and works toward a more robust conception of "meaningful access." Doing so has the potential to authorize significantly broader anti-discrimination legislation for the dying.

Given the difficulty of such an approach, it might be better to begin with the more limited claim that section 1557 of the Affordable Care Act (ACA) include discrimination on the basis of terminal illness. Section 1557 creates a new civil right to health care (Watson 2011). It does so by extending anti-discrimination protection to Medicare, Medicaid, health insurance marketplaces, and the plans offered by insurers that participate in those marketplaces. If Section 1557 was extended to the terminally ill, it might be used to ameliorate discrimination that keeps terminally ill individuals on hospice from access to Medicaid-funded personal assistance services. Alternatively, it could eliminate barriers to hospice access amongst dying people without familial caregivers. As 12% of U.S. hospices do not accept dying people in such circumstances, such discrimination is significant (Aldridge Carlson et al. 2012). Similarly, the same study found that 78% of U.S. hospices had enrollment policies that might restrict care for patients with high-cost medical needs (Aldridge Carlson et al. 2012). Extending Section 1557 protection to dying people might provide a means of combatting such discrimination in access. Even without such an extension, focusing on the end of life can, as the above examples show, highlight other potential forms of discrimination on the basis of factors such as race, gender, and socio-economic status.

Such measures are potentially very important. However, they may not be enough, by themselves, to ameliorate the unjustified segregation of dying Americans in the U.S. hospice system. Such segregation is but one example of the kind of discrimination experienced by the dying. A disability rights framework provides a theoretical foundation for recognizing this discrimination. However, existing disability rights legislation does not provide suitable civil rights grounds for either it recognition, nor its amelioration. It is thus necessary to move beyond the existing legislation to create civil rights legislation for dying people.

It is beyond the scope of this paper to provide a model for such legislation. However, its theoretical framework would be drawn from the ADA: the description of dying as a condition that is not primarily medical but socio-political, the identification of discrimination against terminally ill people, and the move from a "social benefits" approach to rights. More specifically, terminally ill people should be considered entitled to long-standing disability rights, such as the right to the least restrictive environment and the right to self-determination (Dhanda 2006; Mégret 2008; Weber 2004). In both the cases of Simon and Mary, which I describe above, I would argue that such disability rights were violated, even if such a violation could not be (easily) perceived or remedied within the framework of the ADA. In this sense, the rights of dying people should be understood to be consistent with—and an extension of—disability rights. And it is, I believe, in the interests of disability rights advocates to support them.

10. Conclusions

In the section above, I argued that the ADA would be of limited direct utility to dying people. This is true. However, this should not diminish its enormous indirect utility. Indeed, the ADA, as I have also argued, provides an essential theoretical basis for the recognition of the civil rights of terminally ill people. More than that, it is of immense practical benefit to terminally ill people. The creation of a more accessible society, through the ADA's Title II and III, benefits dying patients in home care, and has some potential—through a reinterpretation of *Olmstead*—to give them significantly more autonomy over where they spend their final months of life. Even Title I is of indirect benefit. Most people are disabled before they are dying, and increased employment during that time likely augments both the social and economic capital that they will have available to them when they come to life's end. Even with its limitations, the ADA thus is of significant benefit to dying people.

Similarly, the establishment of civil rights for dying people, while not directly applicable to the long-term disabled, would likely benefit them. Such rights will be different than disability rights. However, they could be different in a way that fills some of the existing gaps in the ADA. For example, most dying people cannot work. This makes ADA Title I not applicable to them. But Title I has been of limited utility in boosting employment amongst disabled people. The Urban Institute has found that high unemployment among disabled people is not primarily due to workplace discrimination. Rather, it can be attributed to other factors, including social isolation, family responsibilities, a lack of transportation, a lack of training, and a fear of the loss of benefits (Loprest and Maag 2001, cited in (Colker 2005, p. 70)). Many of these factors also impact dying people. If crafted appropriately, civil rights legislation for the dying might address them and, by doing so, bring additional help to disabled people.

Such legislation could include, for example, a greater availability of long-term care for dying people. But advocates for the dying could also take what Samuel Bagenstos has termed a more "universalist" approach: establishing a general political right to long-term care or perhaps just palliative care. Indeed, as suggested to me by one of this article's anonymous reviewers, the lack of long-term care in the MHB can itself be considered symptomatic of (and perhaps secondary to) the limits that Medicare places on non-skilled services in general. This is a question of legal and political strategy that is beyond the purview of this article. My point here is that either approach would be beneficial to disabled people: indirectly, the provision of long-term care to the dying could create the grounds for the statutory or legislative expansion of long-term care for disabled people; or directly, a universalist approach would provide coverage to both disabled people and people who are dying.

There are many such areas of overlap: accessible housing, public transportation, access to palliative medicine, the reformulation—and perhaps abolition—of nursing homes, personal attendants, and meal delivery services, to name a few. Progress for dying people in these and other areas will be closely related to, and at times indistinguishable from, progress for disabled people. And, ultimately, such shared progress is more likely to happen if advocates for dying people and disability rights advocates understand their interests as aligned. Such an alliance will expand the political capital of both groups. It will also lead to more sophisticated and creative interplay of how to advance disability and dying rights.

References and Notes

Abel, Emily K. 2013. *The Inevitable Hour: A History of Caring for Dying Patients in America*. Baltimore: JHU Press.

Abel, Emily K. 2017. *Living in Death's Shadow: Family Experiences of Terminal Care and Irreplaceable Loss*. Baltimore: JHU Press.

Aldridge, Melissa D., and Amy S. Kelley. 2015. The Myth Regarding the High Cost of End-of-Life Care. *American Journal of Public Health* 105: 2411–15. [CrossRef] [PubMed]

Aldridge Carlson, Melissa D., Colleen L. Barry, Emily J. Cherlin, Ruth McCorkle, and Elizabeth H. Bradley. 2012. Hospices' enrollment policies may contribute to underuse of hospice care in the United States. *Health Affairs* 31: 2690–98. [CrossRef] [PubMed]

Aragon, Katherine, Kenneth Covinsky, Yinghui Miao, W. John Boscardin, Lynn Flint, and Alexander K. Smith. 2012. Use of the Medicare posthospitalization skilled nursing benefit in the last 6 months of life. *Archives of Internal Medicine* 172: 1573–79. [CrossRef] [PubMed]

Bagenstos, Samuel R. 2009. *Law and the Contradictions of the Disability Rights Movement*. New Haven: Yale University Press.

Batavia, Andrew I. 1997. Disability and physician-assisted suicide. *New England Journal of Medicine* 336: 1671–73. [CrossRef] [PubMed]

Batavia, Andrew I., and Kay Schriner. 2001. The Americans with Disabilities Act as engine of social change: Models of disability and the potential of a civil rights approach. *Policy Studies Journal* 29: 690–702. [CrossRef]

Befort, Stephen F. 2013. An Empirical Examination of Case Outcomes under the ADA Amendments Act. *Washington and Lee Law Review* 70: 2027.

Behuniak, Susan M. 2011. Death with "dignity". *Politics and the Life Sciences* 30: 17–32. [PubMed]

Braswell, Harold. 2018. Putting the "right to die" in its place: Physician-assisted suicide: Disability Rights and Physician-Assisted Suicide in the Context of US End-of-Life Care. *Studies in Law, Politics, and Society*. Forthcoming.

Byock, Ira. 2012. *The Best Care Possible: A Physician's Quest to Transform Care Through the End of Life*. New York: Avery.

Carlson, Eric M. 2007. Disability Discrimination in Long-Term Care: Using the Fair Housing Act to Prevent Illegal Screening in Admissions to Nursing Homes and Assisted Living Facilities. *Notre Dame Journal of Law, Ethics & Public Policy* 21: 363–404.

Chambers, Megan. 2009. Integration as Discrimination against People with Disabilities-Olmstead's Test Shouldn't Work Both Ways. *California Law Review* 46: 177–209.

Chamusco, Binaca G. 2017. Revitalizing the Law That Preceded the Movement: Associational Discrimination and the Rehabilitation Act of 1973. *The University of Chicago Law Review* 84: 1285.

Colker, Ruth. 2005. *The Disability Pendulum: The First Decade of the Americans with Disabilities Act*. New York: NYU Press.

Colker, Ruth. 2008. *When is Separate Unequal? A Disability Perspective*. Cambridge: Cambridge University Press.

Davis, Lennard J. 2013. *The End of Normal*. Ann Arbor: University of Michigan Press.

Dhanda, Amtia. 2006. Legal capacity in the disability rights convention: Stranglehold of the past or lodestar for the future. *Syracuse Journal of International Law and Commerce* 34: 429–62.

Dowbiggin, Ian. 2007. *A Concise History of Euthanasia: Life, Death, God, and Medicine*. Lanham: Rowman & Littlefield.

Emens, Elizabeth F. 2012. Disabling attitudes: US disability law and the ADA amendments act. *The American Journal of Comparative Law* 60: 205–34. [CrossRef]

Francis, Leslie, and Anita Silvers. 2017. Reading Alexander V. Choate Rightly: Now is the Time. *Laws* 6: 17. [CrossRef]

Gill, Carol. 1998. The False Autonomy of Forced Choice: Rationalizing Suicide for Persons with Disabilities. In *Contemporary Perspectives on Rational Suicide*. Edited by James L. Werth. Philadelphia: Taylor & Francis, pp. 171–80.

Gill, Carol. 2010. No, we don't think our doctors are out to get us: Responding to the straw man distortions of disability rights arguments against assisted suicide. *Disability and Health Journal* 3: 31–38. [CrossRef] [PubMed]

Hacker, Jacob S. 2002. *The Divided Welfare State: The Battle over Public and Private Social Benefits in the United States*. Cambridge: Cambridge University Press.

Halabi, Sam. 2014. Selling Hospice. *The Journal of Law, Medicine & Ethics* 42: 442–54.

Harpur, Paul. 2012. Embracing the new disability rights paradigm: The importance of the Convention on the Rights of Persons with Disabilities. *Disability & Society* 27: 1–14.

Harrington, Charlene, Helen Carrillo, and Rachel Garfield. 2015. Nursing Facilities, Staffing, Residents and Facility Deficiencies, 2009 through 2014. Kaiser Family Foundation Report. Available online: http://files.kff.org/attachment/REPORT-Nursing-Facilities-Staffing-Residents-and-Facility-Deficiencies-2009-2015 (accessed on 12 December 2017).

Heyer, Katharina. 2011. Rejecting rights: The disability critique of physician assisted suicide. In *Special Issue Social Movements/Legal Possibilities*. Bingley: Emerald Group Publishing Limited, pp. 77–112.

Hoyer, Thomas. 1998. A history of the Medicare hospice benefit. *Hospice Journal* 13: 61–70. [CrossRef] [PubMed]

Institute of Medicine. 2014. Dying in America: Improving Quality and Honoring Individual Preferences Near the End of Life. Available online: http://www.nationalacademies.org/hmd/Reports/2014/Dying-In-America-Improving-Quality-and-Honoring-Individual-Preferences-Near-the-End-of-Life.aspx (accessed on 1 September 2017).

Jennings, Bruce. 2013. Solidarity, Mortality: The Tolling Bell of Civic Palliative Care. In *Our Changing Journey to the End: Reshaping Death, Dying, and Grief in America [2 volumes]: Reshaping Death, Dying, and Grief in America*. Edited by Christina Staudt and J. Harold Ellens. Westport: Praeger, vol. 2, pp. 271–90.

Johnson, Harriet McBryde. 2003. The disability gulag. *New York Times Magazine* 23: 58–64.

Kidder, David. 1992. The effects of hospice coverage on Medicare expenditures. *Health Services Research* 27: 195–217. [PubMed]

Kohn, Nina A. 2010. The Lawyer's Role in Fostering an Elder Rights Movement. *William Mitchell Law Review* 37: 49.

Linda H. Krieger, ed. 2003. *Backlash against the ADA: Reinterpreting Disability Rights*. Ann Arbor: University of Michigan Press.

Levitsky, Sandra R. 2014. *Caring for Our Own: Why There Is No Political Demand for New American Social Welfare Rights*. Oxford: Oxford University Press.

Longmore, Paul K. 2005. Policy, Prejudice, and Reality Two Case Studies of Physician-Assisted Suicide. *Journal of Disability Policy Studies* 16: 38–45. [CrossRef]

Lunney, June R., Joanne Lynn, Daniel J. Foley, Steven Lipson, and Jack M. Guralnik. 2003. Patterns of functional decline at the end of life. *JAMA* 289: 2387–92. [CrossRef] [PubMed]

Lynn, Joanne, Frank Harrell, Felicia Cohn, and Mary Hamel. 1996. Defining the terminally ill: Insights from support. *Duquesne Law Review* 35: 311–36. [PubMed]

Mégret, Frédéric. 2008. The disabilities convention: Human rights of persons with disabilities or disability rights? *Human Rights Quarterly* 30: 494–516.

Mor, Vincent, and David Kidder. 1985. Cost savings in hospice: final results of the National Hospice Study. *Health Services Research* 20: 407–22. [PubMed]

National Hospice and Palliative Care Organization. 2012. NHPCO Facts and Figures: Hospice Care in America. Available online: https://www.nhpco.org/sites/default/files/public/newsline/2012/NL_March_12.pdf (accessed on 12 December 2017).

National Hospice and Palliative Care Organization. 2015. The Medicare Hospice Benefit. Available online: https://www.nhpco.org/sites/default/files/public/communications/Outreach/The_Medicare_Hospice_Benefit.pdf (accessed on 12 December 2017).

Neumann, Ann. 2016. *The Good Death*. Boston: Beacon Press.

North Carolina Division of Medical Assistance. 2016. Medicaid and Health Choice, Clinical Coverage Policy No. 3D. Available online: https://files.nc.gov/ncdma/documents/files/3D_2.pdf (accessed on 12 December 2017).

Paradis, Lenora Finn, and Scott B. Cummings. 1986. The evolution of hospice in America toward organizational homogeneity. *Journal of Health and Social Behavior* 27: 370–86. [CrossRef] [PubMed]

Perry, Joshua E., and Robert C. Stone. 2011. In the Business of Dying: Questioning the Commercialization of Hospice. *The Journal of Law, Medicine & Ethics* 39: 224–34.

Rabow, Michael W., Joshua M. Hauser, and Jocelia Adams. 2004. Supporting family caregivers at the end of life: They don't know what they don't know. *JAMA* 291: 483–91. [CrossRef] [PubMed]

Sampson, Robert J. 2012. *Great American City: Chicago and the Enduring Neighborhood Effect*. Chicago: University of Chicago Press.

Schriner, Kay, and Richard Scotch. 2003. The ADA and the Meaning of Disability. In *Backlash against the ADA: Reinterpreting Disability Rights*. Edited by Linda Hamilton Krieger. Ann Arbor: University of Michigan Press, pp. 164–88.

Scotch, Richard. 2001. *From Good Will to Civil Rights: Transforming Federal Disability Policy*. Philadelphia: Temple University Press.

Shakespeare, Tom. 2013. The Social Model of Disability. In *The Disability Studies Reader*. Edited by L. Davis. London: Routledge, pp. 214–21.

Stevenson, David G., and Jeffrey S. Bramson. 2009. Hospice care in the nursing home setting: A review of the literature. *Journal of Pain and Symptom Management* 38: 440–51. [CrossRef] [PubMed]

The Connecticut Hospice. 1982. Administrator Testifies on Hospice Legislation. In *The Connecticut Hospice Newsletter*, vol. 8, No.1. Box 6, Folder 74, Florence and Henry Wald Papers, Sterling Memorial Library, Yale University.

Watson, Sidney D. 2011. Section 1557 of the Affordable Care Act: Civil Rights, Health Reform, Race, and Equity. *Howard LJ* 55: 855.

Weber, Mark C. 2004. Home and community-based services, Olmstead, and positive rights: A preliminary discussion. *Wake Forest Law Review* 39: 2692–90.

Wyatt, Karen. 2015. Social Model Hospice Homes May Revolutionize End-of-Life Care in the U.S. *Huffington Post*. Available online: http://www.huffingtonpost.com/karen-m-wyatt-md/social-model-hospice_b_7641916.html (accessed on12 December 2017).

2

Disability, Procreation and Justice in the United States

Kimberly Mutcherson

Rutgers Law School, 217 N. 5th Street, Camden, NJ 08102, USA; kim.mutcherson@rutgers.edu

Abstract: Parenting and procreation have long been contested legal terrain in the United States as exemplified by a history of abuses against marginalized populations including people with disabilities. While some of the most egregious abuses, such as state sponsored sterilization programs, are relics of the past, it remains true that people with disabilities face distinct and at times insurmountable roadblocks to procreation and parenting. This article details ongoing forms of procreative discrimination against people with disabilities, rejects common justifications for that discrimination, and offers proposals for better protecting the rights to procreate and parent for disabled people.

Keywords: disability; procreation; parenting; discrimination

1. Introduction

In its history, the U.S. Supreme Court has issued decisions sanctioning bigotry, discrimination, and dehumanization in a number of forms, including based on race, gender, and national origin. It is no surprise, then, that the Court has failed in key moments to protect people living with disabilities from ill treatment at the hands of law and policymakers. Such was the case in 1927 when the Court decided the fate of a young woman named Carrie Buck in the landmark case of *Buck v. Bell*. Ms. Buck's legal caretakers failed to protect her from a sexual assault at the hands of one of their relatives that left her pregnant and unmarried at the age of 17. Compounding their failure, Carrie's caretakers responded to the assault and pregnancy by having Carrie committed to the Virginia State Colony for Epileptics and the Feebleminded.[1] After her commitment and the birth of her daughter, Ms. Buck was targeted for sterilization as authorized by a Virginia law that permitted permanent sterilization for any person who was a "mental defective" and for whom the "the health of the patient and the welfare of society may be promoted by [ ] sterilization ... under careful safeguard ... [and] without serious pain or substantial danger to life."[2]

Testimony at Ms. Buck's trial sought to establish that Carrie Buck came from a family in which the affliction of mental infirmity was widespread. An expert in eugenics[3] testified that Carrie's mother, Emma Buck, was also a resident at the Virginia Colony, where she had been committed because she was mentally deficient and morally degenerate, as evidenced by her purported promiscuity and the fact that she had given birth to several children outside of marriage.[4] Other witnesses testified that multiple members of Carrie's family were odd and a nurse claimed that she had compared Carrie's

---

1 *Buck v. Bell*, 274 U.S. 200 (1927).

2 *Id. at* 205.

3 I use the term "expert" here loosely as these were people who lacked connection to any scientifically sound methods of evaluating the quality of an individual's genes and determining the risk that any so-called faulty genes would be passed from parent to child.

4 See (Lombardo 2001).

infant daughter, Vivian, to another infant of the same age and that Vivian did not look "normal" though the nurse was unable to offer any specifics of what was abnormal about the child.[5] The historical record would later reveal that Carrie Buck did not have an intellectual or developmental disability (IDD), nor did her daughter. Nevertheless, Justice Oliver Wendell Holmes wrote an opinion for the Court that upheld the statute and the order that Ms. Buck be sterilized. Reflecting on the specious evidence that Ms. Buck was the daughter of a developmentally disabled woman and the mother of a developmentally disabled child, Justice Holmes wrote, "Three generations of imbeciles are enough."[6] The Court's decision in the *Buck* case has never been overruled.

Carrie Buck's experience, and that of the hundreds of people also forcibly sterilized during this particular period of eugenic popularity in the United States,[7] are stark reminders that access to parenting and procreation has long been an area of contestation in the law. The United States has a history of sterilization abuse against poor women, women of color, and, as is clear from *Buck v. Bell*, people living with disabilities of various sorts. Overt forced sterilization laws are a relic of the past in the U.S., but people with disabilities face distinct and at times insurmountable roadblocks to procreation and parenting. These roadblocks include discrimination by the healthcare providers and fertility experts who could facilitate efforts to become pregnant; caretakers who reject the idea of sexual agency for people living with physical, intellectual, or developmental disabilities; inadequate social supports to facilitate parenting by people living with disabilities; and widespread cultural assumptions that those living with disabilities do not deserve or desire foundational life experiences that many people without disabilities take for granted, including the experience of reproduction and parenting.

This article details ways in which disability continues to act as a barrier to procreation and parenting, argues for the importance of recognizing and protecting the constitutional and human right to procreate for people living with disabilities, and offers practical ways that law and policy could be utilized to further the procreative desires of people living with disabilities.

2. The Nature of Disability

The umbrella term disability is inadequate to cover the range of life experiences that can all be said to be disabling.[8] A person with a profound developmental disability experiences life differently than a person who is blind and the person who is blind experiences life differently than a person living with bipolar disorder, who, in turn, experiences life differently than a person who uses a wheelchair because she has lost use of her legs. All of these people fall under the label of being disabled according to the law, but the ways in which their disabilities impact their lived experiences, including how they are perceived by the world around them can be strikingly different. The heterogeneity of the community of people living with disabilities makes it difficult to write about disability as an all-encompassing category. However, it is fair and largely accurate to say that disability as a category, across a range of presentations, has been a space in which state sponsored or at least state approved efforts to control procreative and parental decision-making has been longstanding. Beyond the forced sterilization laws described above, private parties have used the courts to seek permission to sterilize adults living with

---

5 *Id.*

6 *Id.*

7 For a detailed account of the broad impact of eugenic thought in America, see (Lombardo 2016).

8 I use the term disabling here in a way that I hope indicates the complex scholarly discussion about the nature of disability that has spawned rich and persuasive literature about disability as a social construct that rejects or a least substantially complicates the medical model of disability. See, e.g., (Liachowitz 1988). I absolutely acknowledge that what makes something a disability can be the way that societies fail to accommodate the needs of bodies and minds that come in a variety of packages. That being said, it is true that a person who cannot hear or see or who is paralyzed has a condition that impacts that individual's ability to engage in certain basic life functions such that accommodation of some sort becomes necessary. This premise is what underlies the legal definition of a disability as found in the laws like the Americans with Disabilities Act, which protects those who have a "physical or mental impairment that substantially limits one or more major life activities of such individual." 42 U.S.C. §12102.

disabilities,[9] reinvigorating debates about the circumstances, if any, in which one person should be able to consent to sterilization on behalf of another. People with disabilities too frequently have to defend their right to parent, sometimes even in court, because of assumptions about their abilities or lack thereof as caretakers.[10] People with disabilities who seek infertility treatment may find themselves shunned by physicians who make presumptions of parenting ability even when they have no expertise in making such judgments[11] or because they fear the impact of a pregnancy on a particular patient's health.[12] Finally, people with disabilities may find themselves defending their right to have children who share their disability by taking deliberate steps to increase the chance of having a child with a disability[13] or by declining to use technology that could virtually guarantee the birth of a child who would not have a disability. Obviously, not all people living with disabilities have the same life experiences, just as not all people of color and not all women share the same experiences though they sit in a similar identity category. Nevertheless, there is a subset of shared discrimination worthy of attention.

The lives of countless people living with a range of disabilities have improved in the decades since *Buck v. Bell*. Key federal statutes such as the Rehabilitation Act,[14] the Americans with Disabilities Act ("ADA"),[15] and the Individuals with Disabilities Education Act (IDEA)[16] create obligations for various actors, including public accommodations such as schools, stores, and physician offices to make themselves accessible to people with disabilities. The idea that people with disabilities should be shunned or dismissed from the goods offered to others in society no longer holds sway in the context of lawmaking. Nevertheless, procreation and parenting remain areas in which there is a righteousness about the belief that some choices should be limited or forbidden altogether generally to benefit children or the larger society.

3. The Right to Procreate

Issues of procreative discrimination based on disability span the globe. However, this article focuses on the United States as a specific site of such discrimination. In the United States, procreation is ostensibly a fundamental right for all under the U.S. Constitution. In 1942, the U.S. Supreme Court again faced a case that involved a challenge to a non-consensual sterilization law different in scope from the law at issue in *Buck v. Bell*, but with similar intent—prevent procreation by those deemed to possess unworthy genes. Unlike Carrie Buck, the mark against Jack Skinner was his status as a recidivist felon

---

9 See, e.g., (Supreme Court of California 1985) (parents sought a court order allowing them to consent to a sterilization procedure for their adult developmentally disabled daughter); *In re Moe*, 432 N.E.2d 712 (mother of developmentally disabled adult daughter sought court permission to consent to a tubal ligation for her daughter); *In re Guardianship of Hayes*, 608 P.2d 635 (1980) (mother sought permission to consent to sterilization for her adult developmentally disabled daughter); *In the Matter of C.D.M., K.C.M. & B.L.M.*, 627 P.2d 607 (1981) (parents sought permission to consent to tubal ligation on behalf of their developmentally disabled daughter); *In re Grady*, 426 A.2d 467(1981) (parents sought permission to consent to sterilization on behalf of their daughter who was living with Down Syndrome.); *In re Johnson*, 263 S.E.2d 805 (1980) (court allowed unconsented sterilization of developmentally disabled woman under N.C. statues over the woman's objections).

10 See (National Council on Disabilities 2012), ("Removal rates where parents have a psychiatric disability have been found to be as high as 70 percent to 80 percent; where the parent has an intellectual disability, 40 percent to 80 percent. In families where the parental disability is physical, 13 percent have reported discriminatory treatment in custody cases. Parents who are deaf or blind report extremely high rates of child removal and loss of parental rights.").

11 *Id.* at 23–24.

12 Some health conditions that increase pregnancy risks for women include Turner syndrome, a genetic disorder experienced only by women, or women with significant cardiac conditions such as peripartum cardiomyopathy (weakening of the heart muscle), and persistent left ventricular dysfunction. See (Ethics Committee of the American Society for Reproductive Medicine 2016).

13 See (Spriggs 2002); see (Sanghavi 2006).

14 The Rehab Act was an early piece of legislation that prohibits discrimination against people with disabilities in Federal programs, including programs that receive federal funding, and federal employment, including companies that receive contracts from the federal government.

15 The ADA extends the protections of the Rehab Act to state and local governments, public accommodations, commercial facilities, transportation and telecommunications.

16 The IDEA creates affirmative obligations for public schools to make education available to children with living disabilities in the least restrictive environment.

and he was slated to be sterilized without his consent in keeping with Oklahoma's Habitual Criminal Sterilization Act.[17] The law targeted individuals who had been convicted of at least three "felonies involving moral turpitude", though some felonies, mostly white-collar crimes, were excluded from the statute.[18] For those whose crimes were included in the statute's purview, the state could require vasectomy for men or tubal ligation for women to render them surgically sterile, which would avoid the risk that they would pass on their criminal tendencies to their children through their genes or simply parent their children into a life of crime. In *Skinner*, without overruling *Buck*, the Supreme Court took the position that this forced sterilization statute offended the Constitution's guarantee of equal protection by allowing sterilization for some felons and not others.[19] Though the Court spent little time considering the value of procreation in its *Buck* opinion, in *Skinner*, the justices wrote:

> [M]arriage and procreation are fundamental to the very existence and survival of the race. The power to sterilize, if exercised, may have subtle, far-reaching and devastating effects. In evil or reckless hands[,] it can cause races or types which are inimical to the dominant group to wither and disappear. There is no redemption for the individual whom the law touches. Any experiment which the State conducts is to his irreparable injury. He is forever deprived of a basic liberty.[20]

Many scholars and subsequent courts have construed this language as standing for the proposition that procreation is a fundamental right.[21] Like all fundamental rights, the right to procreate is not boundless, and the Court stopped short of making a claim that the state could never force sterilization. The Justices did, however, make clear that when statutes touched on this "basic liberty", the right to procreate, courts would subject those statutes to an exacting level of judicial scrutiny.

The U.S. Constitutional scheme is but one source of a broadly protected right to procreate. Such a right also exists in foundational human rights documents. As recognized by the United Nations:

> [R]eproductive rights embrace certain human rights that are already recognized in national laws, international laws and international human rights documents and other consensus documents. These rights rest on the recognition of the basic rights of all couples and individuals to decide freely and responsibly the number, spacing and timing of their children and to have the information and means to do so, and the right to attain the highest standard of sexual and reproductive health. It also includes the right to make decisions concerning reproduction free of discrimination, coercion and violence, as expressed in human rights documents.[22]

Specifically, in the context of people living with disabilities, the Convention on the Rights of Persons with Disabilities (CRPD), to which the United States is a signatory, makes clear that the general rights to found a family and raise one's children extend equally to people living with disabilities.[23] The Convention holds that States Parties "shall take effective and appropriate measures to eliminate discrimination against persons with disabilities in all matters relating to marriage, family, parenthood and relationships on an equal basis with others . . . "[24] The Convention requires States to recognize the right of people living with disabilities to make procreative decisions, such as the number of children to have, if any, the spacing of those children, and access to appropriate education about family planning and the means to plan their families as they choose.[25] Critically, the Convention

---

17 *Skinner v. Oklahoma*, 316 U.S. 535 (1942).
18 *Id.* at 536–537 (1942).
19 *Id.* at 538–539.
20 *Id.* at 541.
21 *See, e.g., Carey v. Population Servs. Int'l*, 431 U.S. 678, 684–85 (1977); *Stanley v. Illinois*, 405 U.S. 645, 651 (1972).
22 International Conference on Population and Development, Programme of Action, Para 7.3.
23 Convention on the Rights of Persons with Disabilities (CRPD), Article 23(1)(a)-(b).
24 Convention on the Rights of Persons with Disabilities, Article 23(1).
25 *Id.*

makes clear that "Persons with disabilities, including children, retain their fertility on an equal basis with others"[26] thus, responding to and rejecting the acceptability of forced sterilization for people living with disabilities, including children.[27] Finally, in the realm of parenting, in addition to requiring that states protect the rights of parentage and caretaking for people with disabilities, States are also exhorted to "render appropriate assistance to persons with disabilities in the performance of their child-rearing responsibilities."[28] Assistance of this type is critical where a parent with a disability needs social support, financial or otherwise, in order to parent adequately her children.

As a matter of U.S. Constitutional law and human rights principles, people with disabilities have the same rights of procreation and parenting afforded to all people. The constitutional rights to procreate and parent are largely negative rather than positive, meaning that the government is limited in its ability to interfere with a disabled individual's right to parent or to have children, but typically has no affirmative obligation to assist a disabled person who is seeking pregnancy or who has needs that must be met in order to facilitate her ability to parent.[29] Where there are surmountable barriers to parenting, however, human rights principles require a more robust response from the State and affirmative efforts to aid those who procreate or parent while living with a disability. Taken together, the law and human rights principles make a strong case for increased focus on making the law more friendly to and cognizant of the needs of parents or would-be parents who are disabled. Despite this, barriers to parenting and procreation persist largely due to myths and misconceptions about the lives of people with disabilities.

4. Justifications for Limiting Access to Procreation for People with Disabilities

The treatment of disability in law and policy related to procreation must be understood within the broader context of what Ricki Solinger has called reproductive politics. According to Solinger, reproductive politics refers "most basically to the question, *Who has power over matters of pregnancy and its consequences?*"[30] While the U.S. constitutional order often locates rights related to procreation and parenting in the sphere of privacy, the existence of reproductive politics makes clear that what is private for some is a matter of public concern and state control for others. And when the state exercises control over matters of procreation involving people with disabilities, it frequently relies on justifications that cannot legitimately support burdening a fundamental right.

Limitations on access to parenting for the disabled can be structural and systemic as well as personal and localized. State sponsored sterilization programs were a systemic way to prevent certain people from ever having children when possible including people with disabilities, but those programs were also racist and classist. This truth is exemplified by the experience of the Relf sisters, two developmentally disabled Black girls, sterilized in 1973 at the ages of 14 and 12 at a federally funded healthcare facility after their mother signed a consent form with an "X" because she was illiterate.[31] The Relf sisters were part of a long line of women (poor, disabled, Black or Brown) for whom people with power decided procreation was a luxury best denied largely because of myths about so-called irresponsible procreation, inadequate parenting, and hyper sexuality. Thus, intersectional identities, including the intertwining of disability with other indicia of marginalization, impact the power dynamics of reproductive oppression, such that being young, poor, Black, and disabled all played a role in the sterilization experience of the Relf sisters. I make this point to make clear that I do

---

26 CRPD, Article 23(1)(c).
27 CRPD, Article 23(2).
28 *Id.*
29 There are statutory exceptions to the general rule that these rights are negative such as when the state child welfare system becomes involved with a family due to accusations of abuse or neglect and the state assumes an obligation to assist the parent in correcting the conditions that led to state supervision.
30 See (Solinger 2005).
31 This particular act of state sponsored abuse eventually led to change in consent procedures under guidelines to that public hospital and other facilities receiving public funds are bound to follow. See (Southern Poverty Law Center n.d.).

not seek to essentialize the experiences of all disabled women, but to make clear that there are women within the disabled community whose rights are at greater risk than is true for others.

More personalized discrimination comes in the form of individual healthcare providers who are unwilling or unable to provide a level of care necessary to help a woman with a disability become pregnant or carry a pregnancy to term. Some healthcare professionals have been candid about the medical field's failure to provide sufficient healthcare resources to women with disabilities who are pregnant and seeking care noting that "[m]any women with disabilities report difficulty finding a health care provider with experience in providing obstetrical care to women with disabilities or who is willing to assume care for them during pregnancy".[32] Furthermore, "women with disabilities that limit their mobility have reported inaccessible physician offices and clinics, not being weighed even once during their pregnancy, and receiving no help in transferring to a high, non-adjustable exam table in the absence of an adjustable table".[33] Unsurprisingly, when women cannot find adequate obstetrical care, it can discourage them from seeking pregnancy at all or can make their pregnancies less safe for them and the babies they seek to carry to term.

Two primary lines of thought used to justify procreative and parenting restrictions for women with disabilities have deep historical roots. The first is the idea that people living with disabilities risk passing those disabilities to their children thereby keeping supposedly flawed genes in the gene pool. The second is that people with disabilities will be inadequate parents and therefore should not have children who will suffer from their abuse or neglect. To this, I add a third claim which is that people with disabilities, or at least some people with IDDs, are presumed incapable of consenting to sex and therefore should not be able to have the kind of intimate relationships that could lead to a child being born. I will respond to each of these claims in turn.

4.1. Sex and Disability

Starting with the third claim, a significant source of difficulty for people living with disabilities is that the wider world does not always view them as having sexual desires and sexual agency, which precludes them from having the ability to be sexually active on their own terms, especially when doing so requires assistance from others. As one author explained, for decades "[t]he public discourse surrounding sex and severe disability ... largely focused on protecting vulnerable populations from abuse".[34] Studies have revealed that sex and access to sex are fraught for many people living with significant physical or intellectual disabilities both because of concerns about abuse, which lead to laws and policies that impede access to sex, and because physical or other limitations can make it difficult to find sexual partners.[35] As one author wrote, "We live in a society where many individuals seem unaware that disabled people have sex, enjoy sexuality, and are at some unique risks in terms of reproductive health".[36] Unfortunately, it continues to be the case that many people infantilize and desexualize people who are living with disabilities, especially IDDs.[37] The presumption that people are childlike simply because their bodies are small or that they lack sexual desire because they cannot walk or that they are incapable of understanding or consenting to sex because they have a mental illness are all reasons that the sexual dynamics of procreation are too often seen as outside of the capabilities or interests of people with disabilities. This failure to treat people with disabilities as individuals with sexual desires and sexual agency can lead to unintended consequences. As one author explains,

---

32 See (National League for Nursing 2017).

33 *Id.*

34 See (Appel 2010), (arguing for a positive right to sex for people living with disabilities, including altering rules forbidding sexual relationships in institutional settings and creating carve out in prostitution prohibitions on behalf of people with disabilities). But see (Di Nucci 2011), (arguing against the existence of a positive right to sexual pleasure that could require financing by the state).

35 See (Kulick and Rydström 2015).

36 See (Smith 2014a).

37 See (Friedman and Owen 2017).

"because society as a whole thinks that disabled people do not and cannot have sex, members of the public, law enforcement, policymakers, and even medical professionals have difficulty conceiving of the idea that they might be targets for rape and assault. This leaves disabled people, particularly those in institutional care or under the 'care' of abusive individuals, vulnerable to danger".[38]

It is well documented that some individuals take advantage of vulnerabilities possessed by some people with disabilities. Abuse takes place in private homes, in public facilities, and in other settings.[39] Among developmentally disabled adults, one study found that 85% of females and 32% of males are sexual assault survivors.[40] In another study, forty percent of women with physical disabilities reported being sexually assaulted.[41] These numbers are unconscionable and speak to a deep need to find more and better ways to eliminate sexual assault across the board and especially in communities whose members are victimized at such high rates. That being said, for individuals who are capable of consenting to sexual activity, the stereotypes of sexless people with disabilities are unsupportable. For others, though, who are truly incapable of understanding or consenting to a sexual relationship, the concern that they should be protected from those who would hurt them and from the potential consequences of sexual exploitation is valid.

Protecting those who need it from sexual assault involves a number of potential policy shifts, including providing better sexual health education to people living with disabilities, including adolescents, to ensure that they have the tools to recognize and report sexual exploitation;[42] ensuring that healthcare providers and caretakers respect the capacity for consent that people with disabilities possess; and, of course, enforcement of laws and policies that punish perpetrators and remove them from roles that allow them to do harm. Equally as important, attempts to protect the vulnerable should not bar the hopefully rich and fulfilling life experiences of procreation and parenting, or just sexual pleasure, for those people living with disabilities who desire it. Walking this line is difficult, but it is a critical distinction to make so that people are not unfairly deprived of rights.[43] Part of the necessary work here is making sure that courts and decision makers do not paint all people with disabilities with a single brush, but take the time to ascertain both the capacity to consent and the presence of actual consent when faced with a question of sexual contact involving a person with disabilities. These evaluations will not always be easy, but they are required to protect the decisional autonomy of disabled people with the capacity to make their own decisions about sexual experiences, even if those decisions are not always well-considered or in their best interest, just as is true for any person with the capacity to consent to sexual activity.

4.2. Disability and Parenting

The second issue is the concern that people who are living with disabilities will be neglectful or abusive parents. This concern partially explains why parents with disabilities, especially those with mental health disorders, are overrepresented in the ranks of parents forced to interact with state child welfare systems.[44] Further, disability is an acceptable status for rejecting would-be parents who wish to adopt children[45] or for selecting one parent over another in a child custody proceeding.[46]

---

38 s.e. Smith, *supra* note 36.

39 See, e.g., (Euser 2016) (citing research concluding that children with disabilities have an increased prevalence of all kinds of abuse, include sexual abuse).

40 See (Johnson and Sigler 2000).

41 See (Young et al. 1997).

42 s.e. smith, *supra* note 36.

43 For a devastating case of how difficult questions of consent and agency can become when people with significant disabling conditions are involved, see the case of Anna Stubblefield, a tenured university professor convicted of sexually assaulting a profoundly disabled man with whom she claimed to be able to communicate using controversial facilitated communication techniques. See (Engber 2015).

44 National Council on Disability, ROCKING THE CRADLE, *supra* note 10, at 17–21.

45 *Ibid.* at 20.

46 *Ibid.* at 22.

While few people would claim that parenting ability is an irrelevant factor when it comes to the welfare of children, the question of who should be able to make assessments of such ability, the criteria for those assessments, and when assessment is warranted are the crux of this discussion.

Ascertaining what kind of parent a person will be is an imprecise process unless and until a person actually assumes a parental role. Suppositions based on stereotypes about people living with disabilities are a poor substitute for individualized assessments of capacity. Further, it is questionable whether anyone should take it upon themselves to play the role of decision-maker about someone else's parenting prowess in the absence of quality information about what that person brings to the table as a parent. Many people living with disabilities have rich support systems in place that play a critical role in how they parent, something that all parents, no doubt, could use. In keeping with the precepts of the CRPD, where such support does not exist, it is appropriate for public funding to exist to assist parents with disabilities in maintaining close ties to their children and parenting to the best of their ability. Further, having learned to live and thrive with their own disabilities, many parents, especially those living with a disability that their children share, will be able to instill a measure of resilience in their children that parents who do not have disabilities might not be able to replicate. Thus, parenting ability should not be measured in a vacuum, but must be contextualized based on individual ability and the scaffolding of support from others that can enhance that individual ability.

Though not always discussed as such, the issue of parenting by people with disabilities cannot be separated from the reality that the right to procreate in the first instance may depend on a forward-looking supposition about ability to parent. Thus, the relationship between procreation and parenting warrants further exploration in this context. Typically, in the general population, the instances in which parenting ability acts as an initial barrier to procreation are few. In other words, for most people, the point at which parenting becomes questioned by the state in a way that has consequences is if and when a parent comes into contact with the child welfare system after a child is born or when a subsequent child is born into a family that has already had dealings with child welfare.[47]

People living with disabilities who seek to procreate must battle overblown or unfounded fears that their parenting poses risks to children simply by dint of their existence as people with disabilities. This narrative of parental incompetence exemplifies how the social construction of disability, in this case crippling low expectations for people living with disabilities who parent, become what disables the parental aspirations of disabled people rather than the disabilities themselves. These low expectations of parental ability can mask prejudice toward people living with disabilities and give those who wield them the chance to claim that they are acting not to disadvantage parents with disabilities, but to protect future children from the harm of substandard parenting.

Using this concern for children to support discrimination in procreation and parenting for people living with disabilities illustrates how assumptions that a right to procreate depends on an interest and ability to parent works to the disadvantage of people living with disabilities.[48] No doubt, many, if not most, people who procreate, do so with the intent to parent, even if reluctantly. But to the extent that a right to procreate exists, it need not be premised on either a desire to or an aptitude for parenting.

---

47 To be clear, I do not mean to suggest that the government is completely hands off when it comes to procreation, especially when it comes to disenfranchised populations. Welfare caps for poor women, ongoing sterilization abuse, overrepresentation of people of color in state child welfare systems, and abortion restrictions are all ways in which reproduction is tiered in the United States. But, it remains the case that our Constitution seems to disfavor pre-emptive bans on procreation.

48 For a more fleshed out analysis of the distinctions among sex, parenting, and procreation, see (Mutcherson 2015), in which the author argues that it is vital to recognize that parenting, sex, and procreation are distinct experiences all worthy of Constitutional recognition and protection and none of which should necessarily rely on the others in order to have such protection. Examples of how these three significant life experiences can exist without either of the others include women who contract to act as gestational carriers and give birth to children with whom they will have no genetic connection who they will not parent. Intended parents who commission a surrogacy may parent without procreating and without having sex. Similarly, a woman who sells her eggs to another so that the purchaser can produce a child can be said to be procreating in the sense that she is replicating her genes, but, like the gestational surrogate, she does so without an intent or interest in parenting. Thus, these separate strands of human experience can be intertwined or distinct.

This position was articulated by a dissenting justice in *Conservatorship of Valerie N.*—a case decided by the California Supreme Court in 1985.

In that case, the justices were faced with making a decision about surgical sterilization for Valerie, an adult woman living with Down syndrome, whose parents and conservators sought to consent to a sterilization procedure on Valerie's behalf.[49] The California statutory scheme, created in response to California's history of eugenic sterilizations of people living with disabilities, did not allow for the sterilization of a person who was incapable of consenting to the procedure. In other words, it was not possible for a guardian to consent to sterilization on behalf of a decisionally incompetent ward, which meant that a ward in that situation could never be sterilized.[50]

Given the larger statutory scheme that sought to maximize opportunities for personal fulfillment for people living with disabilities, the majority of the members of the California Supreme Court took the position that Valerie's right to avoid procreation was violated within a statutory scheme that did not allow someone to consent to sterilization on her behalf when she was incapable of consenting for herself. The Court's rationale hinged on the idea that for a person like Valerie, who lacked decisional capacity, being fertile meant that her parents felt obliged to restrict her activities in a way that was otherwise not beneficial to her in order to avoid the risk of sexual exploitation and potential pregnancy.[51] Valerie's caregivers testified that she was sexually aggressive with men and that she had not been amenable to taking birth control pills.[52]

In dissent, Chief Justice Bird wrote that the right to procreate is "constitutional" not in the sense of deriving from our Constitutional order but in the sense that it is a truly natural right that precedes and supersedes the Constitution. She explained:

> [T]he right to procreate is more than a byproduct of a right of choice. Its roots go deeper; they are constitutional in the physical sense, implicating the individual's rights to physical integrity and to retention of the biological capabilities with which he or she was born into this world. Hence, even in the case of a mentally competent individual, it is somewhat illogical to treat the right to procreate solely as a matter of control over basic personal decisions.[53]

Thus, according to Justice Bird, in keeping with this view of the roots of a right to procreate, one need not be capable of parenting, desirous of parenting, or engaging in conscious decision making about procreation in order to possess a right to procreate. This is a broad vision of the right to procreate that casts a wide net of protection.

In sharp contrast to this idea that procreation and parenting need not, indeed, should not be intertwined, others have taken the position that one who cannot parent in accordance with some minimum standard of quality parenting has no right to procreate at all. In her writing about procreation and individuals with IDDs, Professor Bonnie Steinbock has argued that the right to procreate presupposes an ability to provide a minimum standard of parenting. She explains that the right to procreate encompasses more than "mere genetic replication" which would lead to the conclusion that "anyone capable of reproducing has the right to reproduce . . . " Instead, the bedrock of a right to procreate is that "it is the usual way of establishing a family, of creating children that one will rear . . . Genetic replication where this is not linked to rearing children may be an interest that

---

49 *Conservatorship of Valerie N.*, 707 P.2d 760, 761–763 (1985).

50 *Id.* at 770.

51 The Court ultimately did not allow for the sterilization to take place because of procedural failures in the lower court proceeding. Among other issues, the Court raised concern that there had been no evidence in the trial court that Valerie was fertile or that other forms of birth control, besides contraceptive pills, had been tried before resorting to a request for surgical sterilization. *Id.* at 777–778.

52 *Id.* at 763.

53 *Id.* at 786 (C.J. Bird dissenting).

some people have, but it is not an interest that society should be concerned to protect".[54] For Steinbock, then, a person who lacks the capacity to parent has no claim to a right to procreate.

Justice Bird's conception of the right to procreate sounds in law, while Steinbock's conception sounds in philosophy and morality, but they represent distinct and conflicting visions of the relationship among disability, parenting, and procreation. Justice Bird's articulation of the right is more in line with the broader right to procreation and fertility espoused in the CRPD and the fundamental nature of the right to procreate.

A broad articulation of a right to procreate that does not hinge on parenting ability does not mean that the law should ignore the needs of children born to parents living with disabilities. As is true of any child, the state has an obligation to act in the role of parens patriae for children of parents with disabilities. Thus, where these parents are incapable of meeting a minimum standard of parenting, the state is obliged and allowed to act in the interest of those children up to and including removing the children from the care of their parents or even terminating parental rights. However, when the state acts, it must do so without prejudice about the parenting abilities of people living with disabilities.

Unfortunately, stories abound of governmental entities that acted without due regard for both the rights and abilities of parents living with disabilities. In 1988, a deaf mother of two young children, who was also a domestic violence survivor, battled the child welfare system in New York City to keep her children out of foster care. According to a lawyer for the children, city workers failed to make required efforts to help the woman find adequate housing for herself and her two children and never found a sign language interpreter to assist them in communicating with the mother.[55] In 2014, a British couple, both of whom are developmentally disabled, lost custody of their child for 18 months before a court returned the child to them and awarded them damages.[56] It is estimated that 40 to 80% of parents with IDDs have their children taken away from them by the state.[57] Though the ADA does provide some protection for parents with disabilities who find themselves battling the child welfare system for the right to raise their own children, if parents do not have qualified legal representation to pursue their rights, they risk losing their relationships with their children.

Combatting discrimination against parents and would-be parents with disabilities requires recognizing the complexity of lived experiences of people with a variety of disabilities. First, parenting ability should not act as a blanket legal barrier to procreation. Second, existing anti-discrimination laws must be enforced both so that people with disabilities can access needed health services to assist in becoming pregnant and maintaining healthy pregnancies, and so that they are privy to the services they need and to which they are entitled in order to keep their families intact. Third, judges, child welfare workers, law and policymakers, and others who make decisions about the rights of disabled parents must be well educated about the strengths of people living with disabilities who parent.[58]

It is vital to explode myths about the parenting abilities of people living with disabilities because those myths hurt those who parent and are equally pernicious for children deprived of parental nurturing or care because of such myths. Additionally, de facto or de jure limitations on parenting imposed on adults living with disabilities send a message to children with disabilities about their worth and about the futures that they can and should imagine for themselves. To the extent that a person living with a disability desires procreation and parenting, she should benefit from an assumption of competence unless proven otherwise.

---

54 See (Steinbock 1994).
55 See (Barbanel 1988).
56 See (Smith 2014b).
57 See (Reeves 2013).
58 ROCKING THE CRADLE, *supra* note 10.

4.3. Reproducing Disability

The third concern used to justify limitations on parenting for people living with disabilities is that in some instances those would-be parents risk passing along their disability to their children. Of course, most people living with disabilities do not have transmissible disabilities. For others, if they so choose, there are ways to avoid passing on disabilities. For instance, a woman living with HIV who becomes pregnant can access interventions that make the risk of HIV transmission from the woman to a child to whom she gives birth less than one percent.[59] But, for some number of those who live with disabilities that are genetic in origin, every pregnancy raises the possibility of giving birth to a child who shares his/her parent's condition. As described earlier, cases such as *Buck v. Bell* made clear that the state has an interest in preventing the legacy of disability being passed down from parent to child and the presumed cycle of dependence that would flow from that genetic legacy. Though *Buck* remains good law, societal understanding of and tolerance for disability has increased along with our knowledge of genetic transmission and the knee jerk belief that disability should be avoided at all costs is a more complicated conversation than it was in the early twentieth-century.

The availability of prenatal testing and pre-implantation genetic diagnosis (PGD) used in conjunction with IVF makes it possible for future parents who have a genetically based disability to opt to discover information about an embryo or fetus that will allow them to discard any embryo or abort any fetus that shares a parent's disability. For those who believe that it is always better to avoid giving birth to a child with a disability if that is possible, these technologies are a boon. For other women, however, for whom sharing a disability with a child is a preference, PGD can be used to detect the presence of disability specifically to create a child who will be disabled. In either case, selecting for or selecting against disability, the parental choices are controversial.

Debates about prenatal testing and disability are not new and they resonate just as strongly in the world of PGD. As Adrienne Asch and Erik Parens explained in their seminal article outlining the disability rights critique of prenatal testing, "using prenatal tests to prevent the birth of babies with disabilities seems to be self-evidently good to many people".[60] However, for those who believe that "living with disabling traits need not be detrimental either to an individual's prospects of leading a worthwhile life, or to families in which they grow up, or to society at large", decisions to avoid the birth of a child with a disability are made based on misinformation in the context of pervasive discrimination against people with disabilities, and express disdain for the lives of people with disabilities.[61] The cure for disability offered by prenatal or pre-implantation testing is to prevent a life from coming to fruition if the person living that life will be disabled. As new technologies bloom, such as gene editing with CRISPR,[62] we can expect that the pressure for women to use technology to avoid disability in children will be strong.

Many in the disability community fear that actions of this sort encourage or justify negative attitudes toward disability in general by promoting the idea that it is better not to be born at all than to be alive and disabled.[63] Thus, the push for prenatal and pre-implantation testing works in a circular way to reinforce the negative attitudes about disability that lead to women with disabilities being treated as "'unfit' for sexual relations and for motherhood".[64] While U.S. society has progressed sufficiently so that many within and outside of the disability community see great value in the

---

59 See (U.S. Department of Health and Human Services 2017).

60 See (Asch and Parens 1999).

61 *Ibid* at S2.

62 CRISPR is gene editing technology that holds promise for the prevention and treatment of several genetic diseases. (U.S. National Library of Medicine 2017), What are genome editing and CRISPR-Cas9? Available at https://ghr.nlm.nih.gov/primer/genomicresearch/genomeediting.

63 See (Kaplan 1994).

64 See (Solinger 2013).

"forms of variation"[65] that disability brings to the human experience, others, including too many medical professionals, still see disabled bodies as unworthy of reproduction and unworthy of life.

Given the broadly held belief that women with disabilities, and all women, should seek to avoid having children who will have disabilities when the option to do so exists,[66] women who opt to create a child with a disability will find that this choice does not receive universal praise. In 2006, an article in the journal Fertility and Sterility revealed that about 3% of clinics providing IVF in the United States had used PGD intentionally to select an embryo that would produce a child with a disability at the request of the parents.[67] Many other clinics and practitioners make clear that they will not transfer genetically anomalous embryos even at the patient's request.[68] Even without PGD, it is possible for people with disabilities to select for genetic anomalies. For instance, a Deaf[69] lesbian couple used deaf sperm donors to increase the chances that they would bring Deaf children into their family, which they succeeded in doing. When their story received media attention, they were the subject of broad criticism for their procreative decisions.[70] Choices of this type have been described as negative enhancement,[71] and, unsurprisingly, have caused raucous ethical debate.

In considering the decision to seek a deaf sperm donor to increase the chances of giving birth to a deaf child, well-known bioethicist and law professor R. Alta Charo said, "I think all of us recognize that deaf children can have perfectly wonderful lives . . . The question is whether the parents have violated the sacred duty of parenthood, which is to maximize to some reasonable degree the advantages available to their children. I'm loath to say it, but I think it's a shame to set limits on a child's potential".[72] The issues here return us to the discussion of what it means to be a person with a disability and how to value and understand the lives of those who are disabled.

It is easy to dismiss the desires of someone who explicitly wants to replicate her genes by having a child, even if those genes include genetic anomalies, but everyone who engages in coital reproduction is also replicating genes often with no knowledge or care about potential genetic anomalies lurking in their own genome. Part of what it means to have a fundamental right to procreate and to found a family is that one gets significant latitude in terms of when, with whom, and how to make babies and parent them. While it is not a perfect comparison, it is certainly the case that the state could not infringe the fundamental right of a deaf person to marry and procreate with another deaf person for fear of creating of deaf child. Similarly, the state could not prevent two people with dwarfism from using technology to avoid implanting an embryo that was destined to be a person with dwarfism. For the state to deny a person with a disability the opportunity to procreate on the same basis as someone who is not disabled is both to deny equality and the fundamental liberty of procreation to people on the basis of disability.

None of this is to say that any specific healthcare provider is bound to engage in any medical practice that she finds unethical. As the ASRM explains, "Valid and reasoned arguments exist to support provider decisions to assist in transferring genetically anomalous embryos, and in declining to assist in such transfers. Principles of reproductive liberty, physician autonomy, and child welfare are invoked in the clinical setting creating challenges in the prioritization and application of these and other principles as clinics work to establish guiding policies".[73] A case can undoubtedly be made that

---

65 Asch and Parens, *supra* note 60.

66 For an account of what would-be parents owe to the children who they seek to create, see (Savulescu 2001). Savulescu argues that "couples (or single reproducers) should select the child, of the possible children they could have, who is expected to have the best life, or at least as good a life as the others, based on the relevant, available information." Savulescu at 415.

67 See (Ethics Committee of the American Society for Reproductive Medicine 2017).

68 *Id.*

69 I capitalize Deaf where appropriate to signify that the physical state of being deaf is considered to be cultural identity by many members of the Deaf community for whom hearing impairment is not a disability.

70 See (Mundy 2002).

71 See (Karpin 2007).

72 Mundy, *supra* note 68.

73 ASRM, *supra* note 67, at 1134.

having a child who is destined to suffer and die in infancy or as a toddler is a morally suspect choice, though one against which we would not legislate. Similarly, a person with an elevated risk of giving birth to a child with a clubfoot certainly would not be discouraged from experiencing the wonder of procreation using her own gametes. And again, while a moral case might be made about people at risk of passing on Cystic Fibrosis or Huntington's disease or an elevated risk of breast cancer, the law does not countenance denying access to procreation to these people.

In the context of people living with certain kinds of disabilities, the willingness and desire to replicate can be a profound act of self-love and a way to create connection with their child. As one author wrote, "Many parents share a touching faith that having children similar to them will strengthen family and social bonds".[74] Whether sharing a disability does in fact create closer familial bonds is perhaps a calculation that can only be measured subjectively, but it certainly cannot be anathema across the board and across types of disability.

Women with disabilities may be especially discouraged by parents, friends, healthcare providers and others from having children at all or having children without the use of embryo screening technologies for fear that they will have children like themselves. Only those for whom disability is deeply undesired and thought to be a radical failing would be so bold as to tell a person that she should avoid having a child who is too much like her. By having a child without concern about parenting a child with a disability or with the goal of parenting such a child, people living with disabilities make clear the value that they place on their lives, even when others do not.

5. Conclusions

Having a child is often a profoundly selfish act in that it is done to satisfy the needs and desires of people already in existence, not to serve the interests of a person who will come into being. This is an observation of procreative behavior, not a critique of such behavior. While law and policy have long supported this desire for some people, the right to procreate in the first instance and then parent one's children has been hard won for others, and, for still others, it is a right still being pursued. That our right to procreate and parent is recognized by constitutional authority and guiding human rights documents speaks to the importance and centrality of procreation and parenting for many people. Like anyone else, some people living with disabilities want to procreate and law and policy must be shaped so as to support this right. This requires taking steps to ensure that people with disabilities get appropriate education about sex and reproductive health; that healthcare providers and caretakers respect the sexual and procreative desires of competent people with disabilities; and that the state enforce its laws against discrimination and educate employees about the diversity among people with disabilities. Standing alone, none of these shifts will protect all people with disabilities from disparate treatment in the realms of parenting and procreation. Nevertheless, each step toward dismantling the structures that diminish the quality of the lives that disabled people can lead moves us closer to the future that people with disabilities deserve, which includes the right to experience the highs and lows of procreation and parenting and to do so with minimal roadblocks and as much support as can be reasonably mustered on their behalf.

References

Appel, Jacob M. 2010. Sex rights for the disabled? *Journal of Medical Ethics* 36: 152–54. [CrossRef] [PubMed]

Asch, Adrienne, and Erik Parens. 1999. The Disability Rights Critique of Prenatal Testing-Reflections and Recommendations. *The Hastings Center Report* 29: S1–S22.

Barbanel, Josh. 1988. Return of Children to Deaf Mother Is Ordered. *New York Times*, April 27.

[74] Sanghavi, *supra* note 13.

Di Nucci, Ezio. 2011. Sexual rights and disability. *Journal of Medical Ethics* 37: 158–61. [CrossRef] [PubMed]
Engber, Daniel. 2015. The Strange Case of Anne Stubblefield. *New York Times Magazine*, October 20.
Ethics Committee of the American Society for Reproductive Medicine. 2017. Transferring Embryos with Genetic Anomalies Detected in Preimplantation Testing: An Ethics Committee Opinion. *Fertility and Sterility* 107: 1130–35.
Ethics Committee of the American Society for Reproductive Medicine. 2016. Provision of fertility services for women at increased risk of complications during fertility treatment of pregnancy: An Ethics Committee opinion. *Fertility and Sterility* 106: 1319–21.
Euser, Saskia. 2016. The prevalence of child sexual abuse in out-of-home care: Increased risk for children with a mild intellectual disability. *Journal of Applied Research in Intellectual Disabilities* 29: 83–92. [CrossRef] [PubMed]
Friedman, Carli, and Aleksa L. Owen. 2017. Sexual health in the community: Services for people with intellectual and developmental disabilities. *Disability and Health Journal* 10: 387–93. [CrossRef] [PubMed]
Johnson, Ida M., and Robert T. Sigler. 2000. Forced sexual intercourse among intimates. *Journal of Interpersonal Violence* 15: 95–108.
Kaplan, Deborah. 1994. Prenatal Screening and Diagnosis: The Impact on Persons with Disabilities. In *Women & Prenatal Testing*. Edited by Karen Rothenberg and Elizabeth Johnson. Columbus: Ohio State University Press, vol. 57, pp. 49–61.
Karpin, Isabel. 2007. Choosing Disability: Preimplantation Genetic Diagnosis and Negative Enhancement. *Journal of Law and Medicine* 15: 89–103. [PubMed]
Kulick, Don, and Jens Rydström. 2015. *Loneliness and Its Opposite: Sex, Disability, and the Ethics of Engagement*. Durham: Duke University Press.
Liachowitz, Claire M. 1988. *Disability as a Social Construct: Legislative Roots*. Philadelphia: University of Pennsylvania Press.
Lombardo, Paul. 2001. Carrie Buck's Pedigree. *The Journal of Laboratory and Clinical Medicine* 138: 278–80. [CrossRef] [PubMed]
Lombardo, Paul. 2016. *A Century of Eugenics in America: From the Indiana Experiment to the Human Genome Era*. Edited by Paul Lombardo. Bloomington: Indiana University Press.
Mundy, Liza. 2002. A World of Their Own. *Washington Post*, March 31.
Mutcherson, Kimberly M. 2015. Procreative Pluralism. *Berkeley Journal of Gender, Law & Justice* 30: 22–75.
National Council on Disabilities. 2012. *Report—Rocking the Cradle: Ensuring the Rights of Parents with Disabilities and Their Children*; Washington: National Council on Disabilities.
National League for Nursing. 2017. Pregnancy in Women with Disabilities. Available online: http://www.nln.org/professional-development-programs/teaching-resources/ace-d/additional-resources/pregnancy-in-women-with-disabilities (accessed on 20 November 2017).
Reeves, Stefanie. 2013. *Protecting the Rights of Parents with Disabilities*. Washington: American Psychological Association.
Sanghavi, Darshak M. 2006. Wanting Babies Like Themselves, Some Parents Choose Genetic Defects. *New York Times*, December 5.
Savulescu, Julian. 2001. Procreative Beneficence: Why We Should Select the Best Children. *Bioethics* 15: 414–26. [CrossRef]
Smith, S. E. 2014a. Discussing Disabled Sexuality Is a Radical Act. *Rewire.Com*, October 22.
Smith, S. E. 2014b. The Fight for Reproductive Rights Too Often Excludes Disabled Parents. *Rewire.Com*, November 7.
Solinger, Rickie. 2005. *Pregnancy and Power: A Short History of Reproductive Politics in America*. New York: NYU Press.
Solinger, Rickie. 2013. *Reproductive Politics: What Everyone Should Know*. Oxford: Oxford University Press.
Southern Poverty Law Center. n.d. Relf v. Weinberger-Sterilization Abuse. Available online: https://www.splcenter.org/seeking-justice/case-docket/relf-v-weinberger (accessed on 20 November 2017).
Spriggs, Merle. 2002. Lesbian Couple Create a Child Who Is Deaf Like Them. *Journal of Medical Ethics* 28: 283. [CrossRef] [PubMed]
Steinbock, Bonnie. 1994. Reproductive rights and Responsibilities. *The Hastings Center Report* 24: 15–16. [CrossRef] [PubMed]
Supreme Court of California. 1985. *Conservatorship of Valerie N, 707 P.2d 760-793*. San Francisco: Supreme Court of California.

U.S. Department of Health and Human Services. 2017. Preventing Mother-To-Child Transmission of HIV. Available online: https://aidsinfo.nih.gov/understanding-hiv-aids/fact-sheets/20/50/preventing-mother-to-child-transmission-of-hiv (accessed on 20 November 2017).

U.S. National Library of Medicine. 2017. What are genome editing and CRISPR-Cas9? Available online: https://ghr.nlm.nih.gov/primer/genomicresearch/genomeediting (accessed on 20 November 2017).

Young, Mary Ellen, Margaret A. Nosek, Carol Howland, Gall Chanpong, and Diana H. Rintala. 1997. Prevalence of abuse of women with physical disabilities. *Archives of Physical Medicine and Rehabilitation* 78: S34–S38. [CrossRef]

3

Models of Disability and Human Rights: Informing the Improvement of Built Environment Accessibility for People with Disability at Neighborhood Scale?

Mary Ann Jackson [1,2]

[1] School of Architecture and Built Environment, Deakin University, Geelong 3220, Australia; jmary@deakin.edu.au

[2] Visionary Design Development Pty Ltd., North Melbourne 3051, Australia; majarch@vdd.com.au

Abstract: In the 21st century, even with the advent of the United Nations Convention on the Rights of Persons with Disabilities (UNCRPD), the existing built environment still fails the neighborhood accessibility needs of people with disability. People with disabilities' human right to the neighborhood is, at face value, enshrined in legislation and 'much' built environment accessibility legislation is in place. But, built environment accessibility practice has been, and continues to be, shaped by a hidden discourse based on theoretical underpinnings little understood by built environment practitioners. Similarly, built environment practitioners have little understanding of either the diversity of the human condition or the accessibility needs of people with disability. In Australia, the operationalization of built environment accessibility rights is, via opaque legislation, not necessarily reflective of the lived experience of people with disability, and weak in terms of built environment spatial coverage. Empirically, little is known about the extent of built environment inaccessibility, particularly neighborhood inaccessibility. Therefore, the question explored in this paper is: How might an understanding of models of disability and human rights inform the improvement of built environment accessibility, for people with disability, at a neighborhood scale? Literature related to disability and human rights theory, built environment accessibility legislation primarily using Australia as an example, and built environment accessibility assessment is drawn together. This paper argues that built environment practitioners must recognize the disabling potency of current built environment practice, that built environment practitioners need to engage directly with people with disability to improve understanding of accessibility needs, and that improved measure, at neighborhood scale, of the extent of existing built environment inaccessibility is required.

Keywords: models of disability; human rights; people with disability; built environment; accessibility; legislation; assessment; neighborhood

---

1. Introduction

Worldwide, a decade after the adoption of the United Nations Convention on the Rights of Persons with Disabilities (UN 2006), the existing built environment encompassing infrastructure, public buildings, commercial buildings and private dwellings still fails to meet the accessibility needs of people with disability. 'Neighborhood' is a location of participation notoriously hard to define, but one that has received attention as a key spatial and social construct and focus of policy and practice across a variety of fields including planning, community development, and health (Jenks and Demsey 2007; Bevan and Croucher 2011; Oliver et al. 2015). Many, if not most, neighborhood activities, ranging from the essential (residing somewhere, attending school) to the ordinary (grocery shopping) to the discretionary (recreation), still require the negotiation of discontinuous travel chains and/or are completely impeded by the presence of barriers (Deane and The National People with Disabilities and Carer Council 2009; Jackson and Green 2012; Pineda and Dard 2016; Stephens et al. 2017). Empirical evidence of the frequency and severity of impediments, the causes contributing to impediment, and clear insight into prioritizing rectification of impediments is still, however, sorely lacking (Green 2011). Furthermore, reflective of outmoded models of disability, the meaningful input of people with disability is still rarely sought (Oliver 1987, 1992; Imrie and Wells 1993; DRC 2004; Boys 2017). Why, at almost the end of the second decade of the 21st century, are the human rights of people with disability still being ignored?

Through more than 30 years of transdisciplinary built environment experience, I have come to the realization that built environment practice and academia around built environment practice does not have a history of understanding disability, or human rights legislation pertaining to built environment accessibility, or people with disabilities' lived experience of neighborhood accessibility. Furthermore, these three arenas appear to be rather siloed and the 'neighborhood', as a mediator between individual experience and community inclusion, is rarely considered. Imrie (2000) notes that '[w]ritings about disabled people are usually aspatial or lack geographical frames of reference' and believes that 'geographical and/or spatial terms of reference are important in understanding disabled people's lives.' (p. 5).In an attempt to draw together literature related to disability and human rights theory, built environment accessibility legislation primarily using Australia as an example, and built environment accessibility assessment, this paper is somewhat exploratory in nature. Focusing largely on literature from, and the built environment in the global north, the paper primarily seeks to illuminate the Australian context. Spanning across all sectors, the terms 'built environment practice' and 'built environment practitioner' are intentionally broader than conventional disciplinary descriptors of architecture/architect, planning/planner, and the like, and signify all those involved in legislating, shaping, funding, forming, making, and researching the built environment. 'People with disability' encompasses the diversity of experience of people with diverse impairments given all are users of the same/single built environment.

How might an understanding of models of disability and human rights inform improving built environment accessibility, for people with disability, at neighborhood scale? The following article sets out to probe this question. Firstly, salient Models of Disability, considered from a built environment perspective, are briefly presented. The topic of Human Rights in the context of the built environment, concentrating mainly on built environment accessibility legislation relevant to Australia, is then briefly covered. Common themes of inaccessibility, as experienced by people with disability, are tabled and various methods of assessing neighborhood accessibility are noted and/or outlined. Interactions between models of disability, built environment accessibility legislation, and current methods of neighborhood-scale accessibility assessment are then discussed. In conclusion, I propose a way forward to improving the accessibility of the existing built environment for people with disability at neighborhood scale.

2. Models of Disability: A Built Environment Perspective

Within and across the disability knowledge domain much research from many nuanced, and contested, perspectives has been, and continues to be, undertaken, much of it interdisciplinary. Built environment practitioners, however, have scant acquaintance with such endeavors (Imrie 2015; Boys 2017). Therefore this paper seeks to bring disability concepts, via the central notions of established disability models, into the view of mainstream, built environment practitioners; it does not purport to add to disability studies scholarship per se. Disability models considered to be the most salient to this paper are the well-established charity, medical, social, relational, and diversity models, and the currently developing human rights model of disability. Relationships between the selected models and the existing built environment are explored in greater detail in the following paragraphs.

2.1. Charity Model of Disability

Terminology such as moral model, charity model, and religious model, in relation to disability signposts an approach to disability characterized by notions of caretaking and protection, both in terms of the vulnerable 'other' needing protection and care and, later, the need to protect the economic and social order by controlling, via segregation, 'deviant members' of society (Braddock and Parish 2001, p. 31). Construction of institutions was a core response to this viewpoint. In Australia, UK, and USA, asylums for the 'mentally ill, retardates, degenerates, and defectives'[1] were a common landmark of the late 1800s and early 1900s; workhouses have a long history in the UK (Higginbotham 2018). Often large, imposing, containing cavernous dormitories, and sited within extensive grounds away from town centers, such structures are a clear-built manifestation of the institutional nature of the charity model of disability. Usually less architecturally imposing than workhouses and asylums but not necessarily better located in terms of nearby community services, segregated schools for 'the blind and the deaf' were also common. In Melbourne, Australia, full closure of 'Kew Asylum/Kew Cottages' only occurred in 2008, a decade ago, and Victoria's last disability institution with 76 remaining residents, Colanda House in Colac in western regional Victoria, was to be closed in 2014; the facility was constructed in 1976.Institutional care for elderly persons in facilities such as workhouses, infirmaries, almshouses, homes for the aged and infirm, and 'homes' was common in the UK and USA until the middle of the 20th century (Peace 2003; Fisher 1953). Similarly, within Australia, institutional care for elderly persons was provided by a combination of charitable benevolence and government intervention, within recognizably institutional physical environments until approximately post-WW2. Due to changes in government policy and subsidies, rapid growth in (institution-like)nursing homes occurred in the 1962–1972 period in Australia, with hostels for older persons subsequently also appearing (Le Guen 1993).

Historically therefore significant proportions of the population, being not only 'the disabled' but also 'the mentally disturbed', 'the elderly', and 'defective' children, have not been publicly visible and have been congregated into institutional care settings at a distance, both geographically and culturally, from wider society (Wolfensberger 1969; Barnes and Mercer 2003). It could be argued that a crucial consequence of the historically pervasive ideology of institutionalization is that much of the general built environment is inaccessible for people with disability. In the UK, USA, and Australia people with disability, particularly people with intellectual disability, are not now generally institutionalized as a first resort. However, a common consequence of de-institutionalization is the inability to access other built environments, at the neighborhood scale, particularly, due to the legacy of poor urban-scale design. Imrie (1998) observed that "western cities are characterized by a design apartheid where building form and design are inscribed with the values of an 'able-bodied' society" (p. 129)—a somewhat inevitable consequence of the charity model's invisible segregation of people with disability.

2.2. Medical Model of Disability

The medical model of disability is essentially a normative one, based on classifying levels of deviance or deficiency compared to a normative state (Nankervis 2006). Central tenets of the medical model of disability are that firstly, a person's 'impairment' can be diagnosed, cured, or at least rehabilitated, by modern medicine and/or medical technology, and secondly, such interventions will be provided by all-knowing professionals (Oliver 1998; Scotch 2000; Pfeiffer 2001). Espousing the view that medicine should treat and/or correct impairment for the social good, the thoughts and approaches of influential American sociologist Talcott Parsons (1951) contributed to the continued preeminence of

---

1 Indicative of the terminology used at the time (Wolfensberger 1969).

the medical model of disability (Pfeiffer 2001). Other, similar descriptors such as: personal tragedy model, individual model, and rehabilitation model, are often used interchangeably.

Inherently influenced by the medical model of disability, institutionalization reached its peak in the late 1960s in most western countries (Stainton [1998] 2017). Although imposing Victorian-era structures may have fallen out of favour at that time, resulting in less immediately identifiable built forms, sheltered workshops and dormitory-style living arrangements were still common. Much existing public transport infrastructure has also been built under the legacy of the charity and medical models of disability and is, therefore, inaccessible for many people with disability. In Australia, much of Melbourne's public transport infrastructure for trains and trams dates from the early 20th century, or before. Melbourne's above-ground train system went through major rebuilding in the 1950s and 1960s but, clearly, accessibility was not much considered. Melbourne's underground city loop train system was constructed in the 1970s with many accessibility shortcomings. Current tram stop upgrading work, in Melbourne, highlights the lack of thought originally given to people with disabilities' accessibility needs.

In 2015, people with disability comprized 18.3% of the Australian population (ABS 2017). Although the oft-repeated statistic of 'approximately 20%' is intended to communicate the substantial number of people with disability in the Australian population, it tends to imply a static 20% minority–majority 80% people without disability. In reality, membership of either statistical group is always in flux with all (100%) people likely to experience mobility and/or other built environment use difficulties at some stage during the course of life (Zola 1993). Compounding such problems is that reporting of disability demographics is often categorized under a 'primary' disability such as intellectual disability, autism, vision-impairment, hearing-impairment, wheelchair user, or user of another mobility aid such as walker, crutches, or walking stick, and as arrived at through precisely categorized medical diagnosis (Nankervis 2006). Therefore, medical model ideology tends to lead to the (unacknowledged) belief among built environment practitioners that built environment accessibility needs of people with disability will be resolved by individual provision of personalized, medical intervention and/or assistive technology. In reality, many people with disability have multiple impairments affecting built environment use in differing ways and significant swathes of the built environment are inaccessible at neighborhood scale.

Engendered by people with disabilities' low public profile, conformist societal attitudes, design precedents, weak legislation, and poor understanding of built environment accessibility needs of people with disability, a significant extent of the existing built environment, whether historical or 'modernist', has been designed within a paradigm of a charity-medical model of disability, albeit unconsciously.

2.3. Social Model of Disability

Significant social and rights movements of the 1960s around race, gender, sexuality, and disability led to profound questioning of the imbalances of power, knowledge, and rights of the status quo. This, however, tended to play out differently in different parts of the world. During this period in the UK of 'new ways of thinking', Finkelstein and Hunt (British researchers, disability activists, and major theorists) developed their social relational theory concluding that social exclusion of people with disability was an outcome 'of the materialist landscape of the industrial era' rendering them economically unviable (Hunt 1966; Finkelstein 1993; Finkelstein 2001; West 2012, p. 76). Viewed through such a lens, design of factories and workplaces, schools, public transport systems, and infrastructure was heavily influenced by the attitudes of the designers' clientele. It is likely, however, that built environment form-makers were not conscious of the effect on accessibility outcomes.

Moving beyond the previous, narrow, medical view of disability to a new, wider, societal view Oliver (1983, 1998, 2013), a British academic and disability activist, developed the social model of disability in the early 1980s. Essentially, in moving disablement from an internal, individual pathology location to a primarily, external, societal environment, the social model critiques and challenges the medical model approach (Oliver 1983; Scotch 2000; Pfeiffer 2001). The Social Model explains that disability arises from barriers within 'an oppressive and discriminating society' rather than impairment per se (Soder 2009). This shifts the onus of response away from the individual (to be cured) to society (to dismantle barriers that construct disability).

New ways of thinking also extended to built form. 'Post-modernist' architecture started to emerge in the 1960s.However the Australian version, popular in the 1980s, was rarely manifested in more than facade form and decoration, with little attention paid to post-modernism's underlying hallmark concerns of diversity and discrimination. Therefore, throughout this time in Australia in terms of accessibility for people with disability, urban layouts and building design remained largely untouched by the concerns of either post-modern social theorists or proponents of the social model of disability, thereby remaining as inaccessible as ever. The Social Model of Disability, in recognizing that the built environment is a disabling instrument in itself, is of great significance to built environment practice. Invariably, however, built environment practitioners in Australia are, still unaware of such concerns. This lack of understanding can be partly explained from a regulatory perspective. Although various state-based Building Regulations may have previously contained some provision for 'disabled access' the Australian *Disability Discrimination Act* (DDA, (Australian Government 1992)) was not enacted until 1992, the *Building Code of Australia* (BCA, (ABCB 2016)) was not fully adopted nation-wide until 1998, and the (Australian) *Disability (Access to Premises—Buildings) Standards 2010* (Premises Standards, (Australian Government 2010)) was not in force until 2011!

Oliver (2013) lamented thirty years on, that even though the social model had taken on a life of its own somewhat over-reaching his original intentions, 'still talking' rather than observable progress appeared to be the main outcome. Furthermore, in an environment of funding cuts to major services due to post-global financial crisis austerity measures and associated disability movement fragmentation, Oliver (2013) acknowledges that new disability models are warranted. The influence of broader social theories of: feminism, post-modernism, and post-structuralism, on the development of other disability models is, therefore, salient (West 2012).

2.4. Relational Model of Disability

In the late 1960s Nirje, a Swedish social theorist, formulated the principles of normalization emphasizing strong support of deinstitutionalization, recognition of the diversity of the human condition, and belief that people with disability and 'normal' (ordinary) life, including access to the built environment, are not mutually exclusive. This work represents part of an emerging grand idea of social inclusion for people with disability in the community and within the neighborhood (Nirje [1969] 1994). Following on in this continuum of Nordic interest in people–environment interaction, a new disability model developed around the end of 1990s–early2000s, and has subsequently been recognized as the (Nordic) Relational Model of Disability (Goodley 2011).

As identified by UK-based Critical Disability Studies scholar Goodley (2011), restated by Lid (2013) in Norway, and Carling-Jenkins (2014) in Australia, the Nordic Relational Model of Disability revolves around three main tenets being that disability is a person-environment mismatch, situational (contextual), and relative. In work underpinned by Relational Model of Disability theory Lid (2016) posits that accessibility for wheelchair users and people with vision impairment in urban areas requires a sound understanding of person-environment interaction.

The preceding discussion is of interest because it provides at least a partial explanation of why the Nordic-Scandinavian countries are considered, in many ways, to be at the vanguard of contemporary built environment accessibility policy. Norway, for instance, is to be 'universally designed by 2025' (Norwegian Ministry of Children, Equality and Social Inclusion (NMCEandSI 2016)). However, although those involved in disability studies in Australia, Carling-Jenkins for example, are somewhat cognizant of the relational model of disability, reference to this does not appear to exist in Australian built environment literature. In a further vindication of Imrie's concerns (Imrie 2015) of built environment practitioner indifference to disability, none of the people mentioned in this subsection are from a built environment disciplinary background.

2.5. *Diversity Model of Disability*

In the USA, Shriner and Scotch, professors specializing in social work, and sociology and political economy respectively, were also very concerned about the under-representation of people with disability in employment, reduced educational attainment, and the discriminatory nature of the existing built environment. Scotch and Shriner (1997) postulate that the *Americans with Disabilities Act* of 1990 (ADA, (USDoJ CRD 2017)) with its concomitant *Title II Regulations*, Title *III Regulations*, and *ADA Standards for Accessible Design*, has arisen out of the previously dominant minority group model of disability (a political strategy which relies on advocating for justice for a disadvantaged minority, (Bickenbach et al. 1999)) and as such is a deficient approach. Instead they proposed and explored, 'Disability as Human Variation', an alternative model intended to focus attention on how society's systems respond to variation introduced by disability (Scotch and Shriner 1997). Under this model, accessibility in the built environment, for example, is not solely achieved by antidiscrimination regulation requiring a 'universal' solution; the diversity of disability must be acknowledged (Scotch and Shriner 1997). Shriner and Scotch (2001) further question the socio-political definition of disability, in which (all) barriers faced by people with disability are (built-environment) imposed and therefore removable, feeling that this common underlying ideology of disability rights activists and independent living movements insufficiently recognizes that 'impairment' does have a bearing on accessibility outcomes.

Seeking to overcome the false dichotomy of ability/disability, Bickenbach et al. (1999) pursue the concept of universalism, proposing:

> While the 'social' model is now universally accepted, it is argued that universalism as a model for theory development, research and advocacy serves disabled persons more effectively than a civil rights or 'minority group' approach. (p. 1173)

Bickenbach et al. (1999) explain that universalism reflects the view that 'disablement is a universal human phenomenon' rather than a minority one (p. 1179). A universal approach to disability shifts the focus from 'special responses for special needs' (where such needs are competing with those of the general population, Zola 1989 in (Bickenbach et al. 1999) to an approach that 'accepts difference and widens the range of normal' along an ability–disability continuum that can be applied to all humanity (Bickenbach et al. 1999, p. 1182).

Spanish researchers Palacio and Romanach (2006) also sought to overcome the false dichotomy of ability/disability in the development, via the fields of bioethics and human rights, of the diversity model of disability. Palacio and Romanach (2006) intentionally use the all-encompassing term 'diversity', adding a somewhat postmodern outlook. The similarities and differences between the diversity model and universalism cannot be debated here, but both offer new ways of thinking to built environment practitioners. Nonetheless, Hamraie (2016) whose interdisciplinary scholarship bridges critical disability, race, feminist studies, architectural history, and science and technology studies argues that a 'normate template' notion continues to underpin present-day built environment theory and practice concluding that [built environment practitioners need to] 'foreground the political, cultural, and social value of [diverse] disability embodiments.' (p. 304).

2.6. *Human Rights Model of Disability*

As with previous disability models explored in this paper, the Human rights model of disability did not spontaneously appear, but rather, evolved within a continuum of rights-based approach thinking (Quinn et al. 2002; Degener 2016). In line with the USA's standing as a significant site for rights activism, social responses to impairment were heavily predisposed towards Human Rights discourses and resultant frameworks as proposed by the United Nations (Quinn et al. 2002). An early signpost towards the human rights model of disability is the UN Universal Declaration of Human Rights adopted, in 1948, shortly after the end of WW2 (Berghs et al. 2016). Declarations of rights often arise in response to established power imbalances constraining the ability of marginalized and/or minority groups to fully participate in all aspects of society and are hallmarked by written articulation, at high legislative level, of who does and doesn't have rights and what those rights are and are not. Content is usually informed by contemporaneous sociopolitical movements, such as civil rights, women's rights, children's rights, and, of course, disability rights (Berghs et al. 2016). In the built environment space, in response to the worldwide phenomenon of emphasis on rights and deinstitutionalization, disability research and activism work in the USA investigated 'needs based assessments' (characteristic of welfare policy) and (fairer) 'rights based assessments' in relation to independent living; building on such work the independent living movement emerged in Berkeley, California, in the early 1970s (Berghs et al. 2016).

The 1980s were pivotal in disability discourse and activism, globally. Along with the emergence of Oliver's social model of disability in the early 1980s, 1981 was the UN-decreed International Year of Disabled Persons, 1983–1992 was the UN Decade of Disabled Persons, Universal Design (UD) arrived in 1984, and the UN Convention of Rights of the Child encompassing children with disability was adopted in 1989. Continuing on into the 1990s saw an expanded commitment to disability antidiscrimination legislation, for example, the ADA (USA 1990), the Australian DDA (Australian Government 1992), and the UK *Disability Discrimination Act 1995* (now the Equality Act 2010, legislation.gov.uk). Notwithstanding such positive events, Hahn (2000), a pioneer in rights-based approaches, concluded a decade after the introduction of the ADA that it 'has not fulfilled many of the hopes of its proponents' (p. 192). Nonetheless, a (human) rights model of disability is evolving and continuing to gain traction, particularly in light of the UNCRPD, adopted by the UN in 2006. In discussing the development towards the UNCRPD, Bruce (2014) restates the views of prominent Disability Studies writers (e.g., Zola, Oliver, and Hahn) in explicitly problematizing inaccessible built environments for people with disability.

Increasingly, critiques of both the built environment and legislation regarding it, have been framed from discrimination and rights viewpoints. Schindler (2015) acknowledges that the ADA has achieved progress for people with disability but highlights the power of the built environment over people's lives and its discriminatory ability, through design and planning mechanisms, to segregate thereby reducing opportunity and autonomy. Theresia Degener (2016) characterizes the inaccessibility of the built environment as a human rights problem, suggesting that Disability Studies has moved beyond the debate of medical versus social models of disability and is now in a new era of human rights model of disability as epitomized by the UNCRPD.

It is perhaps the case that the human rights model of disability is in danger of becoming narrowly defined as being the UNCRPD. There is no doubt that in its various explicit and implicit references, the UNCRPD effectively requires all the built environment to be accessible for people with disability of all ages. Disability advocates believe that the UNCRPD's rights-based sociopolitical approach to barrier removal will engender both nondiscrimination and social inclusion (Berghs et al. 2016). On the other hand, weaknesses identified by various analyses include potential for no enforcement generally, toothlessness at nation-state level, ill-defined linkages with other legislative boundary-crossing bodies, and misinterpretation leading to ill-considered modified environments (Berghs et al. 2016). Perhaps the greatest danger, however, is that in advocating for individuals' rights its use will be restricted to personal protection and safeguard, rather than being the go-to tool to precipitate enabling environments (Berghs et al. 2016). This would mark an unwelcome return to disability being considered an individualized problem, suggesting that 'a continued role for the more established social model of disability' is defensible (Berghs et al. 2016).

2.7. Disability Models: A Conundrum for Built Environment Practice?

As highlighted in the preceding pages, built environment accessibility outcomes are critically affected by the way society positions and views disability. Built environment accessibility practice has been, and continues to be, shaped by a hidden discourse. Unless exposed, this will remain uncritiqued. It is a hope that the above analysis of disability models, provides some insights from a built environment perspective.

The various models are reflective of their different historical periods. The particular value of the social model to built environment practice is the emphasis on the way environment, including the built environment, constructs disability. Disability is not a preexisting, independent, condition; the nature and experience of disability is directly linked to the built environment, among other factors. More recent models emphasize diversity of human experience—this also has implications for built environment accessibility practice. The UNCRPD specifically draws attention to the wide-ranging extent of the built environment, for example, housing, public buildings, transport, and social/cultural/recreational locations. Notions of 'community' and 'inclusion' that focus attention on geographical areas, or neighborhoods, are embedded in the UNCRPD and the way people are supported to interact with their environment is considered crucial. Therefore, the human rights model of disability, via the UNCRPD, potentially offers very strong direction and breadth for built environment accessibility legislation and practice.

From a built environment perspective, the preceding discussion raises somewhat of a conundrum, particularly in relation to built environment practice in Australia. Worldwide, including Australia, enforcement of existing built environment accessibility legislation is widely cited as a problem (NZHRC 2012; USDoJ CRD 2017; AFDO 2015; DARU 2016; NMCEandSI 2016; Sawadrsi 2011; Ariffin 2016; ACPF 2014; IDRM 2004). Nonetheless, in my experience there is a perception within critical/disability studies that a human rights model of disability, with associated UNCRPD-derived 'prescriptive' built environment accessibility legislation, would achieve more tangible results more quickly. Unfortunately, my experience indicates that built environment accessibility is already being treated, thoughtlessly, as a regulatory exercise by most built environment practitioners. As highlighted in the following Section 3 of this paper, much of the Australian built environment is not directly subject to built environment regulatory controls. Therefore, I believe there is real danger that a solely rights-based, prescriptive, approach, even if comprehensive, would merely further entrench the current tick-box mentality, with unimproved outcomes at the neighborhood scale.

3. Human Rights Legislation and the Built Environment: An Australian Viewpoint

At face value, people with disabilities' right to inclusion in the neighborhood is enshrined in 'disability' legislation. However, we know from disabled peoples organizations (DPOs), disability advocates, human rights commissions' complaints lists, media reports, and people with disability themselves, that significant difficulty in exercising such rights is still being experienced. Is this due to inadequacies in legislation? Built environment accessibility legislation is indeed somewhat opaque, as illustrated by the following paragraphs.

3.1. Accessibility Legislation

3.1.1. At International Level: UNCRPD

Within disability policy and legislation in Australia, and elsewhere, it is acknowledged that the UNCRPD is the umbrella human rights instrument addressing disability (Commonwealth of Australia 2018). Beyond the specific directives contained in Article 9 Accessibility various other Articles, (such as Article 19 Living independently and being included in the community, Article 20 Personal mobility, Article 24 Education, Article 27 Work and employment, Article 28 Adequate standard of living and social protection, Article 29 Participation in political and public life, and Article 30Participation in cultural life, recreation, leisure and sport) effectively require all the built environment to be accessible for people with disability (UN 2006). The UNCRPD also mandates the inclusion of people with disability, in communicating views about built environment experience (UN 2006). Therefore, from an 'Accessibility in the Built Environment' perspective, the content of the UNCRPD, is ground breaking.

However, there are several layers of procedure between a UN member state signing the convention and the convention being directly enforceable through domestic legislation within that country.

Although only a miniscule number of UN member states have no involvement in the convention, there are significant differences in official commitment levels. Only approximately half of the world's countries have fully committed in signing and ratifying both the convention and its accompanying optional protocol. Amongst other potential benefits for people with disability, only full commitment, that is, signing and ratifying both the convention and the optional protocol, allows (individual) claimants to take a case directly to the UN. Notably, the USA's commitment had not (mid-2017) extended beyond signing (UN 2017). A contributing factor to USA's non-UNCRPD ratification is a governmental view that the USA's ADA, with its attendant standards, is sufficiently *prescriptive* to achieve an accessible built environment (Hamraie 2012). This governmental view is, however, contested as evidenced by numerous media reports and advocacy organizations' electronic communication platforms. [2]

Australia has signed and ratified both the Convention and the Optional Protocol. Australia's ratification expresses acceptance of the inherent obligations (ALRC 2014). However, unless Australia passes appropriate domestic law the UNCRPD is not directly enforceable within the Australian judicial system (McSherry 2014). Effectively, in the Australian built environment context, it is *policy*, not enacted legislation. Furthermore, most built environment practitioners within Australia are neither familiar with UNCRPD content nor aware of its significance in relation to built environment accessibility practice.

3.1.2. Built Environment Accessibility Legislation: At National Level

In response to difficulties experienced by returned servicemen, laws specifically referencing the welfare, and rights, of people with disability started gaining momentum after WW2, particularly in the USA (The Guardian 2017). As previously highlighted, the 1960s–1990s period saw significantly strengthened legal provisions concerning rights throughout the world. Nonetheless, prior to the adoption of the UNCRPD, '[a]ccording to the Inter-Parliamentary Union, only one third of countries have antidiscrimination and other disability-specific laws.'(UN 2008). Over a decade later however, most countries have various laws and multiple official government policies in place proscribing discrimination, upholding rights, and enhancing wellbeing of people with disability; the content of same is, however, somewhat variable (DREDF 2017). The USA legislative package of ADA, ADA Regulations, and integral *ADA Standards for Accessible Design* (the latter running to hundreds of pages), is rights-based. *ADA Standards for Accessible Design* are also 'prescriptive', that is, there is much detailed information about what *must* be done within the built environment to satisfy the stipulated accessibility requirements.

Australia's DDA is a complaints-based document. In a sense, it is also 'performance-based' in that detailed prescriptive requirements are not contained within the act, rather, it is necessary to satisfy the 'objects' of the act. These are contained in one paragraph consisting of three brief, explanatory parts. Only part of the first part appears to be of direct relevance to the built environment:

(a) to eliminate, as far as possible, discrimination against persons on the ground of disability in the areas of:

 (i) work, accommodation, education, access to premises, clubs and sport; and

---

2 For example: http://usicd.org/index.cfm/crpd, https://www.hrw.org/news/2013/07/26/us-ratify-disability-rights-treaty, http://www.catholicethics.com/forum-submissions/the-us-fails-to-ratify-the-un-convention-on-the-rights-of-persons-with-disabilities, https://www.ahead.org/CRPD/Myths%20and%20Facts, https://www.huffingtonpost.com/2013/10/08/ada-violations_n_4064270.html, https://dredf.org/2017/10/04/ada-under-attack-tell-house-representatives-oppose-h-r-620/, https://dredf.org/web-log/2017/06/23/no-roll-backs-civil-rights-past-plaintiff-opposing-h-r-620-ada-notification-act/.

(ii) the provision of goods, facilities, services and land; and... (Australian Government 1992, p. 1)

However, notwithstanding its central 'do not discriminate' intention, implementation detail is somewhat lacking. Therefore, built environment practitioners do not understand the significance of DDA requirements which are thus commonly ignored.

To address perceived gaps and to further Australia's DDA implementation outcomes, subordinate *legislation* via a suite of 'Disability Standards', being the: *Disability Standards for Accessible Public Transport 2002* ((Australian Government 2002), Transport Standards), *Disability Standards for Education 2005* ((Commonwealth of Australia 2006), Education Standards), and the Premises Standards (2010), has subsequently been enacted. Each of these standards has limitations in terms of directing built environment practice effectively. The first half, approximately, of the Premises Standards covers 'legalities', for example: Preliminaries, Scope of Standards, Commission Exemptions, and Review, before moving on to (technical) Deemed-to-satisfy provisions. Premises Standards technical content generally aligns with that of the BCA in numbering, presentation and detail. However all three Disability Standards, and the BCA, have complex inclusions and exclusions.

In terms of built environment accessibility, oversight of transport *premises* has now been transferred to the Premises Standards. Potential shortcomings of this legislative move include: nullifying compliance target date timetabling, the relationship between compliance-timetabled rolling stock and compliance un-timetabled built infrastructure impacting people with disabilities' built environment accessibility, and the restricting of public sector scrutiny by effectively putting transport premises into the (individual) buildings regulatory system. In addition, the Premises Standards do not apply to most private dwelling stock nor to public realm-pedestrian environment infrastructure. Each of the Disability Standards features largely inaccessible language. The Education Standards are written in 'policy-speak' and hence ignored by built environment practitioners whereas the Transport Standards and Premises Standards are written in built environment regulatory code language incomprehensible to those without sufficient background technical knowledge and access to all referenced documents; the latter are not freely available.

The Premises Standards and the BCA, in the context of built environment accessibility, are commonly referred to as being harmonized. The BCA is a national-level, *performance-based,* document and has been since 1996 (ABCB 2017). Nonetheless, the on-going inclusion of technical-looking deemed-to-satisfy provisions has contributed to a continued perception of prescription. It is a common misconception that the technical detail presented in the deemed-to-satisfy provisions, in both the premises standards and the BCA, is prescriptive. This is not the case. Ultimately, the legislated requirement is to satisfy the performance requirements, compliance with Deemed-to-satisfy provisions is merely an undemanding way to acceptably demonstrate so-called satisfaction. However, if one looks closely one will discover that significant portions of buildings, for example, fit-out, fixtures, and fittings are not directly covered in deemed-to-satisfy provisions which mainly focus on wheelchair-accessible paths of travel and toilets.

Although the Premises Standards and BCA are commonly referred to as being harmonized, some BCA Performance Requirements are omitted from the Premises Standards and the 'legalities' part of the Premises Standards is not included in the BCA at all. What has been 'harmonized' is, predominantly, the replication of deemed-to-satisfy provisions. However, Deemed-to-satisfy provisions Parts D4 Braille and tactile signs and D5 Accessible water entry/exit for swimming pools in the Premises Standards are appended to Part D3 in the BCA, confoundingly called Specifications (deemed-to-satisfy), and numbered differently. The BCA's: Part D3 Access for people with a disability, Part E3 Lift installations, and Part F2.4 Accessible sanitary facilities, all being deemed-to-satisfy provisions, do not make any direct, or inferred reference, to either the *Disability Discrimination Act,* or the Disability Standards.

Bourne out by my extensive consulting and provision of professional education experience, architects and building designers tend to rely on the BCA as their only built environment accessibility regulatory source. This is rather problematic on three counts. Firstly, referenced documents such

as Australian Standards[3] are published by private sector entity SAI Global and are not freely available. Secondly, effectively, the BCA does not cover the accessibility of either public realm infrastructure, including the pedestrian environment, or most private dwellings. This is particularly concerning as, in terms of spatial coverage, those categories of built form comprise most of the built environment. The 'public realm', being, roads and other transport infrastructure, the pedestrian environment, parks and the like, *not buildings*, is thus not subject to building permit regulation. Building accessibility legislation requirements are also therefore not directly triggered. Current built environment accessibility legislation in Australia being not directly applicable to private dwellings is reflective of conventional content which can be traced back to the USA's ANSI (1961) *A117.1 Accessible and Usable Buildings and Facilities* first issued in 1961. Detached and semi-detached housing comprise approximately 87% of Australia's private dwellings (Heath 2017). Thirdly, if the fine print is closely read, it can be discerned that the deemed-to-satisfy provisions of the BCA (and the Premises Standards) allow plenty of opportunity for suboptimal outcomes and/or 'avoidance'. Such avoidance does not obviate the DDA complaint process but complainants' capacity to complain is often limited by meagre resources.

4. Assessing Neighborhood Accessibility

An essential component of this tripartite paper is the lived experience of people with disability, at the neighborhood scale. Illustrated in Table 1: Accessing the neighborhood? an extensive survey, undertaken as part of my current PhD studies, has established that across 'anglophone' countries, Europe, Asia-Pacific, Africa, and Latin America, many people with disability find their everyday environments a daily, overwhelming struggle. Within the literature common themes are very obvious: social inclusion stymied by inability to navigate broken travel chains; built environment areas of greatest concern being housing, public realm pedestrian environment (at the community/neighborhood scale), and public transport; lack of enforcement of existing legislation identified as a very significant problem; and inconsistent and/or misinterpretation of existing legislation also identified as problematic.

Table 1. Accessing the neighborhood?

Themes	Social exclusion • Community/neighborhood inclusion stymied by broken travel chains Inequitable built environment • Unsuitable housing • Deficient public realm pedestrian environment • Unusable public transport infrastructure Legislation inadequacies • Legislation not enforced • Legislation misinterpreted
Regions	'Anglophone' countries, Europe, Asia Pacific, Africa, Latin America
Countries	UK, New Zealand, Canada, USA, Australia; France, Turkey, Slovenia, Poland, Germany, Kosovo, Sweden, Norway; Malaysia, Thailand, Japan, China, India, Singapore, Pacific Islands; Ethiopia, Sierra Leone, Uganda, Zambia, Egypt, Ghana; Mexico, Belize, Honduras, Suriname, Brazil, Chile
References	(HoC WEC 2017; NZHRC 2012; Stephens et al. 2017; USDoJ CRD 2017; AFDO 2015; Rains and Butland 2012; DARU 2016; Sander et al. 2005; Baris and Uslu 2009; Zajac 2013; Basha 2015; NMCEandSI 2016; Sawadrsi 2011; Sarma 2016; Ariffin 2016; Wee et al. 2015; ACPF 2014; Tudzi et al. 2017; IDRM 2004; Pereira Martins et al. 2016; Rotarou and Sakellariou 2017)

[3] There is much confusion around the difference between Australian Standards and Disability Standards. In the built environment accessibility context, the former are, effectively, merely guidelines and the latter are indeed legislation.

Given the breadth of the existing built environment inaccessibility problem as articulated above, what processes are in place for improving same? As a starting point, what tools are available to empirically assess the accessibility for people with disability, at neighborhood scale, of the existing built environment?

Generally positioned within the 'expert' domain, access auditing refers to assessment by experts for compliance against accessibility legislation. In the prescriptive USA system this involves working through the very lengthy ADA and associated detailed standards. Although still available, the *ADA Best Practices Tool Kit for State and Local Governments* does not appear to have been updated since 2008 (USDoJ CRD 2008). In 2016, the (USA) Institute for Human Centered Design, through its New England ADA Center, produced *ADA Checklist for Existing Facilities* (Existing Facilities) along with various other recreational facilities checklists including, for example, amusement rides, various water-based recreational activities, and shooting facilities. The publicly available Existing Facilities checklist, based on the USA *2010 ADA Standards for Accessible Design*, is technical-compliance based requiring equipment, expert knowledge, many Yes/No boxes checked, accumulated photographic record dealt with, and possible solutions noted, after which it is expected that the possible solutions will be costed, a plan developed, changes made, and progress annually monitored (IHCD 2016). Typologically, more and more of the USA's built environment is being covered by ADA checklists. Nonetheless, although ongoing development of publicly available Access Auditing tools is occurring via new, and updated, ADA checklists for example, such assessment tools are invariably compliance-based without input from people with disability. Data collected remains as discrete, islands of information. Although checklist content may include cost estimates, compliance-achieving rectification recommendations are the intended main output. Neither interrogating the legislation itself nor identifying user preference prioritization is contemplated. The process, therefore, is invariably reduced to a financial transaction, not an upholding of rights.

In Australia's performance-based system 'compliance' is interpreted, by experts, against various deemed-to-satisfy provisions often referencing Australian Standards but not covering off all aspects of building structure, form, or fit out. Also in Australia, similarly to the USA, esoterically comprehensive spreadsheets of information are produced and input from people with lived experience of disability is generally not sought. Prioritization of rectifications is arrived at through combinations of expert opinion and costing differentials. In both the USA and Australian legislative systems, public and commercial building accessibility is the customary target. Lack of specific accessibility legislation directly applicable to private housing, public space, and pedestrian environments makes 'compliance' auditing of such areas, in Australia, a flawed undertaking. In Australia the Access Institute, a private sector registered training organization, runs various 'accessibility in the built environment' programs at diploma, certificate iv, and short course level. Short courses offered vary in duration from two–three hours to one–two days and access audit templates for attendees' future use are issued (Access Institute 2017). Nonetheless, courses are applicable to discrete parts of the built environment in isolation only and offered on a commercial transaction basis. There is no expectation that data obtained from subsequent assessments will be used for any wider, community oriented, benefit. No publicly available, peer-reviewed, standardized checklists are in widespread use amongst the Australian Access Consulting community. The lack of attention paid to developing, and maintaining, publicly available access auditing tools is, perhaps in Australia at least, a reflection of the now privatized nature of built environment 'compliance' consulting services, resulting in private-practice-developed methods being treated as commercial-in-confidence. Operationalization of (expert) Access Auditing invariably involves tick-boxing a list of pre-determined items corresponding to defined regulations. Underpinning theoretical concepts, for example adherence to any particular disability model or acknowledgement of human rights requirements, are not communicated–the list is the list.

Beyond the type of access auditing described above, there are a range of other measurement approaches. In relation to fitness and recreation environments an assessment tool, *Accessibility Instruments Measuring Fitness and Recreation Environments* (AIMFREE), was first used in assessing

35 health clubs and fitness facilities in a US national field trial (Rimmer et al. 2005). A major driver of AIMFREE development was the identification of highly inaccessible, neighborhood-scale, public realm pedestrian environments for people with disability, and in this context, 'health clubs may present a viable alternative for participating in physical activity' (Rimmer et al. 2005, p. 2022). Several further studies, in either full or modified form, have been undertaken in Canada, USA, Kuwait, and Singapore (Arbour-Nicitopoulos and Ginis 2011; Calder and Mulligan 2014; Rimmer et al. 2017). Albeit with limitations, principally being length of 422 questions and some problematic psychometric properties, AIMFREE methodology is considered satisfactory, particularly regarding content validity and development of appropriate scoring calculations (Calder and Mulligan 2014). Various AIMFREE Manuals in both professional and consumer versions can be ordered from National Center on Health, Physical Activity and Disability (NCHPAD); purchase price and content unknown (NCHPAD 2017). AIMFREE is specifically applicable to sport/fitness and recreation centers, a rather esoteric component of the built environment, typologically, locationally, and spatially.

Lau et al. (2015) proposed the *Building Inclusiveness Assessment Score* (BIAS) for assessing the disability inclusiveness of university buildings. Originally intended to be conveyed as one final score, the development and testing process conducted in Hong Kong indicated that making the Physical Disability Inclusion Subscore (PDIS) and the Visual Impairment Inclusion Subscore (VIIS) explicit was warranted (Lau et al. 2015). Assessment items included in BIAS are intentionally derived from international accessible design guidelines, built environment accessibility legislation and standards, and universal design principles; 'subjective' input from people with disability is not sought (Lau et al. 2015). Such attitudes are indicative of, firstly, the tension between compliance-based built environment assessment and sidelined disability studies lived experience and, secondly, the naive belief that standards and guidelines are 'right', and properly reflective of people with disability accessibility needs. Several built environment accessibility assessment methodologies developed in other parts of the world, including BIAS, are referenced in literature back grounding development of the *Composite Disability Design Inclusiveness Score* (CDDIS), a method of assessing the inclusivity of university buildings in Ghana specifically (Tudzi et al. 2017). Further development of the methodologies mentioned is not apparent.

A range of other nonconventional accessibility investigation tools, designed to determine public realm accessibility for people with disability, do not appear to be in use or undergoing further development.[4] Elsewhere and across a range of, mainly, public realm environments, several research projects investigating built environment accessibility for people with disability have developed measurement methods and generated data (Kadir and Jamaludin 2012; Zajac 2013; Wee et al. 2015; Pereira Martins et al. 2016; Buhler et al. 2015; Stephens et al. 2017). Production of replicable built environment accessibility assessment tools was not, however, a defined intention. Findings arrived at using conventional accessibility/walkability tools in the interdisciplinary *Street Mobility and Network Accessibility* project indicated high accessibility/walkability potential (Mindell et al. 2017). Fine grain analysis, however, found that people with disability were disproportionately affected by poor quality pedestrian environments, particularly deficient pedestrian crossings and footpaths (Mindell et al. 2017).

In Australia, Green (2011) devised a new tool, the *Universal Mobility Index* (UMI), purporting to quantitatively measure, comparatively rate, and longitudinally track equity of access across all parts of the built environment using a participatory approach. The UMI is explicitly founded on the social model of disability and methodologically intended to function as a rights-based indicator (Green 2011). The UMI tool consists of two main components—built environment component and

---

4 See, for example: *Access Audit Tool*, Lewis, McQuade, and Thomas, early 2000s; the oft-referenced 2009 Ankara work of Baris and Uslu; *International Transportation Accessibility Survey* (ITAS), 2010 International Conference on Mobility and Transport for Elderly and Disabled Persons; *A Methodology for Enhancing Life by Increasing Accessibility* (AMELIA-AUNT-SUE), (Evans 2010; AUNT-SUE 2010; Mackett et al. 2012); and *Rating of Accessibility and Safety* (ValeAS), (Biocca 2014).

policy environment component—the latter considers whether the opinions of people with disabilities on the built environment are meaningfully acknowledged and included (Green 2011). The built environment component requires neighborhood accessibility assessment being undertaken by people with disability themselves. Therefore, its characteristics, in underpinning theory, components, and measurement methods, are markedly different to conventional access auditing. The first pilot of the UMI was undertaken for my Masters research project in the Kensington (Victoria, Australia) neighborhood in 2011 with results published in 2012 (Jackson and Green 2012).

Therefore, although various work is being done in various specialized directions it appears there is not any overall neighborhood scale built environment accessibility assessment tool in widespread use. Other than the UMI, current and past built environment accessibility assessment tools and methods commonly lack explicit theoretical regard to disability models and/or human rights requirements. Furthermore, excluding the concept of access auditing, tools and/or assessment methods presented above are virtually unknown in built environment practice. Many have been developed from a non-built environment disciplinary perspective. Given the general spatial scale of assessment this is somewhat understandable; the nuances of built environment production are, however, difficult to comprehend from a non-built environment perspective. On the other hand, reflective of the lack of understanding within the built environment knowledge domain of the lived experience of people with disability, accessibility assessment tools developed from a built environment perspective, BIAS for example, tend to be building typology specific, expert-driven, and compliance-based with, at first impression, complicated calculating processes.

5. Putting it All Together

5.1. Disability Models: Application in the Built Environment Context

Deeply entrenched ways of thinking exemplified by the charity and medical models of disability have had a profound influence on the shaping, forming, and making, of our existing built environment. While it is doubtful that most built environment practitioners in the past sat at drawing boards dreaming up ways to deliberately design-out 'the disabled', the net result of their exclusionary 'othering' actions is the same: a built environment that continues to fail the accessibility needs of many people with disability. This has occurred not just at the individual building scale but is also evident in enduring urban layouts, for example, poor pedestrian environments, deficient public transport provision, and unsatisfactory location of residential and other services. Deinstitutionalization, now considered a societal norm has, doubtless, resulted in reduced incidence of full-time institutional care. However many residents of group homes are routinely unable to access local pedestrian environments, services, and public transport; children with disability and their carers community access needs are not addressed; and the laudable ideal of ageing in place is an accessibility nightmare in many cases, both at home and within the neighborhood. Although some current urban planning and design practices such as tactical urbanism and biophilic design may be post-modernist in their participatory-ness and natural-world focus, outcomes are still informed by entrenched design-school attitudes, the result being that the accessibility needs of people with disability are still ignored.

The medical model of disability is generally accepted to lack social focus and typical disability reporting, of 'primary' impairment or medical diagnosis of 'greatest severity', does not convey the multifactorial lived, person + environment, experience of many people with disability. Therefore, in the quest to improve built environment accessibility, the social model of disability serves as a powerful wake-up call. Firstly, it shifts the focus away from the individual, but perhaps more importantly, at least in the context of built environment practice, it recognizes that the built environment is a disabling instrument in itself. The relational model of disability, being tied in with the Nordic way of life, legislation, policy, and professional proficiency also provides some pointers, particularly given Nordic/Scandinavian standing at the vanguard of built environment accessibility practice. In figuring out how to improve the accessibility of the existing built environment, at neighborhood scale, we surely need to consider all users. But who is ALL? The false dichotomy of ability/disability is a pitfall to be avoided; the post-modernist diversity model of disability aids understanding in this regard. The human rights model of disability is a forceful reminder of the rights of people with disability.

Built environment practitioner ignorance of people with disabilities' accessibility needs is compounded by slow rates, overall, of built environment renewal. Pinnegar et al. (2008) concluded that the Australian built environment changes at a rate of only around 1.25% per year. Therefore much of the existing built environment has indeed been informed by the charity and medical models of disability. The social model of disability has now been in existence for approximately four decades, the relational, diversity, and human rights, disability models are more recent. Unfortunately though, the concept of models of disability is virtually unknown in Australian built environment circles.

5.2. Built Environment Accessibility Rights Instruments: Implementation Issues

Neighborhood inclusion for all is apparently enshrined in law via various rights declarations and national-level regulatory mechanisms, and the groundbreaking advent of the UNCRPD. However in many ways, albeit unconsciously, the ways of thinking derived from the charity and medical models of disability are still underpinning current building regulations at the within-country level. Entrenched and poorly built environment accessibility outcomes at the neighborhood scale thereby continue.

Human rights instruments vary markedly in content, format, and prescription versus performance orientation, profoundly influencing interpretation. However, those that call for more certainty, via more prescription along the lines of the standards integral to the USA's ADA, perhaps do not understand the nuances of built environment design, the wide variation in built environment existing conditions, and the particularities of project-specific challenges. It is physically impossible to write detailed prescriptive requirements covering every possible situation, and attempting to do so risks reduction to tick-box compliance devoid of understanding of the diversity of the human condition. Additionally, reducing design outcomes to a set of pre-determined, potentially outmoded, solutions risks stifling innovation, an essential component in the quest to obviate disability-related inequality of existing built environment access. On the other hand Australia's performance-based system, theoretically encouraging endless innovation, is not necessarily superior in all respects, if one's aim is to improve the existing built environment sooner rather than later.

Evidently, there are also resources imbalances at the nation-state level throughout the world. Nonetheless, living in a developed country does not automatically translate to all its citizens enjoying full access to the built environment. In Australia, if we are not mindful, our charity-medical model inaccessible built environment legacy is likely to be further entrenched. Replacement and/or renewal of the overall existing built environment and particularly of the public realm is, historically, slow. Increasing appreciation of the value of retaining existing structure, which in the context of sustainability concepts such as embodied energy and carbon and virtual water is to be encouraged, is likely to decelerate, rather than increase, 'natural' renewal.

Due to the various factors discussed in the preceding paragraphs it is likely that built environment (in)accessibility, in Australia at least and particularly within the public realm and housing, will continue to be problematic if reliance on the current legislative framework is continued in isolation. Perhaps there are other processes that can also be utilized to improve the accessibility of the built environment, at neighborhood scale, for people with disability?

5.3. Improving Neighborhood Accessibility: Measure

There is still not any overall neighborhood scale built environment accessibility assessment tool, in widespread use. In Australia, as elsewhere, within either the academy or professional practice, concerted research and development of neighborhood-scale accessibility assessment tools aimed at evaluating the lived experience of diverse people with disability has not, to date, occurred. Without such information and given the extent of the problem, it is difficult to see how a well thought-out, rather than reactionary, program of improvement can be determined. As a first step, measurement of existing conditions is essential, particularly in the face of scarce resources (Green 2011).

6. Conclusions

The fact that the built environment is still inaccessible in the 21st century is staggering. Self-evidently, built environment practitioners are unfamiliar with contemporary accessibility expectations and fail to realize that historically entrenched ways of practice continue to construct disability. The social model of disability, compelling practitioners to confront the disabling nature of built environment practice, is fundamental to improving built environment accessibility outcomes.

Improving built environment accessibility outcomes also requires built environment practitioners to understand the accessibility needs of people with disability. People with disability are not a homogenous group. People with disability are diverse, as are all of the members of a society. There is, however, only one built environment. To ensure that our built environment is as accessible as possible for all people, built environment shapers, formers, and makers, must engage directly with people with disability—an uncommon activity, historically. Furthermore, to ensure that people with disabilities' built environment accessibility needs are not inadvertently overlooked, *a la* charity and medical models of disability, a human rights model of disability is warranted.

Globally, significant built environment accessibility rights legislation and policy frameworks already exist, for example, the groundbreaking UNCRPD, national disability discrimination acts, 'disability standards', building code accessibility requirements, and other guidelines within-country. However, in attempting to achieve built environment accessibility, existing legislation does not, nor can it, provide all the answers. Nonetheless, built environment practitioners take for granted that it does, due to lack of understanding, encountering, or interacting, with disability. Furthermore most built environment practitioners are not aware of the full content or significance of built environment accessibility legislation. People with disability experiencing major difficulties accessing the existing built environment within the neighborhood therefore continues. Areas of greatest concern are housing, the public realm's pedestrian environment, and public transport. These areas comprise the greatest spatial content of neighborhoods, and in Australia these areas are, coincidentally, the areas of the built environment with the weakest, least direct, accessibility legislation. Current codifying of built environment accessibility (human) rights via legislation within-country is opaque, risking stymieing positive outcomes flowing from the UNCRPD.

Also coincidentally, empirical data regarding the extent of the existing built environment inaccessibility problem, particularly at the neighborhood scale, is not readily available. Cogent processes of improvement are unlikely without such information. Various ways of measuring neighborhood accessibility have shown promise in the past but have not progressed. Subject to further piloting—perhaps the UMI, originally devised by Green and consciously underpinned by social model of disability and rights-based approach—might fill this gap.

Understanding disability models and acknowledging human rights can beneficially inform improvement of accessibility of built environment for people with disability at neighborhood scale. However, built environment practitioners must firstly recognize that, exemplified by the charity and medical models of disability and best explained by the social model of disability, built environment practice is a potent disabling instrument in itself. Secondly, it is essential for built environment practitioners to always engage with people with disability directly, rather than assuming tick-box compliance of codified human rights is sufficient. Thirdly, if existing built environment conditions are not well-understood, accessibility improvement progress is likely to be impeded.

Acknowledgments: Publishing cost fully funded by Deakin University through the Knowledge Unlatched initiative. No other funding has been received.

References

Australian Building Codes Board (ABCB). 2016. *National Construction Code NCC 2016 Building Code of Australia—Volume One (BCA);* Canberra: The Australian Building Codes Board.

Australian Building Codes Board (ABCB). 2017. Available online: http://www.abcb.gov.au/Connect/Articles/2017/11/Celebrating-21-years-of-the-performance-base-code (accessed on 29 November 2017).

Australian Bureau of Statistics (ABS). 2017. 4430.0—Disability, Ageing and Carers, Australia: Summary of Findings, 2015. Available online: http://www.abs.gov.au/ausstats/abs@.nsf/mf/4430.0 (accessed on 12 January 2018).

2017. Access Institute. Available online: https://accessinstitute.com.au/events/category/courses/ (accessed on 10 November 2017).

African Child Policy Forum (ACPF). 2014. *Access Denied Voices of Persons with Disabilities from Africa.* Addis Ababa: The African Child Policy Forum.

Australian Federation of Disability Organizations (AFDO). 2015. *The National Disability Strategy: Five Years on.* Melbourne: Australian Federation of Disability Organizations.

Australia Law Reform Commission (ALRC). 2014. Available online: https://www.alrc.gov.au/publications/equality-capacity-and-disability-commonwealth-laws/legislative-and-regulatory-framework (accessed on 12 January 2018).

American National Standards Institute (ANSI). 1961. *A117.1 Accessible and Usable Buildings and Facilities.* Washington: American National Standards Institute.

Arbour-Nicitopoulos, Kelly P., and Kathleen Martin Ginis. 2011. Universal Accessibility of "Accessible" Fitness and Recreational Facilities for Persons with Mobility Disabilities. *Adapted Physical Activity Quarterly*, 28. [CrossRef]

Ariffin, Affifah. 2016. Existing Buildings to Meet New Accessibility Requirements from 2017. *Channel News Asia.* Available online: https://www.channelnewsasia.com/news/singapore/existing-buildings-to-meet-new-accessibility-requirements-from-2-7929208 (accessed on 11 October 2017).

2010. Accessibility and User Needs in Transport for Sustainable Urban Environments (AUNT-SUE). Available online: http://aunt-sue.lboro.ac.uk/toolkit/amelia/ (accessed on 10 November 2017).

Australian Government. 1992. *Disability Discrimination Act (DDA) 1992 (as Amended).* Canberra: Office of Parliamentary Counsel.

Australian Government. 2002. *Disability Standards for Accessible Public Transport 2002 (as Amended).* Canberra: Attorney-General's Department.

Australian Government. 2010. *Disability (Access to Premises—Buildings) Standards 2010 (as Amended).* Canberra: Attorney-General's Department.

Baris, Mehmet E., and Aysel Uslu. 2009. Accessibility for the disabled people to the built environment in Ankara, Turkey. *African Journal of Agricultural Research* 4: 801–14.

Barnes, Colin, and Geof Mercer. 2003. *Disability.* Cambridge: Polity Press.

Basha, Rozafa. 2015. Disability and Public Space—Case Studies of Prishtina and Prizren. *International Journal of Contemporary Architecture "The New ARCH"* 2. [CrossRef]

Berghs, Maria, Karl Atkin, Hilary Graham, Chris Hatton, and Carol Thomas. 2016. Chapter 3 Scoping models and theories of disability. In *Implications for Public Health Research of Models and Theories of Disability: A Scoping Study and Evidence Synthesis.* Southampton: NIHR Journals Library, Public Health Research, No. 4.8. [CrossRef]

Bevan, Mark, and Karen Croucher. 2011. *Lifetime Neighborhoods.* London: Department for Communities and Local Government, ISBN 978-1-4098-2973-7.

Bickenbach, Jerome E., Somnath Chatterji, Elizabeth M. Badley, and T. Bedirhan Ustun. 1999. Models of disablement, universalism and the international classification of impairments, disabilities and handicaps. *Social Science & Medicine* 48: 1173–87.

Biocca, Luigi. 2014. ValeAS: Uno strumento ICT per valutare l'accessibilità e la sicurezza dell'ambiente costruito = ValeAS: An ICT tool to assess accessibility and safety of the built environment. *TECHNE: Journal of Technology for Architecture &Environment* 132–39. [CrossRef]

Boys, Jos. 2017. Introduction. In *Disability, Space, Architecture: A Reader.* Edited by Jos Boys. London and New York: Routledge, ISBN 978-1-315-56007-6 (ebk).

Braddock, David L., and Susan L. Parish. 2001. Chapter 2: An Institutional History of Disability. In *Handbook of Disability Studies*, 2nd ed. Edited by Gary L. Albrecht, Seelman K and Michael Bury. Thousand Oaks: Sage Publications. [CrossRef]

Bruce, Anna. 2014. Which Entitlements and for Whom? The Convention on the Rights of Persons with Disabilities and Its Ideological Antecedents. Ph.D. thesis, Lund University, Lund, Sweden.

Buhler, Christian, Roland Borosch, and Gertrud Servos. 2015. Implementing UNCRPD—Barrier Free Access to Buildings in NRW—Database and Signet "NRWInklusiv". In *Assistive Technology*. Edited by Cecilia Sik-Lanyi, Evert-Jan Hoogerwerf, Klaus Miesenberger and Peter Cudd. Amsterdam: IOS Press. [CrossRef]

Calder, Allyson M., and Hilda Mulligan. 2014. Measurement properties of instruments that assess inclusive access to fitness and recreational sports centers: A systematic review. *Disability and Health Journal* 7: 26–35. [CrossRef] [PubMed]

Carling-Jenkins, Rachel. 2014. *Disability and Social Movements: Learning from Australian Experiences*. Series: Interdisciplinary Disability Studies; Farnham: Routledge.

Commonwealth of Australia. 2006. *Disability Standards for Education 2005*. Canberra: Attorney-General's Department.

Commonwealth of Australia. 2018. Rights of People with Disability. Available online: https://www.ag.gov.au/RightsAndProtections/HumanRights/Human-rights-scrutiny/PublicSectorGuidanceSheets/Pages/Rightsofpeoplewithdisability.aspx (accessed on 12 January 2018).

Disability Advocacy Resource Unit (DARU). 2016. 3. Advocacy Issues. Available online: http://www.daru.org.au/disability-advocacy-by-the-numbers-statistics-from-july-2012-to-june-2016/3-advocacy-issues (accessed on 11 October 2017).

Deane, Kirsten, and The National People with Disabilities and Carer Council. 2009. *SHUT OUT: The Experience of People with Disabilities and their Families in Australia*. Canberra: Commonwealth of Australia, ISBN 978-1-921380-54-9.

Degener, Theresia. 2016. Disability in a Human Rights Context. *Laws* 5: 35. [CrossRef]

Disability Rights Commission UK (DRC). 2004. Towards Access Standards: The Work of Local Access Groups in England and Wales. Available online: http://disability-studies.leeds.ac.uk/library/titles/T/ (accessed on 19 February 2018).

2017. Disability Rights Education & Defense Fund (DREDF). Available online: https://dredf.org/legal-advocacy/international-disability-rights/international-laws/ (accessed on 29 July 2017).

Evans, Graeme. 2010. Accessibility, Urban Design and the Whole Journey Environment. *Built Environment* 35: 366–85. [CrossRef]

Finkelstein, Vic. 1993. Disability: A social challenge or an administrative responsibility? In *Disabling Barriers, Enabling Environments*. Edited by John Swain, Vic Finkelstein, Sally French and Mike Oliver. London: Sage.

Finkelstein, Vic. 2001. A Personal Journey into Disability Politics. Presentation Held in Independent Living Institute Library Collection. Available online: www.independentliving.org/docs3/finkelstein01a.html (accessed on 12 January 2018).

Fisher, Jacob. 1953. Trends in Institutional Care of the Aged. *The Bulletin*, October.

Goodley, Dan. 2011. *Disability Studies: An Inter-Disciplinary Introduction*. London: Sage.

Green, Ralph J. 2011. An Introductory Theoretical and Methodological Framework for a Universal Mobility Index (UMI) to Quantify, Compare, and Longitudinally Track Equity of Access across the Built Environment. *Journal of Disability Policy Studies* 21. [CrossRef]

Hahn, Harlan. 2000. Accommodations and the ADA: Unreasonable Bias or Biased Reasoning. *Berkeley Journal of Employment and Labour Law* 21. [CrossRef]

Hamraie, Aimi. 2012. Proximate and Peripheral: Ableist Discourses of Space and Vulnerability surrounding the UNCRPD. In *The Politics of Space and Place*. Edited by Chiara Certoma, Nicola Clewer and Doug Elsey. Newcastle upon Tyne: Cambridge Scholars Publishing, pp. 145–69, ISBN (10): 1-4438-4073-4.

Hamraie, Aimi. 2016. Universal Design and the Problem of "Post-Disability" Ideology. *Design and Culture*. [CrossRef]

Heath, David. 2017. Meeting the Housing Needs of Australia's Booming Population. Available online: http://builtoffsite.com.au/issue-06/meeting-housing-needs-australias-booming-population/ (accessed on 19 February 2018).

Higginbotham, Peter. 2018. The Workhouse. Available online: http://www.workhouses.org.uk/ (accessed on 19 February 2018).

House of Commons Women and Equalities Committee (HoC WEC). 2017. Building for Equality: Disability and the Built Environment. Available online: www.parliament.uk/womenandequalities (accessed on 11 October 2017).

Hunt, Paul. 1966. A Critical Condition. In *Stigma: The Experience of Disabilitty*. Edited by Paul Hunt. London: Geoffrey Chapman.

International Disability Rights Monitor (IDRM). 2004. *International Disability Rights Monitor Regional Report of the Americas*. International Disability Network; Chicago: Center for International Rehabilitation.

2016. Institute for Human Centred Design (IHCD). Available online: http://adachecklist.org/checklist.html (accessed on 10 November 2017).

Imrie, Rob. 1998. Oppression, Disability and Access in the Built Environment. In *Disability Reader: Social Science Perspectives*. Edited by Tom Shakespeare. London: Bloomsbury Pubishing PLC, ISBN13: 9780304339761.

Imrie, Rob. 2000. Disabling Environments and the Geography of Access Policies and Practices. *Disability & Society* 15: 5–24.

Imrie, Rob. 2015. Doing disability differently: An alternative handbook on architecture, dis/ability and designing for everyday life. *Disability & Society* 30: 486–88.

Imrie, Rob F., and Peter Wells. 1993. Disablism, Planning, and the Built Environment. *Environment and Planning C, Government and Policy* 11: 213–31. [CrossRef]

Jackson, Mary Ann, and Ralph J. Green. 2012. The Role of Access in Achieving Healthy Buildings: Universal Mobility Index. Paper presented at the 10th International Conference on Healthy Buildings, Brisbane, Queensland, Australia, July 8–12.

Jenks, Mike, and Nicola Demsey. 2007. Defining the Neighborhood: Challenges for Empirical Research. *The Town Planning Review* 78: 153–77. [CrossRef]

Kadir, Syazwani A., and Mariam Jamaludin. 2012. Users' Satisfaction and Perception on Accessibility of Public Buildings in Putrajaya: Access Audit Study. *Procedia—Social and Behavioral Sciences* 50: 429–41. [CrossRef]

Lau, Wai Kin, Daniel Chi Wing Ho, and Yung Yau. 2015. Assessing the disability inclusiveness of University buildings in Hong Kong. *International Journal of Strategic Property Management* 20: 184–97. [CrossRef]

Le Guen, Roxane. 1993. *Residential Care for the Aged: An Overview of Government Policy from 1962 to 1993*. Canberra: Parliamentary Research Service.

Lid, Inger Marie. 2013. Developing the theoretical content in Universal Design. *Scandinavian Journal of Disability Research* 15: 203–15. [CrossRef]

Lid, Inger Marie. 2016. Implementing Universal Design in a Norwegian Context: Balancing Core Values and Practical Priorities. Available online: http://dsq-sds.org/article/view/3234/4303 (accessed on 19 February 2018).

Mackett, Roger L, Helena Titheridge, and Kamal Achuthan. 2012. Consulting Older and Disabled People about their Local Accessibility Needs. Paper presented at the International Conference on Mobility and Transport for Elderly and Disabled Persons (TRANSED 2012), Delhi, India, September 17–21.

McSherry, Bernadette. 2014. *Australia's International Human Rights Obligations*. Paper prepared for Mental Health Commission of NSW to support the development of the Strategic Plan for Mental Health in NSW 2014–2024; Gladesville: Mental Health Commission of NSW.

Mindell, Jenny S., Paulo R. Anciaes, Ashley Dhanani, Jemima Stockton, Peter Jones, Muki Haklay, Nora Groce, Shaun Scholes, and Laura Vaughan. 2017. Using triangulation to assess a suite of tools to measure community severance. *Journal of Transport Geography* 60: 119–29. [CrossRef]

Nankervis, Karen. 2006. Conceptions of disability. In *Community Disability Services: An Evidence-Based Approach to Practice*. Edited by Ian Dempsey and Karen Nankervis. Sydney: UNSW Press, pp. 3–26.

2017. NCHPAD. Available online: https://www.nchpad.org/426/2254/AIMFREE~Manuals (accessed on 10 November 2017).

Nirje, Bengt. 1994. The Normalization Principle and Its Human Management Implications*. *SRV-VRS: The International Social Role Valorization Journal* 1: 2. First published 1969.

Norwegian Ministry of Children, Equality and Social Inclusion (NMCEandSI). 2016. *The Government's Action Plan for Universal Design 2015–2019*. Oslo: Norwegian Ministry of Children, Equality and Social Inclusion.

New Zealand Human Rights Commission (NZHRC). 2012. *Better Design and Buildings for Everyone: Disabled People's Rights and the Built Environment Book 1 of 3*. Auckland: Human Rights Commission New Zealand, ISBN 978-0-478-35631-1 (Online).

Oliver, Mike. 1983. *Social Work with Disabled People*. Basingstoke: MacMillan.

Oliver, Mike. 1987. Re-Defining Disability: Some Issues for Research. *Research, Policy and Planning* 5: 9–13.

Oliver, Mike. 1992. Changing the social relations of research production? *Disability Handicap & Society* 7: 101–15.

Oliver, Mike. 1998. Theories in Health Care and Research: Theories of Disability in Health Practice and Research. *British Medical Journal* 317: 1446–49. [CrossRef] [PubMed]

Oliver, Mike. 2013. The social model of disability: Thirty years on. *Disability & Society*, 28. [CrossRef]

Oliver, Melody, Suzanne Mavoa, Hannah Badland, Karl Parker, Phil Donovan, Robin A. Kearns, En-Yi Lin, and Karen Witten. 2015. Associations between the neighborhood built environment and out of school physical activity and active travel: An examination from the Kids in the City study. *Health & Place* 36: 57–64.

Palacio, Agustina, and Javier Romanach. 2006. El modelo de la diversidad: la bioética y los derechos humanos como herramientas para alcanzar la plena dignidad en la diversidad funcional. Available online: https://e-archivo.uc3m.es/handle/10016/9899 (accessed on 17 February 2018).

Parsons, Talcott. 1951. *The Social System*. E-book produced by Social Theory in collaboration with Univerity of Chicago; Glencoe: Free Press.

Peace, Sheila M. 2003. The development of residential and nursing home care in the United Kingdom. In *End of Life in Care Homes: A Palliative Approach*. Edited by Jeanne Samson Katz and Sheila M. Peace. Oxford: Oxford University Press, pp. 15–42.

Pereira Martins, Kaisy, Tatiana Ferreira da Costa, Thayris Mariano de Medeiros, Maria das Graças Melo Fernandes, Inácia Sátiro Xavier de França, and Kátia Nêyla de Freitas Macêdo Costa. 2016. Internal structure of Family Health Units: Access for people with disabilities. *Ciência & Saúde Coletiva* 21: 3153–60.

Pfeiffer, David. 2001. The conceptualization of disability. In *Exploring Theories and Expanding Methodologies: Where We Are and Where We Need to Go (Research in Social Science and Disability, Volume 2)*. Edited by Sharon N. Barnartt and Barbara M. Altman. Bingley: Emerald Group Publishing Limited, pp. 29–52.

Pineda, Victor S., and Benjamin Dard. 2016. The Inclusion Imperative: Towards Disability-inclusive and Accessible Urban Development. Available online: http://www.ohchr.org/Documents/Issues/Housing/Disabilities/CivilSociety/CBM-TheInclusionImperative.pdf (accessed on 19 February 2018).

Pinnegar, Simon, Jane Marceau, and Bill Randolph. 2008. *Innovation and the City: Challenges for the Built Environment Industry*. Report prepared for Department of Innovation, Industry, Science and Research by City Future Research Centre; Sydney: UNSW, ISBN 9781740440974 (pbk.).

Quinn, Gerard, Theresia Degener, Anna Bruce, Christine Burke, Joshua Castellino, Padraic Kenna, Ursula Kilkelly, and Shivaun Quinlivan. 2002. *Human Rights and Disability the Current Use and Future Potential of United Nations Human Rights Instruments in the Context of Disability. Report, to the United Nations*. New York and Geneva: United Nations.

Rains, Madeleine, and Rowena Butland. 2012. Lifting the Barriers: Planning for Increased Mobility and Accessibility through the Adelaide CBD. Paper presented at State of Australian Cities National Conference, Sydney, Australia, November 26–29.

Rimmer, James H., Barth Riley, Edward Wang, and Amy Rauworth. 2005. Accessibility of Health Clubs for People with Mobility Disabilities and Visual Impairments. *American Journal of Public Health* 95: 2022–28. [CrossRef] [PubMed]

Rimmer, James H., Sangeetha Padalabalanarayanan, Laurie A. Malone, and Tapan Mehta. 2017. Fitness facilities still lack accessibility for people with disabilities. *Disability and Health Journal* 10. [CrossRef] [PubMed]

Rotarou, Elena S., and Dikaios Sakellariou. 2017. Inequalities in access to health care for people with disabilities in Chile: The limits of universal health coverage. *Critical Public Health*. [CrossRef]

Sander, Marie-Sylvie, Marie-Christine Bournot, Françoise Lelièvre, and Anne Tallec. 2005. Les personnes ayant un handicap visuel Les apports de l'enquête Handicaps-Incapacités–Dépendance. Available online: https://www.epsilon.insee.fr/jspui/bitstream/1/12824/1/er416.pdf (accessed on 17 February 2018).

Sarma, J. 2016. Accessibility to the built environment in Delhi, India: Understanding the experience of disablement through the intersectionality paradigm. *Knowledge Management for Development Journal* 11: 104–21.

Sawadrsi, Antika. 2011. Embodiment in the disabling built-environment: An experience of daily life. *FORUM Ejournal* 10: 53–66.

Schindler, Sarah. 2015. Architectural Exclusion: Discrimination and Segregation through Physical Design of the Built Environment. *The Yale Law Journal* 124: 1836–2201. Available online: https://www.yalelawjournal.org/article/architectural-exclusion (accessed on 17 February 2018).

Scotch, Richard K. 2000. Models of Disability and the Americans with Disabilities Act. *Berkeley Journal of Employment & Labor Law* 21. [CrossRef]

Scotch, Richard K., and Kay Shriner. 1997. Disability as Human Variation: Implications for Policy. *The Annals of the American Academy of Political and Social Science* 549: 148–59. [CrossRef]

Shriner, Kay, and Richard K. Scotch. 2001. Disability and Institutional Change: A Human Variation Perspective on Overcoming Oppression. *Journal of Disability Policy Studies* 12: 100–6. [CrossRef]

Soder, Marten. 2009. Tensions, perspectives and themes in disability studies. *Scandinavian Journal of Disability Research* 11: 67–81. [CrossRef]

Stainton, Tim. 2017. Intellectual Disability, Oppression and Difference. In *Countering Discrimination in Social Work*. Edited by Bogdan Lesnik. London and New York: Routledge. First published 1998.

Stephens, Lindsay, Karen Spalding, Henna Aslam, Helen Scott, Sue Ruddick, Nancy L. Young, and Patricia McKeever. 2017. Inaccessible childhoods: Evaluating accessibility in homes, schools and neighborhoods with disabled children. *Children's Geographies* 15. [CrossRef]

2017. The Guardian. Available online: https://www.theguardian.com/global-development-professionals-network/ng-interactive/2016/jun/22/disability-rights-around-the-world-from-1944-to-the-present-day (accessed on 10 November 2017).

Tudzi, Eric P., John Bugri, and Anthony Danso. 2017. Towards Accessible Built Environments in Universities in Ghana: An Approach to Inclusiveness Assessment. *Disability, CBR & Inclusive Development* 28. [CrossRef]

United Nations. 2006. Convention on the Rights of Persons with Disabilities—Articles. Available online: https://www.un.org/development/desa/disabilities/convention-on-the-rights-of-persons-with-disabilities/convention-on-the-rights-of-persons-with-disabilities-2.html (accessed on 10 November 2017).

2008. United Nations (UN). Available online: https://www.un.org/development/desa/disabilities/backgrounder-disability-treaty-closes-a-gap-in-protecting-human-rights.html (accessed on 10 November 2017).

2017. United Nations (UN). Available online: http://www.un.org/disabilities/documents/maps/enablemap.jpg (accessed on 10 November 2017).

Civil Rights Division of the United States Department of Justice (USDoJ CRD). 2008. Available online: https://www.ada.gov/pcatoolkit/abouttoolkit.htm (accessed on 10 November 2017).

United States Department of Justice Civil Rights Division (USDoJ CRD). 2017. Information and Technical Assistance on the Americans with Disabilities Act (Enforcement). Available online: https://www.ada.gov/enforce_current.htm (accessed on 11 October 2017).

Wee, Judy, Julie Babinard, Christopher Bennett, and Christine McMahon. 2015. *Improving Accessibility to People with Disabilities in the Pacific*. Sydney: PRIF Coordination Office (PCO).

West, Raelene. 2012. What Do We Mean by Support? The Receipt of Disability Services and Compensation for People with a Spinal Cord Injury (SCI) in Victoria. Ph.D. thesis, University of Melbourne, Melbourne, Australia.

Wolfensberger, Wolf. 1969. The Origin and Nature of Our Institutional Models. In *Changing Patterns in Residential Services for the Mentally Retarded*. Washington: President's Committee on Mental Retardation. Available online: http://www.disabilitymuseum.org/dhm/lib/detail.html?id=1909&page=all (accessed on 12 February 2018).

Zajac, Adam P. 2013. Public Space That Excludes: A Case Study of Warsaw. Paper presented at the International RC21 Conference 2013, Berlin, Germany, August 29–31.

Zola, Irving K. 1993. Disability Statistics, What We Count and What It Tells Us A Personal and Political Analysis. *Journal of Disability Policy Studies* 4. [CrossRef]

4

Prioritising Supported Decision-Making: Running on Empty or a Basis for Glacial-to-Steady Progress?

Terry Carney [1,2]

[1] School of Law, University of Sydney, Eastern Ave., Camperdown, NSW 2006, Australia; terry.carney@sydney.edu.au

[2] Faculty of Law, University of Technology Sydney, 15 Broadway, Ultimo, NSW 2007, Australia

Abstract: Honouring the requirement of the Convention on the Rights of Persons with Disabilities to introduce supported decision-making (SD) has largely been a case of much talk and little real action. As a socio-economic right, actualising support is resource-intensive as well as being fairly uncharted territory in terms of what works, to what degree and for how long benefits last. This paper, drawing lightly on mainly Australian examples, considers unexplored (and sometimes unorthodox) approaches such as the 'needs-based' principle for setting social welfare priorities as possible ways of revitalising SD through progressive realisation, whether through civil society programs or under the law. It argues that pure repeal of proxy decision-making *on its own* is not viable in realpolitik terms so progressive realisation of 'repeal with adequate support' must instead be devised for SD implementation to progress.

Keywords: supported decision-making; socio-economic rights; progressive realisation; program priorities

1. Introduction

Article 12 of the *Convention on the Rights of Persons with Disabilities* (2006)[1] ('CRPD') is widely, but certainly not universally, understood in line with the views of the monitoring Committee as calling for the repeal of substitute decision-making regimes—such as adult guardianship or proxy decision-making for involuntary mental health patients—and for their replacement with supported-decision-making ('SD') which does not transfer *any* decision making away from the person. The repeal arm located in Article 12(1), (2) advances a civil right (elimination of capacity-based denials of legal capacity and autonomy), while the provision of support subject to 'safeguards' arm found in Articles 12(3), (4), arguably is a socio-economic right (and certainly is treated as such in the realpolitik of government). Like the socio-economic right to health (generally Tobin 2012; Magnusson 2017), SD however presently remains a fairly 'empty' right, even in first world economies. While there are many law reform blueprints (e.g., VLRC 2012; ALRC 2014; Law Commission of Ontario 2017), concepts and principles remain in flux (Carney 2014), legislation is scant,[2] and—despite a proliferation of legislative and non-legislative programs and schemes (Then 2013; Boundy and Fleischner 2013; Browning 2010; Power et al. 2013; Van Puymbrouck 2017)—there is no rigorous evidence of

---

[1] *Convention on the Rights of Persons with Disabilities* 999 UNTS 3. Australia was an original signatory when the CRPD and its Optional Protocol opened for signature on 30 March 2007, and ratified the CRPD in July 2008 (entering into force on 16 August 2008) followed by the Optional Protocol in 2009.

[2] Australia has been slower to legislate supported decision-making than Canada or Sweden (Gooding 2014; Gordon 2000; Law Commission of Ontario 2014). So far, other than a bit of dabbling in South Australia, Victoria is the only Australian state to legislate new 'support' measures which avoid conferring proxy decision-making power, limited so far to appointments which the person makes for themselves or in health and mental health: *Powers of Attorney Act 2014* (Vic) ss 87–89; *Mental Health Act 2014* (Vic) Part 3, ss 12–27; *Medical Treatment and Planning Act 2016* (Vic) ss 31, 32 [from March 2018]; also see *Advance Care Directives Act 2013* (SA), s 10(d); *Disability Services Act 1993* (SA) as amended, s 3A (Carney 2015a).

effectiveness (Kohn and Blumenthal 2014; Kohn et al. 2013; Carney 2015b; Davidson et al. 2015). Why is this so?

Have we lost sight of the bigger picture (or given it too little attention)? Such as that law has a patchy record at best in securing rights in general and socio-economic rights such as SD in particular; that neoliberal governance reforms and fiscal austerity have increased pressures on accessing scarce public resources (e.g., for the UK: UN Committee on the Rights of Persons with Disabilities 2017; UK Independent Mechanism 2017, pp. 22–27); that we have bold 'capacity-building' visions of how to harness the potential of informal civil society supports, but little understanding of how to operationalise the marshalling of that non-state 'support' (family or otherwise), and even less appreciation of associated 'risks' of hidden paternalism in the absence of appropriate safeguards? Or that there can be unintended consequences[3] and that competition for access to finite resources carries risks of unfair and unequal outcomes, such as favouring the more powerful or more articulate in the absence of a needs principle or other means of ensuring proportional allocation? Alternatively, have we perhaps simply misread what SD realisation entails?

This paper suggests that the answer to such questions is more 'yes' than 'no', and in addressing some of these themes, it sketches some ideas on how SD implementation may begin to be reimagined and the stalled progress rectified. In doing so it characterises the SD arm of Article 12 as a socio-economic right due to its capacity-building personal development and associated significant resourcing implications for supporters, meaning both that progressive realisation (and non-retrogression) tests must be met, and that there is salience to conversations closer to traditional welfare allocation (and priority setting) debates. Due to the tension in the link between the civil rights and socio-economic arms of Article 12 (and a realpolitik unwillingness of government to move on the civil rights front in isolation) it is also argued that the withdrawal or winding back of most proxies is contingent on delivery of *adequate* Article 12(3) support in those settings. In short it is contended that there is a neglected theoretical and operational indivisibility of the two types of rights in Article 12. Channelling Jenny Goldschmidt's CRPD focus on pursuit of transformative equality and justice—engaging principles of equality, accessibility, autonomy, participation and inclusion (Goldschmidt 2017)—this paper takes a broad brush look at new ways of realising CRPD substantive equality rights in the world of realpolitik, lightly engaging some concrete examples from Australia regarding possible priorities to be favoured.

2. Some (Re-)Conceptualisations?

When confronted with challenging issues it is sometimes helpful to strip out the technical detail to isolate the real shape of the underlying concepts. But first, some clarification of what SD involves.

2.1. SD as a 'Relational' Socio-Economic Right to Scarce Resources?

A short but simplistic answer to the question of the meaning of SD as expressed in Article 12(3) of the CRPD that 'States Parties shall take appropriate measures to provide access by persons with disabilities to the support they may require in exercising their legal capacity', when read with the rest of Article 12, is that it is provision of any needed 'support' to enable people to exercise legal capacity to make their own authentic decisions. Article 12(3) follows articulation of the rights to 'recognition everywhere as persons before the law' (Art 12(1)) and to 'enjoy legal capacity on an equal basis with others in all aspects of life' (Art 12(2)). As is well known, the General Comment issued by the monitoring Committee for the CRPD reads Article 12 as requiring immediate withdrawal of any 'substitute' decision-making such as adult guardianship, or proxy-decisions such as under involuntary mental health powers (UN Committee on the Rights of Persons with Disabilities 2014;

3 Disability history reminds us of egregious unintended consequences of lofty principles such as deinstitutionalisation (Gooding 2016; Wiesel and Bigby 2015).

Arstein-Kerslake and Flynn 2015, pp. 5–6). This is mainly because of the egregious abuses associated with exercise of those powers, but also by implication in reading Article 12 as entirely concerned with civil rights which therefore do not permit progressive realisation.

As now explained, I read SD implementation within Article 12 as a 'package', and a package where civil and socio-economic rights are in some tension. On this reading, any imperative to withdraw substitute decision-making extends beyond proxy decisions made under the law (e.g., adult guardianship and mental health involuntary treatment) to also include any unconsented and 'significant'[4] proxy decision-making occurring in natural relationships in civil society (as with the paternalism associated with say a worryingly subordinated dependent or abusive relationship). And that the withdrawal or winding back of most proxies, especially outside mental health treatment, is contingent on delivery of *adequate* Article 12(3) support in those settings.[5] This is because the right to SD is properly characterised as a socio-economic right (Carney 2015a). Fundamentally, then, SD as conceived in Article 12(3) is about ensuring that everyone has *access to* the necessary resources and assistive relationship(s) to enable full expression of their human agency as a *relational* being (see for example Herring 2016, p. 18; Gooding 2012, p. 435).

Despite the artificiality and deficiencies of taxonomies distinguishing say civil from socio-economic rights (see generally, Marks 2009) or first from so-called second or third generation rights (Tushnet 2016) and conceding the seamless relationships of such rights with each other, there *are* some useful markers. Socio-economic rights, such as to health or education, are often distinguished as imposing 'positive' liberties (claims on the state for expenditure or access to resources) while civil rights can be realised in a 'negative' or protective way, such as in describing civil rights to privacy or autonomy as the 'right to be left alone' (simply guaranteed by the state against interference with enjoyment). Although SD in the CRPD is only about ensuring equal access to agency as legal capacity, most SD programs to date offer a much wider spectrum of supports for greater agency in decision-making, so viewing SD *purely* as a 'civil and political right' (De Bhailís and Flynn 2017, pp. 17–18) is not persuasive. It is not persuasive because even though civil and political rights are not cost-free (protection of say the right to liberty, or freedom from torture all have machinery-of-enforcement costs), the resources to be marshalled to realise SD in *any* form are I contend both central to the right in question and are *very* much more substantial than those associated with civil and political rights. Like the rights to health or to social security, this *quantitative* difference in required resourcing is one of the characteristics that marks them out as socio-economic rights (attracting the correlative principle of progressive realisation). It is also that heavy resourcing implication that engages principles of realpolitik, which likewise presses for progressive realisation. I therefore find it no answer to deflect from engaging with this socio-economic character of SD, or its resource burden, by instead pointing to say the 'myriad ways' in which support can be delivered, or to requirements of personal tailoring of support to individual circumstances; for socio-economic rights share both of those attributes. It is the resourcing attributes, not these latter ones, which are critical in my analysis.

The socio-economic right to support includes among other things any necessary resources associated with reading a person's will and preferences when unable to verbalise choices, and facilitation of choice through provision of information or other assistance required in order to understand and select between options. This in itself can be costly and time-consuming to deliver. But as Jonathan Herring observes, its realisation also entails a radical paradigm shift. Writing about the role of law (but by extension also encompassing any SD program) under this re-conception, the object is explained as not so much to 'emphasize independence, liberty, and autonomy; but

[4] The qualifying caveats are necessary because everyone tacitly or expressly accepts a degree of paternalist influence by others over what might be termed the minutiae of everyday life and social interaction.

[5] The adequacy of SD too is a subjective question, where reasonable minds will differ. My point is simply that not having any SD, or only having an empty 'opportunity' for SD to emerge within civil society settings such as family and other networks, without asking about the substance of that support, *fails* the test.

rather ... to *uphold relationships and care*' (Herring 2016, p. 18). For the friendless this necessarily entails establishing or finding equivalents for missing relationships (e.g., recruiting supporters or finding other sources of advice and support), while the correlative 'safeguards' obligation of Article 12(4) calls attention to ensuring an acceptable 'quality' of those relationships, including avoiding the risk of a relationship of dependence or domination (Arstein-Kerslake and Flynn 2017). All of this explains why SD trials have proved to be so resource intensive (Bigby et al. 2017; Purcal et al. 2017), even though their goals and achievements were often quite modest.[6] But of course it also highlights the matrix of socio-economic contributors to overlapping and cumulative barriers and disadvantages encountered by those to be assisted by SD, such as poverty or problematic behaviours compounding reliance on care, and heightening levels of 'control' or surveillance of their lives (for an introduction, (Goggin et al. 2017)). Despite what some may wish, the evidence so far is that SD simply cannot be delivered 'on the cheap', at low cost.

2.2. *Conceptual Language for SD Realisation and the Role of Law*

Metaphorical mapping of conceptual debates and choices arguably highlights some important distinctions between the legal or program outcomes sought or able to be realised for the lived lives of people. These distinctions I suggest are the difference between actual and token or symbolic realisation of SD as a socio-economic right.

Many laws and many debates focus on the *making* of orders or accessing services. These may be thought of as 'gateway' issues, since they are about how easy or difficult it is to pass through the gate, and because little if any attention is paid to what occurs once a person has gained access (e.g., there is little monitoring and few if any safeguards beyond the access point or 'time'). Involuntary civil commitment and adult guardianship laws for instance tend to be weighted towards the gateway issues of the *making* of a sound and procedurally fair order rather than what happens afterwards. Other laws and debates are about finding an access route to a desired legal benefit, service or resource. These may be thought of as 'pathway' issues, because the focus is on the ability (or not) of a person to become *connected* to the social good in question, with little if any attention on whether the good in question is beneficial or not, or for how long any benefit subsists (Community Treatment Orders in mental health exemplify provision of such a pathway—an opportunity to have priority access to community mental health resources, but leaving debatable what is actually provided, or its benefits, if any: (Segal et al. 2017)). Other laws and debates by contrast are about seeking to achieve or guarantee access to a resource for a person. These may be thought of as akin to 'ticket to service' issues, because the focus here is on *requiring* the state or other providers to actually *deliver* the service or resource in question (as exemplified in say a legally enforceable *right* to social security), or at least in showing the service arrived (see Tait et al. 1995).

Of these labels, I suggest that SD as conceived in Article 12(3) is a 'ticket to services' product. But is this ticket to service mainly realised by adopting a treaty or passing a domestic law? What is the power of such laws in delivering on this? The answer I suggest is rather deflating. Making a normative 'ought' statement is one thing; but *operationalising* it so it translates into changes to the lived lives of people is quite another. International treaties like the CPRD certainly are among the most powerful of normative statements. But treaties do not automatically become part of the domestic law of a country, and their normative position may have little traction with the public at large (or what is often termed the 'beltway' of everyday politics). They are not self-actualising and may not even change culture and values, for as Jenny Goldschmidt (2017, pp. 12–13) notes, rights have lost purchase recently; and if actively opposed by ordinary folk they may even result in a backwards step (constituting what would

6 Those modest aims—such as increasing understanding of the difference between substitute and supported decision-making or providing 'assistance with decision-making' rather than some theoretical purity of human agency which is beyond us all—are not necessarily objectionable. However, it highlights how difficult it is to define 'success' in realising the aims of SD, and draws attention to another 'cost-benefit' calculus when prioritising allocation of scarce community resources.

be a breach of the 'non-retrogression' test for implementation of socio-economic rights if the product of government action).

Even when normative statements of international law command widespread popular acceptance, as say with the 'right to health', and even when such propositions are incorporated in the 'peak' constitutional documents of nations (as is often the case with the right to health), the operational impact may be negligible or slight. Thus at best it can be argued that a constitutional right to health 'changes the conversation' of the body politic (DeLaet 2015), even though there is, as yet, no empirical evidence of its ability to generate *any* additional resourcing at all (Chilton and Versteeg 2016). This is true also of US jurisprudence, as hopes of substantive change following adoption of a 'right to treatment' in mental health were dashed by experience (Carney et al. 2008). Nothing lasting really came of US and Canadian court jurisprudence laying down minimum criteria for civil commitment (Fischer 2006, p. 158; Appelbaum 1994), the qualified rights of competent patients to refuse treatment, or the limited 'right to treatment' for those detained (see Case Comment 1973; Eisenberg and Yeazell 1980, pp. 468–69; Perlin 2011).

So how does all this conceptual mapping help to understand the policy challenges associated with the limited implementation of SD to date?

3. Some Policy Challenges

One thing that is crystal clear from the Australian pilot programs for SD is that, irrespective of whether they achieve the desired outcomes or not, programs of support piloted so far in Australia are very costly (Bigby et al. 2017; Purcal et al. 2017, pp 32–33, 49). So, in a real-world context, even though not everyone needs support (e.g., some in mental health) and costs will vary with the individual, some priority setting is inevitable: for no government has unlimited resources.

Now these priorities can either be set by default (through inaction or by responding to the most vocal pressure groups) or result from explicit policy choices. Australia's introduction of provision for 'plan nominees' and support in its National Disability Insurance Scheme ('NDIS') is a (crude) legislative and program example of the latter. Appointment of a nominee and/or funding for support are both now seen as potential inclusions in personal plan packages, though the costs of any SD support mean its inclusion is rare and rarely is it fully funded. Further, the NDIS covers only small numbers of people (just 475,000 of the 4.3 million Australians with some form of disability: (Productivity Commission 2017, pp. 5, 16, 70)), and predominantly those with an intellectual disability and autism. This highlights some of the equity and distributional issues entailed when priorities are set in this ad hoc way. People with only marginally lesser needs than NDIS participants (or greater 'complex' needs such as associated criminal justice or poverty issues: (Steele et al. 2016)), simply miss out on either form of support. Skewing of access towards intellectual disability and autism results in inequality of access for otherwise apparently similar support needs of people with acquired brain injuries or mental illness/ psychosocial disabilities,[7] while NDIS design features mean that older citizens with mild dementias miss out entirely due to its age ceiling (other than for people already in the scheme prior to reaching retirement age).

So firstly, what 'does' Article 12 require of governments? Is repeal of proxy powers alone ever acceptable in the absence of support, and would this ever be ethically acceptable to any government? And, secondly, if progressive realisation is either the proper reading of Article 12(3) or is the only realistic pathway ever perceived to be available by governments, are there any insights to be drawn from debates about the merits or otherwise of needs-based allocation of welfare resources? These two questions are dealt with below.

---

[7] Mental illness or psychosocial disability is the third most common disability after intellectual disability and autism, but accounts for only 6% of NDIS scheme participants: (Productivity Commission 2017, p. 16).

3.1. Repealing Substitute Decision-Making First/in Isolation?

Whether expressly or by implication, many commentators have accepted that the most immediate priority is giving effect to the CRPD Committee's insistence on eliminating all coercive powers (repealing all involuntary mental health and guardianship laws). This also is not happening, so is it time to 'tell 'em they're dreamin' in the memorable line from the Australian film *The Castle* (Wikipedia 1997), or is the reason for lack of legislative action due to a misreading? I suggest it is a misreading of how Article 12 in general is to be operationalised,[8] or at least that this is so in the world of realpolitik.

I argue that the first reason for such sluggish progress in either repealing laws like adult guardianship, or even adding some SD options to the statute book, lies in the neglected *indivisibility* of the civil and the socio-economic rights contained in Article 12. For legislatures (or indeed for social policy programs in general), winding back or eliminating most instances of substitute decision-making *needs to go hand in glove* with establishment of meaningful SD programs or arrangements. One way of demonstrating this for Australia is to pose the thought experiment of asking how life was for most such people (not involuntary mental health patients who were already under proxy treatment regimes) around half a century ago—*before* substitute decision-making laws were fashioned into something close to current guardianship legislation. This is interesting because in practice for many (or most) people, essentially there were *no laws at all*: the only options were the rarely used costly and cumbersome avenue of the inherent superior court protective jurisdiction; *automatic* property guardianship on becoming an involuntary patient; and—in some states such as Victoria—*administrative* procedures of medical certification of need for management (Carney 1982). This was the situation rectified by reforms introducing accessible least restrictive but substitute decision-making guardianship reforms, as recommended by an enquiry which sat between 1982 and 1984 (an Orwellian date, though not actually enacted until 1986: (Carney 1989)).

Of course, it is always problematic to ignore the cultural, organisational and other differences between historical eras, but since no-one found the then prevailing situation acceptable in the 1980s, it is surely difficult to argue that abolition of say guardianship laws *alone* would now be acceptable (the case for repeal alone is much easier to make in mental health where support may not be required). To the contrary, I contend that this is the whole purpose of the CRPD's inclusion in Article 12 of the *correlative* socio-economic right to support. Absent such support all that results from repeal is that state paternalism for all (under guardianship) is replaced, in the case of too many people for comfort, by civil society paternalism (by family or citizens who are generally well-meaning but unschooled in how properly to realise assistance and avoid paternalism). A paternalism that is less visible and less open to scrutiny, even if delivered by people theoretically likely to hold values closer to those of the person being assisted/subtly coerced, and even if unprotested by (i.e., notionally 'chosen by') the person. That is ethically unacceptable for most (some of course would judge it the lesser of evils). No government is likely to readily go down that path when that risk is judged excessive.

It is of course possible to argue that the remit of Article 12 as a whole is confined to realising rights of legal agency, meaning that the only way situations of domination trigger Article 12 scrutiny at all is where the person subject to paternalism turns to (or 'potentially' turns to) law to escape paternalism's clutches (as nicely argued by (Arstein-Kerslake and Flynn 2017, p. 27)).[9] Only rights such as to independent living under Article 19 would then be accepted as genuine socio-economic rights in the CRPD on this basis. Even if this were to be accepted (contrary to my reading), the language of Art 12(3)

---

[8] For analysis questioning the conceptual weaknesses of a strong reading of the CRPD on the basis of 'meshing' of articulated will/preferences and presumed autonomy goals, such as read from prior life history or 'diachronic identity' (Burch 2017, p. 394–97).

[9] ... problem sought to be addressed is that '[i]n the informal sphere of familial relationships and services for daily ...on-making ... many of the decisions made ... do not appear to have legal consequences or rise to the level of an ... of legal agency. However, for many people with cognitive disabilities, some of the most damaging decision-making ...cur within these informal spheres' (Arstein-Kerslake and Flynn 2017, p. 24).

at the very least surely still sets provision of SD as a hard, *practical precondition* to any step to realise legal capacity, such as through repeal of guardianship (much perhaps as a right to a fair trial often requires funding for advocacy). Legislators and policy-makers certainly will not take unilateral repeal or other action in the face of the possibility of things being *worse* for affected citizens; so, repeal is not unconditional however we read Article 12.

While repeal of guardianship is easy, realising the correlative socio-economic right to support without incurring an all too common resultant paternalism and undue influence within the civil society settings which remain is not at all easy to address. Since it is rare indeed for people to *actually* ever make an entirely independent autonomous decision without taking into account external views of others (or community 'expectations'), merely removing barriers to autonomous decision-making as an end in itself cannot take us far at all; we need to know to what extent autonomy is *achieved* (Carney 2017c). Rather than such a starry-eyed consequential 'status' of self-actualisation, I would contend that the focus is better placed on a more modest notion such as the *means* by which people can be assisted to more fully and/or more often exercise their 'will' and/or 'preferences' (since the two are not necessarily the same: Szmukler 2017 IALMH paper summarised in (OPA 2017, p. 51)).

Seen in this light, the definition of 'success' in realising this Article 12(3) CRPD right to SD becomes quite debatable. Is it enough simply to 'try' to facilitate SD (a perhaps largely symbolic gain) or as argued below should there be insistence on a showing of progress? If so, how much progress and how durable should progress be? Is it enough that a new culture and language is adopted between the person being 'supported' and those around them (which may yield 'slow-burn' gains over time), or should, as suggested below, attention be on measuring change in the *number* and *type* of decisions *actually* being made? And, if so, can trends of expanded confidence in the number and magnitude of decisions being made be taken at face value without considering any (offsetting?) enhanced 'risk' of any unfortunate outcomes of those decisions? Surely not. Surely nor should the answers to these questions differ between SD schemes that are legislated as against being program or civil society initiatives (the range sketched in (Carney and Beaupert 2013)).

Since SD is something delivered to assist someone other than the supporter to realise their Article 12 rights, I argue that the contribution made by law and policy primarily must surely be on achievement of some minimum level of competence and understanding of SD by supporters, and where this does not exist naturally (as rarely it does) then it turns on the success and durability of capacity-building of SD among supporters. And since Article 12 is about ensuring/promoting optimal achievable equality, regard surely must then be had to the *substantive* as distinct from symbolic achievements of supporters in serving as the instrumental agents for realising optimal decision-making autonomy of those being assisted. This might for the purposes of the present discussion be translated into some crude conceptual labelling of the forms of SD. Labelling which deliberately here is pitched to be inclusive in the sense of catching not only SD under some legal auspice but also the much larger numbers of people receiving it under a formal civil society scheme, or the even larger numbers living and supported 'informally' by family or friends in natural civil society settings.

For simplicity, the 'substance' of such arrangements, on an evaluative spectrum from good to awful, might be badged as SD which is: (i) sensitive/substantive (i.e., SD at its optimal best); (ii) symbolic/empty (i.e., well-intentioned SD, but in name only); and (iii) abusive/oppressive (i.e., SD which is paternalistic substitute decision-making 'in disguise', whether by default or design (or as Matthew Burch evocatively puts it, '[w]hat happens when manipulation dons the mantle of support': (Burch 2017, p. 397)). The latter is of the greatest concern, not only because in practice CRPD autonomy enhancing is being contradicted, but also because in some instances it is the result not of lack of capacity of the supporter to do the right thing, instead involving deliberate abuse and exploitation of the person being supported (Arstein-Kerslake and Flynn 2017). However, the middle category is of concern too, since its symbolic window-dressing deflects public policy attention by conveying a false appearance of CRPD compliance. Only the first category passes CRPD muster, but so far there is no evidence (other than unscientific anecdotal evidence) that *any* law or program *actually* is entitled to the label (though the same could of course be said of proxy decision-making).

So, what is entailed by priority setting and what 'language' maps the conceptual territory of laws and programs associated with that part of the challenge of 'properly' realising SD in the way sketched so far?

3.2. Setting Priorities for Allocating Limited Resources for SD

The second reason for sluggish progress in implementing SD (beyond the indivisibility point discussed in 3.1) I suggest may be due to a failure to address the realpolitik of implementing socio-economic rights in times of real or perceived austerity.[10] Now I recognise that some will regard it as almost heretical to speak about setting 'priorities' for the realisation of human rights. Yet socio-economic rights have always provided for 'progressive realisation' by State Parties (especially in recognition of the challenges of developing states), subject to a correlative 'non-retrogression' obligation (not going backwards);[11] and it is hard to find examples even of wealthy countries not taking a similar progressive (i.e., staged) and/or selective (i.e., needs-based) approach to their realisation. Despite the jurisprudence on the obligation to 'respect, protect and fulfil' (Wills and Warwick 2016; Forman et al. 2016), progressive realisation of universal socio-economic rights does of course risk glacial progress at best or constant postponement to the 'never-never land' at worst, especially in the face of neoliberal fiscal austerity which constrains public funding options even in wealthy first-world economies.

Welfare policy seems particularly well adapted to addressing progressive realisation issues because it constantly engages with the competition and choices arising between the three principles of distributive justice for setting priorities about allocation of necessarily scarce resources: the competing principles of (i) equality (universal provision but at the risk of spreading resources too thinly); (ii) equity (proportionate return on prior contributions); and (iii) 'need' such as by means testing (see Carney 2006, chp. 4; Devereux 2016, pp. 168–78). The realpolitik of governing, especially in the age of neoliberal austerity, is that the needs principle will often be selected (and on its own) unless the case can be made for some selective *supplementary* application of a more costly principle, such as illustrated by Steven Devereux's argument for supplementary provision of universal access to 'essential' services (Devereux 2016, pp. 178–79). In just this vein the right to health has been refined to stipulate a limited number of 'minimum core obligations' (the specification or measurement of which proves problematic: (Forman et al. 2016)), effectively elevating the core ahead of the right generally. Selective provision of a social good such as income or a service (such as by means-testing access or rates, or other forms of rationing) reflects prioritisation of the most pressing or acute need, including any redistributive pursuit of greater equality in access to the social good in question; though over the long history of welfare both 'social investment' (capacity-building initiatives) and needs-based programs are evident (see for example, Smyth and Deeming 2016).

Indulge for a moment engaging with the heretical thought exercise of asking how to isolate a 'minimum core' for SD, or how otherwise to provide a rank order of possible priority targets for early roll out of SD. Possible inclusions on such a 'shopping list' of possible steps towards realising the ultimate goals of the 'support-with-safeguards' principle of Article 12(3) of the CRPD might include:

(a) addressing the most egregious breaches (perhaps people languishing under heavy drug restraints in care homes, though for an argument to cover family settings too, see: (OPA 2017, p. 38));

---

10 Targetting (priority setting allocation such as through means testing) is one of the three fundamental choices/tension in welfare provision (the others being universal provision and provision proportionate to say prior contributions or years of work/citizenship: (Devereux 2016)).

11 For elaboration of these twin principles in the context of neoliberal shrinking of public resources, see the insightful discussion of the *International Covenant on Economic Social and Cultural Rights*, one of the two main 'parents' of the CRPD (Wills and Warwick 2016, especially pp. 640–46, 653–55).

(b) addressing the most pervasive but more routine support needs (such as for a supporter or nominee/representative payee in social security);
(c) prioritising the needs of the least visible and most vulnerable (such as people lacking friends or relatives, or overly reliant on a very 'protective' carer; or those who are criminalised or labelled with complex needs);
(d) tackling issues where law or policy has the strongest track record in being brought into actual practice (perhaps by operationalisation of advance directives);
(e) concentrating on groups fortunate to be more plentifully resourced (such as Australia's NDIS population); or
(f) picking the issues where the impact is most cost-effective (such as legislation allowing people to authorise someone else to convey information or access records on their behalf)?

I suggest a case can be made for putting almost *any* of the above items first on the list, and for choosing almost any subsequent running order of the remaining items. For instance calls have been made for more attention to be paid to the routine needs of large numbers of ordinary people (i.e., item (b): (Carney 2015a)) and concern expressed about neglect of the needs of people who are socially isolated (item (c)). But adapting Anna Arstein-Kerslake et al.'s observation that NDIS resourcing is already adequate to also properly fund SD, a start could very well be made with that population (noting however the authors difficult to avoid worry that SD may just become 'another service' controlled and delivered by others rather than by those being supported: (Arstein-Kerslake et al. 2017)). Reasonable minds will differ. Others may rightly urge keeping item (a) at the top of the list due to the depth of infringement of liberty and strong presence of actual or de facto coercion (actual in the case of involuntary treatment or restraint; often de facto where people are living in 'total institution' settings and/or feeling beholden to their carers). But there are several ethical and social values and standpoints potentially in play even here: of the just mentioned measure of diminution of individual autonomy; of the alternative measure of empowering or allowing 'others to decide' (the amount of paternalism or disempowerment); or by the measure of how much 'harm' is visited on the person (from consequential harms and risks[12]). So, in varying ways, prioritising any one (or putting others into a rank order for realisation) inevitably reprises the choice between, or weighting of, the just mentioned values of equality, equity and need (whether assessed by measurable variables like severity or more amorphous concepts such as 'vulnerability').

However, the problems are not yet finished. For knowing when Article 12(4) safeguards are called for involves yet another of those tricky 'threshold' questions. Certainly, as already argued, Article 12(3) extends a correlative entitlement to 'support' as the required replacement for some form of substitute decision-maker. In that sense, it provides the answer to the concern that reading Article 12 simply as outlawing substitute decision-making would merely return people to say Victoria's 'pre-1984' situation of having neither an accessible substitute decision-maker (just costly and ultra-paternalistic Supreme court actions) nor any practical support (at least outside institutional or coercive orders). This would involve a return to what I have characterised above as the morally unsupportable position of being 'free' of substituted decision-making but with nothing but a theoretical (and unrealisable in practice) ability to enjoy autonomous decision-making unless blessed with access to 'perfect' natural or civil society supporter(s). But, as Linus Broström (2017) points out, there is a vast literature about the ease with which even the most conscientious and well-intentioned informal supports can rapidly degrade to operate paternalistically, under the thrall of forms of undue influence (Broström 2017). So finding ways to bring about the paradigm shift in values and skills of civil society members to genuinely realise 'support-with-safeguards' free of undue influence in the way envisioned by the CRPD, is a

---

12 Indeed it was this latter lack of adequate safeguard protections against the risk of large social security debts that led me to focus on the 'mass/mundane' issues facing representative payee arrangements (Carney 2017a, pp. 10–13).

major empirical challenge in capacity building of supporters (Carney 2017c). But first there is the thorny question of where any bright line is set for 'undue' influence.

For its part, operationalising such a threshold of undue influence is very challenging. Common law principles of equity on undue influence could in theory make a contribution (Sloan 2012, chp. 7), but they do not readily lend themselves to simple application outside the higher courts. Concepts of vulnerability have been advanced by some in the related context of guardianship reform or elsewhere (Hall 2012 [as basis for guardianship]; Herring 2016, pp. 83–85 [inherent parens patriae], 243–49 [contracts]) . Here the focus on webs of relationships and 'layering' of contributions to vulnerability (Luna 2009; Luna and Vanderpoel 2013) holds the promise of a richer calibration of individual and social-contextual dimensions (such as being socially isolated). However, vulnerability too remains a very woolly concept (Kohn 2014; Smith et al. 2010; Herring 2016, chp. 2, especially pp. 6–11). Vulnerability, then, is no generic standard or test, but one which calls for conceptual clarity between different formulations, along with specification in particular contexts (such as in quarantining special disability trusts: (Carney 2017b)). That specification may in turn be open to the criticism that it is a 'stark binary' capacity test in disguise, unless framed along the lines of Martha Fineman or Amartya Sen's 'universal vulnerability' or 'spatial/environmental' terms (for a detailed review: (Brown et al. 2017; Clough 2017), also the four articles underpinning [and fully republished within] her doctoral thesis: (Clough 2015)).

Turning to the risk of contravention of CRPD autonomy maximising values by civil society actors in ordinary relationship settings, it is again important to take a grounded real-world approach. Arguably all citizens are prone to adapt behaviour and choices to some degree in response to forms of external influence (Herring 2016, chp. 2). So, it is only when influence is judged to be a form of 'undue' influence that it becomes of concern legally, ethically, or socially. But as just shown, there probably is no bright line test which identifies the threshold beyond which concern is properly raised. At best there sometimes may be some assistance to be derived in posing a crude counterfactual, such as by comparing the lived-life autonomy enjoyed by someone under as against a person without guardianship or its companions. For surely it is unacceptable to argue that it is 'better' that a person enjoys *less* autonomy, or is subject to more paternalism in a civil society setting, than would be the case under say guardianship.

Might all of these worries about finding and prioritising resources and resolving design and safeguards issues be contributing to the very slow progress being made towards realising the legislative or program 'package' for SD as I argue is conceived in Article 12 of the CPRD? Does it not help to understand in realpolitik terms if no other, why legislatures such as Victoria have combined some minor 'easing back' of civil committal powers in mental health with the enunciation of rights to nominate supporters (*Mental Health Act 2014* (Vic), s 24)? A measure sure to be criticised by the CRPD Committee for its failure to repeal involuntary treatment but which it seems has already proved rather empty on the supporter side due to low take-up (Brophy 2017), as evidenced by the presence of nominated supporters at just four per cent of committal hearings (MHT 2016, p. 15). How can Victoria be faulted on a 'priority of needs' basis for at least *starting with* an area as rights-sensitive and fraught as mental health (especially if that support is not forthcoming in the way envisaged)? For self-evidently this is a strong candidate for inclusion on any hypothetical 'minimum core' for progressive realisation of the right to SD.

If this analysis has purchase, where does it leave Article 12 'repeal in conjunction with adequate SD' in the longer term? With a de facto status quo and glacial progression for much of the duration? Surely if simple repeal of substitute decision-making without more is not an option on ethical grounds or because it is unattractive to government realpolitik, and only the resource-intensive 'repeal & replace' avenue is open, as argued above, then the answer is 'yes.' Now this undoubtedly is an unsettling conclusion. But it is nothing other than the standard approach regarding implementation of other socioeconomic rights such as the rights to housing, to health, or to social security.

4. Conclusions

This paper was stimulated by the apparently glacial progress made in the decade since the CRPD enunciated the right to support. It has explored—well more accurately perhaps it has 'lightly sketched'—some less orthodox conceptual and distributional frames (such as welfare's 'priority of needs principle') as possible ways of injecting greater momentum into the implementation of SD by looking at it through a different lens than that of what might be termed the 'capacity-analysis' literature.

In doing so I am mindful that some may object that a lot of 'below the radar' support programs and pilot schemes have already been generated internationally (e.g., Power et al. 2013; Van Puymbrouck 2017), or that SD resourcing costs are overstated, so we should remain patient. Others will object that even if progress is inadequate, it would be positively sacrilegious to isolate particular beneficiaries or to contemplate progressive realisation of what was framed as a universal entitlement. Both may be right. And there are no doubt other lenses which could be applied, such as a justice-reinvestment analysis (for an overview Brown et al. 2016) designed to boost resources available for SD by earmarking and reallocating savings from lowering the load on say the already costly adult guardianship and mental health machinery (while remaining alert to avoiding the past failure of deinstitutionalisation to hypothecate similar 'savings' while States congratulated themselves on their purist 'reforms': (Mansell and Ericsson [1996] 2013; Caplan and Ricciardelli 2016, p. 33)). However as I have previously written about the right to health, even John Tobin's optimistic book about actualising the right to health closes by writing that: 'Following Lauterpacht,[13] it can safely be said that if economic and social rights are at the vanishing point of human rights law, as a surprising number of jurists and philosophers still seem to think, then the right to health is at the vanishing point of economic and social rights' (Tobin 2012, p. 371).

The worry tackled in this paper is that the socio-economic right to SD risks dropping below even that vanishing point; hence canvassing of some rather heretical paradigm shifting thought experiments as a way of assessing progress to date and the way forward. Rather than pessimism about Article 12 in general and SD in particular 'running on empty', I suggest that the slow but measured progressive realisation so far is also the course to stay for the future. After all, isn't that the history of pursuit of substantive equality, with its messy needs priority and other principles (Fredman 2016; Goldschmidt 2017)? If so, does it not become even more imperative to know when SD serves to build capacity, for how long benefits subsist and at what economic cost, as a current study is designed to reveal (further, LIDS 2017)?

Acknowledgments: I am indebted to Linda Steel and Fleur Beaupert for helpful critiques, leads and insightful suggestions which contributed greatly to this paper; needless to say, they are not responsible for any of my remaining errors or wrong turnings.

References

ALRC. 2014. *Equality, Capacity and Disability in Commonwealth Laws: Final Report*. Sydney: Australian Law Reform Commission.

Appelbaum, Paul S. 1994. *Almost a Revolution: Mental Health Law and the Limits of Change*. Oxford: Oxford University Press.

Arstein-Kerslake, Anna, and Eilionóir Flynn. 2015. The General Comment on Article 12 of the Convention on the Rights of Persons with Disabilities: A roadmap for equality before the law. *The International Journal of Human Rights* 20: 1–20. [CrossRef]

---

13 Adapting the wry 1952 comment by Sir Hersch Lauterpacht about the limited normative power of the international law of war ('if international law is the vanishing point of law...the law of war is the vanishing point of international law').

Arstein-Kerslake, Anna, and Eilionóir Flynn. 2017. The Right to Legal Agency: Domination, disability and the protections of Article 12 of the Convention on the Rights of Persons with Disabilities. *International Journal of Law in Context* 13: 22–38. [CrossRef]

Arstein-Kerslake, Anna, Joanne Watson, Michelle Browning, Jonathan Martinis, and Peter Blanck. 2017. Future Directions in Supported Decision-Making. *Disability Studies Quarterly*. [CrossRef]

Bigby, Chris, Jacinta Douglas, Terry Carney, Shih-Ning Then, Ilan Weisel, and Lizzie Smith. 2017. Delivering Decision-making Support to People with Cognitive Disability—What has been learned from pilot programs in Australia from 2010–2015. *Australian Journal of Social Issues* 52: 222–40. [CrossRef]

Boundy, Marcia, and Bob Fleischner. 2013. *Supported Decision Making Instead of Guardianship: An International Overview*. Washington: TASC [Training & Advocacy Support Center], National Disability Rights Network.

Brophy, Lisa. 2017. Nominated supporters in mental health. Paper presented at IALMH Congress Session, Prague, Czech Republic, July 14.

Broström, Linus. 2017. Due and Undue Influence in Supported Decision Making: Mapping the moral landscape. Paper presented at XXXV International Congress of Law and Psychiatry, Charles University, Prague, Czech Republic, July 9–14.

Brown, David, Chris Cunneen, Melanie Schwartz, Julie Stubbs, and Courtney Young. 2016. *Justice Reinvestment: Winding Back Imprisonment*. Basingstoke: Palgrave Macmillan.

Brown, Kate, Kathryn Ecclestone, and Nick Emmel. 2017. The Many Faces of Vulnerability. *Social Policy and Society* 16: 497–510. [CrossRef]

Browning, Michelle. 2010. *Report by Michelle Browning 2010 Churchill Fellow To Investigate New Models of Guardianship and the Emerging Practice of Supported Decision Making*. Canberra: Winston Churchill Memorial Trust.

Burch, Matthew. 2017. Autonomy, Respect, and the Rights of Persons with Disabilities in Crisis. *Journal of Applied Philosophy* 34: 389–402. [CrossRef]

Caplan, Mary, and Lauren Ricciardelli. 2016. Institutionalizing Neoliberalism: 21st-Century Capitalism, Market Sprawl, and Social Policy in the United States. *Poverty & Public Policy* 8: 20–38.

Carney, Terry. 1982. Civil and Social Guardianship for Intellectually Handicapped People. *Monash University Law Review* 8: 199–232.

Carney, Terry. 1989. The Limits and the Social Legacy of Guardianship. *Federal Law Review* 18: 231–66.

Carney, Terry. 2006. *Social Security Law and Policy*. Sydney: Federation Press.

Carney, Terry. 2014. Clarifying, Operationalising and Evaluating Supported Decision Making Models. *Research and Practice in Intellectual and Developmental Disabilities* 1: 46–50. [CrossRef]

Carney, Terry. 2015a. Supported Decision-making for People with Cognitive Impairments: An Australian perspective? *Laws* 4: 37–59. [CrossRef]

Carney, Terry. 2015b. Supporting People with Cognitive Disability with Decision-making: Any Australian law reform contributions? *Research and Practice in Intellectual and Developmental Disabilities* 2: 6–16. [CrossRef]

Carney, Terry. 2017a. Australian Guardianship Tribunals: An adequate response to CRPD disability rights recognition and protection of the vulnerable over the lifecourse? *Journal of Ethics in Mental Health* 10: 1–17. Available online: http://www.jemh.ca/issues/v9/theme3.html (accessed on 11 October 2017).

Carney, Terry. 2017b. Financial Planning Mechanisms (Lasting Power of Attorney, Guardianship, and SNT) for persons with ID in Australia? Paper presented at International Symposium on Special Needs Trusts, Faculty of Law, The University of Hong Kong, Hong Kong, October 13–14.

Carney, Terry. 2017c. Supported Decision-making in Australia: Meeting the challenge of moving from capacity to capacity-building? *Law in Context*. forthcoming.

Carney, Terry, and Fleur Beaupert. 2013. Public and Private Bricolage-Challenges balancing law, services & civil society in advancing CRPD supported decision making. *University of New South Wales Law Journal* 36: 175–201.

Carney, Terry, David Tait, and Fleur Beaupert. 2008. Pushing the Boundaries: Realising rights through mental health tribunal processes? *Sydney Law Review* 30: 329–56.

Case Comment. 1973. Wyatt v Stickney and the Right of Civilly Committed Mental Patients to Adequate Treatment. *Harvard Law Review* 73: 1282–306.

Chilton, Adam S., and Mila Versteeg. 2016. *Rights Without Resources: The Impact of Constitutional Social Rights on Social Spending*. Coase-Sandor Working Paper Series in Law and Economics No. 781; Chicago: University of Chicago.

Clough, Beverley. 2015. Exploring the Potential of Relational Approaches to Mental Capacity Law. Ph.D. Thesis, School of Law, University of Manchester, Manchester, UK.

Clough, Beverley. 2017. Disability and Vulnerability: Challenging the Capacity/Incapacity Binary. *Social Policy and Society* 16: 469–81. [CrossRef]

Davidson, Gavin, Berni Kelly, Geraldine Macdonald, Maria Rizzo, Louise Lombard, Oluwaseye Abogunrin, Victoria Clift-Matthews, and Alison Martin. 2015. Supported Decision Making: A review of the international literature. *International Journal of Law and Psychiatry* 38: 61–67. [CrossRef] [PubMed]

De Bhailís, Clíona, and Eilionóir Flynn. 2017. Recognising Legal Capacity: Commentary and analysis of Article 12 CRPD. *International Journal of Law in Context* 13: 6–21. [CrossRef]

DeLaet, Debra L. 2015. What a Wonderful World it Would Be: The Promise and Peril of Relying on International Law as a Mechanism for Promoting a Human Right to Health. *Global Health Governance* 9: 92–113.

Devereux, Stephen. 2016. Is Targeting Ethical? *Global Social Policy* 16: 166–81. [CrossRef]

Eisenberg, Theodore, and Stephen C. Yeazell. 1980. The Ordinary and the Extraordinary in Institutional Litigation. *Harvard Law Review* 93: 465–517. [CrossRef] [PubMed]

Fischer, Jennifer. 2006. A Comparative Look at the Right to Refuse Treatment for Involuntarily Hospitalized Persons with a Mental Illness. *Hastings International and Comparative Law Review* 29: 153–86.

Forman, Lisa, Luljeta Caraoshi, Audrey R. Chapman, and Everaldo Lamprea. 2016. Conceptualising Minimum Core Obligations under the Right to Health: How should we define and implement the 'morality of the depths. *The International Journal of Human Rights* 20: 531–48. [CrossRef]

Fredman, Sandra. 2016. Substantive Equality Revisited. *International Journal of Constitutional Law* 14: 712–38. [CrossRef]

Goggin, Gerard, Linda Steele, and Jessica Robyn Cadwallader. 2017. Normality and disability: Intersections among norms, law, and culture. *Continuum* 31: 337–40. [CrossRef]

Goldschmidt, Jenny E. 2017. New Perspectives on Equality: Towards Transformative Justice through the Disability Convention? *Nordic Journal of Human Rights* 35: 1–14. [CrossRef]

Gooding, Piers. 2012. Supported Decision-Making: A Rights-Based Disability Concept and its Implications for Mental Health Law. *Psychiatry, Psychology and Law* 20: 431–51. [CrossRef]

Gooding, Piers. 2014. Supported Decision-Making: A Disability and Human Rights-Based Concept for Mental Health Law. Ph.D. Thesis, Monash University, Clayton, Australia.

Gooding, Piers. 2016. From Deinstitutionalisation to Consumer Empowerment: Mental health policy, neoliberal restructuring and the closure of the 'Big bins' in Victoria. *Health Sociology Review* 25: 33–47. [CrossRef]

Gordon, Rob. 2000. The Emergence of Assisted (Supported) Decision-making in the Canadian Law of Adult Guardianship and Substitute Decision-Making. *International Journal of Law and Psychiatry* 23: 61–77. [CrossRef]

Hall, Margaret. 2012. Mental Capacity in the (Civil) Law: Capacity, autonomy and vulnerability. *McGill Law Journal* 58: 61–94. [CrossRef]

Herring, Jonathan. 2016. *Vulnerable Adults and the Law*. Oxford: OUP.

Kohn, Nina A. 2014. Vulnerability Theory and the Role of Government. *Yale Journal of Law and Feminism* 26: 1–27.

Kohn, Nina A., and Jeremy A. Blumenthal. 2014. A Critical Assessment of Supported Decision-making for Persons Aging with Intellectual Disabilities. *Disability and Health Journal* 7: S40–S43. [CrossRef] [PubMed]

Kohn, Nina A., Jeremy A. Blumenthal, and Amy T. Campbell. 2013. Supported Decision-Making: A Viable Alternative to Guardianship? *Penn State Law Review* 117: 1111–57. [CrossRef]

Law Commission of Ontario. 2014. *Legal Capacity, Decision-Making and Guardianship. Discussion Paper May 2014*. Toronto: Law Commission of Ontario.

Law Commission of Ontario. 2017. *Legal Capacity, Decision-Making and Guardianship: Final Report*. Toronto: Law Commission of Ontario.

LIDS. 2017. Effective Decision-Making Support. La Trobe University Living With Disability Research Centre. Available online: http://www.latrobe.edu.au/lids/research/support-for-decision-making/decision-making-support (accessed on 11 September 2017).

Luna, Florencia. 2009. Elucidating the Concept of Vulnerability: Layers not labels. *International Journal of Feminist Approaches to Bioethics* 2: 121–39. [CrossRef]

Luna, Florencia, and Sheryl Vanderpoel. 2013. Not the Usual Suspects: Addressing Layers of Vulnerability. *Bioethics* 27: 352–32. [CrossRef] [PubMed]

Magnusson, Roger. 2017. *Advancing the Right to Health: The Vital Role of Law*. Geneva: World Health Organization.

Mansell, Jim, and Kent Ericsson. 2013. *Deinstitutionalization and Community Living: Intellectual Disability Services in Britain, Scandinavia and the USA*. Dordrecht: Springer, First published 1996.

Marks, Stephen P. 2009. The Past and Future of the Separation of Human Rights into Categories. *Maryland Journal of International Law* 24: 209–43.

MHT. 2016. *Mental Health Tribunal Annual Report 2015–2016*. Melbourne: Mental Health Tribunal.

OPA. 2017. *Designing a Deprivation of Liberty Authorisation and Regulation Framework*. Melbourne: Office of the Public Advocate.

Perlin, Michael L. 2011. The Right to Treatment and the Road Ahead: "Abandoned Love": The Impact of Wyatt v. Stickney on the Intersection Between International Human Rights and Domestic Mental Disability Law. *Law & Psychology Review* 35: 121–239.

Power, Andrew, Janet Lord, and Allison de Franco. 2013. *Active Citizenship and Disability: Implementing the Personalisation of Support, Cambridge Disability Law and Policy Series*. Cambridge: Cambridge University Press.

Productivity Commission. 2017. *National Disability Insurance Scheme (NDIS) Costs*. Canberra: Productivity Commission.

Purcal, Christiane, Trish Hill, Kelly Johnson, and Rosemary Kayess. 2017. *Evaluation of the Supported Decision Making Phase 2 (SDM2) Project: Final Report*. Sydney: Social Policy Research Centre, UNSW.

Segal, Steven P., Stephania L. Hayes, and Lachlan Rimes. 2017. The Utility of Outpatient Commitment: I. A Need for Treatment and a Least Restrictive Alternative to Psychiatric Hospitalization. *Psychiatric Services*. [CrossRef] [PubMed]

Sloan, Brian. 2012. *Informal Carers and Private Law*. Oxford: Hart Publishing.

Smith, Maxwell J., Carrie Bernard, Kate Rossiter, Sachin Sahni, and Diego DSilva. 2010. Vulnerability: A Contentious and Fluid Term. *The Hastings Center Report* 40: 5–6. [CrossRef] [PubMed]

Smyth, Paul, and Christopher Deeming. 2016. The 'Social Investment Perspective' in Social Policy: A Longue Durée Perspective. *Social Policy & Administration* 50: 673–90. [CrossRef]

Steele, Linda, Leanne Dowse, and Julian Trofimovs. 2016. Who is Diverted: Moving beyond Diagnosed Impairment towards a Social and Political Analysis of Diversion. *Sydney Law Review* 38: 179–206.

Tait, David, Terry Carney, and Kirsten Deane. 1995. *Ticket to Services or Transfer of Rights?: Young People and Guardianship*; Canberra: National Youth Affairs Research Scheme.

Then, Shih-Ning. 2013. Evolution and Innovation in Guardianship Laws: Assisted decision-making. *Sydney Law Review* 35: 133–66.

Tobin, John. 2012. *The Right to Health in International Law*. Oxford: Oxford University Press.

Tushnet, Mark. 2016. Notes on Some Aspects of the Taxonomy of 'Generations' of Rights. *Journal of Institutional Studies [Revista Estudos Institucionais]* 2: 475–85. [CrossRef]

UK Independent Mechanism. 2017. Disability Rights in the UK: Submission to inform the CRPD list of issues on the UK. Available online: https://www.equalityhumanrights.com/en/our-human-rights-work/monitoring-and-promoting-un-treaties/un-convention-rights-persons-disabilities (accessed on 3 September 2017).

UN Committee on the Rights of Persons with Disabilities. 2014. *General Comment No. 1 (2014)*. Geneva: UN Committee on the Rights of Persons with Disabilities.

UN Committee on the Rights of Persons with Disabilities. 2017. List of Issues in Relation to the Initial Report of the United Kingdom of Great Britain and Northern Ireland. Available online: http://tbinternet.ohchr.org/_layouts/treatybodyexternal/Download.aspx?symbolno=CRPD%2fC%2fGBR%2fQ%2f1&Lang=en (accessed on 3 September 2017).

Van Puymbrouck, Laura. 2017. *Supported Decision Making in the United States: A White Paper by CQL*. Towson: Council on Quality and Leadership.

VLRC. 2012. *Guardianship: Final Report*. Melbourne: Victorian Law Reform Commission.

Wiesel, Ilan, and Christine Bigby. 2015. Movement on Shifting Sands: Deinstitutionalisation and People with Intellectual Disability in Australia, 1974–2014. *Urban Policy and Research* 33: 178–94. [CrossRef]

Wikipedia. 1997. The Castle. Available online: https://simple.wikipedia.org/wiki/The_Castle_(movie) (accessed on 18 August 2017).

Wills, Joe, and Ben Warwick. 2016. Contesting Austerity: The potential and pitfalls of socioeconomic rights discourse. *Indiana Journal of Global Legal Studies* 23: 629–64. [CrossRef]

5

Protection for Privacy under the United Nations Convention on the Rights of Persons with Disabilities

Mark C. Weber

College of Law, DePaul University, Chicago, IL 60604, USA; mweber@depaul.edu

Abstract: Article 22 of the Convention on the Rights of Persons with Disabilities (CRPD) protects personal and family privacy and reputation. This paper examines the antecedents of the CRPD privacy article in other international instruments and selected domestic law. It traces the history of the article through the deliberations that led up to the final version of the CRPD, which has now been ratified by 173 nations. It analyzes the text of the article and discusses its limited administrative and judicial applications. Finally, it describes the article's place in current thinking about disability human rights.

Keywords: disability rights; disability; privacy; Convention on the Rights of Persons with Disabilities; reputation

---

1. Introduction

Article 22 of the Convention on the Rights of Persons with Disabilities (CRPD) protects personal and family privacy and reputation. Article 22 reads:

> Respect for Privacy
>
> 1. No person with disabilities, regardless of place of residence or living arrangements, shall be subjected to arbitrary or unlawful interference with his or her privacy, family, home or correspondence or other types of communication or to unlawful attacks on his or her honour and reputation. Persons with disabilities have the right to the protection of the law against such interference or attacks.
>
> 2. States Parties shall protect the privacy of personal, health and rehabilitation information of persons with disabilities on an equal basis with others (UNGA 2006)[1].

International Human Rights Law protections for privacy are generally thought to include privacy of personal information, privacy of communications, privacy of personal environment, such as one's dwelling and other personal spaces, and freedom from attacks on personal honor or reputation (UMHRC 2012). United States Supreme Court Justice Louis Brandeis described privacy—in his words "the right to be let alone"—as the "most comprehensive of rights and the right most valued by civilized men."[2] A recent commentary on data privacy states: "The values thought to be protected by privacy . . . include physical security, liberty, autonomy, intimacy, dignity, identity, and equality" (Francis and Francis 2014[3], p. 2 of 25). Privacy is a value in itself, and its protection furthers other values that human beings cherish (Wachter 2017).

---

1 Hereafter, CRPD.
2 *Olmstead v United States*. 1928. 277 U.S. 438, 478 (Brandeis, J., dissenting).
3 Hereafter Francis and Francis, Privacy.

2. Relation to Other International and National Privacy Protection Regimes

The privacy article of the CRPD aligns closely with privacy protections in other international human rights instruments; those instruments served as inspiration for the CRPD provision (United Nations Ad Hoc Committee n.d.a). The International Covenant on Civil and Political Rights states: "(1). No one shall be subjected to arbitrary or unlawful interference with his privacy, family, home or correspondence, nor to unlawful attacks on his honour and reputation. (2). Everyone has the right to the protection of the law against such interference or attacks." (UNGA 1976). The language of the Universal Declaration of Human Rights is similar (UNGA 1948).[4] The Convention on the Rights of the Child states: "(1). No child shall be subjected to arbitrary or unlawful interference with his or her privacy, family, home or correspondence, nor to unlawful attacks on his or her honour and reputation. (2). The child has the right to the protection of the law against such interference or attacks." (UNGA 1990a). The Convention on Migrant Workers provides: "No migrant worker or member of his or her family shall be subjected to arbitrary or unlawful interference with his or her privacy, family, home, correspondence or other." (UNGA 1990b). Various regional and other instruments also protect a person's private information and reputation (ICRC n.d.). The CRPD itself, in its article on statistics and data collection, requires that state parties will collect appropriate information to implement policies in accordance with the Convention, but in collecting and maintaining the information state parties must obey safeguards to ensure confidentiality and respect for the privacy of people with disabilities.[5]

The connection between the CRPD's privacy article and the terms of the other human rights instruments distinguishes the CRPD's treatment of privacy from its treatment of some other rights. The point has been made that although the United Nations' own materials on the CRPD stress that it does not create new rights and instead applies existing rights in a way that responds to the situation of persons with disabilities (Kayess and French 2008[6], p. 20), in fact the treaty does contain new rights for people with disabilities, for example, rights to research and development (Article 4), raising of awareness (Article 8), poverty reduction and economic security (Article 28), and other entitlements not found or not expressed as affirmative rights in other pacts (Kayess and French 2008, pp. 32–33). The privacy article only modestly expands on the language found in other instruments. The consistency of the language, however, should not be taken to mean that the article requires mere formal equality of treatment between people with disabilities and others, as discussed at greater length in Section 6, below.

Many regional and national legal regimes afford protection for privacy rights. The European Convention on Human Rights guarantees privacy (Council of Europe 2010). A celebrated recognition of privacy in European Union law is the "right to be forgotten" case, *Google Spain SL v. Agencia Española de Protección de Datos* (*Google v. Spain*), in which the European Union Court of Justice ruled that European citizens have the right to request search engine firms that gather personal information for profit to remove links to private information if the information is no longer relevant (The Court (Grand Chamber) (2014).[7] The court relied on European Union Directive 95/46, implementing Articles 7 and 8 of the Charter of Fundamental Rights of the European Union. It ruled that Google may be forced to de-link its search engine from personal information searched for by a person's name even when the information is true and was lawfully published. The court required a balancing of the conflicting interests of the subject of the information and the general public.[8]

National privacy legislation is found in many places. For example, Argentina enacted a wide-reaching *Personal Data Protection Act* in 2000.[9] New Zealand's *Privacy Act* establishes principles

---

4 For a discussion see (Hurley 2015).

5 CRPD, Art. 31(1)(a).

6 Citing UN online sources.

7 For a critical review, see (Perotti 2015).

8 Case C-131/12, para 99. For discussion of the privacy jurisprudence of the European Court of Human Rights and how it might be applied in the interpretation of Article 22, see (Della Fina 2017).

9 Act 25,326 (30 October 2000).

for the collection, use, and disclosure of individuals' information by private and public agencies, as well as access by the individuals affected to the information held by the agencies.[10] Sweden's *Personal Data Act* protects people against violation of personal integrity when personal data is processed.[11] Privacy protections exist in Canadian law, although the position has been advanced that existing domestic law is insufficient to protect against employer misuse of genetic information (Labman 2004). In the United States, constitutional protections exist against unreasonable searches by government actors[12] and many legal sanctions exist for nongovernmental intrusions into individuals' privacy (Dobbs 2000). In U.S. constitutional law, privacy concepts are closely linked to bodily autonomy and fundamental rights to make decisions about sexuality,[13] medical treatment,[14] abortion[15] and other matters,[16] free from government prohibitions. The idea of privacy rights being connected with rights to bodily autonomy surfaced in the comments of a number of contributors to the drafting of Article 22.

As with other aspects of the CRPD, any overlap with other international human rights instruments and national legislation does not diminish the need for particularized protections for individuals with disabilities, given the unique nature of much disability discrimination. In the words of one commentator, "the reality of persons with disabilities' rights experience in most contexts is more complex than simply outright denial. Even when their entitlement to rights has been formally recognized and uncontentious, their disability has often effectively excluded them from rights enjoyment." (Mégret 2011, p. 263).[17] The CRPD provides a means to challenge the barriers to the realization of basic human rights for persons with disabilities.

3. The History of Article 22

During the Second Session of the Ad Hoc Committee on the Convention in 2003, the Secretary General appraised the World Programme of Action, acknowledging advances in medical research, genetics, and biotechnology, and discussing implications for the privacy rights of individuals with disabilities (United Nations Ad Hoc Committee 2003a).[18] The Second Session also considered a letter from Morten Kjaerum, the Executive Director of the Danish Institute for Human Rights concerning the "concept of autonomy" (United Nations Ad Hoc Committee n.d.b). The letter pointed out that autonomy rights include: "[1.] right to personal development, to create ideas and goals for life; [2.] right to privacy; [3.] right to integrity, liberty and freedom from coercion; [4.] right to inclusion in community life; and, [5.] right to participate actively in political process" (United Nations Ad Hoc Committee n.d.b). The letter went on to state: "Issues of privacy are also highly relevant for persons with disabilities whose dependence on technical and personal aids may lead to situations of vulnerability" (United Nations Ad Hoc Committee n.d.b). The Bangkok delegation referred to respect for privacy in its initial proposals for the Convention (United Nations Ad Hoc Committee 2003b). The delegation's discussion mentioned the link between respect for private and family life, freedom of expression, and the right to sexuality for individuals with disabilities.

Following the Second Session, the Ad Hoc Committee established a Working Group. The Working Group's proposed text included an article establishing protection for privacy, home, and family. The portion of the text relating to privacy and reputation was close to what would become the final wording of Article 22:

---

10 Privacy Act 1993 (assent 17 May 1993).
11 Personal Data Act (1998:204) (issued 29 April 1998).
12 *Bivens v Six Unknown Named Agents of the Federal Bureau of Narcotics*. 1971. 403 U.S. 388; Mapp v Ohio. 1961. 367 US 643.
13 *Lawrence v Texas*. 2003. 539 U.S. 558.
14 *Parham v JR*. 1979. 442 US 584.
15 *Roe v Wade*. 1973. 410 US 113.
16 *Griswold v Connecticut*. 1965. 381 US 479.
17 The truth of Mégret's observation should not, of course, diminish the attention paid to outright denial of rights.
18 UN Doc CRPD/A/AC 265/2003/1. For an account of the history of the CRPD as a whole, see (Degener and Begg 2017).

> 1. Persons with disabilities, including those living in institutions, shall not be subjected to arbitrary or unlawful interference with their privacy, and shall have the right to the protection of the law against such interference. States Parties to this Convention shall take effective measures to protect the privacy of the home, family, correspondence and medical records of persons with disabilities and their choice to take decisions on personal matters (United Nations n.d.).

The Working Group suggested that the Ad Hoc Committee consider replacing the word "correspondence" in the first paragraph with the broader term "communications." (United Nations n.d.).

Various Working Group participants submitted commentaries and proposals concerning the privacy language to be included in the Convention (Martin and Lachwitz n.d.). Great Britain suggested protecting privacy under a provision covering autonomy in general (Martin and Lachwitz n.d.). The United States highlighted the need for privacy with regard to voting and employment (United Nations 2004). The nongovernmental organization (NGO) Inclusion International noted the threat to privacy from institutional living arrangements imposed on people with mental disabilities and discussed the need to protect privacy rights of individuals with disabilities (United Nations 2003). Another NGO suggested a specialized article on the privacy of records (WNUSP 2003).

The Third Session of the Ad Hoc Committee for disability rights discussed proposals for the privacy article extensively (United Nations Ad Hoc Committee n.d.c). Costa Rica's draft entitled "Respect for Privacy" read:

> 1. Persons with disabilities shall not be subjected to arbitrary or unlawful interference with their privacy, and have the right to the protection of the law against such interference in all fields. States Parties to this Convention shall take effective measures to protect the privacy of the communications, information and documents of persons with disabilities (United Nations Ad Hoc Committee n.d.c).

The European Union's early draft was somewhat more detailed:

> 1. Persons with disabilities, including those living in institutions, shall not be subjected to arbitrary or unlawful interference with their privacy, and shall have the right to the protection of the law against such interference. States Parties to this Convention shall take effective measures to protect the privacy of the home, family, correspondence and medical records of persons with disabilities and their choice to take decisions on personal matters (United Nations Ad Hoc Committee n.d.c).

Wording changes to this draft were discussed. Kenya suggested including the term "communication" (United Nations Ad Hoc Committee n.d.c). South Africa suggested the article should provide protection of "all forms of privacy of an individual" and "reflect the full range of human rights protection" (United Nations Ad Hoc Committee n.d.c). An Australian NGO suggested separating privacy and family into separate articles and broadening the scope of the language used in the Committee's draft concerning medical records (United Nations Ad Hoc Committee n.d.c). The materials from the Fourth Session of the Ad Hoc Committee in 2004 continued to combine privacy and family rights, but added protection for privacy in government data collection activities (United Nations Ad Hoc Committee 2004).

During the Fifth Session of the Ad Hoc Committee, privacy was split off from family rights and became its own article, as reflected in the final version of the Convention (United Nations Ad Hoc Committee 2005a). The committee said, "There was broad support to split the substance of the text prepared by the Working Group for draft article 14 into two separate articles." The privacy draft now read:

> No persons with disabilities, regardless of place of residence or living arrangements, shall be subjected to arbitrary or unlawful interference with his or her privacy, family, home

> or correspondence or other types of communication, or to unlawful attacks on his or her honour and reputation. All persons with a disability have the right to the protection of the law against such interference or attacks (United Nations Ad Hoc Committee 2005a).

There remained an active draft concerning the privacy of medical records, and there was concern about providing for advances in communication technologies (United Nations Ad Hoc Committee 2005a). On behalf of the EU, Luxemburg favored the broad language "regardless of their place of residence or living arrangements" over language that specified institutional settings (United Nations Ad Hoc Committee 2005b). Yemen and Serbia and Montenegro expressed support for the language on arbitrary and unlawful interference and revived the proposal to replace correspondence with "communications" (United Nations Ad Hoc Committee 2005b). Serbia and Montenegro suggested covering all records pertaining to people with disabilities. The United Arab Emirates favored retaining language about persons living in institutions to make sure that privacy rights are protected while the institutions are monitored (United Nations Ad Hoc Committee 2005b). Japan favored conforming usage to that in the Covenant on Civil and Political Rights, and supported the broader language about place of residence over that specifying institutional settings (United Nations Ad Hoc Committee 2005b). Russia opposed the splitting of family rights and privacy rights into two articles, stating that the issues were closely related, but it supported some of the changes to the language while suggesting modified versions of others (United Nations Ad Hoc Committee 2005b). At the Seventh Session, Article 22 appeared in its final version (United Nations Ad Hoc Committee 2006, pp. 17–18).

4. The Text of Article 22

Several features of Article 22's text merit comment. As indicated above, the language "regardless of place of residence or living arrangements" was the product of extensive discussions over whether to single out institutional arrangements or to embrace broader terminology that would avoid reinforcing the stereotyped idea that people with disabilities will reside in institutional settings. The broader language should not be taken as minimizing the unique threats to personal privacy that life in institutions poses for the people with disabilities who live in them. Article 22 may provide authority by which to challenge the use of large institutions that not only make privacy impossible but also breed abusive conditions (Perlin 2007, p. 344). The CRPD elsewhere addresses the opportunity of individuals to choose where they live and to have access to resources that support living an inclusive life in the community rather than a segregated or isolated institutional existence.[19]

The textual provision "arbitrary or unlawful interference with his or her privacy, family, home or correspondence or other types of communication" is also noteworthy. The drafters opted for breadth of coverage for privacy protections by explicitly addressing both correspondence and other forms of communication, expanding the terms of earlier human rights instruments. As illustrated by the rise of social media communication in the present era and the temptation for both public and private actors to make use of personal information on social media platforms, making rights protection keep pace with communications technology remains a continuing, even an increasing, challenge.[20]

The language "or to unlawful attacks on his or her honour and reputation," which echoes that in other human rights instruments, holds promise for efforts to diminish the stigma that frequently is imposed on persons with disabilities.[21] The protections in the other instruments inspired the drafters of Article 22 to include parallel provisions regarding defense against attacks on honor and reputation. State-sponsored segregation of people with disabilities and the history of eugenics and other attacks on those with disabilities make them uniquely subject to reputational harm.[22]

---

19 CRPD, Art 19.
20 e.g., (Horowitz 2016).
21 See (Goffman 1963, p. 5).
22 See (Weber 2007, pp. 18–20).

The term of Article 22 recognizing "the right to the protection of the law against such interference or attacks" imposes an affirmative duty on the state to prevent and remedy interference with privacy and attacks on reputation. Of course, nations will differ in the domestic law they create to effectuate this duty and the avenues of enforcement available. In countries influenced by the English Common Law, private suit is the default method by which victims of intrusion or damage to reputation may obtain redress.[23] States with other traditions will address violations of the norms of privacy and reputation protection in other ways,[24] although, as noted below, even in places that do not follow common law approaches, individual litigation has included claims under Article 22.

The language in Article 22 providing that "States Parties shall protect the privacy of personal, health and rehabilitation information of persons with disabilities on an equal basis with others" reflects special concerns about health-related information and the potential that its disclosure will lead to discrimination against persons with disabilities. The same concern inspired the *Genetic Information Nondiscrimination Act*[25] in the United States and the present debate in the U.S. over the collection and use of medical information in employee wellness programs (Abelson 2016). Aisling De Paor and Charles O'Mahony have declared: "By implication, the right to genetic privacy is ... protected under the UN CRPD and other human rights instruments ... " (De Paor and O'Mahony 2016, p. 13). They note that Article 22 rights may be interpreted to require states to prohibit employers from genetically testing employees (De Paor and O'Mahony 2016, p. 19). Questions linger whether people with disabilities should be afforded special protections given their vulnerability to the misuse of personal, health, and rehabilitation information, but the language of Article 22 simply provides that the protection for people with disabilities shall be "on an equal basis with others."

The dominant approach in affording protection of health information privacy is to ensure that no personally identifiable information is disclosed without the informed consent of the individual. Recent research has criticized that approach as incomplete, however, because individuals may be subject to discrimination based on correlations between characteristics they have and aggregate predictions of risk of disease or disability. As two prominent authorities state: "For example, employers or insurers might learn from [data analytics] that particular demographic categories of patients have especially high rates of chronic conditions (including HIV) or especially high costs of treating these conditions and alter plan design accordingly."[26]

5. Article 22 Applications and Interpretations

Application and interpretation of Article 22 may be found in the reports of the Committee on the Rights of Persons with Disabilities reviewing the progress of the parties adopting the CRPD, as well as in administrative and judicial decisions in cases involving the CRPD. As an example of Committee observations, Denmark's 2014 review led to an expression of concern that psychiatric hospitals continued to be allowed to transfer private information about patients without the patients' consent (UNCRPD 2014). Reports by internal authorities in countries that have ratified the CRPD also describe challenges and responses with regard to implementing Article 22.[27] The report from Argentina, for example, noted the nation's law protecting the rights of persons living with HIV infections (UNCRPD 2010a). China's report pointed to the ability of individuals whose privacy rights have been violated to seek civil liability for damage to reputation (UNCRPD 2010b). The Austrian report cautioned: "In civil society there are doubts about whether people who live or work in homes or institutions are sufficiently protected against the passing on of personal data" (UNCRPD 2010c). Peru

---

23 See Restatement 2nd of Torts. 1977. § 558 (elements of defamation), § 652A (principles for liability for invasions of privacy).
24 See (Harpur and Bales 2010).
25 Pub. L. No 110-233 (2008).
26 Francis and Francis, Privacy (n. 4) p. 12; see (Hoffman 2017, pp. 7–9 of 17).
27 E.g., (UNCRPD 2011).

noted that it has a national registry of persons with disabilities but that the information is confidential and subject to disclosure only by court order (UNCRPD 2010d).

Independent bodies have also issued reports on CRPD implementation that include Article 22. A draft monitoring report for India from 2013 commented on dissatisfaction with privacy protections for persons with disabilities and recommended that disability and other relevant laws explicitly provide for the right to privacy, specifically for personal, health, and rehabilitation information, and that rehabilitation and medical professionals receive training in privacy rights of persons with disabilities (Gupta et al. 2013, pp. 160–64). A report on Singapore stated that the *Personal Data Protection Act* governed collection, use, and disclosure of personal data, but concluded that it did not cover persons with chronic mental illness who have to report their conditions for medical insurance and was unclear with regard to protections of personal data of people with chronic mental illness (Disabled People's Association Singapore 2015, p. 27).

The European Commission has studied the European Union's implementation of the CRPD. The Commission's Staff Working Document of 2014 commented on a directive and regulation that established a framework for protecting health and other personal data. Under the directive, consent is generally required except when processing the information is necessary to protect the vital interests of the person to whom the information pertains or another person, if the subject of the information is physically or legally not able to provide consent (EC 2014). Further protections were under discussion at the time of the report, and the European Data Protection Supervisor was responding to complaints alleging misuse of information pertaining to individuals with disabilities (EC 2014, pp. 26, 56).

A number of cases alleging violations of Article 22 are pending before the UN's Committee on the Rights of Persons with Disabilities (Office of High Commissioner, UN Human Rights 2017). In an adjudicated case involving the United Kingdom, the Committee, applying Article 2 of the CRPD Optional Protocol, considered the communication of an insulin-dependent service delivery manager for Oracle Corporation who had been laid off (UNCRPD 2012). The government's Employment Tribunal decided against the complainant on his allegation that Oracle failed to make reasonable adjustments and otherwise discriminated against him on the basis of disability. The communication to the Committee alleged that the Employment Tribunal, by finding him not to be a credible witness, attacked his honor and reputation in violation of Article 22 of the CRPD. The Committee found that the dismissal and judicial review took place before the entry into force of the Convention and Optional Protocol in the U.K., so the communication was ruled inadmissible.

6. The Relation of Article 22 to Disability Human Rights Ideas

Professor Degener has recently argued that the CRPD embodies a human rights model of disability, a model that "encompasses the values for disability policy [and] that acknowledges the human dignity of disabled persons." (Degener 2016, p. 3). Privacy and reputation are key aspects of human dignity, so their protection fits neatly into an international treaty based on human dignity principles. The first paragraph of Article 22 is an absolute protection for privacy and reputation rights, couched in language that does not make any comparison with the rights of nondisabled persons. In this respect and using Degener's terms, Article 22 provides for something "more than anti-discrimination." (Degener 2016, p. 4). Professor Kanter has also stressed the departure of the CRPD from anti-discrimination measures that rely on equalizing opportunities to establish a right to substantive equality so that outcomes, not just treatment, will be equal (Kanter 2015, pp. 842–44). The rights set out in the first paragraph of Article 22 are substantive and call for different treatment when the protections society generally affords are not sufficient to guard privacy and reputational interests of those who have disabilities. Like Degener, Kanter contends that the CRPD embodies a human rights approach to disability. Unlike Degener, she sees the human rights approach as fundamentally consistent with a social model of disability, and finds both to be present in the terms of the CRPD (Kanter 2015, pp. 845–48).[28]

In work roughly contemporaneous with the UN General Assembly's consideration and adoption of the CRPD, Professor Stein articulated a human rights model of disability that he found immanent in the draft Convention (Stein 2007). Like Degener, he emphasizes the Convention's focus on the dignity and inherent worth of each person, and the importance of developing the capabilities of all (Stein 2007, pp. 83–85, 106–10). Stein is not the only authority who supports a capabilities approach in understanding and enforcing the rights of persons with disabilities under the Convention (Lang et al. 2011). Following Stein's and others' ideas, guarantees against intrusion and misuse of information would appear central both to dignity and to permitting individuals to achieve basic minimums needed for a meaningful life, as well as to reach toward achieving their full potential free from stereotyping assumptions and discriminatory treatment. Privacy losses are prominent among the negative consequences of disability discrimination that results from institutionalization, fear of contagion, and imposition of stigma.

The privacy provisions of the CRPD are thus consistent with disability rights thinking. Moreover, as a practical matter, quite apart from considerations of theory, privacy protections often safeguard against the most common forms of discrimination and so contribute to the overall goal of the CRPD and disability rights in general. As Professor Roberts notes, "[I]n certain circumstances, discriminators need information to discriminate ... Restricting potential discriminators' access to information about protected status can significantly reduce the chances of subsequent discrimination" (Roberts 2015, pp. 2099–2100). She cites the example of protecting the confidentiality of genetic information to prevent employment discrimination on that basis (Roberts 2015, pp. 2101, 2132). She further concludes that even at a theoretical level, privacy and anti-discrimination are symbiotic and can advance the same interests and values (Roberts 2015, p. 2121).

It is true that furthering the anti-subordination aims of laws forbidding disability discrimination may require abandoning privacy to some extent and in some situations, as when one requests an accommodation from an employer, or the modification of rules from a public accommodation or government entity (Areheart 2012, p. 714). Disclosure of personal information about disability may also promote solidarity among those with disabling conditions (Areheart 2012, p. 715). There is a loss of privacy involved in coming out as a person with a disability, a step that includes embracing an identity as disabled and joining the community of persons with disabilities. Coming out as disabled has been described as a political matter for precisely that reason (Michalko 2002, pp. 69–70, 78–79). Deciding not to invoke a shield of privacy, whether for strategic, moral, or ideological reasons, ought to be a voluntary decision, however. Legal protections need to be present to prevent unwanted, unwarranted, or abusive intrusion into a person's private sphere.

7. Conclusions

Just what constitutes unwanted, unwarranted, or abusive intrusion into a person's private sphere is an issue that remains to be developed, both in the context of the rights of persons with disabilities and in the context of human rights in general. Authorities have questioned whether typical privacy protection legislation, which relies on notice and consent, can be effective in an era when corporate and government information gathering is pervasive and fully informed consent is rare (Symposium 2013). Because people with disabilities are uniquely at risk of discrimination when privacy protections fail, and because institutional and other settings in which people with disabilities often live are particularly subject to private and public intrusion, people with disabling conditions are canaries in the coal mine for loss of privacy by everyone. The coming years will demonstrate how effectively governments will "protect the privacy of personal, health and rehabilitation information of persons with disabilities on

---

28 For a view consistent with Kanter's, expressed in relation to the views of Professor Stein, see (Weber 2011, pp. 2530–31).

an equal basis with others." (UNGA 2006). Article 22 of the CRPD holds promise for the protection of personal information, dignity, and reputation of individuals with disabilities, but that promise is the beginning of the story, not its end.

Acknowledgments: Mallory Morgan, DePaul University College of Law Class of 2017, provided extensive research assistance for this article. Her contributions are gratefully acknowledged.

References

Abelson, Reed. 2016. AARP Sues U.S. Over Rules for Wellness Programs. *New York Times*. October 24. Available online: https://www.nytimes.com/2016/10/25/business/employee-wellness-programs-prompt-aarp-lawsuit.html?_r=0 (accessed on 30 March 2017).

Areheart, Bradley A. 2012. GINA, Privacy, and Antisubordination. *Georgia Law Review* 46: 705–18.

Council of Europe. 2010. European Convention on Human Rights. Art. 8 (Right to respect for private and family life). Available online: http://www.echr.coe.int/Documents/Convention_ENG.pdf (accessed on 13 June 2017).

De Paor, Aisling, and Charles O'Mahony. 2016. The Need to Protect Employees with Genetic Predisposition to Mental Illness? The UN Convention on the Rights of Persons with Disabilities and the Case for Regulation. *Industrial Law Journal* 45: 525–55. [CrossRef]

Degener, Theresia. 2016. Disability in a Human Rights Context. *Laws* 5: 35. [CrossRef]

Degener, Theresia, and Andrew Begg. 2017. From Invisible Citizens to Agents of Change: A Short History of the Struggle for the Rights of Persons with Disabilities at the United Nations. In *The United Nations Convention on the Rights of Persons with Disabilities*. Edited by Valentina Della Fina, Rachele Cera and Giuseppe Palmisano. Cham: Springer.

Della Fina, Valentina. 2017. Article 22 (Respect for Privacy). In *The United Nations Convention on the Rights of Persons with Disabilities*. Edited by Valentina Della Fina, Rachele Cera and Giuseppe Palmisano. Cham: Springer.

Disabled People's Association Singapore. 2015. Singapore and the UN CRPD. Available online: http://www.dpa.org.sg/wp-content/uploads/2015/06/Singapore-and-UN-CRPD.pdf (accessed on 1 April 2017).

Dobbs, Dan B. 2000. *The Law of Torts*. St. Paul: West Pub. Co., chap. 29.

European Commission. 2014. Report on the implementation of the UN Convention on the Rights of Persons with Disabilities (CRPD) by the European Union. June 5 26 SWD 182. Available online: http://ec.europa.eu/justice/discrimination/files/swd_2014_182_en.pdf (accessed on 1 April 2017).

Francis, John G., and Leslie P. Francis. 2014. Privacy, Confidentiality, and Justice. *Journal of Social Philosophy* 45: 408–31. [CrossRef]

Goffman, Erving. 1963. *Stigma: Notes on the Management of Spoiled Identity*. New York: Simon & Schuster.

Gupta, Shivani, Meenakshi Balasubramaniam, Sudha Ramamoorthy, Rama Chari, and Bhargavi Davar. 2013. Monitoring Report of Civil Society, United Nations Convention on Rights of Persons with Disabilities—India. Available online: http://www.dnis.org/FINAL-MONITORING%20CRPD%20-%20ZERO%20DRAFT%20REPORT.doc (accessed on 1 April 2017).

Harpur, Paul, and Richard A. Bales. 2010. The Positive Impact of the Convention on the Rights of Persons with Disabilities: A Case Study on the South Pacific and Lessons from the U.S. Experience. *Northern Kentucky Law Review* 37: 363–88.

Hoffman, Sharona. 2017. Big Data and the Americans with Disabilities Act. *Hastings Law Journal*. Available online: https://papers.ssrn.com/sol3/papers.cfm?abstract_id=284143 (accessed on 31 March 2017).

Horowitz, Josh. 2016. WhatsApp's encryption could make it a target of the Chinese government. Available online: https://qz.com/655778/whatsapps-encryption-could-make-it-a-target-of-the-chinese-government/ (accessed on 31 March 2017).

Hurley, Deborah. 2015. Taking the Long Way Home: The Human Right of Privacy. In *Privacy in the Modern Age: The Search for Solutions*. Edited by Marc Rotenberg, Julia Horwitz and Jeramie Scott. New York: The New Press, Available online: https://ssrn.com/abstract=2676864 (accessed on 9 June 2017).

International Committee of the Red Cross. n.d. Practice Relating to Rule 105. Respect for Family Life Customary IHL. Available online: https://ihl-databases.icrc.org/customary-ihl/eng/docs/v2_rul_rule105_sectiona (accessed on 31 March 2017).

Kanter, Arlene S. 2015. The Americans with Disabilities Act at 25 Years: Lessons to Learn from the Convention on the Rights of Persons with Disabilities. *Drake Law Review* 63: 819–83.

Kayess, Rosemary, and Phillip French. 2008. Out of Darkness into Light? Introducing the Convention on the Rights of Persons with Disabilities. *Human Rights Law Review* 8: 1–34. [CrossRef]

Labman, Shauna. 2004. Genetic Prophecies: The Future of the Canadian Workplace. *Manitoba Law Journal* 30: 227–47.

Lang, Raymond, Maria Kett, Nora Groce, and Jean-Francois Trani. 2011. Implementing the United Nations Convention on the rights of persons with disabilities: Principles, implications, practice and limitations. *ALTER-European Journal of Disability Research* 206: 216–17. [CrossRef]

Martin, Robert, and Klaus Lachwitz. n.d. Some reflections regarding the Preparation of a Comprehensive and Integral Convention on the Promotion and Protection of the Rights and Dignity of Persons with Disabilities. Available online: http://www.un.org/esa/socdev/enable/rights/wgcontrib-EU.htm (accessed on 31 March 2017).

Mégret, Frédéric. 2011. The Disabilities Convention: Toward a Holistic Concept of Rights. *International Journal of Human Rights* 12: 261–78. [CrossRef]

Michalko, Rod. 2002. *The Difference that Disability Makes*. Philadelphia: Temple University Press.

Office of High Commissioner, UN Human Rights. 2017. Committee on the Rights of Persons with Disabilities. Table of Pending Cases. Available online: http://www.ohchr.org/EN/HRBodies/CRPD/Pages/Tablependingcases.aspx (accessed on 30 March 2017).

Perlin, Michael. 2007. International Human Rights Law and Comparative Mental Disability Law: The Universal Factors. *Syracuse Journal of International Law and Commerce* 34: 333–57.

Perotti, Elena. 2015. The European Ruling on the Right to be Forgotten and its Extra-EU Implementation. Available online: http://dx.doi.org/10.2139/ssrn.2703325 (accessed on 9 June 2017).

Roberts, Jessica L. 2015. Protecting Privacy to Prevent Discrimination. *William & Mary Law Review* 56: 2097–174.

Stein, Michal Ashley. 2007. Disability Human Rights. *California Law Review* 95: 75–121.

Symposium. 2013. Privacy and Technology. *Harvard Law Review* 126: 1880–2041.

The Court (Grand Chamber). 2014. App. No. C-131/12 (Grand Chamber 13 May 2014). Available online: http://curia.europa.eu/juris/document/document.jsf?text=&docid=152065&pageIndex=0&doclang=EN&mode=req&dir=&occ=first&part=1&cid=305802 (accessed on 31 March 2017).

University of Minnesota Human Rights Center (UMHRC). 2012. *Human Rights Yes!: Action and Advocacy on the Rights of Persons with Disabilities*, 2nd ed. Minneapolis: Human Rights Resource Center, chap. 7; Available online: http://hrlibrary.umn.edu/edumat/hreduseries/HR-YES/chap-7.html (accessed on 31 March 2017).

United Nations Committee on the Rights of Persons with Disabilities (UNCRPD). 2010a. Initial Reports submitted by States parties under article 35: Argentina. October 6 CRPD/C/ARG/1. Available online: http://www.un.org/ga/search/view_doc.asp?symbol=CRPD/C/ARG/1 (accessed on 1 April 2017).

United Nations Committee on the Rights of Persons with Disabilities (UNCRPD). 2010b. Initial Reports submitted by States parties under article 35: China. August 30 CRPD/C/CHN/1. Available online: http://www.refworld.org/docid/4efc32622.html (accessed on 1 April 2017).

United Nations Committee on the Rights of Persons with Disabilities (UNCRPD). 2010c. Initial Reports submitted by States parties under article 35: Austria. November 2 CRPD/C/AUT/1. Available online: https://documents-dds-ny.un.org/doc/UNDOC/GEN/G11/462/79/PDF/G1146279.pdf?OpenElement (accessed on 1 April 2017).

United Nations Committee on the Rights of Persons with Disabilities (UNCRPD). 2010d. Initial Reports submitted by States parties under article 35: Peru. July 8 CRPD/C/PER/1. Available online: https://documents-dds-ny.un.org/doc/UNDOC/GEN/G11/462/79/PDF/G1146279.pdf?OpenElement (accessed 1 April 2017).

United Nations Convention on the Rights of Persons with Disabilities (UNCRPD). 2011. First New Zealand Report on Implementing the United Nations Convention on the Rights of Persons with Disabilities. Available online: https://www.odi.govt.nz/united-nations-convention-on-the-rights-of-persons-with-disabilities/un-reviews-of-nzs-implementation-of-the-convention/first-nz-report-on-implmentation-march-2011/first-new-zealand-report-on-implementing-the-un-convention-on-the-rights-of-persons-with-disabilities/ (accessed on 1 April 2017).

UNCRPD. 2012. McAlpine v United Kingdom of Great Britain and Northern Ireland (13 November 2012) CRPD/C/8/D/6/2011. Available online: http://repository.un.org/bitstream/handle/11176/298831/CRPD_C_8_D_6_2011-EN.pdf?sequence=3&isAllowed=y (accessed on 1 April 2017).

United Nations Committee on the Rights of Persons with Disabilities (UNCRPD). 2014. Concluding observations on the initial report of Denmark. October 30 CRPD/C/DNK/CO/1. Available online: http://repository.un.org/bitstream/handle/11176/310320/CRPD_C_DNK_CO_1-EN.pdf?sequence=1&isAllowed=y (accessed on 1 April 2017).

United Nations General Assembly (UNGA). 1948. Universal Declaration of Human Rights. Available online: http://www.un.org/en/documents/udhr/ (accessed on 9 June 2017).

United Nations General Assembly (UNGA). 1976. International Covenant on Civil and Political Rights. Art. 17. Available online: http://www.ohchr.org/EN/ProfessionalInterest/Pages/CCPR.aspx (accessed on 31 March 2017).

United Nations General Assembly (UNGA). 1990a. Convention on the Rights of the Child. Art. 16. Available online: http://www.ohchr.org/EN/ProfessionalInterest/Pages/CRC.aspx (accessed on 31 March 2017).

United Nations General Assembly (UNGA). 1990b. Convention on the Protection of the Rights of All Migrant Workers and Members of Their Families. Art. 14. Available online: http://www.ohchr.org/EN/ProfessionalInterest/Pages/CMW.aspx (accessed on 31 March 2017).

United Nations General Assembly (UNGA). 2006. Convention on the Rights of Persons with Disabilities. Available online: https://www.un.org/development/desa/disabilities/convention-on-the-rights-of-persons-with-disabilities/convention-on-the-rights-of-persons-with-disabilities-2.html (accessed on 13 June 2017).

United Nations. n.d. Working Group on a Convention. Available online: http://www.un.org/esa/socdev/enable/rights/ahcwgreporta14.htm (accessed on 31 March 2017) (footnotes omitted).

United Nations. 2003. Inclusion International. Available online: http://www.un.org/esa/socdev/enable/rights/wgcontrib-inclintl.htm (accessed on 31 March 2017).

United Nations. 2004. United States Contribution: Disability Rights. Available online: http://www.un.org/esa/socdev/enable/rights/wgcontrib-usa.htm (accessed on 31 March 2017).

United Nations Ad Hoc Committee. 2003a. Issues and Emerging Trends Related to Advancement of Persons with Disabilities. Paper presented at Second Session of Ad Hoc Committee, New York, NY, USA, June 16–27.

United Nations Ad Hoc Committee. 2003b. Bangkok Recommendations on the Elaboration of a Comprehensive and Integral International Convention to Promote and Protect the Rights and Dignity of Persons with Disabilities. June 2–4 UN Doc CRPD/A/AC 265/2003/CRP/10. Available online: http://www.un.org/esa/socdev/enable/rights/a_ac265_2003_crp10.htm (accessed on 3 August 2017).

United Nations Ad Hoc Committee. 2004. Report of the Ad Hoc Committee on a Comprehensive and Integral International Convention on the Protection and Promotion of the Rights and Dignity of Persons with Disabilities on its fourth session. September 14. Available online: https://www.un.org/esa/socdev/enable/rights/ahc4reporte.htm (accessed on 31 March 2017).

United Nations Ad Hoc Committee. 2005. Report of the Ad Hoc Committee on a Comprehensive and Integral International Convention on the Protection and Promotion of the Rights and Dignity of Persons with Disabilities on its fifth session. February 23. Available online: https://www.un.org/esa/socdev/enable/rights/ahc5reporte.htm (accessed on 31 March 2017).

United Nations Ad Hoc Committee. 2005. Daily summary of discussion at the fifth sessions, UN Convention on the Human Rights of People with Disabilities. February 2. Available online: http://www.un.org/esa/socdev/enable/rights/ahc5sum2feb.htm (accessed on 1 April 2017).

United Nations Ad Hoc Committee. 2006. Report of the Ad Hoc Committee on a Comprehensive and Integral International Convention on the Protection and Promotion of the Rights and Dignity of Persons with Disabilities on its seventh session. February 13. Available online: https://www.un.org/esa/socdev/enable/rights/ahc7docs/ahc7report-e.pdf (accessed on 31 March 2017).

United Nations Ad Hoc Committee. n.d.a References: Article 22: Respect for Privacy. Available online: https://www.un.org/esa/socdev/enable/rights/ahcstata22refinthr.htm (accessed on 31 March 2017).

United Nations Ad Hoc Committee. n.d.b Letter dated 26 May 2003 from the Executive Director of the Danish Institute for Human Rights addressed to the Secretary of the Ad Hoc Committee on a Comprehensive and

Integral International Convention on the Protection and Promotion of the Rights and Dignity of Persons with Disabilities. UN Doc CRPD/A/AC.265/2003/CRP/9. Available online: https://digitallibrary.un.org/record/496630?ln=en (accessed on 31 March 2017).

United Nations Ad Hoc Committee. n.d.c Third Session: Comments, proposals, and amendments submitted electronically. Available online: https://www.un.org/esa/socdev/enable/rights/ahcstata22tscomments.htm (accessed on 31 March 2017).

Wachter, Sandra. 2017. Privacy: Primus Inter Pares: Privacy as a Precondition for Self-Development, Personal Fulfilment and the Free Enjoyment of Fundamental Human Rights. Available online: https://ssrn.com/abstract=2903514 (accessed on 9 June 2017).

Weber, Mark C. 2007. *Disability Harassment*. New York: NYU Press.

Weber, Mark C. 2011. Disability Rights, Welfare Law. *Cardozo Law Review* 32: 2483–531.

World Network of Users and Survivors of Psychiatry (WNUSP). 2003. Submission to the United Nations Ad Hoc Committee on a Comprehensive and Integral International Convention to Promote and Protect the Rights and Dignity of Persons with Disabilities. Available online: http://www.un.org/esa/socdev/enable/rights/contrib-wnusp.htm (accessed on 31 March 2017).

6

The Inclusion of the Lived Experience of Disability in Policymaking

Laufey Löve [1,*], Rannveig Traustadóttir [1], Gerard Quinn [2] and James Rice [3]

1 Centre for Disability Studies, Faculty of Social and Human Sciences, University of Iceland, 101 Reykjavik, Iceland; rannvt@hi.is
2 Centre for Disability Law & Policy, National University of Ireland, H91 TK33 Galway, Ireland; gerard.quinn@nuigalway.ie
3 Centre for Disability Studies, Faculty of Social and Human Sciences, and Department of Anthropology, University of Iceland, 101 Reykjavik, Iceland; james@hi.is
* Correspondence: lel2@hi.is

Abstract: This paper examines the process under way in Iceland to align national law with the UN Convention on the Rights of Persons with Disabilities, focusing on the Convention's call for the active involvement of disabled people and their representative organizations in policy and decision making on matters that affect them. The paper draws on comments submitted by Icelandic DPOs on draft legislation intended to replace the existing law on services for disabled people, focusing on comments relating to their ability to participate in and affect the policymaking process. Furthermore, it draws on interviews with leaders of representative organizations of disabled people that solicited their views on the issue. The findings indicate that there is a reluctance on behalf of Icelandic authorities to make changes to the established process, which limits the active participation of disabled people and their representative organizations. The draft legislation has neither been revised to include provisions for expanding the participation of DPOs in policy and decision making, nor to ensure that disabled people themselves participate in the process.

Keywords: disability; CRPD; inclusion; policymaking

---

1. Introduction

The United Nations Convention on the Rights of Persons with Disabilities (CRPD) reflects the fundamental principle that those most affected have the right to participate in decisions that impact them, a contribution that has been called "one of the most progressive developments in human rights law provided by the CRPD" (Stein and Lord 2010, p. 698). There is an emphasis on participation that runs throughout the Convention that embeds within it an advocacy role for civil society organizations representing disabled people, which also extends to disabled people themselves (Meyers 2016; Stein and Lord 2010; Sabatello 2014). The preamble sets the stage by proclaiming that "Persons with disabilities should have the opportunity to be actively involved in decision making processes about policies and programs, including those directly concerning them" (United Nations 2007). Further emphasizing this stand in Article 4(3), the Convention demands that State parties "closely consult with and actively involve persons with disabilities, including children with disabilities, through their representative organizations when developing and implementing policies and legislation concerning persons with disabilities." The Convention maintains a focus on the importance of participation in the monitoring processes where it states that civil society, in particular persons with disabilities and their representative organizations, shall be involved and participate fully (Article 33(3)), requiring states parties to recognize the obligation set out in Article 4(3). Finally,

Article 34(3) encourages states parties to give "due consideration" to representation by persons with disabilities on the monitoring body (Stein and Lord 2010).

The CRPD sets out to create a new politics of disability and calls for changes to the process norms with regard to how disability policy is made. Bearing in mind how the Committee on the Rights of Persons with Disabilities (CRPD Committee), the body of independent experts that monitors implementation of the Convention by the States Parties, defines representative organizations of disabled people, this paper asks the question whether the new draft legislation on disability services currently before the Icelandic parliament, intended to bring national legislation into compliance with the CRPD, sufficiently embodies the Convention's call for changes to the process norms, particularly the principle that those most affected have to right to participate in decisions that most impact them. This is a question that may have wider relevance to other States Parties in the process of aligning national legislation with the CRPD. To shed light on this, the paper draws attention to the important role of DPOs in the drafting of the Convention and highlights those articles that lay the foundation for the argument that disabled people should be recognized as decision makers in their own affairs. Furthermore, it draws on theories that focus on the active involvement of marginalized groups, including disabled people, as a necessary component of changing their position of oppression. The paper then goes on to address the process underway in Iceland and examines comments submitted by Icelandic DPOs on the draft legislation pertaining to their views on the policymaking process. Furthermore, it draws on interviews with leaders of DPOs about their perceptions of their ability to affect decision making.

The prominent role afforded to civil society, particularly disabled people and their representative organizations, in the implementation and monitoring of the CRPD can be attributed to the unprecedented involvement of non-governmental organizations (NGOs), and in particular disabled persons' organizations (DPOs), in the drafting process of the Convention (Brennan et al. 2016; Degener 2016; Kanter 2014). Over 400 NGOs were accredited by the Ad Hoc Committee, the body responsible for the drafting of the treaty, which was at the time a historically high number for a UN process (Degener 2016; Kanter 2014). The involvement of civil society extended to a Working Group established by the Ad Hoc Committee to produce the first draft of the Convention. An unusual feature of the Working Group, which met in January 2004, was that it was equally composed of States, NGOs/DPOs and National Human Rights Institutions (NHRIs).[1] The DPOs were mostly led by and composed of disabled people themselves and much of the language of the Convention, when it was finally adopted, reflected their inputs during the Working Group. Further, many State delegations included disabled people who also helped shape the dialogue. This unique way of working—affording equal status to civil society in a treaty drafting process—gave the Convention an edge it would otherwise have lacked. It built relationships of trust with States and demonstrated how the lived experience of disabled people could enrich the process of developing norms and international standards.

An emphasis on the lived experience of disability was high on the agendas of many of the DPOs. The International Disability Caucus (IDC), a coalition of over 70 world-wide, regional and national DPOs that worked together to coordinate their efforts during the Ad Hoc Committee, put forth a suggestion that the Monitoring Committee be composed entirely or of a majority of disabled people (Stein and Lord 2010; Kumpuvuori and Virtanen 2017). The suggestion was rejected by the Ad Hoc Committee, as was the proposal that the Chair of the CRPD Committee be a disabled person

---

1 Membership of the Working Group included 27 States from every region of the world and six global NGOs/DPOs who had equal standing with the States in the Working Group's deliberations. NHRIs were represented by one person nominated by the International Coordination Committee (ICC) of NHRIs; there were three in all throughout the entirety of the process (Anuradha Mohit from the Indian National Human Rights Commission, Charlotte McLain-Nhlapo of the South African Human Rights Commission and, in the latter stages, Gerard Quinn of the Irish Human Rights Commission). The NGOs/DPOs included the World Blind Union, the World Federation of the Deaf, Inclusion International, and Rehabilitation International. They were mostly led by and composed of disabled people themselves.

(Stein and Lord 2010). However, it is worth noting that the call for disabled people themselves to have significant representation and a leading role in the Convention's monitoring body has materialized. As Degener (2016) points out, in 2016 the CRPD Committee consisted of 18 independent experts who were all disabled people except for one.

As a human rights convention, the CRPD aims not only to ensure disabled people their full human rights; it also recognizes that a part of having full human rights is the right to participate in decision making with regard to one's own affairs. In fact, as Gerard Quinn (Quinn 2009) points out, one of the key changes that the CRPD brings with it is that it treats disabled people as subjects capable of making decisions regarding their own lives and not as objects to be managed or cared for. The recognition of the right to be in charge of one's own life and affairs draws on Articles 12 and 19 of the CRPD, which lay the foundation for actualizing the right to make decisions regarding one's own life and to effective inclusion in society. Article 12 emphasizes the right to legal capacity for people with disabilities "on an equal basis with others and in all areas of life." As Quinn (2010) argues, legal capacity is instrumental to the recognition of a person as a human being and of full personhood. Having legal capacity provides recognition of the right to make decisions for oneself and to enter into contracts (O'Donnell and O'Mahony 2017; Quinn 2010). Article 19 provides further support for the right to personal autonomy by recognizing the right to independent living and community inclusion as a human rights issue (Brennan et al. 2016). While the Article does not include a definition of the term "independent" (O'Donnell and O'Mahony 2017), it reflects the principles of autonomy and choice, which align with the key principles outlined in Article 3 of the Convention. These include "independence of persons", "freedom of choice", and "full and effective participation in society". In addition, the two Articles, 12 and 19, are interdependent (Committee on the Rights of Persons with Disabilities 2014a; Keys 2017; O'Donnell and O'Mahony 2017). In order to live independently, it is necessary to have the legal capacity to make decisions and enter into agreements. In turn, the right to live independently and in accordance with one's own choices provides a platform to exercise the right to legal capacity and individual autonomy. Furthermore, the rights stated in Articles 12 and 19 are fundamental for the active participation of disabled people in policy and decision making that affects them, as stated in Article 4(3). As Mary Keys points out, it is necessary to have the right to choose to be able to actualize the right to participate actively in political life at all levels, including in policymaking (Keys 2017).

The importance of full and active participation by marginalized groups in the policymaking process has been recognized by many, including Young (1990), Oliver (1990), Charlton (2000), Guldvik et al. (2013), Keys (2017) and Priestley et al. (2016). Young argues that society's structures and norms are a reflection of existing power relations, created and defined by dominant groups to maintain the status quo (Young 1990). To change their position of oppression, marginalized groups must be a part of the political structure, engage in setting the agenda and defining the issues, and redefining the concepts that relate to their lives. Without their active involvement, their position of marginalization and oppression will be maintained (Young 1990). Keys adopts a similar focus and points out that to be able to leave behind the paternalistic approach that has created and maintained the historic disadvantages that disabled people have experienced, it is necessary that they themselves participate in policymaking to change laws and policies that do not reflect their experiences (Keys 2017). This focus draws attention to Dorothy Smith's argument that recognizing lived experience as knowledge is pivotal to the ability of marginalized groups to assert themselves. Smith maintains that all knowledge is socially constructed and that people's understanding of the world is derived from how they are differently socially located (Smith 1990). However, "privileged forms of discourse [are] claimed by master narratives", meaning that the knowledge produced by some people and groups are given greater acceptance (Mann and Kelley 1997, p. 395). Smith points out that, traditionally, everyday life experiences have been undervalued as the basis for knowledge, weakening the position of marginalized groups. Recognizing knowledge that emerges from lived actualities will strengthen the knowledge claims of marginalized and oppressed people (Smith 1990). Smith's focus on the need to value the knowledge provided by everyday lived experiences reflects the emphasis of the DPOs during the drafting of the CRPD, as well as the subsequent focus of the Convention on ensuring the full participation of both disabled people and their representative organizations in policy and lawmaking in all matters affecting them.

It is important that the participatory focus is maintained as states parties assume the task of aligning national laws with the CRPD, particularly as it pertains to the lived experience of disability. A state commits to develop and reform national laws and bring them in line with the CRPD when ratifying the Convention (Stein and Lord 2009). As of 30 September 2017, 175 countries have ratified the CRPD and are in various stages of fulfilling this obligation. This includes Iceland, which ratified the CRPD in 2016 and is in the process of finalizing draft legislation that has as its stated goal to bring Icelandic law into alignment with the Convention. This draft legislation, entitled "Laws pertaining to services for disabled people with significant support needs" (Althingi 2016–2017), is the central legislation concerned with disability issues in Iceland. In combination with other draft legislation on social services provided by local authorities in general (i.e., not specific to disabled people), it is intended to replace the existing Icelandic law on services for disabled people from 1992, the Act on the Affairs of Disabled People (No. 59/1992) (Althingi 1992). (Amendment 1055/2010 was passed in 2010, reiterating the obligation to uphold the aims of the CRPD.) The draft legislation states that the authorities shall ensure that disabled people and their representative organizations have the ability to influence policy and decision making in matters that pertain to their affairs (Article 1 of the draft legislation). This point is further reiterated in Article 4 of the draft legislation, which states that disabled people shall have the opportunity for active participation in policymaking in matters that concern them.

It is important to recognize, as Quinn points out, that adopting a legal text will not automatically translate into changes on the ground. "There is no guarantee that the new values that are embedded in the text of the Convention will be internalized and then operationalized" (Quinn 2009, p. 216). There are indeed hurdles to be cleared. As Arstein-Kerslake points out with regard to legal capacity and Article 12, not only does it require states parties to make changes to their existing legal systems; it also tests people's ability and willingness to change their often ingrained perceptions of disabled people as lacking in decision making skills (Arstein-Kerslake 2017). Furthermore, it is important to recognize that the full and active participation of disabled people does not mean that their opinions, suggestions and comments will translate directly into law and policy outcomes. The final decision making remains in the hands of democratically elected representatives.

2. Methods

This paper draws on qualitative data from two sources: transcripts of interviews with leaders of Icelandic disabled people's representative organizations; and comments submitted by representative organizations on the draft legislation "Laws pertaining to services for disabled people with significant support needs" (Althingi 2016–2017).

2.1. The Interviews

Eleven semi-structured in-depth interviews were conducted with leaders of nine disability groups and organizations in Iceland in 2016 and 2017. The focus of the interviews was to obtain the leaders' perceptions and experiences of their ability to affect the changes underway aimed at implementing the CRPD in Iceland. This focus is derived from the belief that disabled people themselves are best positioned to judge whether policies aimed at delivering equality have been successful or not, a perspective adopted by Sherlaw and Hudebine (2015), as well as Disability Rights Promotion International (Samson 2015). To this end, semi-structured interviews were chosen as a method of inquiry to gain knowledge of the subjective understanding, perspectives and meaning that participants attach to the issues. They enable the interviewees to direct the discussion to what they find to be of importance and to express the meaning they attach to concepts, while at the same time allowing the discussion to be directed toward predetermined topics in keeping with the theme of the research (Esterberg 2002; Taylor et al. 2016).

Purposeful sampling was used to identify and recruit participants as it allows researchers to select participants who have experience or particular insight and knowledge into the concepts being explored (Creswell and Plano Clark 2017). The leaders selected were of both genders. Six of the 11 leaders were women and five were men. Their ages and educational background varied. While the participants differed as to how long they had served as leaders of their organizations, they all had considerable experience in promoting disabled people's rights in various capacities, and all had spoken in public on the issue.

An effort was made to provide a balanced representation of leaders of both established disability organizations and grassroots and activist groups. The five established organizations that were a part of this study, including three large umbrella organizations, are comprised of both disabled people and non-disabled people. Their rules vary with regard to whether or not non-disabled members can serve in leadership positions or on their boards. Some of these organizations own and operate services for disabled people and are thus in some cases employers of staff and specialists, as well as being interest organizations. Six interviews were conducted with leaders of established organizations. Of these six leaders, three were disabled and three non-disabled. In addition, five interviews were conducted with leaders of activist groups; in the case of a horizontally organized group, a representative was interviewed. The activist groups referred to in this paper are all comprised of, run and directed by disabled people. All five leaders interviewed were disabled. The groups and organizations represented varied considerably with regard to how long they had been operational, ranging from less than five years to more than fifty. Membership also varied greatly, with one of the three established umbrella organizations claiming approximately 30 thousand members, with some of the activist groups having fewer than 50. This fact was not considered to be of concern as the focus of the study was predominantly on their views and experiences with regard to the ability of disability groups and organizations to participate in policy and decision making on matters of concern to disabled people.

All the interviews were conducted in Icelandic and direct quotations were translated by the first author of this paper. In addition, keeping in mind the small size of the Icelandic population, both names and identifying details have been omitted to the extent possible to ensure confidentiality. All participants gave informed consent and agreed to have the interviews recorded. In one instance, a list of topics to be discussed was provided in advance to give room for preparations.

2.2. *Comments on the Draft Legislation*

Following the initial discussion by Althingi (the Icelandic Parliament) during its 146th session (2016–2017) of the draft legislation on "Laws pertaining to services for disabled people with significant support needs", it was sent to the Althingi's Welfare Committee, which opened it for public comment. A total of 36 comments on the draft legislation were submitted by public, private and academic institutions, as well as groups, organizations, associations, local authorities and individuals. Of these, 12 were submitted by 10 different disability groups and organizations (Althingi 2017a). (Two organizations submitted two comments).

The comments submitted by disability groups and organizations differed in scope. A number of the organizations submitted comments that were primarily focused on areas specific to the interests and needs of their membership. This includes the Communication Center for the Deaf and Hearing-Impaired (Samskiptamidstöd heyrnarlausra og heyrnarskertra), which primarily focused on the draft's omission of reference to disabled deaf citizens, as Icelandic sign language is now recognized as an official language in Iceland (Althingi 2011). In the same manner, the Center for User-led Personal Assistance (CUPA) (NPA Midstödin) focused predominantly on the need to secure the right to personal assistance, as did the Icelandic Federation of Physically Disabled People (Sjálfsbjörg) and the Association of Rehabilitated People with Spinal Cord Injuries (Samtök endurhæfdra mænuskaddadra), for the most part. These and other comments that do not relate to the focus of the paper are not addressed in the findings.

Four of the 10 disability organizations that submitted comments on the draft legislation addressed the issue that is the focus of this paper—the active participation of disabled people and their representative organizations in policy and decision making processes on issues that concern them—but to varying degrees. The paper examines predominantly the comments of two of the organizations, the umbrella organization the Organisation of Disabled in Iceland (ODI) (Öryrkjabandalag Íslands) and the activist feminist disability group Tabu, as these two organizations made the most extensive comments relating directly to the subject of the paper. The two other organizations that touch on the issue, the umbrella organization the National Association of Intellectual Disabilities (NAID) (Landssamtökin Throskahjálp) and CUPA, did so without making it a focus area of their comments in the same manner that ODI and Tabu did.

The analysis of the data, as it pertains to the interviews and the comments submitted by the representative organizations was based on an inductive process (Creswell 2009). To analyze the data, the grounded theory method was employed. This method reflects the premise that theory can be developed from rigorous analysis of empirical data (Charmaz 2014). In keeping with this approach, the collection and analysis of data was directed by the constant comparative method of grounded theory. This method calls for data gathering to be continued while data is simultaneously coded and analyzed, and analytical memos developed, with the goal of identifying central themes to help direct further data collection and theory building (Charmaz 2014). The goal of this approach is to identify central themes while the process is ongoing to help direct further data collection and theory building (Charmaz 2014). To this end, interviews were conducted in three intervals, in December 2016, April 2017 and July 2017, until it was concluded that new information obtained had ceased to provide further insight. Initially, broad questions were posed to leaders of the representative organizations about their approaches to advancing the rights of disabled people. As the research progressed and themes began to emerge from the analysis of the interviews, the questions were narrowed. The interviews were recorded, transcribed and coded. Coding consisted of detailed reading of the transcripts followed by sorting and organization of the codes, revealing patterns in the data that helped develop a deeper understanding of the issues at hand (Creswell 2009). Based on the findings, the information relating to the theme of this study was selected and further analyzed.

3. Findings

On 17 February 2014, the Icelandic Minister of Social and Housing Affairs established a working group tasked with drafting the new legislation on services for disabled people; it completed its work in October 2016. The draft legislation (Althingi 2016–2017) opened for comments toward the end of Althingi's 146th session in the spring of 2017, was based on the group's proposal. The working group was initially comprised of 12 persons, who included the appointed representatives of Althingi, government ministries, local authorities, and several interest groups and NGOs, including two umbrella organizations representing disabled people, ODI and NAID.[2] Representatives of organizations representing disabled people thus made up only one-sixth of the working group, or 17%. In addition, only one of the two representatives designated by these organizations was a disabled person. This person resigned in March 2015 and was replaced by a non-disabled person. As a result, for 19 months no disabled person served on the working group.

The two umbrella organizations representing disabled people on the working group are also the two representative organizations of disabled people that have the right, according to Icelandic law, to be consulted on policy and decision making on issues affecting disabled people. It is important to note here that neither fulfills the criteria established by the CRPD Committee in its Guidelines on the

2 An additional representative of the Ministry of Welfare was added at a later date.

Participation of Disabled Persons' Organizations (DPOs) and Civil Society Organizations in the work of the Committee (Committee on the Rights of Persons with Disabilities 2014b). DPOs, according to the Guidelines, are organizations that are "comprised by a majority of persons with disabilities—at least half of its membership—governed, led and directed by persons with disabilities (Committee on the Rights of Persons with Disabilities 2014b). Following the example of Sturm et al. (2017), this paper will henceforth use "disability organizations" (DO) as a general term when both organizations that do and do not fulfill the criteria are concerned.

The comments submitted by ODI and Tabu on the draft legislation stand out as both the most comprehensive and critical in nature. They are also the most relevant to this discussion as they make the issue that is the subject of this paper—ensuring the active involvement of disabled people and their representative organizations in policy and decision making processes on matters that concern them—a special focus of attention. Their comments provide valuable insight into how they perceive their ability to be heard by the authorities and to affect the policymaking process.

The two other representative organizations that address to some extent the issue of active involvement are NAID and CUPA. In the case of NAID, which like ODI, was part of the working group tasked with drafting the new legislation, it expresses frustration in one instance about not being heard on its objection to the omission of a requirement for a minimum number of residents living in a service area. In addition, NAID emphasizes the importance of ensuring active consultation with disabled people and their representative organizations with regard to future regulations to be set by the Ministry on the basis of the draft legislation. In a second comment, NAID stresses the need to ratify the Optional Protocol to the Convention to strengthen the ability of disabled people to pursue their rights in their interactions with the authorities. As for CUPA, it had been granted observer status in a project group established in 2011 by the Ministry of Social and Housing Affairs to lay the groundwork for the introduction of personal assistance as a legally mandated service option in the draft legislation. In its comments on the draft legislation, CUPA states that comments received from DPOs had been taken into account in the proposal submitted by the project group to the working group, which then incorporated them into the draft legislation. In other regards, the comments submitted by NAID and CUPA do not focus on the subject of this paper.

Pointing to the obligations stated in the CRPD, both ODI and Tabu strongly criticize the very limited amount of time granted to civil society for the submission of comments on the draft legislation (Althingi 2017a). "It is important to note that this way of working is very inaccessible and unprofessional, and contradicts the objectives and principles of the CRPD," states ODI. When the legislation was initially opened for comments, only 10 days were allocated to the process. The perceived rush led the DOs to comment that the lack of time devoted to the process was in contravention of the CRPD, which places an obligation on states to ensure the active participation of disabled people and their representative organizations. The Welfare Committee of Althingi, which was responsible for reviewing the draft legislation before submission for further parliamentary action, responded to the criticism at its meeting of 29 May 2017 (Althingi 2017b). It recognized its obligation pursuant to Article 4(3) of the CRPD and suggested that further parliamentary action on the draft legislation be postponed so that additional time could be given, until 7 September 2017, for comments to be submitted.

3.1. Organisation of Disabled in Iceland (ODI)—The Ability to Affect Outcomes

One of the concerns expressed by ODI is that the draft legislation does not sufficiently reflect the need to ensure the full participation of disabled people through their representative organizations in policymaking in matters pertaining to them, as stated in Article 4(3) of the CRPD. "The authorities have failed greatly in its compliance with this Article," ODI states in its comment (Althingi 2017a). Furthermore, ODI emphasizes the need to clarify that wherever the draft refers to "participation", the wording "active participation" should be used, and suggests that the law specify in certain articles collaboration with umbrella organizations. ODI cites Kumpuvuori and Virtanen's (2017) analysis of what constitutes full DPO participation, according to which two conditions must be met, the first being that the participation of DPOs extend from the very beginning of the policy formulation process to the very end, and, secondly, that the opinions, perspectives and suggestions presented by DPOs are taken into account and not ignored. Keeping in mind that ODI is one of two DOs appointed to the working group that drafted the legislation and that it participated from when it was first convened until the conclusion of its work, ODI's criticism seems to be directed more toward the second point, that is a lack of meaningful participation, where the perspectives and suggestions made by the DOs are not taken into account in the policy outcome. ODI's comments on the draft legislation, which are both extensive and critical, seem to bear this out.

Among the issues raised by ODI are the need to review and rewrite a number of articles of the draft legislation to sufficiently reflect the intent of the CRPD. Furthermore, it points to the need to redefine the definition of disability contained in the draft legislation's first Article on Objectives to sufficiently reflect the CRPD's understanding of the interplay between society and impairment. "ODI respectfully suggests that a real collaboration with disabled people, their representative organizations and academic institutions take place in order to avoid inconsistency" in how disability is defined (Althingi 2017a). ODI points out that the draft neglects to sufficiently state the right of disabled parents to assistance, as stipulated in the CRPD, Article 23(2), and to a lack of understanding of the independent living ideology behind personal assistance. All in all, ODI proposes changes in one form or another to about half of the 42 articles of the draft legislation, suggesting that despite having participated in the work of the committee, its perception is that it was not sufficiently able to affect the policy outcome. ODI's overall position is summed up with the comment that if the proposed legislation becomes law, it is clear that the Icelandic state still has a considerable distance to go to achieve compliance with the CRPD (Althingi 2017a).

3.2. *Tabu—Giving a Voice to Disabled People Themselves*

In its comments, Tabu also criticizes what it maintains is a lack of meaningful involvement by disabled people and their representative organizations in the drafting of the proposed legislation. Unlike ODI's criticism, which seems to be predominantly concerned with not being able to affect policy outcomes, Tabu focuses on disabled people themselves being given a proper voice and recognized as having valuable expertise to offer.

Tabu's criticism is two-pronged. First, it criticizes the inadequate representation of disabled people and their representative organizations in the working group preparing the draft legislation, which amounted to 17% of the membership (Althingi 2017a). To rectify the problem, Tabu suggests increasing the number of representatives of disabled people. Secondly, Tabu criticizes the fact that the participation of disabled people themselves is not ensured and points out: "According to the current law on the affairs of disabled people, ODI and NAID are the only ones with the legal right to be consulted on matters pertaining to disabled people. It's clear that times have changed and it is appropriate to increase the number of seats for disabled people at the table where decisions are made," Tabu further states in its comments on the draft legislation. "ODI and NAID have made important contributions in the past decades in the fight for disabled people's rights but it is clear that it is very problematic that more often than not they send non-disabled people to the table. This is in contradiction with the CRPD." (Althingi 2017a). Tabu draws attention to the need to make a clear distinction between the two types of disabled people's organizations, those that are led by disabled people and those that are led by non-disabled people representing disabled people's interests. Or, put another way, organizations of disabled people and organizations for disabled people. This echoes the importance that the CRPD Committee attaches to this distinction, as evidenced by its Guidelines on the Participation of DPOs (Committee on the Rights of Persons with Disabilities 2014b).

In its comments, Tabu emphasizes that the expertise of disabled people when it comes to their needs and lives, based on their own lived experience, must be effectively harnessed in policy and decision making. To this end, Tabu offers its expertise, in addition to identifying two other activist groups comprised of and led by disabled people themselves, CUPA and the Self-Advocacy Group of People with Intellectual Disabilities (Átak—Félag fólks med throskahömlun), and calls for all three to be given consultative status on issues pertaining to disabled people's affairs on an equal footing with the two umbrella organizations stating that, "All these groups are led by disabled people and our contribution, knowledge and experience are a necessary addition to working groups, committees and other policymaking that concerns disabled people." (Althingi 2017a). In addition, Tabu emphasizes the CRPD's call to also include the participation of disabled children and youth. The increase in representation suggested by Tabu would have raised the percentage of disabled people and their representatives to about 30% of the working group's membership, which, for the purposes of comparison, is closer to what Sherlaw and Hudebine (2015) report being the case in France, for example. Furthermore, it would have ensured the inclusion of at least three disabled people. Tabu maintains that such a change would not only lead to a better work product, drawing on the expertise and lived reality of disabled people themselves, but also serve to empower disabled people by giving them an opportunity to serve in such a capacity. Tabu points out how challenging it is for a single disabled person to be put in a position of having to face a committee comprised almost exclusively of non-disabled people, many of whom represent the interests of the authorities.

3.3. Interviews with Leaders—Pro Forma Consultations

The experience of not being "heard" by the authorities and not being able to affect policy outcomes, is supported by the findings of the in-depth interviews that this paper draws on. While the leaders of the established organizations focus primarily on advancing the rights of disabled people through collaboration with authorities, they shared with the activist groups interviewed the experience of having difficulty at times being heard by the authorities in the sense that their comments and suggestions were either not taken into account in the formulation of policy or in other ways acted upon. A lack of funds was frequently cited as a reason for inaction. "You experience an incredible reluctance," said a leader of an established organization. Another commented: "And of course, we always get the same answer. It doesn't matter what issue category you ask about, it's always just money." Reflecting on the collaboration with the authorities, one of the leaders stated "sometimes it feels to me as if it's pro forma. They have to include us. And then it's like decisions have already been made at some kind of pre-meeting, where you have the feeling that all the decisions have been made in advance." A leader also mentioned having to remain vigilant about ensuring that the comments made by DO representatives were included in minutes of the meetings. A leader of an activist group recounted similar experiences and reported feeling that other meeting participants were sometimes either not interested in what he had to say or just ignored his comments.

The issues highlighted by Tabu also find support in the in-depth interviews with leaders of other activist groups. They reveal feelings of frustration over not being given due access to decision making bodies. "We are the ones who have experienced disability on our own skin. Without this experience, it is really impossible for people to fully understand," stated a leader of an activist group. Another leader expressed a similar sentiment, "If you're not disabled, you don't have the experience to draw from. You can't imagine what being disabled is like, no matter how hard you try." A third said "Nobody can properly see things with our eyes." All the leaders expressed the importance of ensuring that disabled people themselves have a leading voice in matters that concern them. Similar to Tabu's comment on the draft legislation, the activist leaders also pointed to the need for the authorities to make more of a distinction between DPOs for disabled people and DPOs of disabled people. "These old organizations have been around for so long," said one leader. "Sometimes you get the feeling that they're protecting the rights of their staff or the interests of some system. Maybe it's a bit difficult to sit on both sides of the negotiating table," said one leader referring to the fact that some of the established organizations own and operate services for disabled people.

The activist leaders also reported a lack of responsiveness on the part of the authorities and a feeling of being ignored at times when trying to speak up for disabled people's interests. "Sometimes we feel that because we are critical of the system, we are not popular with the authorities and they want to minimize their engagement with us," stated a leader of an activist group. The leaders described how they sought to counter this apathy and to gain recognition of disabled people as experts in their own affairs and as leaders in the fight to secure full rights, a role that has traditionally been occupied exclusively by others. The means they employed were intended to establish disabled people themselves as the ones on the front lines, speaking up, taking to the streets in demonstration, delivering declarations to the authorities, taking the initiative of drafting proposed legislation for submission to the authorities, and writing and publishing first-person accounts of the lived realities of disabled people (Löve et al. 2017).

3.4. The Active Participation of Disabled People

The data gathered indicates that there is less focus on ensuring the participation of disabled people, and thereby the lived experience of disability, among both the established DOs and the authorities, compared to activist groups made up of and run by disabled people themselves.

The draft legislation under consideration in Iceland does not include a reference to the criteria contained in the guidelines issued by the CRPD Committee on what constitutes a DPO, and therefore seems to lack the emphasis embodied in the CRPD on ensuring the inclusion of the lived experience of disability in decision making. While the draft legislation stipulates, in Chapter 1 on Objectives and Definitions (Article 1) and Chapter 2 on Governance and Organization (Article 4), that disabled people shall have the opportunity to actively participate in policy and decision making that relate to their affairs, other articles refer to consultations with representative organizations without specifying how such organizations should be defined (Althingi 2016–2017). In Althingi's first discussion (and only one to date) of the draft legislation, on 2 May 2017, one member of Althingi raised the need to clarify how disabled people and service users would be able to convey their views on matters that affect them. "This whole regulatory framework is rather confusing," she noted, "and points to a lack of a coordinated strategy as to how consultations with users, representative organizations and others will be managed". Changes to the decision making process were otherwise not mentioned and there was no discussion of the need to increase DPO representation, as defined by the CRPD Committee. Nor did the Minister address the issue in his response to questions.

While being critical of the process, ODI does not raise the need to increase the number of DOs with the right to participation on matters pertaining to disability issues, nor does it mention the need to ensure the inclusion of disabled representatives. ODI does suggest the addition of a sentence to a number of articles of the draft legislation stating the obligation to engage in active collaboration with umbrella organizations, thereby excluding the grassroots and activist groups. There is only one reference to the need to include disabled people themselves, in ODI's comments on Article 9 on housing where it suggests adding a reference to active collaboration with disabled people and their umbrella organizations, while again excluding reference to other types of organizations (Althingi 2017a).

Finally, as stated earlier, the Welfare Committee of Althingi, in its meeting of 29 May 2017, responded to the comments it had received at that time. While suggesting an extension of the time provided for submission of comments and that consideration of the draft legislation be delayed until Althingi's fall session of 2017, the Committee did not suggest accommodating changes that would either increase DOs representation in general or ensure the participation of disabled people themselves. Furthermore, nor did it in general respond to other comments and criticism concerning the need to ensure the active participation of disabled people and their representative organizations.

4. Discussion

The drafting process initiated by the Icelandic authorities, intended to align Icelandic disability law with the CRPD, was criticized by both ODI and Tabu as inadequate in terms of ensuring the full participation of disabled people and their representative organizations in setting laws and policies pertaining to their rights and matters that concern them. Referring to Article 4(3), ODI stated that "[t]he authorities have failed greatly in its compliance with this article" (Althingi 2017a). However, the two

DOs criticize the process from different perspectives. ODI, which was involved in the drafting process from start to finish, is critical of the policy outcome and submits extensive and critical comments on the draft legislation. In its comments, ODI calls attention to the fact that having representation doesn't ensure a DO's ability to impact outcomes if its suggestions and opinions are ignored. The experience of not being able to affect decision making, even when participating in the decision making process, is not unique to ODI or the leaders of the Icelandic DOs interviewed. A study carried out in nine European countries on the ability of organizations representing disabled persons to affect the implementation of the CRPD on a national level found mixed results, with some organizations reporting having difficulty affecting policy outcomes despite being represented in the process (Waldschmidt et al. 2017). Other international research—including in Italy (Biggeri et al. 2011); Bulgaria (Mladenov 2009); Canada, the U.S. and the U.K. (Levesque and Langford 2016); and Africa (Lang et al. 2011)—has also pointed to mixed results with regard to the ability of DOs to affect policy and have concluded that both structural and attitude changes are needed, as well as ensuring sufficient resources and capacity building among disabled people and DOs, to effectively participate in policymaking processes. There is, however, as stated earlier, a need to differentiate between, on the one hand, the right to full and active participation in the policymaking process on equal footing with others, and, on the other, the demand that one's opinions, perceptions and suggestions be included in the policy outcome. Such a demand, which this paper does not make, can be seen as running counter to the principles of representative democracy, which allocate the ultimate policymaking power to elected representatives.

While ODI focuses on its impact on the policy outcome, Tabu and the other activist groups focus predominantly on the lack of recognition of the need for disabled people themselves to be a part of the policymaking process. As the composition of the working group bears out, DOs had very limited representation during the drafting of the legislation. In addition, for more than a year-and-a-half (19 months), the working group did not have any disabled persons among its members. Moreover, no representative organizations made up of, run and directed by disabled people—the criteria established by the CRPD Committee—were represented in the working group. This lack of significant participation is in stark contrast to the prominent focus on the participation of DPOs and disabled people themselves during the drafting of the CRPD, an emphasis that became embedded into the Convention, and is reflected in its recognition of the lived experience of disability and that the persons most affected have the right to participate in decisions that impact them (Stein and Lord 2010).

The two other DOs that comment on participation in decision making, NAID and CUPA, are less critical in their comments, with CUPA expressing a positive experience in the project group that worked on articles of the draft legislation pertaining to personal assistance. Like ODI, NAID has a seat at the table in the established policymaking process and may, therefore, have less of a reason than those not included to suggest changes to it. Moreover, as the interviews reveal, the leaders of the established organizations express a commitment to working within the established process. This may also apply to the other established organizations that did not address the issue of participation in their comments on the draft legislation. CUPA, for its part, has succeeded in gaining partial access to the process on the one issue that dominates its agenda, personal assistance, and that may explain why—when it comes to this matter—it does not specifically address the need for change. As for the activist groups, which do not have access to the process as it is currently constructed, one can speculate that they may feel that the process is so closed and the barriers to entry so high that they do not feel sufficiently empowered to demand access. As Sherlaw and Hudebine point out, all participatory processes involve tension. "Participation of the vulnerable and needy often involves institutions and persons giving up a degree of power, which is no easy option, and is often unwelcome and strenuously resisted" (Sherlaw and Hudebine 2015, p. 15). Changing the status quo requires a radical approach. Tabu has challenged the status quo by demanding entrance, possibly leading the way for others.

The importance of the participation of disabled people in policy and decision making is emphasized by Young and Keys, who point out that without disabled people's active contribution and involvement in setting the political agenda, defining the issues that relate to their lives from their own perspectives and needs, their marginalization will be maintained, leaving in place laws that have created and maintain their historical disadvantage (Keys 2017; Young 1990). The work of the Icelandic activist groups, and Tabu's comments on the draft legislation, reflect Young's and Keys's positions. Furthermore, they embrace Smith's position on the validation of everyday lived experience as knowledge. This understanding is also echoed in the responses by the leaders of the activist groups interviewed; they assert that only with the lived experience of disability can one fully comprehend "what it is really like", underlining the importance of disabled people themselves having a leading voice in matters that concern them.

The Icelandic activist groups have set out to change the perception of disabled people as lacking the capacity to be in charge of their own affairs, and to introduce and gain recognition of this position in the political arena. However, as the draft legislation and the response of the Welfare Committee to the comments received show, their efforts seem to have made limited inroads with the authorities and the established disability organizations.

The draft legislation makes no reference to establishing the participation of DPOs as defined by the CRPD Committee in its guideline for DPOs, which would ensure recognition of the lived experience of disability and pave the way for changes to the process norms with regard to how disability policy is made. This is of particular concern as ODI and NAID, the two representative organizations that have the right to consultative status on disability issues according to Icelandic law, and which therefore represent the interests of disabled people in shaping policy and legislation, fail to meet the CRPD Committee's criteria for DPOs (Committee on the Rights of Persons with Disabilities 2014b).

Furthermore, it is of interest that while ODI, for its part, emphasizes the need to ensure full and effective participation, it does not suggest increasing the number of representative organizations that have consultative status in order to strengthen and embolden the voice of the disability community, nor does it suggest that disabled people themselves be ensured representation. Further, ODI appears to actively distance itself from organizations by disabled people by stating in its comments on the draft legislation that "consultation with umbrella organizations for disabled people", to the exclusion of other types of disability organizations, should be specified in three articles of the draft legislation (Althingi 2017a).

The Welfare Committee, which makes suggestions on changes to draft legislation during the legislative process, before Althingi votes on it, did not in its meeting of 29 May 2017 address Tabu's request to increase the overall representation of DOs on matters pertaining to disability, or the request to ensure the participation of disabled representatives. To date, the Committee appears to have paid little attention to calls for increased and effective participation by disabled people and their representative organizations, apart from its decision to extend the time for submitting comments from the initial ten days to over three months. In that instance, the Committee stated that its decision to do so was in recognition of its obligations under Article 4(3) of the CRPD (Althingi 2017b).

As far as the process of aligning Icelandic disability law with the CRPD is concerned, there seems to be a reluctance to fully embrace the fundamental principle reflected in the CRPD, that the persons most affected have the right to participate in decisions that impact them (Stein and Lord 2010). The CRPD's call for new process norms with regard to how disability policy is made seems to require more changes to the current consultation process than the Icelandic authorities are prepared to initiate. This is particularly the case with regard to making a distinction between the two types of representative organizations, ensuring the participation of disabled people themselves, and recognizing the value of their contribution and their expertise based on their everyday lived experience of disability.

This draws attention to Quinn's point that there is no guarantee that by setting laws, new values will be internalized (Quinn 2009, p. 216). The lack of confidence in the ability of disabled people to be in charge of their own affairs is deeply rooted. Throughout history, disabled people have been identified as different, kept at the margins of society and perceived as having little to contribute (Braddock and Parish 2001). Their status as non-producers and dependents led, in great part, to their segregation and marginalization, and robbed them of the opportunity to participate as citizens and exercise full civic and political rights (Snyder and Mitchell 2006).

Article 4(3) sets out to create a new politics of disability. It calls for changes to the process norms with regard to how disability policy is made. In the past, disabled people were commonly excluded from the process of policymaking on matters that pertained to them, reflecting the position of the medical model on disability, which views disabled people as having to be taken care of and managed by others. The result has been laws that have mostly fallen short by curbing the rights of disabled people and their quality of life. By expanding the policymaking process as Article 4(3) of the CRPD does, to include disabled people through their representative organizations, it enables a new politics of disability to emerge. The laws and policies produced as a result are likely to better serve and reflect the needs and perspectives of disabled people themselves. However, in order to live fully up to the intent of the CRPD and its emphasis on incorporating the lived experience of disability, it is important that States Parties adopt the CRPD Committee's criteria as to what constitutes a disabled people's representative organization, namely that they are governed, led and directed by persons with disabilities.

It is important to recall that the full and active participation of disabled people should not be taken to mean that their opinions, suggestions and comments will automatically translate into law and policy outcomes. Rather, the new politics of disability bring disabled people and their representative organizations into the democratic process as contributing participants in the development of solutions to policy issues that take into account different perspectives and needs, in addition to their own. Thus, Article 4(3) should be seen to describe a process whereby social policy is co-produced.

5. Conclusions

The findings indicate that the new draft legislation on disability services in Iceland does not sufficiently embody the Convention's call for changes to the process norms with regard to how disability policy is made. The new process calls for the active involvement of disabled people through their representative organizations, as defined by the CRPD Committee in its guidelines on DPOs, that are led and directed by disabled people. The criteria established by the Committee are aimed at ensuring that the lived experience of disability is incorporated into the policymaking process. It seems that this priority is not given due attention in the draft legislation, which makes no reference to the need for changes to the current process to ensure that the lived experience of disability is brought to bear in policy and decision making. The limited representation of DOs, and the fact that those represented do not meet the CRPD Committee's criteria for what constitutes a DPO, is a cause for concern. It seems to contradict the fundamental principle embodied in the CRPD that those most affected have the right to participate in decisions that impact them. Accepting disabled people as full participants with valuable knowledge and expertise means letting go of ingrained perceptions of disabled people as lacking in capacity for decision making and management of their own affairs. With this in mind, it is important to recognize that the call for a new politics of disability embodied in Article 4(3) of the CRPD provides a path forward toward the co-production of social policy with the active and effective contribution of civil society. The need to fully take into consideration the CRPD Committee's criteria for how to define DPOs in the context of the CRPD may be of relevance to other States Parties as they align their national legislation with the Convention as part of the ratification process. Furthermore, the co-production of social policy described above may have a wider application, not exclusive to the case of disability policy but to social policy making in general.

Author Contributions: Laufey Löve and Rannveig Traustadóttir conceived and designed the study; Laufey Löve carried out the research and had the lead role in analyzing the data; Laufey Löve, Gerard Quinn and Rannveig Traustadóttir contributed to defining the analytical direction and legal context; James Rice contributed to the theoretical context of the study; Laufey Löve wrote the paper; Rannveig Traustadóttir, Gerard Quinn and James Rice contributed to editing.

References

Althingi. 1992. *Lög um Málefni Fatlads Fólks (The Act on the Affairs of Disabled People)*. Law No. 59/1992; Reykjavik: Althingi.

Althingi. 2011. *Lög um Stödu Íslenskrar Tungu og Íslensks Táknmáls (Law on the Status of the Icelandic Language and Icelandic Sign Language)*. Law No. 61/2011; Reykjavik: Althingi, Available online: https://www.althingi.is/lagas/nuna/2011061.html (accessed on 18 September 2017).

Althingi. 2016–2017. *Frumvarp til Laga um Thjónustu vid Fatlad Fólk Med Miklar Studningstharfir (Draft Legislation Pertaining to Services for Disabled People with Significant Support Needs)*. Parliamentary Document No. 571-438; Reykjavik: Althingi.

Althingi. 2017a. Welfare Committee: Comments by Representative Organizations of Disabled People on Draft Legislation Pertaining to Services for Disabled People with Significant Support Needs. Available online: http://www.althingi.is/pdf/erindi_mals/?lthing=146&malnr=438 (accessed on 6 October 2017).

Althingi. 2017b. Summary of the 42, Meeting of The Welfare Committee Held on 29 May 2017. Available online: https://www.althingi.is/thingnefndir/fastanefndir/velferdarnefnd/fundargerdir/?faerslunr=8925 (accessed on 8 August 2017).

Arstein-Kerslake, Anna. 2017. Legal Capacity and Supported Decision-Making: Respecting Rights and Empowering People. In *Disability Law and Policy: An Analysis of the UN Convention*. Edited by Charles O'Mahony and Gerard Quinn. Dublin: Clarus Press.

Biggeri, Mario, Nicolò Bellanca, Sara Bonfanti, and Lapo Tanzj. 2011. Rethinking policies for persons with disabilities through the capability approach: The case of the Tuscany Region. *Alter, European Journal of Disability Research* 5: 177–91. [CrossRef]

Braddock, David L., and Susan L. Parish. 2001. An Institutional History of Disability. In *Handbook of Disability Studies*. Edited by Gary L. Albrecht, Katherine D. Seelman and Michael Bury. Thousand Oaks: Sage Publications.

Brennan, Ciara, Rannveig Traustadóttir, Peter Anderberg, and James Rice. 2016. Are Cutbacks to Personal Assistance Violating Sweden's Obligations under the UN Convention on the Rights of Persons with Disabilities? *Laws* 5: 23. [CrossRef]

Charlton, James I. 2000. *Nothing about Us without Us: Disability Oppression and Empowerment*. Berkeley: University of California Press.

Charmaz, Kathy. 2014. *Constructing Grounded Theory*, 2nd ed. Los Angeles: Sage.

Committee on the Rights of Persons with Disabilities. 2014a. *General Comment No. 1 (2014). Article 12: Equal Recognition before the Law*. CRPD/C/GC/1; Geneva: CRPD.

Committee on the Rights of Persons with Disabilities. 2014b. *Guidelines on the Participation of Disabled Persons Organizations (DPOs) and Civil Society Organizations in the Work of the Committee*. CRPD/C/11/2, Annex II; Available online: https://goo.gl/7bqnCW (accessed on 5 August 2017).

Creswell, John W. 2009. *Research Design: Qualitative, Quantitative, and Mixed Methods Approaches*, 3rd ed. Thousand Oaks: Sage.

Creswell, John W., and Vicki L. Plano Clark. 2017. *Designing and Conducting Mixed Methods Research*, 3rd ed. New York: SAGE Publications.

Degener, Theresia. 2016. Disability in a Human Rights Context. *Laws* 5: 35. [CrossRef]

Esterberg, Kristin G. 2002. *Qualitative Methods in Social Research*. Boston: McGraw Hill.

Guldvik, Ingrid, Ole P. Askheim, and Vegard Johansen. 2013. Political citizenship and local political participation for disabled people. *Citizenship Studies* 17: 76–91. [CrossRef]

Kanter, Arlene S. 2014. *The Development of Disability Rights Under International Law: From Charity to Human Rights*. New York: Routledge Press.

Keys, Mary. 2017. Article 12 of the UN Convention on the Rights of Persons with Disabilities and the European Convention on Human Rights. In *Disability Law and Policy: An Analysis of the UN Convention*. Edited by Charles O'Mahony and Gerard Quinn. Dublin: Clarus Press.

Kumpuvuori, Jukka, and Riku Virtanen. 2017. Are we right or are we right?: 'Right approach' in the advocacy work of organization of persons with disabilities. In *Disability Law and Policy: An Analysis of the UN Convention*. Edited by Charles O'Mahony and Gerard Quinn. Dublin: Clarus Press.

Lang, Raymond, Maria Kett, Nora Groce, and Jean-Francois Trani. 2011. Implementing the United Nations Convention on the rights of persons with disabilities: Principles, implications, practice and limitations. *Alter, European Journal of Disability Research* 5: 206–20. [CrossRef]

Levesque, Mario, and Brynne Langford. 2016. The role of disability groups in the development and implementation of the UN Convention on the Rights of Persons with Disabilities. *Canadian Journal of Disability Studies* 5: 62–102. [CrossRef]

Löve, Laufey, Rannveig Traustadóttir, and James Rice. 2017. Achieving Disability Equality: Empowering Disabled People to Take the Lead (under review). *Social Inclusion, Special Issue on Disability Equality*. Forthcoming.

Mann, Susan A., and Lori R. Kelley. 1997. Standing at the Crossroads of Modernist Thought: Collins, Smith, and the New Feminist Epistemologies. *Gender and Society* 11: 391–408. [CrossRef]

Meyers, Stephen. 2016. NGO-Ization and Human Rights Law: The CRPD's Civil Society Mandate. *Laws* 5: 21. [CrossRef]

Mladenov, Teodor. 2009. Institutional woes of participation: Bulgarian disabled people's organisations and policy-making. *Disability & Society* 24: 33–45.

O'Donnell, Sinead, and Charles O'Mahony. 2017. The UN Convention on the Rights of Persons with Disabilities: Exploring the synergy between Article 12 and Article 19. In *Disability Law and Policy: An Analysis of the UN Convention*. Edited by Charles O'Mahony and Gerard Quinn. Dublin: Clarus Press.

Oliver, Michael. 1990. *The Politics of Disablement: Critical Texts in Social Work and the Welfare State*. London: Macmillan.

Priestley, Mark, Martha Stickings, Ema Loja, Stefanos Grammeons, Anna Lawson, Lisa Waddington, and Bjarney Fridriksdóttir. 2016. The political participation of disabled people in Europe: Rights, accessibility and activism. *Electoral Studies* 42: 1–9. [CrossRef]

Quinn, Gerard. 2009. Resisting the 'Temptation of Elegance': Can the Convention on the Rights of Persons with Disabilities Socialise States to Right Behaviour? In *The UN Convention on the Rights of Persons with Disabilities: European and Scandinavian Perspectives*. Edited by Oddný Mjöll Arnardóttir and Gerard Quinn. Leiden: Martinus Nijhoff Publishers.

Quinn, Gerard. 2010. Personhood & legal capacity: Perspectives on the paradigm shift of Article 12 CRPD. Paper presented at the HPOD Conference, Harvard Law School, Boston, MA, USA, February 20.

Sabatello, Maya. 2014. A short history of the international disability rights movement. In *Human Rights & Disability Advocacy*. Edited by Maya Sabatello and Marianne Schulze. Philadelphia: University of Pennsylvania Press.

Samson, R. M. 2015. Securing the full participation of persons with disabilities and their representative organizations in disability rights monitoring. In *Rights Monitoring, and Social Change: Building Power out of Evidence*. Edited by Marcia H. Rioux, Paula C. Pinto and Gillian Parech. Toronto: Canadian Scholars' Press.

Sherlaw, William, and Hervé Hudebine. 2015. The United Nations Convention on the Rights of Persons with Disabilities: Opportunities and tensions within the social inclusion and participation of persons with disabilities. *ALTER, European Journal of Disability Research* 9: 9–21. [CrossRef]

Smith, Dorothy E. 1990. *The Conceptual Practices of Power: A Feminist Sociology of Knowledge*. Boston: Northeastern University Press.

Snyder, Sharon L., and David T. Mitchell. 2006. *Cultural Locations of Disability*. Chicago: The University of Chicago Press.

Stein, Michael A., and Janet E. Lord. 2009. Future Prospects for the United Nations Convention on the Rights of Persons with Disabilities. In *The UN Convention on the Rights of Persons with Disabilities: European and Scandinavian Perspectives*. Edited by Oddný Mjöll Arnardóttir and Gerard Quinn. Leiden: Martinus Nijhoff Publisher.

Stein, Michael A., and Janet E. Lord. 2010. Monitoring the Convention on the Rights of Persons with Disabilities: Innovations, lost opportunities, and future potential. *Human Rights Quarterly* 32: 689–728. [CrossRef]

Sturm, Andreas, Anne Waldschmidt, Anemari Karacic, and Timo Dins. 2017. Exercising influence at the European level: Political opportunity structures for disability rights advocacy and the impact of the UN CRPD. In *The Changing Disability Policy System: Active Citizenship and Disability in Europe Volume 1*. Edited by Rune Halvorsen, Bjorn Hvinden, Jerome Bickenback, Delia Ferri and Ana Marti Guillén Rodriquez. New York: Routledge.

Taylor, Steven J., Robert Bogdan, and Marjorie L. DeVault. 2016. *Introduction to Qualitative Research Methods: A Guidebook and Resource*, 4th ed. New York: John Wiley & Sons.

United Nations. 2007. *The Convention on the Rights of Persons with Disabilities and Optional Protocol*. New York: United Nations.

Waldschmidt, Anne, Andreas Sturm, Anemari Karacic, and Timo Dins. 2017. Implementing the UN CRPD in European countries: A comparative study on the involvement of organisations representing persons with disabilities. In *The Changing Disability Policy System: Active Citizenship and Disability in Europe Volume 1*. Edited by Rune Halvorsen, Bjorn Hvinden, Jerome Bickenback, Delia Ferri and Ana Marti Guillén Rodriquez. New York: Routledge.

Young, Iris M. 1990. *Justice and the Politics of Difference*. Princeton: Princeton University Press.

7

Victims of Violence: The Forced Sterilisation of Women and Girls with Disabilities in Australia

Laura Elliott

Graduate student, Melbourne Law School, University of Melbourne, 185 Pelham St, Carlton, VIC 3053, Australia; lelliott1@student.unimelb.edu.au

Abstract: This paper considers the issue of forced sterilisation of women and girls with disabilities in the Australian context. It examines the history and ideological underpinning of this practice, the current Australian regime and the present rationales for court or tribunal authorisation of a sterilising procedure. It is by no means an exhaustive coverage, but aims to critically analyse the current system and make recommendations for reform of Australian law and policy. This paper ultimately concludes that the practice of forced sterilisation in Australia should be criminalised, save for exceptional circumstances.

Keywords: disability; human rights; sterilisation; violence; medical procedures; legal capacity; consent; women; girls; Convention on the Rights of Persons with Disabilities

---

1. Introduction

In recent years, the forced sterilisation of people with disabilities in Australia has been a topic of considerable focus and debate, both nationwide and internationally. Despite a barrage of recommendations from people with disabilities, their allies and international bodies to criminalise forced sterilisation, this practice is still legal and sanctioned in Australia. This paper will focus on the forced sterilisation of girls and women as they are disproportionately affected by this procedure (Frohmader 2013). It is an intersectional issue and a gendered practice, the 'result of both gender and disability-based discrimination' (Australian Human Rights Commission 2013, p. 3).

The current legislative and policy framework in Australia permits gross violations of human rights and dignity to occur on a regular basis. Furthermore, consistently authorising this form of violence puts Australia in breach of its international human rights obligations. As such, this paper contends that the involuntary sterilisation of women and girls with disabilities in Australia should be criminalised in all circumstances, save for exceptional situations in which an individual is completely unable to make a decision or, for minors, where there is a serious risk to an individual's health or life. The inadequacy of the current system necessitates a new regime that aligns more closely with the social model of disability: rather than viewing the individual as the problem, attention should be paid to reducing the societal or environmental barriers that lead to the factors that underpin the justifications for the sterilisation of women and girls with disabilities (Shakespeare 2002).

Section 2 of this paper provides an overview of forced sterilisation in Australia, including its recent history and socio-political basis. Section 3 details Australia's human rights obligations under international law, and examines how specific provisions under the *Convention on the Rights of Persons with Disabilities* (Convention on the Rights of Persons with Disabilities 2008a) (CRPD) relate to the practice of forced sterilisation. Sections 4 and 5 outline the current Australian legislative framework in which applications for forced sterilisation of women and girls can be authorised by a court or tribunal and the rationales for authorising forced sterilisation. This background paves the way for a critical analysis of the current Australian system, which is provided in Section 6. This section addresses the ultimate question: should the forced sterilisation of women and girls with disabilities be made illegal in Australia? After asserting that it should, Section 7 details the author's recommendations for legislative and policy reform in Australia.

The forced sterilisation of women and girls with disabilities in Australia must be put to an end. It is time for the Australian Government to jettison their callous indifference towards the life-long impact on individuals that are affected by this practice and bring Australia in line with its human rights obligations.

2. Overview of Forced Sterilisation in Australia

Women with Disabilities Australia (WWDA) have defined forced sterilisation as the 'performance of a procedure which results in sterilisation in the absence of the free and informed consent of the individual who undergoes the procedure' (Frohmader 2013, p. 22). This definition is inclusive of situations in which sterilisation has been authorised by a third party such as a parent, legal guardian, court, tribunal or judge (Frohmader 2013). The CRPD defines persons with disabilities as those who have 'long-term physical, mental, intellectual or sensory impairments which in interaction with various barriers may hinder their full and effective participation in society on an equal basis with others' (Convention on the Rights of Persons with Disabilities 2008a, article 1).

It is broadly recognized that sterilisation is a 'process or act that renders a person unable to produce children' (Senate Community Affairs References Committee 2013, p. 6). Various kinds of procedures constitute a sterilising practice. These include permanent or irreversible sterilising procedures, such as a hysterectomy (removal of the uterus and sometimes the cervix, fallopian tubes, ovaries or part of the vagina), tubal litigation (blocking or closing of the fallopian tubes) and endometrial ablation (laser technology used to destroy the uterine lining for purposes of stopping menstruation). This definition also includes non-permanent contraceptive measures such as oral contraceptives, diaphragms, intrauterine devices and long acting reversible contraceptives such as injections (Depo Provera) and implants (Implanon) (Senate Community Affairs References Committee 2013).

For over 20 years, disability advocates have been demanding the Australian Government undertake comprehensive reforms to stop the involuntary and coerced sterilisation of women and girls with disabilities, and develop policies and programs that allow women and girls with disabilities to be afforded respect of their human rights on an equal basis with others (Frohmader 2013). There have been numerous studies undertaken and reports published recommending reform in the sterilisation sphere in Australia. In 1994, the Family Law Council (Family Law Council 1994) concluded that a uniform and consistent approach was needed for all children regardless of their geographical location within Australia. The Council also stated that sterilisation of a child should only be authorised if it is necessary to save the child's life or prevent serious damage to their health (Family Law Council 1994). The Australian Human Rights Commission published reports in 1997 and 2001 propounding that the number of sterilisations being performed on children and women with disabilities in Australia was greater than those that had been authorised by a court or tribunal and that it was clear that the law was failing to protect individuals from involuntary sterilisation (Brady and Grover 1997; Brady et al. 2001). These reports did trigger some minor changes, such as Medicare amending their policies to require that claims for sterilisation of children be accompanied by a court order or medical details of the need for the procedure (Brady et al. 2001). However, there have been no substantial changes made to legislation or policy regarding the forced sterilisation of women and children with disabilities.

The Australian Government has spent a considerable amount of time investigating the issue of forced sterilisation of women and girls with disabilities. The main concern of public policy in this area has focused on "piecemeal development of mechanisms, protocols and guidelines in an attempt to 'minimise the risk of unauthorised sterilisations occurring'" (Standing Committee of Attorneys-General 2004 as cited in Frohmader 2013, p. 26). In December 2000, the Government tabled in the Senate the report '*Sterilisation of women and young girls with an intellectual disability*' which, on the basis of data from the Australian Institute of Health and Welfare, submitted that, between 1993 and 1999, there were few sterilisations of girls with disabilities in Australia (Senate Community Affairs References Committee 2013). In reality, there has been a substantial dearth of quantitative research undertaken in regards to forced sterilisation. Brady et al. (2001) reported in 2001 that 28 authorisations occurred between 1992 and 1998, with eight rejections. In contrast, Brady and Grover (Brady and Grover 1997) adduced Health Insurance Commission data to claim that at least 1045 women and girls had been sterilised during the same period, and noted that there would be others who were treated in public hospitals without attracting Medicare benefits. This lack of concrete data has led to considerable uncertainty around the exact frequency of the practice of forced sterilisation in Australia, a concern that has not been addressed by the Australian Government. In August 2003, Australian Governments, through the then *Standing Committee of Attorneys-General* (SCAG) agreed that a nationally uniform framework for the authorisation of the sterilisation of children was required (Frohmader 2013). From 2003 to 2007, notwithstanding strong resistance from human rights and disability advocates, the SCAG developed proposed legislation that aimed to regulate the authorisation of sterilisation of children with a 'decision-making disability', rather than make the practice of sterilisation of children illegal (Frohmader 2013). In November 2006, the SCAG released a draft bill that set out procedures that jurisdictions could adopt in authorising the sterilisation of children who have an intellectual disability[1]. Ultimately, however, the SCAG abandoned this draft Bill in 2008, declaring that there would be limited benefit from developing model legislation. Instead, the Government 'agreed to review current arrangements to ensure that all tribunals or bodies with the power to make orders concerning the sterilisation of minors with an intellectual disability are required to be satisfied that all appropriate alternatives to sterilisation have been fully explored and/or tried before such an order is made' (Standing Committee of Attorneys-General 2008, p. 7).

There is no evidence to date that those reviews were conducted. In 2009, the Australian Government formally declared to the UN that a comprehensive review undertaken in Australia showed that sterilisations of children with an intellectual disability had declined since 1997 to very low numbers (Australian Government 2009 as cited in Frohmader 2013). However, there was again no evidence to support that a comprehensive review had been undertaken (Frohmader 2013).

Furthermore, the issue of forced sterilisation in Australia has received ample international scrutiny. Since 2005, UN treaty monitoring bodies have continuously and formally recommended that the Australian Government enact uniform national legislation outlawing the sterilisation of girls, except where there is a serious threat to their health or life, and adult women with disabilities without their free and informed consent. These bodies include the Committee on the *Convention on the Rights of the Child* (Convention on the Rights of the Child 1990) (CRC), the Committee on the *Convention on the Elimination of all Forms of Discrimination Against Women* (CEDAW) (Convention on the Elimination of all Forms of Discrimination against Women 1981) and the UN Human Rights Council (Committee on the Rights of the Child 2012; Committee on the Elimination of Discrimination against Women 2010; Committee on the Rights of the Child 2005; UN General Assembly Human Rights Council 2011). The Australian Government is yet to comply with any of the recommendations (Frohmader 2013). In 2011, after WWDA lodged a formal complaint, UN Special Rapporteurs Anand Grover and Rashida Manjoo wrote to the Australian Government seeking a formal response on the issue of forced sterilisation (Frohmader 2013, Appendix 2). The Government's response confirmed the absence of a uniform national approach to the authorisation of sterilisation of women and girls with disabilities, and reinforced the Government's view that there are situations in which it can and should be permitted (Frohmader 2013, Appendix 3). International medical bodies, such as the International Federation of Gynaecology and Obstetrics, World Medical Association, International NGO Council on Violence against Children and the WHO, have also become involved, developing new protocols and calls for action to eliminate the practice of forced sterilisation (World Medical Association and the

---

1 *Children with Intellectual Disabilities (Regulation of Sterilisation) Bill* 2006.

International Federation of Health and Human Rights Organisations 2011; International NGO Council on Violence against Children 2012; World Health Organisation 2014). Despite the abundance of debate and discussion around this issue, the forced sterilisation of women and girls with disabilities remains legal and practiced in Australia (Frohmader 2014).

It is also worrying to note that, often due to the cost and formality of court processes in Australia, families and carers wishing to have an individual with a disability sterilised are starting to circumvent the formal procedures. In a 2003 Four Corners report, Peter and Dot King spoke of how they had their 15-year-old daughter Trish sterilised in secret. She was booked into the hospital under her mother's name, and the procedure was carried out without any substantial questions being asked (ABC 2003a). Dr and Mrs Carter, in their submission to the recent Senate inquiry, stated that they 'are aware of instances where parents have taken their daughters to Thailand or New Zealand to have a hysterectomy because their request to have a hysterectomy performed in Australia was rejected' (Carter and Carter 2013, p. 3). It is clear that the current law is continually failing to protect vulnerable individuals at risk of forced sterilisation in numerous ways and that steps need to be taken to ensure that the rights of these individuals are protected on an equal basis with others.

3. International Obligations

WWDA have declared that 'forced sterilisation clearly breaches every international human rights treaty and declaration to which Australia is a party' (Frohmader 2013, p. 70). These include the CRPD, the CRC, the CEDAW, the *International Convention on Civil and Political Rights* (International Convention on Civil and Political Rights 1976), the *International Covenant on Economic, Social and Cultural Rights* (International Covenant on Economic, Social and Cultural Rights 1976) and other key international and national standards and frameworks (Frohmader 2013). This report will focus on the CRPD, in particular how allowing involuntary sterilisation to continue puts Australia in breach of articles 12 and 16.

Australia ratified the CRPD on 17 Australia 2008 and the Optional Protocol on 21 August 2009. It must be noted that in entering into the treaty, Australia declared its view that the Convention allows for substituted decision-making and compulsory medical treatment (Convention on the Rights of Persons with Disabilities 2008b). Whilst the Committee on the CRPD (the Committee) may make recommendations that the Government in Australia take specific action, the CRPD has no binding effect in Australia. To date, no domestic legislation has been enacted that protects the rights affirmed under the CRPD. Whilst bodies such as the Committee can be influential in shaping Australia's policy, it is ultimately the Australian Government's responsibility to enact legislation to enforce Australia's international obligations.

3.1. Article 12: Equal Recognition before the Law

Article 12 provides that persons with disabilities have the right to recognition everywhere as persons before the law. This includes recognising that persons with disabilities enjoy legal capacity on an equal basis with others in all aspects of life. This positive right requires States to take appropriate measures to provide access for persons with disabilities to the support they may require in exercising their legal capacity. It also requires States to ensure that effective safeguards are in place in all measures that relate to the exercise of legal capacity to prevent abuse of human rights (Convention on the Rights of Persons with Disabilities 2008a).

Numerous stakeholders hold the view that article 12 prohibits substituted decision-making. The Committee has clearly stated that article 12 mandates the replacement of substituted decision-making systems with supported decision-making (Committee on the Rights of Persons with Disabilities 2011). WWDA submit that article 12 means that 'an individual's right to decision-making cannot be substituted by decision-making of a third party, but each individual without exception has the right to make their own choices and to direct their own lives, whether in relation to living arrangements, medical treatment or family relationships' (Frohmader 2013, p. 71). People With Disabilities Australia

(People with Disabilities Australia 2013, p. 18) argue that the 'implementation of article 12 requires establishing supported decision-making alternatives to substituted decision-making regimes [and] effective safeguards to be introduced in relation to supported decision-making arrangements to prevent abuse in accordance with international human rights law'. Flynn and Arstein-Kerslake (Flynn and Arstein-Kerslake 2014) also propound that article 12 requires a proactive approach from state parties, where measures are put in place to support individuals in the exercise of their legal capacity, rather than assessing their mental capacity before their decisions will be legally recognized. This article therefore prohibits substituted decision-making regimes, such as that provided in the *Guardianship and Administration Act 1986* (Vic)[2] (Guardianship Act) or at common law in relation to the sterilisation of girls with disabilities.

3.2. Article 16: Freedom from Exploitation, Violence and Abuse

Article 16 requires that States take all appropriate legislative, administrative, social, educational and other measures to protect persons with disabilities from all forms of exploitation, violence and abuse, including their gender-based aspects. It also compels States to provide information, education, assistance and support for persons with disabilities and their families on how to avoid, recognise and report instances of exploitation, violence and abuse. Further, it mandates that States put in place effective legislation and policies, including those focused on the protection of women and children, to ensure that instances of exploitation, violence and abuse against persons with disabilities are identified, investigated and, where appropriate, prosecuted (Convention on the Rights of Persons with Disabilities 2008a).

As will be argued later in this paper, forced sterilisation can be classified as a form of violence. Thus, article 16 requires state parties to take measures to protect individuals from this practice. This includes providing education and support and enacting legislation to prohibit occurrences of forced sterilisation. Under the CRPD, therefore, state parties are prevented from facilitating procedures, such as those in place in Australia, in which the practice of forced sterilisation can be lawfully authorised.

3.3. Other Relevant Articles

Article 23(1)(c) requires States to take effective and appropriate measures to eliminate discrimination against persons with disabilities in all matters relating to marriage, family, parenthood and relationships, on an equal basis with others, so as to ensure that persons with disabilities, including children, retain their fertility on an equal basis with others (Convention on the Rights of Persons with Disabilities 2008a). Allowing women and children with disabilities to be sterilised without their consent clearly violates this provision, as the same law does not affect, on an equal basis, women and girls without disabilities.

4. Australian Legislative Framework and Court Processes

Australia's international treaty obligations are given effect through federal, state and territory legislation. There is much disparity in the legislation and court processes between the states and territories. As such, this paper will focus solely on the Victorian jurisdiction.

4.1. Girls with Disabilities

In Victoria, jurisdiction has not been expressly conferred on any Australian court or tribunal to hear child sterilisation cases. The sterilisation of children with disabilities is dealt with by the common law following the leading decision in *Secretary, Department of Health and Community Services (NT) v JWB and SMB* (1992) 175 CLR 218 (*Marion's Case*)[3]. In that case, the High Court heard an application for

---

2 *Guardianship and Administration Act 1986* (Vic).

3 *Secretary, Department of Health and Community Services (NT) v JWB and SMB* (1992) 175 CLR 218 (*Marion's Case*).

the sterilisation of a 13-year-old girl with an intellectual disability. Marion's parents, who brought the application, were concerned about fertility control and menstruation with its psychological and behavioural problems[4]. The High Court held that, in cases where the child is not 'legally competent', the Family Court is required to give approval before a child is sterilised, unless sterilisation occurs because of an appropriate 'therapeutic' procedure carried out to address an actual health issue (Office of the Public Advocate 2013, p. 6). This case confirmed that the Family Court's child welfare jurisdiction under section 67ZC of the *Family Law Act 1975* (Cth)[5] (Family Law Act) empowers the court to make orders for the sterilisation of a child (Senate Community Affairs References Committee 2013). It also established that it is only for the Courts to decide on such fundamental questions of human rights as the right to reproduce, rather than parents, carers or medical practitioners (Dowse 2004). There were two main reasons for this. Firstly, the risk of making the wrong decision is significant, and secondly, the consequences of a wrong decision would be particularly grave.[6] Before making an order for sterilisation, the Family Court must be satisfied that two conditions are met. First, that the sterilisation is, in the circumstances of the particular case, in the child's best interests, and second, that alternative and less invasive procedures have failed or it is certain that no other procedure or treatment will work (Senate Community Affairs References Committee 2013). Sections 60CB to 60CG of the Family Law Act outline how a court is to determine what is in the child's best interests. However, it must be noted that these provisions were not designed specifically for sterilisation cases; rather, they were enacted to deal with situations in which matters such as where the child will live are being decided (Senate Community Affairs References Committee 2013). Therefore, in hearing child sterilisation cases, the Family Court will apply the general principles regarding the best interests and the welfare of the child in Part VII of the Family Law Act, the factors detailed in Marion's Case in determining that particular child's best interests, as well as the *Family Law Rules 2004* (Cth)[7] developed to govern applications for 'medical procedures'.

Marion's Case was thought to be progress in the human rights sphere, as it considered the rights of children with disabilities through a 'best interests' lens and aimed to prevent parents from being able to sterilise their child without an order of the court. One of the intentions of the decision was to prevent unnecessary sterilisations (Rhoades 1995; ABC 2003b). However, Marion was quickly deemed 'legally incapable' and at no point did any member of the proceedings attempt to understand what Marion's wishes were. This is a trend in most court decisions on sterilisation, and there has been negligible deliberation in the judgements over this issue compared to decisions in cases relating to children without a disability (Steele 2008). Furthermore, the majority of the High Court held that the views of the parents are a relevant consideration for the Family Court, and anticipated that the outcome in sterilisation cases would ordinarily coincide with their wishes[8] (Rhoades 1995). The extent to which Marion's Case tangibly progressed the rights of people with disabilities is therefore debatable, as there was never any discussion of the empowerment of people with disabilities to make decisions. It has also been argued that judicial decisions following Marion's Case have failed to give full effect to its promise. There has been concern that the legal requirements set out in Marion's Case have not consistently been followed and that some sterilisations are being performed illegally with parent approval only, as opposed to court approval (Office of the Public Advocate 2013). Further, it has been said that within the medical practice the distinction between 'therapeutic' and 'non-therapeutic' sterilisations has become blurred (Naik 2012, p. 453). The Family Court has been criticised for effectively ignoring its own rhetoric regarding the rights of women and girls with disabilities and reverting to an archaic and discredited model (Rhoades 1995). It is clear that both legislative reform and greater guidance for

---

4 *Secretary, Department of Health and Community Services (NT) v JWB and SMB* (1992) 175 CLR 218 (*Marion's Case*).
5 *Family Law Act 1975* (Cth).
6 *Secretary, Department of Health and Community Services (NT) v JWB and SMB* (1992) 175 CLR 218 (*Marion's Case*).
7 *Family Law Rules 2004* (Cth).
8 *Secretary, Department of Health and Community Services (NT) v JWB and SMB* (1992) 175 CLR 218 (*Marion's Case*), at p. 260.

decision makers are required to ensure the rights of women and girls with disabilities do not continue to be violated.

4.2. Women with Disabilities

For women over 18 with disabilities, court proceedings differ across States and Territories. In Victoria, the Guardianship Act (s. 39) empowers the Victorian Civil and Administrative Tribunal (VCAT) to make an order giving consent to special medical treatment for persons 18 years of age or older who are incapable of giving consent to the proposed treatment. 'Special procedure' includes any procedure that is intended or is reasonably likely to have the effect of rendering a person permanently infertile (Guardianship Act, s. 3). A person is considered to be incapable of providing consent if he or she is incapable of understanding the general nature and effect of the proposed procedure or treatment, or is incapable of indicating whether or not he or she consents or does not consent to the carrying out of the proposed procedure or treatment (Guardianship Act, s. 36). If it is found that the person does not have capacity to consent, the court or tribunal is to decide whether to authorise the sterilization (Guardianship Act, s. 39).

The tribunal may consent to the carrying out of a special procedure only if it is satisfied that the person is incapable of giving consent and is not likely to be capable, within a reasonable time, of giving consent and the special procedure would be in the person's best interests (Guardianship Act, s. 42E). In determining a patient's best interests, the tribunal must take into account the person's wishes and the wishes of any relative, the consequences if the treatment is not performed, any alternative treatment available, the nature and degree of any significant risks associated with the treatment or any alternative treatment and whether the treatment is to be carried out only to promote and maintain the person's health and wellbeing (Guardianship Act, s. 38). By requiring the tribunal to consider the views of relatives, this legislation explicitly incorporates the opinions and needs of persons other than the individual concerned in the determination of *their* best interests (Senate Community Affairs References Committee 2013).

It is an offence subject to imprisonment for two years and/or a fine of up to $36,400 for a registered practitioner to conduct a special procedure without tribunal consent (Guardianship Act, s. 42G). However, it is not an offence, or professional misconduct, for the registered practitioner to act in response to a medical emergency or in good faith reasonably believing that consent had been obtained (Guardianship Act, s. 42A). It is also an offence to purport to give consent to special medical treatment. A person who gives consent to treatment knowing that he or she is not authorised to do so is guilty of an offence subject to a fine not exceeding 20 penalty units (Guardianship Act, s. 42). In 2016, this means the maximum fine would be around $3300, hardly an excessive figure (Victorian State Government 2016).

Additional regulatory requirements in relation to sterilisation exist at the State and Territory level. States and territories have adopted the Australian Guardianship and Administration Council's *Protocol for Special Medical Procedures (Sterilisation)*[9] (the Protocol), which applies to both women and girls and is intended to promote consistency in similar sterilisation cases regardless of the jurisdiction in which the case is heard. Phase 2 of the Protocol requires tribunals to adopt a two-stage inquiry process. First, the tribunal must consider whether an individual has the capacity to consent to sterilization (the Protocol, cl. 5.8). This involves determining whether the person understands the nature and effect of their decision, whether they are freely and voluntarily making a decision and whether they can communicate their decision in some way (the Protocol, cl. 5.11). However, even though the Protocol requires tribunals to consider capacity as a threshold question, it does not prohibit tribunals from hearing a case where it is determined that the individual does have capacity (Senate Community Affairs References Committee 2013). Second, before authorising a procedure, the tribunal must consider

---

9 *Protocol for Special Medical Procedures (Sterilisation).*

whether sterilisation is required, in the sense that other options have been explored and decided against (the Protocol, cl. 5.17).

5. Current Rationales for the Sterilisation of Women and Girls with Disabilities

WWDA classifies the main contemporary justifications for the sterilisation of a woman or girl with a disability into four broad categories: the genetic/eugenics argument, the good of the state, community or family argument, the incapacity for parenthood argument and the prevention of sexual abuse argument (Frohmader 2013). These rationales are all strongly rooted in the medical model of disability. The medical model views disability as a deficiency or disorder that is a tragedy and causes dependence on others. It sees disability as an essential trait of the person (Parker 2012). Under this model, the focus is placed on 'diagnosis and treatment of what are seen as cognitive and adaptive deficits, measured against norms of intelligence and independent functioning' (Parker 2012, p. 522).

5.1. The Genetic/Eugenic Argument

Historically, the rationale for sterilisation of women and girls with disabilities was a pseudo-scientific theory called eugenics. The aim of sterilisation under the eugenics movement was to stop non-productive members of society from reproducing for the 'benefit' of the rest of society (Gallichan 1929 and Ford 1996 as cited in Spicer 1999). Whilst this justification has been eradicated from legislation in most countries, remnants of it still remain within the attitudes of some sectors of the community (Frohmader 2013). This argument centres on the misconceived fear that women with disabilities will produce children with undesirable genetic 'defects'. The contemporary version of this justification disguises itself behind a 'best interests' veil, attempting to smother any trace of its connections to the Nazi era and genetic 'cleansing'. A recent example is the 2004 case of *BH v CCH* [2004][10] FamCA 496 in which the Family Court authorised the sterilisation of a 12-year-old girl with an intellectual disability and Tuberous Sclerosis. There was a 50% chance that any child she had would be born with Tuberous Sclerosis (TS). Although one in two people born with TS will lead a 'normal' life, the Court nonetheless considered that this was a factor weighing in favour of sterilisation.

5.2. The Good of the State, Community or Family Argument

This justification focuses on the 'burden' that women and girls with disabilities and their potentially disabled children place on the resources and services provided by the state and community (Frohmader 2013). It is also based on the burden of care that the management of menstruation and contraception places on families and carers due to 'conditions' such as challenging or unmanageable behaviour and hygiene issues (Steele 2008; Frohmader 2013). There have been numerous instances where the Court has authorised the sterilisation of women and girls with disabilities for menstrual management[11] (*Attorney-General (QLD) v Parents (In Re S)* (1989) 13 Fam Lr 660; *Re Angela* [2010] FamCA 98[12]; *BH v CCH* [2004] FamCA 496).

The most concerning aspect of this rationale is that it is being used to authorise sterilisations before the individual has even begun menstruating. In *Re Angela* [2010] FamCA 98, the Family Court authorised the hysterectomy of an 11-year-old girl with Rett Syndrome to prevent menstruation. In *Re Katie* (1995) 128 FLR 194,[13] a 15-year-old girl was sterilised at the onset of her menstruation. In *Attorney-General (QLD) v Parents (In Re S)* (1989) 13 Fam Lr 660 and *Re M (An Infant)* (1992) 106 FLR 433,[14] 12-year-old and 15-year-old girls, respectively, were sterilised before they had begun menstruating. Stella Young has also divulged the story of how at the age of four, when being treated

---

10 *BH v CCH* [2004] FamCA 496.
11 *Attorney-General (QLD) v Parents (In Re S)* (1989) 13 Fam Lr 660.
12 *Re Angela* [2010] FamCA 98.
13 *Re Katie* (1995) 128 FLR 194.
14 *Re M (An Infant)* (1992) 106 FLR 433.

for a broken leg, her doctor had suggested to her parents that they perform a hysterectomy to prevent having to deal with the 'inconvenience of menstruation' in the future (Young 2013, p. 1).

As WWDA have promulgated, 'the denial of a young women's human rights through the performance of an irreversible medical intervention with long term physical and psychological health risks is wrongly seen as the most appropriate solution to the social problem of lack of services and support (Frohmader 2013, p. 42). Sterilisation is often easier, faster and less costly than providing the programs, services and supports to enable young women and girls with disabilities to obtain and understand information and competencies about their bodies, relationships, sex, safety and rights (Frohmader 2013). Evidence indicates that the concerns and problems that arise at the onset of menstruation of women and girls with disabilities are often the same types of concerns as for women and girls without disabilities (Brady and Grover 1997 as cited in Spicer 1999). It also indicates that even individuals with high support needs can be accommodated with approaches similar to those taken for non-disabled women (Frohmader 2013). When parents and carers are given the necessary resources and support, the justification of menstrual management loses credibility.

The flip side to this argument focuses on the loss of dignity and reduction in quality of life associated with an inability to manage menstruation. Carter and Carter (Carter and Carter 2013, p. 1) stated that, 'there are many moderate-severe intellectually disabled women who are extremely distressed due to their inability to cope with menstruation leading to loss of dignity'. They stress that menstruation can cause a significant reduction in quality of life and hence damage to an individual's emotional or psychological health. They give the example of instances where 'an intellectually disabled woman has remained in the bathroom at the supported employment with blood over her clothes, due to the onset of menstruation' (Carter and Carter 2013, p. 1).

5.3. The Incapacity for Parenthood Argument

This rationale is based on widely held societal attitudes that women with disabilities, especially intellectual disabilities, are incapable of being good parents. This ideology creates pressure to prevent pregnancy in women with disabilities (Frohmader 2013). Women with disabilities are often seen as perpetually child-like, asexual or over-sexed and therefore inadequate parents (Committee on the Rights of Persons with Disabilities 2013; STAR 1991). Stella Young touches on this misconception in her submission to the recent Senate inquiry, recounting how she was laughed at when telling a doctor that she was sexually active (Young 2013, p. 1).

In Australia, a parent with a disability is up to ten times more likely to have a child removed from their care than a parent without a disability (Victorian Office of the Public Advocate 2012). Often, the removal of a child from a parent with a disability is carried out on the basis of the person's disability, rather than incapacity to care for the child (Victorian Office of the Public Advocate 2012). The mere fact that the parent has a disability is often mistakenly taken for prima facie evidence that they are unable to be a good parent or pose a risk to the child (Frohmader).

5.4. The Prevention of Sexual Abuse Argument

This justification rests on the fact that women and girls with disabilities are particularly vulnerable to sexual abuse, and thus should be sterilised to prevent them from abuse and/or its consequences. For example, in *Re Katie* (1995) 128 FLR 194, it was said that the attractive looks of the girl made her more of a target for sexual predators, and this formed part of the Court's rationale for her to be sterilised at age 16. In other cases, the young girls' over-sexualised or inappropriate behaviour towards men was taken into account in authorising their sterilisation before menstruation (*In re Elizabeth* (1989) 96 FLR 248[15]; *Attorney-General (QLD) v Parents (In Re S)* (1989) 13 Fam Lr 660).

15 *In re Elizabeth* (1989) 96 FLR 248.

The incongruous nature of this rationale can be seen immediately: it is not about preventing abuse, but about preventing the consequences of abuse, i.e., unwanted pregnancies. Research has shown that sterilisation can actually increase the risk of sexual abuse rather than protect against it, as there is no chance of the individual becoming pregnant. This is especially so for women with psychosocial or intellectual disabilities, women in psychiatric or other institutions and women in custody (Committee on the Rights of Persons with Disabilities 2016; Sobsey and Doe 1991). Instead of taking appropriate measures to combat sexual abuse and the reasons why it occurs, sterilisation is used as a Band-Aid solution that places the responsibility on girls and women with disabilities for preventing the consequences that accompany it. As Stella Young so eloquently put it: 'the fact that this burden rests on the shoulders of some of our most vulnerable citizens is a disgrace; it's an insight into how people with disabilities, particularly women, are denied some of the most basic rights of personhood that should be afforded to all human beings, and we should be deeply ashamed of it' (Young 2013, p. 2).

6. Should Forced Sterilisation Be Made Illegal?

6.1. Positions Taken by Stakeholders

WWDA argue for an outright ban of involuntary sterilisation for women and girls with disabilities. 'Forced sterilisation is an act of violence, a form of social control and a clear and documented violation of the right to be free from torture. It is internationally recognized as a harmful practice based on tradition, culture, religion or superstition' (International NGO Council on Violence against Children 2012 as cited in Frohmader 2013, p. 8). They recognise that the issue is part of a more widespread pattern of denial of human and reproductive rights, which includes exclusion from appropriate health care, information and services (Dowse and Frohmader 2001 as cited in Frohmader 2013).

The CRPD Committee has formally asserted that involuntary sterilisation of women and girls with disabilities, and other kinds of reproductive discrimination, violates multiple provisions of the CPRD (Nowak 2008). It has urged state parties to abolish the administration of sterilisation of children and adults with disabilities without the full and informed consent of the individual concerned, including all forms of forced sterilisation, forced abortion and non-consensual birth control (Committee on the Rights of Persons with Disabilities 2013; Committee on the Rights of Persons with Disabilities 2016). In particular, the Committee has recommended that Australia 'enact national legislation prohibiting, except where there is a serious threat to life or health, the use of sterilisation of girls, regardless of whether they have a disability, and of adult women with disabilities in the absence of their fully informed and free consent' (Committee on the Rights of Persons with Disabilities 2013; Committee on the Rights of Persons with Disabilities 2016, p. 8).

The Australian Government argues that an outright ban is inappropriate, stating that it 'potentially denies the rights of persons with disabilities to access all available medical support on an equal basis with persons without a disability. It is a 'one size fits all' solution to a complex problem' (Senate Community Affairs References Committee 2013, p. 94). The Government suggests that all sterilisation should be banned where an individual has the capacity to consent, and if they may develop capacity to consent in the future, then irreversible sterilisation should be banned. It recommends that state and territory legislation regulating the sterilisation of adults with disabilities be amended to explicitly state that it is presumed that persons with disabilities have the capacity to make their own decisions unless objectively assessed otherwise. Finally, it submits that state and territory legislation be amended to clearly dictate that a court of tribunal does not have authority to hear an application for sterilisation where a person has legal capacity (Senate Community Affairs References Committee 2013).

6.2. Forced Sterilisation Should Be Criminalised

No woman or girl with a disability should ever be sterilised without her consent, save for very exceptional circumstances. Involuntary sterilisation is a form of violence, permits gross violations of human rights and puts Australia in breach of its international obligations. Urgent action must be taken to prevent the continued occurrence of this blatant disregard for human rights.

6.2.1. Forced Sterilisation Is a form of Violence

The sterilisation of a woman or girl without her consent is a form of violence. This is recognised by the Committee on the Rights of Persons with Disabilities (Committee on the Rights of Persons with Disabilities 2016) which has stated that forced, coerced and otherwise involuntary sterilisation may be considered not only violence, exploitation and abuse but also cruel, inhuman or degrading treatment or punishment. It is broadly recognized that forced sterilisation has life-long physical and psychological effects, 'permanently robbing women of the reproductive capabilities and causing severe mental pain and suffering' (Frohmader 2013, p. 60). By taking away such a basic bodily function as the ability to reproduce, the physical and mental wellbeing of a woman is adversely impacted and her physical and bodily integrity is violated (Sifris 2010 as cited in Frohmader 2013). Steele (Steele 2013) has called it 'legal violence', which is violence that is made possible by and sanctioned by the law.

It is concerning to note that, despite the significant amount of academic, medical and parental discourse around this issue, there is next to no discussion about sterilisation publicly available from women and girls with disabilities themselves. A prime example is the 2013 Senate Inquiry titled 'Involuntary or Coerced Sterilisation of People with Disabilities in Australia'. A clear majority of the submissions to the Senate Inquiry were made by disability activist bodies and parents arguing for and against forced sterilisation. There are a very limited number of case studies available to demonstrate the real and tangible harm that forced sterilisation causes to women and girls with disabilities. A small insight was provided at a conference held by STAR, where women spoke of experiences such as "I went to hospital and instead of having my appendix out, I had a tubal ligation" and "after trying to have a baby for a long time I finally found out I had been sterilised when I was 14 living in an institution" (STAR 1991). These types of blatant violations of bodily integrity clearly fall within the ambit of violence and abuse. By not only failing to criminalise this practice, but authorising this form of violence to be perpetrated against both women and children, Australia is breaching article 16 of the CRPD.

Australia is further in breach of article 16 by declining to enact effective legislation and policies to ensure that the forced sterilisation of women and girls does not occur. Article 16 specifically mandates that gender-specific legislation and policies be enacted locally. There is currently no legislation prohibiting or even regulating the sterilisation of girls under 18 with disabilities. The legislation regulating the sterilisation of women over 18 with disabilities legalises this form of violence if the individual is deemed by a court not to have 'decision-making capacity', a notion that is arbitrary and decided on a case-by-case basis. This lack of effective legislation is unacceptable and falls far short of meeting the requirements of the CRPD.

Finally, article 16 explicitly dictates that state parties are to provide support and education to avoid, recognise and report instances of exploitation, violence and abuse. The failure to provide appropriate and sufficient assistance, support, information and education for women and girls with disabilities and their families and carers makes the current Australian position inconsistent with its obligations under the CRPD.

6.2.2. Substituted Decision-Making Is Prohibited by the CRPD

As well as the obvious breaches of article 16 mentioned above, the current capacity considerations and 'best interests' tests put Australia further in breach of its human rights obligations. Currently, there is a heavy focus on capacity considerations before an application for the sterilisation of a woman or girl with a disability can be authorised. If an individual is deemed not to have capacity, a decision is made about what is in her best interests according to the court. This means that 'in practice, the choices of women with disabilities, especially women with psychosocial or intellectual disabilities, are often ignored and their decisions are often substituted by those of third parties, including legal representatives, service providers, guardians and family members' (Committee on the Rights of Persons with Disabilities 2016, p. 11). This provision for substituted decision-making violates article 12 of the CRPD, which requires the provision of support for persons with disabilities to exercise their legal capacity. The UN Special Rapporteur on Torture has recently reiterated that the law should never distinguish between individuals on the basis of capacity or disability in order to permit sterilisation, specifically of girls and women with disabilities (Méndez 2013). Flynn and Arstein-Kerslake (Flynn and Arstein-Kerslake 2014) argue that upholding cognition as a prerequisite for personhood or the granting of legal capacity results in the exclusion of people with cognitive disabilities. 'Irrespective of decision-making ability, every person has an inherent right to legal capacity and equal recognition before the law' (Flynn and Arstein-Kerslake 2014, p. 83). This right to be recognized as a person before the law and have one's decisions legally recognized calls for a system of supported decision-making to replace the current substituted decision-making model that allows third parties to make decisions on behalf of individuals. Flynn and Arstein-Kerslake (Flynn and Arstein-Kerslake 2014) note that in recent years there has been growing support for the idea that almost every human being is able to express her will and preferences with the right support. They also argue that 'for the most part, we know very little about how people make decisions and, as a consequence, we should be slow to deny the right to have one's decisions respected by the law to anyone, even when it is difficult to decipher the person's wishes or where the individual has a different worldview, even one which may seem irrational or ill-formed' (Flynn and Arstein-Kerslake 2014, p. 82). The Committee on the Rights of Persons with Disabilities (Committee on the Rights of Persons with Disabilities 2016) has recognised that restricting or removing legal capacity can actually facilitate forced interventions, such as sterilization, abortion or contraception. As such, the current allowance for substituted decision-making is unacceptable.

The 'best interests' test has received a spate of criticism from disability rights advocates. Amnesty International Australia (Amnesty International Australia 2013, p. 44) maintain that the use of a best interests test is prohibited under international law, stating, 'claims that forcing or coercing women and girls into sterilisation is in their 'best interests' contradict the general principles of respect for inherent dignity, individual autonomy including the freedom to make one's own choices, and independence of persons set out in article 3(a) of the CRPD'. The main concern about the best interests test is that it is amorphous, undefined and slanted to give weight to the views and needs of carers (Senate Community Affairs References Committee 2013). It is a 'malleable concept that can fail to address the needs and human rights of persons with disabilities' (Senate Community Affairs References Committee 2013, p. 123). The test provides no adequate safeguards and may allow courts and tribunals to put the wishes of family members or carers above those of the individual with a disability. In the past, the best interests test has been used to justify the authorisation of sterilisations based on inappropriate considerations such as those mentioned in Section 5 of this paper. In reality, the best interests approach has little to do with the individual involved and more to do with the interests or wishes of others, in particular families and carers (Frohmader 2013). Legislative reform must be put into effect, which eliminates capacity considerations and implements a supported decision-making regime to prevent further violations of human rights.

6.2.3. Exceptional Circumstances

There are undoubtedly situations that give rise to a 'moral grey area' and make proposing legislative and policy reforms a toilsome task. These difficult cases necessitate exceptions to an outright ban on sterilisation without consent. This paper does not have the scope to consider a completely comprehensive solution to these controversial issues. However, they must be taken into consideration in any future legislative or policy reform in Australia.

The most obvious such circumstance is where an individual is in a coma or permanent vegetative state, and thus completely unable to make a decision (Flynn and Arstein-Kerslake 2014). Any new legislation would need to be flexible enough to allow for an exception in which a third party may make a decision on the basis of what the individual's will and preference would have been. This may be very difficult to ascertain, but difficulty should not preclude an effort to understand what the individual would have wanted in the circumstances.

Another problematic situation may arise where an individual refuses life-saving treatment. For example, if a woman with an intellectual disability is diagnosed with cancer and requires a hysterectomy to live, but refuses to undergo the operation, should the legislation be drafted such that she is allowed to refuse the treatment and ultimately die? It must be considered that women without disabilities have the right to refuse life-saving treatment, and as such, women with disabilities should be afforded the same right provided they have been supported in making an informed decision. Future legislative drafters would need to consider protecting medical practitioners who comply with the wishes of people with disabilities to refuse lifesaving treatment. Any legislation criminalising forced sterilisation would be otiose if medical practitioners were made liable for declining to perform a sterilisation procedure without the consent of an individual. Different considerations apply to minors. In general, minors are not considered able to make their own decisions in regards to medical treatment as they lack the necessary experience, knowledge and maturity (O'Connor 2009). A further exception may therefore be required for girls under the age of 18 where sterilisation without their consent is necessary due to a serious threat to their health or life.

6.2.4. Other Factors in Favour of Criminalisation

Whilst this paper does not have the scope to deeply delve into this complex subject, the interrelated issue of sexual autonomy weighs in favour of prohibiting forced sterilisation. The Australian Association of Development of Disability Medicine Inc. (Australian Association of Developmental Disability Medicine Inc. 2013, p. 1) has stated that, 'people with disabilities have the same rights as other people to exercise choices regarding sexual expression and relationships and have freedom over their body to make such choices'. The ability of individuals with disabilities to have their sexual and reproductive rights recognized on an equal basis with others should be taken into consideration when drafting rights-protecting legislation and reform.

7. Recommendations

As has been discussed, Australia's current legislative and policy framework regarding forced sterilisation of women and girls with disabilities is failing to protect those at risk of being sterilised without their consent. This paper proposes that a departure from the medical model ideology is needed, and that a new regime founded on the social model of disability should be developed. The social model recognises that disability results from the interaction between persons with impairments and the attitudinal and environmental barriers surrounding them (Parker 2012). This carries the implication that the environment must change to enable individuals living with a disability to participate in society on an equal basis with others. It recognises people with disabilities as an oppressed group in society and distinguishes between impairments and disability; disability being imposed on top of impairments by the way individuals are isolated and excluded from participating fully in society (Davis 2013). Thus, the focus should be shifted from performing a 'quick-fix' on the person who is seen as the problem, and placed on the environmental factors that are contributing to the issues that sterilisation is purportedly trying to address. This includes providing more support, education, resources and information to people with disabilities, their families and carers to enable them to better manage things such as menstruation and behavioural changes. It includes training for medical practitioners to try and change the archaic attitudes within the profession towards the sterilisation of people with disabilities. It includes a national uniform legislative regime to ensure that individuals are provided with consistent treatment regardless of geographical location. It includes the elimination of considerations of capacity and the 'best interests' of the individual, and the introduction of a supported decision making system to allow individuals to make informed decisions about sterilisation. It includes research to obtain a greater understanding of the prevalence of forced sterilisation in Australia. Furthermore, it includes harsher punishment for those who attempt to circumvent the formal procedures.

7.1. Support, Education, Resources and Information

There is an appalling lack of support and resources available for people with disabilities to assist them with choices about relationships and sexuality, sexual and reproductive health and menstrual management (Senate Community Affairs References Committee 2013). Women with disabilities are often denied access to information, communication and education around these issues because of 'harmful stereotypes that assume that they are asexual and do not therefore require such information on an equal basis with others' (Committee on the Rights of Persons with Disabilities 2016, p. 10). Even where there are educational resources available, sex education is often not targeted appropriately, and is undermined by the message that people with disabilities are different and that sex education does not apply to them in the same way that it does to people without disabilities (Senate Community Affairs References Committee 2013). The increase of information, education and support in areas of sex, reproduction and menstruation for both individuals with disabilities and their carers will assist in alleviating some of the stresses that are experienced when dealing with matters such as menstrual management. The Senate has (rightly, in my opinion) recommended that such access to support services should be tailored to each individual, not a one-size-fits-all program (Senate Community Affairs References Committee 2013). An increased level of funding and devoted resources would assist in bridging the gap and providing individuals with disabilities and their families and carers the support they need to realise their rights on an equal basis with others. Further, it would bring Australia in line with its obligation under article 16 of the CRPD to provide support and resources to prevent instances of violence from occurring.

7.2. Training for Medical Practitioners

Medical practitioners are not presently provided with adequate education, training and professional development in relation to people with disabilities, sexual and reproductive health, informed consent, how to assess capacity, and how to communicate with people with disabilities and their carer or advocates effectively (Senate Community Affairs References Committee 2013). This is particularly problematic given that medical professionals are often influential in the decision to sterilise women and girls with disabilities (Frohmader 2013). The judgments of medical professionals are made from a particular perspective that women or girls with disabilities are basically the sum of their biology or physiology (Dowse and Frohmader 2001 as cited in Frohmader 2013). This ideology reinforces notions of the medical model and allows for medical professionals to hold the view that sterilisation will 'fix' the 'problems' that individuals face due to their impairments. Providing more effective education and training for medical practitioners will assist in re-shaping these misconceived attitudes and help to prevent instances of forced sterilisation occurring. This would also enable Australia to more effectively fulfil its obligations under article 16 of the CRPD.

7.3. Legislative Reform

Currently, it cannot be guaranteed that a person with a disability will receive the same treatment regardless of their geographic location. The principal differences between jurisdictions include the requirement of capacity as a threshold issue, the availability of legal representation and the factors considered when determining whether to authorise a sterilisation procedure (Senate Community Affairs References Committee 2013). Uniform national legislation should thus be developed to provide a coherent and consistent framework that criminalises sterilisation for girls, and for women without their free and informed consent. As mentioned, article 16 of the CRPD mandates that legislation be enacted to prevent instances of violence from occurring. Developing legislation to prohibit forced sterilisation would make Australia compliant with this requirement.

This paper will not attempt the arduous task of drafting proposed legislation. However, there are three matters that should undoubtedly be considered in drafting any future legislation:

1. For the reasons submitted, considerations of capacity as a threshold issue should be eliminated. The provision for a substituted-decision making regime once an individual is deemed not to have capacity should also be excluded from any future legislation. Instead, a supported decision-making model should be developed to assist women with disabilities in making free and informed decisions about any sterilisation procedures. This would ensure that Australia realises its obligations under article 12 of the CRPD.
2. Following that, the 'best interests' test should be rejected. This test undermines human rights and would be redundant in a supported decision-making model.
3. As discussed, the provision of a small number of limited exceptions will be necessary to handle exceptional circumstances. These include where an individual does not have any ability to make a decision as they are in a coma or vegetative state, or, where a minor requires life-saving treatment. Any exceptions would need to be very carefully defined and limited in their scope to prevent the existing human rights violations arising from substituted decision-making from happening in the future.

It is vital that any drafters of future legislation keep in mind the general principle that women with disabilities, like all women, have the right to 'have control over and decide freely and responsibly on matters related to their sexuality, including sexual and reproductive health, free of coercion, discrimination and violence' (Committee on the Rights of Persons with Disabilities 2016, p. 10).

7.4. Harsher Punishment for Those Trying to Circumvent Formal Procedures

There have been reported instances of families taking their children to other jurisdictions to have them sterilized (Senate Community Affairs References Committee 2013). To address this issue, similar provisions to the Female Genital Mutilation (FGM) offences under the *Crimes Act 1900* (NSW)[16] could be adopted. Section 45 makes it an offence to aid, abet, counsel or procure a person to perform an FGM act on another person. It carries a penalty of imprisonment for 21 years. Section 45A makes it an offence to take a person or arrange for a person to be taken from the State with the intention of having FGM performed on that person. This also carries a penalty of imprisonment for 21 years. Similar provisions may be implemented to criminalise aiding, abetting or procuring a person to perform a sterilisation procedure on an Australian resident or taking an Australian resident outside of the State to have a sterilization procedure performed without consent. In addition to this, the Law Institute of Victoria (Law Institute of Victoria 2013) recommended that a system be put in place to allow the Australian Federal Police to put a child on an Airport Watch List if necessary. This would ensure that authorities were alerted if a family that had unsuccessfully applied for a sterilisation procedure were attempting to remove an individual from the country.

7.5. Redress for Victims

Article 16 of the CRPD requires that parties take appropriate measures to promote the recovery, rehabilitation and social reintegration of persons with disabilities who become victims of violence. After identifying that forced sterilisation is a form of violence, it is necessary that the Australian Government provide redress to the women and girls who have suffered from this practice. Whether this be in the form of an apology or compensation WWDA recommends that both occur (Frohmader 2013), it is appropriate that the Government publicly recognise that harm has been caused to the individuals affected, and attempt to assist these individuals in their rehabilitation.

---

[16] *Crimes Act 1900* (NSW).

7.6. Data Recording

As mentioned, there is currently a substantial lack of information regarding the exact numbers of forced sterilisations that are occurring in Australia. The Government has not conducted any comprehensive reviews or research to shed light on this issue. It is therefore recommended that a uniform national approach to data recording be implemented to gain a more holistic understanding of the present number of sterilisations being performed and authorised in Australia.

8. Conclusions

Despite the copious attention that the issue of forced sterilisation of women and girls with disabilities in Australia has received from national and international stakeholders in recent years, little to no progress has been made. The Government remains apathetic and indifferent towards this issue. The persistent theme throughout this paper, and in recommendations from disability advocates and international bodies, is the violation of human rights. The current legislative and policy framework is impermissible from a human rights perspective. It puts Australia in breach of not only the CRPD, but almost all other human rights treaties to which it is a party. This paper has propounded that forced sterilisation is a form of violence. Legally authorising violence to be perpetrated against women and children with disabilities is unacceptable and cannot be allowed to continue in Australia. The prevention of this flagrant disregard for human rights begins with a national legislative scheme criminalising forced sterilisation. Coupled with further support and education for individuals with disabilities, their carers, and medical professionals, these reforms will provide a backbone for momentous progress in the Australian human rights sphere. Whilst the recommendations in this paper may not provide a complete and comprehensive solution to the issue of forced sterilisation, they will guide Australia down a path towards the ultimate goal: justice for the victims of this violence.

References

ABC. 2003. Walk in our Shoes. *Four Corners*. June 16. Available online: http://www.abc.net.au/4corners/content/2003/transcripts/s880681.htm (accessed on 7 May 2016).

ABC. 2003. Interview with Chief Justice Alastair Nicholson. *Four Corners*. May 12. Available online: http://www.abc.net.au/4corners/content/2003/20030616_sterilisation/int_nicholson.htm (accessed on 17 June 2017).

Amnesty International Australia. 2013. *Involuntary or Coerced Sterilisation of People with Disabilities in Australia*. Submission No. 48 to Senate Community Affairs References Committee; Broadway: Amnesty International Australia.

Australian Association of Developmental Disability Medicine Inc. *Involuntary or Coerced Sterilisation of People with Disabilities in Australia*. Submission No. 59 to Senate Community Affairs References Committee; Brisbane: Australian Association of Developmental Disability Medicine Inc.

Australian Human Rights Commission. 2013. *Involuntary or Coerced Sterilisation of People with Disabilities in Australia*; Submission No. 5 to Senate Community Affairs References Committee; Sydney: Australian Human Rights Commission.

Brady, Susan M., and Sonia Grover. 1997. *The Sterilisation of Girls and Young Women in Australia—A Legal, Medical and Social Context*; Sydney: Australian Human Rights Commission.

Brady, Susan, John Britton, and Sonia Grover. 2001. *The Sterilisation of Girls and Young Women in Australia: Issues and Progress*; Sydney: Australian Human Rights Commission. Available online: https://www.humanrights.gov.au/our-work/disability-rights/projects/sterilisation-girls-and-young-women-australia-issues-and (accessed on 8 May 2016).

Carter, John, and Merren Carter. 2013. Involuntary or Coerced Sterilisation of People with Disabilities in Australia. Submission No. 20 to Senate Community Affairs References Committee. Available online: https://sydney.edu.au/health-sciences/cdrp/Sterilisation_Submission%2021.pdf (accessed on 8 May 2016).

Committee on the Elimination of Discrimination against Women. 2010. *Concluding Observations of the Committee on the Elimination of Discrimination against Women: Australia*; Geneva: UN Committee on the Elimination of Discrimination against Women (CEDAW). Available online: http://www.refworld.org/docid/52dd07654.html (accessed on 8 May 2016).

Convention on the Elimination of all Forms of Discrimination against Women. 1981. Opened for signature 1 March 1980, 1249 UNTS 13 (entered into force 3 September 1981). Available online: http://www.ohchr.org/Documents/ProfessionalInterest/cedaw.pdf (accessed on 7 May 2016).

Convention on the Rights of Persons with Disabilities. 2008. Opened for signature 30 March 2007, 999 UNTS 3 (entered into force 3 May 2008). Available online: https://www.un.org/development/desa/disabilities/convention-on-the-rights-of-persons-with-disabilities/convention-on-the-rights-of-persons-with-disabilities-2.html (accessed on 7 May 2016).

Convention on the Rights of Persons with Disabilities: Declarations and Reservations (Australia). 2008. Opened for signature 30 March 2007, 999 UNTS 3 (entered into force 3 May 2008). Available online: http://indicators.ohchr.org/ (accessed on 27 June 2017).

Committee on the Rights of Persons with Disabilities. 2011. *Consideration of Reports Submitted by States Parties under Article 35 of the Convention, Concluding Observations of the Committee on the Rights of Persons with Disabilities—Spain*; Geneva: UN Committee on the Elimination of Discrimination against Women (CEDAW). Available online: http://www.refworld.org/docid/54992a7a4.html (accessed on 7 May 2016).

Committee on the Rights of Persons with Disabilities. 2013. *Concluding Observations on the Initial Report of Australia*; Geneva: UN Committee on the Elimination of Discrimination against Women (CEDAW). Available online: http://www.refworld.org/docid/5280b5cb4.html (accessed on 17 June 2017).

Committee on the Rights of Persons with Disabilities. 2016. *General Comment No. 3 (2016) on Women and Girls with Disabilities*; 13th sess. UN Doc CRPD/C/GC/3 25 November 2016. Geneva: UN Committee on the Elimination of Discrimination against Women (CEDAW). Available online: http://tbinternet.ohchr.org/_layouts/treatybodyexternal/Download.aspx?symbolno=CRPD/C/GC/3&Lang=en (accessed on 7 May 2016).

Convention on the Rights of the Child. 1990. Opened for signature 20 November 1989, 1577 UNTS 3 (entered into force 2 September 1990). Available online: http://www.ohchr.org/EN/ProfessionalInterest/Pages/CRC.aspx (accessed on 7 May 2016).

Committee on the Rights of the Child. 2005. Consideration of Reports Submitted by States Parties under Article 44 of the Convention, Concluding Observations: Australia. Available online: http://www2.ohchr.org/english/bodies/crc/docs/co/CRC_C_AUS_CO_4.pdf (accessed on 7 May 2016).

Committee on the Rights of the Child. 2012. *Consideration of Reports Submitted by States Parties under Article 44 of the Convention, Concluding Observations: Australia*; Geneva: Committee on the Rights of the Child (CRC). Available online: http://www2.ohchr.org/english/bodies/crc/docs/co/CRC_C_AUS_CO_4.pdf (accessed on 7 May 2016).

Davis, Lennard J. 2013. *The Disability Studies Reader*, 4th ed. London: Routledge.

Dowse, Leanne. 2004. Moving Forward or Losing Ground? The Sterilisation of Women and Girls with Disabilities in Australia. Paper presented at the Disabled Peoples' International (DPI) World Summit, Winnipeg, MB, Canada, September 8–10. Available online: http://wwda.org.au/issues/sterilise/sterilise2001/steril3/ (accessed on 8 May 2016).

Family Law Council. 1994. *Sterilisation and Other Medical Procedures on Children*; Melbourne: Family Law Council. Available online: https://www.ag.gov.au/FamiliesAndMarriage/FamilyLawCouncil/Documents/Sterilisation%20and%20Other%20Medical%20Procedures%20on%20Children.doc (accessed on 8 May 2016).

Flynn, Eilionoir, and Anna Arstein-Kerslake. 2014. Legislating personhood: Realising the right to support in exercising legal capacity. *International Journal of Law in Context* 10: 81–104. [CrossRef]

Frohmader, Carolyn. *Parenting Issues for Women with Disabilities in Australia: A Policy Paper*; Tasmania: Women with Disabilities Australia. Available online: http://wwda.org.au/wp-content/uploads/2013/12/parentingpolicypaper09.pdf (accessed on 8 May 2016).

Frohmader, Caroyln. 2013. *Involuntary or Coerced Sterilisation of People with Disabilities in Australia*. Submission No. 49 to Senate Community Affairs References Committee; Canberra: Senate Community Affairs Committee Secretariat.

Frohmader, Carolyn. 2014. *Fact Sheet: Forced Sterilisation*; Tasmania: Women with Disabilities Australia. Available online: https://www.pwd.org.au/documents/temp/FS_Sterilization.pdf (accessed on 10 March 2016).

International Convention on Civil and Political Rights. 1976. Opened for signature 19 December 1966, 993 UNTS 171 (entered into force 23 March 1976). Available online: http://www.ohchr.org/Documents/ProfessionalInterest/ccpr.pdf (accessed on 7 May 2016).

International Covenant on Economic, Social and Cultural Rights. 1976. Opened for signature 19 December 1966, 993 UNTS 3 (entered into force 3 January 1976). Available online: http://www.ohchr.org/EN/ProfessionalInterest/Pages/CESCR.aspx (accessed on 7 May 2016).

International NGO Council on Violence against Children. 2012. Violating Children's Rights: Harmful Practices Based on Tradition, Culture, Religion or Superstition. A report from International NGO Council on Violence against Children. New York: International NGO Council on Violence against Children. Available online: http://srsg.violenceagainstchildren.org/document/_844 (accessed on 7 May 2016).

Law Institute of Victoria. 2013. *Involuntary or Coerced Sterilisation of People with Disabilities in Australia*. Submission No. 79 to Senate Community Affairs References Committee; Melbourne: Law Institute of Victoria.

Méndez, Juan E. 2013. *Report of the Special Rapporteur on Torture and Other Cruel, Inhuman or Degrading Treatment or Punishment*. 22nd sess. Agenda Item 3, UN Doc A/HRC/22/53 (1 February 2013). Available online: http://www.ohchr.org/Documents/HRBodies/HRCouncil/RegularSession/Session22/A.HRC.22.53_English.pdf (accessed on 7 May 2016).

Naik, Lesley. 2012. When is the sterilisation of an intellectually disabled child "therapeutic"? A practical analysis of the legal requirement to seek court authorisation. *Journal of Law and Medicine* 20: 453–63. [PubMed]

Nowak, Manfred. 2008. *Report of the Special Rapporteur on Torture and other Inhuman or Degrading Treatment or Punishment*. 7th sess. Agenda Item 3, UN Doc A/HRC/7/3. 15 January 2008. Available online: http://www.ohchr.org/EN/Issues/Torture/SRTorture/Pages/SRTortureIndex.aspx (accessed on 31 May 2017).

O'Connor, Christopher M. 2009. What rights do minors have to refuse medical consent? *Journal of Lancaster General Hospital* 4: 63–65.

Office of the Public Advocate. 2013. *Involuntary or Coerced Sterilisation of People with Disabilities in Australia*. Submission No. 14 to Senate Community Affairs References Committee; Carlton: Office of the Public Advocate.

Parker, Malcolm. 2012. Bioethical Issues: Forced Sterilisation: Clarifying and challenging intuitions and models. *Journal of Law and Medicine* 20: 512–27.

People with Disabilities Australia. 2013. *Involuntary or Coerced Sterilisation of People with Disabilities in Australia*. Submission No. 50 to Senate Community Affairs References Committee; Redfern: People with Disabilities Australia.

Rhoades, Helen. 1995. Intellectual Disability and Sterilisation—An Inevitable Connection? *Australian Journal of Family Law* 9: 234–52.

Senate Community Affairs References Committee, Parliament of Australia. 2013. *Involuntary or Coerced Sterilisation of People with Disabilities in Australia*; Canberra: Commonwealth of Australia. Available online: http://www.aph.gov.au/Parliamentary_Business/Committees/Senate/Community_Affairs/Involuntary_Sterilisation/First_Report (accessed on 10 March 2016).

Shakespeare, Tom. 2002. The social model of disability: an outdated ideology? *Research in Social Science and Disability* 2: 9–28.

Sobsey, Dick, and Tanis Doe. 1991. Patterns of sexual abuse and assault. *Sexuality and Disability* 9: 243–59. [CrossRef]

Spicer, Cathy. 1999. *Sterilisation of Women and Girls with Disabilities—A Literature Review*; Tasmania: Women with Disabilities Australia. Available online: http://wwda.org.au/issues/sterilise/sterilise1995/steril/ (accessed on 7 May 2016).

Standing Committee of Attorneys-General. 2008. Communique. March 28. Available online: http://www.nswbar.asn.au/circulars/scag.pdf (accessed on 31 May 2017).

STAR. 1991. *On The Record—A Report on the 1990 STAR Conference on Sterilisation: 'My Body, My Mind, My Choice'*; Melbourne: Victorian Action on Intellectual Disability (STAR). Available online: http://wwda.org.au/issues/sterilise/sterilise1995/record/ (accessed on 17 June 2017).

Steele, Linda. 2008. Making sense of the Family Court's decisions on the non-therapeutic sterilisation of girls with intellectual disability. *Australian Journal of Family Law* 22: 1–23.

Steele, Linda. 2013. Involuntary or Coerced Sterilisation of People with Disabilities in Australia. Submission No. 44 to Senate Community Affairs References Committee; February 24. Available online: http://www.aph.gov.au/DocumentStore.ashx?id=9880795d-9a5b-4a00-8614-72fb4bad7b6a&subId=16147 (accessed on 7 May 2016).

UN General Assembly Human Rights Council. 2011. *Draft Report of the Working Group on the Universal Periodic Review: Australia*; 10th sess. UN Doc A/HRC/WG.6/10/L. 8 (3 February 2011). Available online: https://www.ag.gov.au/RightsAndProtections/HumanRights/United-Nations-Human-Rights-Reporting/Documents/UniversalPeriodicReview-ReportoftheWorkingGroup.pdf (accessed on 27 June 2017).

Victorian Office of the Public Advocate. 2012. *The Removal of Children from Their Parent with a Disability*. Position Statement; Carlton: Office of the Public Advocate.

Victorian State Government. 2016. Penalties and Values (11 March 2016) Justice and Regulation. Available online: http://www.justice.vic.gov.au/home/justice+system/fines+and+penalties/penalties+and+values/#breadcrumbs (accessed on 10 May 2016).

World Health Organisation. 2014. *Eliminating Forced, Coercive and Otherwise Involuntary Sterilisation: An Interagency Statement*; Geneva: World Health Organisation. Available online: http://www.unaids.org/sites/default/files/media_asset/201405_sterilization_en.pdf (accessed on 7 May 2016).

World Medical Association and the International Federation of Health and Human Rights Organisations. 2011. Global Bodies Call for end to Forced Sterilisation. Press Release. 5 September 2011. Available online: http://wwda.org.au/issues/sterilise/sterilise2011/sterilwma2011/ (accessed on 7 May 2016).

Young, Stella. 2013. Involuntary or Coerced Sterilisation of People with Disabilities in Australia. Submission No. 68 to Senate Community Affairs References Committee.

8

Some Parents are More Equal than Others: Discrimination against People with Disabilities under Adoption Law

Blake Connell

Melbourne Law School, The University of Melbourne, Melbourne 3053, Australia; connellb@student.unimelb.edu.au or blakejconnell@gmail.com

Abstract: Article 23 of the Convention on the Rights of Persons with Disabilities (CRPD) explicitly includes 'the adoption of children' as a right to which people with disabilities are equally entitled. Despite the CRPD having been in force for over nine years, research is yet to consider whether CRPD signatory states have brought their respective adoption regimes in line with their obligations under art 23 of the CRPD. Using the laws of the Australian state of Victoria by way of case study, this article aims to shed light on the difficulties people with disabilities still face when attempting to adopt children. In terms of methodology, this article conducts an interpretive critique of Victoria's adoption law against art 23 of the CRPD, which it interprets mainly through the lens of the social model of disability. Ultimately, this article finds that Victoria's adoption framework closely resembles the adoption regimes of many other CRPD signatories, yet it clearly fails to uphold Australia's obligations under the CRPD. This is both as a result of the words of the legislation as well as their implementation in practice. This article proposes a suite of changes, both legislative and cultural, to bring Victoria's adoption framework in line with art 23, which it hopes will serve as a catalyst for change in other CRPD signatory states.

Keywords: adoption; adoption law; CRPD; disability; disability rights; people with disabilities; social model; medical model; Victorian adoption law

---

1. Introduction

Parenthood is held out to be a transformative part of human life (Chapman et al. 2015). It is therefore unsurprising that many people with disabilities desire to be parents (Shakespeare et al. 1996; Frohmader 2009). While critiques of society's privileging of parenthood exist, these do not detract from the claims of people with disabilities to this right (Warner 2000).

Despite this, recent research has shown that people with disabilities face disproportionate difficulty becoming and being parents—be it as a result of forced sterilisation (Kempton and Kahn 1991; Fennell 1992; Arstein-Kerslake 2015), higher rates of child removal (Llewellyn et al. 2003; Booth et al. 2005; IASSID 2008), over-representation in out-of-home care (Australian Institute of Family Studies 2016) or lack of access to assisted reproductive technologies (Frohmader 2009). Most of this research has focused on supporting the right of people with disabilities to conceive children or to retain custody of children often presumed to be their biological children. Where research has considered the ability of people with disabilities to become parents by other means, it has mostly considered assisted reproductive technologies like in vitro fertilisation (IVF). For example, a recent consideration of parenting laws in a report by the Victorian Law Reform Commission (VLRC 2007) identified disability as a significant barrier to IVF. In contrast, its consideration of adoption was far shorter and identified same-sex attraction as the only hurdle to adoption.

Limited research does exist on the discrimination faced by people with disabilities who attempt to become parents through adoption (Wates 2002; National Council on Disability 2012; Fleming 2015). Yet, often this research stops short of critiquing the legal systems that govern adoption, instead focusing on the prejudices of adoption workers and relinquishing parents (i.e., the biological parents of the adopted child). More importantly, no research has considered adoption as a right protected by the Convention on the Rights of Persons with Disabilities (CRPD)[1]. While art 23 of the CRPD explicitly guarantees the right of people with disabilities to adopt, the question of whether or not CRPD signatory states have actually implemented their art 23 obligations through domestic legislation has so far evaded scrutiny. Now that the CRPD has been in force for over nine years, there is a need for such analysis.

This article seeks to fill this gap in research by conducting an interpretive legal analysis of the adoption regime of one CRPD signatory state, and critiquing that regime against art 23 of the CRPD. Using the adoption regime of the Australian state of Victoria by way of case study, this article will argue that people with disabilities are systematically prevented from becoming parents by the legal systems that govern adoption, in breach of their human rights under the CRPD.

In terms of structure, Part II contextualizes this article by outlining the strong political, social and theoretical connections between adoption and other threads of disability advocacy. Part III discusses this article's methodology, namely how it uses the state of Victoria as a case study to explore how the adoption rights are governed through written law. Part IV discusses the theories of disability relevant to this essay, namely the medical model, the social model and Shelley Tremain's deconstructionist critique of the social model. Part V introduces art 23 of the CRPD which protects people with disabilities' right to adopt. Part VI provides a break-down of the legal structure through which adoption occurs in the state of Victoria. Part VII analyses Victoria's adoption regime against the requirements of the CRPD, which it interprets primarily through the lens of the social model. Part VIII provides recommendations for the Victorian Parliament, the Committee on the Rights of Persons with Disabilities and disability advocates and allies to pursue change to Victoria's adoption regime and more broadly. Part IX discusses the related but tangential issue of 'passing', and how the distinction between hidden and visible impairments can further affect the impact of an adoption system on the disability community.

While this article may sometimes refer to three broad classes of disability—physical, intellectual and mental health—it makes every effort not to conflate all people with disabilities during the course of analysis, and not to extrapolate broad stroke solutions that do not reflect this diversity within the disability community.

2. Snapshot of Adoption in Australia

Adoption is the legal process by which a couple (the 'adoptive parents') become the legal parents of a child under the age of 18, replacing the child's birth or biological parents (which the Victorian legislation refers to as 'relinquishing parents'). Legally speaking, an adoption order extinguishes all rights of the relinquishing parents in relation to the child (unless it specifically mentions such rights), and entitles the adopted child to all the rights of a biological child in their new adoptive family.

This said, there are different types of adoption (and other forms of caregiving), many of which fall outside the scope of this essay. This Part will limit this article's scope of enquiry to local adoptions.

2.1. Local Adoption in Perspective

At the highest level, it is important to distinguish adoption from other ways that non-biological parents may care for children, namely out-of-home care (OOHC). OOHC is a state-based statutory system which includes relative care (where a child is cared for by a relative), foster care (where a child is cared for by an unrelated carer) and residential care (where a child is cared for in a communal

1 Convention of the Rights of Persons with Disabilities, opened for signature 13 December 2006, 2515 UNTS 3 (entered into force 3 May 2008).

residential building). From the outset, it must be stated that the number of adoptions is minuscule compared to the number of children in out-of-home care. In the Australian Institute of Health and Welfare's (AIHW) latest reporting period, there were only 278 adoptions in Australia (Australian Institute of Health and Welfare 2016). This compares to 11,581 Australian children admitted to OOHC in 2014–2015 (Australian Institute of Family Studies 2016).

OOHC can be informal or formal. Informal OOHC is where a biological parent consents to their child going into the OOHC system, whereas formal OOHC occurs as a result of the state forcibly removing a child through a care and protection court order. It is important to establish that biological parents with disabilities, as well as children with disabilities, are both over-represented in the OOHC system (Senate Community Affairs References Committee 2015). While this issue lies outside the scope of the article, future research should focus on this phenomenon, as the rights of such parents clearly also come within the scope of art 23 of the CRPD.

Of the 278 adoptions which occurred in Australia in 2015–2016, there are different types of adoption. This article only deals with Australian child adoption, as distinct from intercountry adoption. Local adoptions accounted for 196 (or 71%) of the adoptions in the last reporting period, compared to 82 intercountry adoptions (29%) (Australian Institute of Health and Welfare 2016). While many of the same processes and issues discussed in this article remain relevant to intercountry adoption, intercountry adoption involves less clear-cut Australian regulation, is highly dependent on the Hague Convention and the legal regimes of foreign jurisdictions and involves other complex issues (such as the consent of birth parents) that can obscure the operation of disability human rights.

Of these adoptions, some are considered 'local adoptions' while others are considered 'known child adoptions'. Local adoptions are where the adopted child has had no previous contact or relationship with the adoptive parents. In contrast, known child adoptions are where such contact has occurred (e.g., where a child adopted by a step-parent or relative). In the latest reporting period, there were 45 local adoptions (23%) versus 151 known child adoptions (77%) in Australia. As the successful adoptive parents in known child adoptions are chosen by virtue of their pre-existing relationship with a child (erasing the need to assess whether they would be good parents), known child adoptions obviously lie outside the scope of this article.

Importantly, the AIHW (Australian Institute of Health and Welfare 2016) report confirms that consent of relinquishing parents is obtained 100% of the time in the case of 'local adoptions'. The presence of consent in cases of local adoption is important for this article, as the input of the relinquishing parent is a factor later discussed. This said, it is important to acknowledge the oftentimes problematic circumstances in which parents 'consent' to the removal of a child, such as duress and economic hardship (Anthony and Rijswijk 2012).

Notably, the statistics relevant to the consent of the relinquishing parents in the case of 'known child adoptions' are omitted from the AIHW report (Australian Institute of Health and Welfare 2016). As parents with disabilities are already known to disproportionately lose their children to state caregivers, the experiences of relinquishing parents in known child adoptions is an important area for other research to consider.

2.2. Demographics of Local Adoption

There are very few publicly available statistics to do with the relinquishing and adoptive parents involved in local adoptions. In their latest article, the AIHW reports only on age and marriage status of relinquishing parents. The median age of relinquishing mothers was 26 (5 years below median age of all Australian mothers), with range of 14–42, and that 93% were unmarried. As for adoptive parents, almost all (96%) were married and 94% were aged 30 or more.

These statistics perhaps create the illusion of a harmonious system where willing birth parents give up children to loving adoptive parents, and obscure the operation of complex societal factors such as race, class and Indigenous status. In its report on the OOHC system, the Senate Community Affairs References Committee (2015) shed light on some of the factors which can prevent biological parents from caring for their children such as family violence, drug and alcohol misuse, poverty and homelessness and lack of family support services. They also pointed to Indigenous Australians and people with disabilities as two groups disproportionately at risk of losing children to a formal child care court order. It would be logical to assume that these same factors play some kind of role in the decision-making of relinquishing parents involved in adoption as well.

Having now established the specific field of enquiry, this article will discuss the context for choosing this field of enquiry, and the important interplay between this field of enquiry and other threads of disability research and advocacy.

3. Context and Critical Connections

Given the relative rarity of adoption, let alone local adoption, the question arises: why focus on adoption? First, the rarity of adoption does not diminish the claim of people with disabilities to this right. An important reason for the choice of this article's topic is, of course, that people with disabilities desire to become parents, including via adoption (Shakespeare et al. 1996; Frohmader 2009).

Second, no country's adoption regime exists in a vacuum. Adoption law is just one aspect of how a country governs how and when its citizens are allowed to parent. In the Australian context, state governance of family formation has a long and sad history which includes the forcible removal of children not only from people with disabilities, but also from Indigenous Australians (known as the Stolen Generations) (Attwood 2001) and more recently, from migrants (Horin 2010). In the context of disability advocacy, adoption law is merely one instance in a well-documented history of the Australian government interfering in the family formation of people with disabilities, from the forcible removal of children to restricted access to alternative parenting procedures like IVF (Frohmader 2009; Arstein-Kerslake 2015). Underpinning and entwining these different restrictions on the parenting rights of people with disabilities is the same unwritten notion that the parenting abilities of people with disabilities are different and lesser, and therefore that it is the state's role to control the reproductive and caring rights of people with disabilities.

Given this interconnectedness between adoption and all the other ways that the state denies people with disabilities the right to parent, writing about—and fighting for—greater adoption rights for people with disabilities has other important legal, political and social consequences for people with disabilities. As adoption is one part of an integrated legal system overseen by a central government, reforming this one part of the system will help spur change in other parts of the system. Often (but not always), these consequences will be positive, in that fighting for greater rights via adoption often reinforces the same arguments that will help people with disabilities achieve advances in other parenting rights. For example, the argument developed in this article that people with disabilities have an equal parenting ability to people without disabilities when societal barriers are removed, could equally be used to argue for greater rights for people with disabilities in relation to IVF, or to argue that people with disabilities should not be sterilised.

Third, on top of developing the topic of disability parenting generally, this article argues that adoption law is a particularly important signpost for how the government—and society more broadly—views the parenting ability of people with disabilities. Adoption differs from other issues to do with the parenting rights of people with disabilities such as child removal, sterilization and IVF in that it is not about restricting the ability of people with disabilities to have or care for their own children. On the contrary, it is about selecting—often from extremely large pools of prospective adoption applicants—the 'ideal' family for a given adoptive children. It therefore has to do with how the government views the idea of family, and how people with disabilities fit into that conception. Accepting that law has the ability to shape societal views (Gelber and McNamara 2015), Victorian adoption law thus has important connections to how our society views the parenting capabilities of people with disabilities.

Having stated these reasons, it is also important to acknowledge that fighting for greater adoption rights does not always align exactly, theoretically speaking, with the other rights movements emanating from within the disability community. An important example of this are the significant issues to do with the forcible removal of children from parents with disability and the over-representation of children with disabilities in state care (Llewellyn et al. 2003; Booth et al. 2005; IASSID 2008). In the context of that debate, strong emphasis is often put on the inalienable and irrevocable rights of the biological parent(s) (Senate Community Affairs References Committee 2015). The issue of adoption by a parent or parents with a disability, by contrast, tends to set up a dichotomy between the rights of the biological or relinquishing parents, and those of the adoptive parents (with a disability).

As is the case with all minorities, not all rights movements emanating from within the one community will always align exactly. Yet, it is important not to eschew progress that has been made in other related fields, nor to close off the opportunity of future progress in those fields. In this instance, where an argument can be used to justify greater rights of adoptive parents can also be used bolster the state's ability to remove children from people with disabilities, then that argument is not preferable because it gives people with disabilities not real net gain in terms of rights. Therefore, this article sees these two issues as inextricably connected and seeks to temper all its arguments—and suggested solutions—so as not to reinforce the phenomenon of child removal from people with disabilities.

Furthermore, it is still possible to advocate for greater adoption rights for people with disabilities without supporting the notion that the state can take children away from people with disabilities. An important distinction to draw between local adoption and the forced removal of children from parents with disabilities is that only in the former situation have the parents consented to the removal of their child. Already, this provides a basis on which the views of the relinquishing parents in local adoptions can be attributed given different weight to the views of relinquishing parents in situations where the state is forcibly removing children.

Therefore, adoption law is an important field of enquiry both in and of itself, as well as because of its important connections to theoretical and political constructions of family. While fighting for greater rights for adoptive parents could, at a surface level, be seen to erode the rights of people with disabilities seeking to maintain custody of their children, it is this article's argument that progress in one sphere is not mutually exclusive with progress in the other. Through nuanced conversation, disability advocates from all theoretical perspectives can bring their causes forward at the same time. This article endeavours to play a part in that conversation.

4. Methodology

This article is concerned with words. More specifically, it is concerned with the capacity of words in legal instruments—from official Acts of Parliament to the regulations and manuals created by bureaucrats—to oppress and to liberate. This article does not only concern itself with the beliefs and prejudices of those who oversee the adoption process; it also seeks to illuminate how the behavior of those decision-makers is often predetermined by the laws, regulations and manuals that they are legally obliged to follow. In this way, this article posits that, despite the common notion of law serving an anti-discrimination function, discrimination can also be insidiously embedded in legal systems (Hellman and Moreau 2013).

It is, however, impossible to speak about the impact of words in the abstract. In order to elucidate how discrimination emanates from the legal instruments that govern adoption, this article has chosen a concrete case study: the adoption regime of the Australian state of Victoria. Methodologically speaking, this article is an interpretative analysis of legal instruments: namely, the CRPD and the myriad legislative instruments that govern adoption in Victoria.

While it may appear that an analysis of Victorian law is of limited import when it comes to addressing the discrimination faced by people with disabilities worldwide, it should be noted that Victoria's adoption regime possesses many of the characteristics typical of adoption regimes around the world: statutorily enshrined health requirements; court orders that a person is a suitable candidate for adoption; and wide-ranging discretion conferred to adoption workers and relinquishing parents.

For example, one problem intrinsic to Victorian law is that in order adopt, a person with a disability will be assessed against legislative criteria such as 'health' and 'financial circumstances' to determine whether they are a 'fit and proper person' to adopt. These very same criteria are present in the equivalent New South Wales[2], Queensland[3] and Western Australian legislation (Department for Child Protection and Family Support 2016). Beyond Australia, Adoption Panels in the UK also assess a person's 'suitability to parent' by considering both health and financial circumstances (Department for Education 2014). The same is true in many states of the United States (Fleming 2015). Hence, the plain words of adoption legislation around the world is often very similar, and even when the words change, the ideas and structures within that legislation that give rise to discrimination against people with disabilities often remain the same.

Other problems discussed in this article—such as the prejudice held by adoption workers and relinquishing parents, or how adoption agencies fail to provide services or information specific to people with disabilities—have nothing to do with the specific words of Victorian legislation, and everything to do with discriminatory attitudes and prejudice against people with disabilities. Such attitudes are well proven to exist far beyond the state of Victoria and therefore such analysis remains relevant to any CRPD signatory state (Sutherland 1981).

Equally, the solutions offered in this article can also have application beyond Victoria. While this article offers the specific wording that the Victorian Parliament should adopt in amending the Adoption Act 1984 (Vic)[4], lawyers and disability advocates could read these suggested changes for their purposive effect, and then advocate for amendments to their own laws that would achieve the same outcome. The legislative amendments suggested by this article seek to bring Victoria's adoption laws in line with Australia's obligations under the CRPD, and therefore they remain relevant to any country that is a signatory to the CRPD who is therefore bound by the same obligations as Australia.

Therefore, this article concerns itself with discrimination through written law. While many of the examples used will come from Victorian legislation, this article is hoping to engage in a larger conversation around how adoption is currently governed, and how existing adoption regimes can be changed to adhere to the CRPD.

5. Theoretical Underpinnings

Disability literature provides several theoretical models through which this article will argue its thesis. As in all bodies of scholarship, there exists a variety of voices and not all those voices are always perfectly reconcilable. In this section, this article will present the main schools of thought to which it refers or relies, while pointing out the various unresolved tensions which exist.

5.1. The Medical Model

The earliest, and sadly the most prevalent, model of disability is the medical model. While the medical model of disability is no longer orthodoxy in academic circles or for disability advocates, it nonetheless continues to pervade societal thinking about people with disabilities (Frohmader 2009).

In essence, the medical model tells us that disability is determined by reference to, and is a result of, a person's 'biological deficit' or impairment (Shakespeare 2013). Inherent in the medical model paradigm is a norm of able-bodiedness from which people with disabilities deviate. Under the medical model, people with disabilities are yoked to their impairment in a way that makes them inherently less functional than a person without a disability (Sutherland 1981; Shakespeare 2002). Under this model, any difficulties that a person with a disability faces flow causally from their impairment. A person with a disability is perceived and studied as a 'personal tragedy' (Barnes and Mercer 1997), and the

---

2 Adoption Regulation 2015 (NSW) reg 45.
3 Adoption Act 2009 (Qld) ss 122 and 124
4 Adoption Act 1984.

corresponding role of research and treatment is to reduce, obscure or otherwise 'cure' the disability or its impact (Hunt 1966; Kayess and French 2008).

Applied in the context of parenthood, the medical model tells us that people with disabilities will be less capable parents on account of their impairment. This is because implicit in the medical model conception of parenthood is the idea that there is a normal way to parent a child (Frohmader 2009; Radcliffe 2008). By virtue of their impairment, people with disabilities are viewed as 'naturally unsuited' to the 'nurturant reproductive' role of parenthood (Frohmader 2009; Collins 1999). The medical model thus offers a zero sum and static conception of parenting: it is not enough that a person with a disability could fulfill the same function in a different way; or moreover, that they would simply provide a different but equally valid version of parenting altogether.

The medical model emerged from the Enlightenment period and dominated academic discourse about people with disabilities until three decades ago (Shakespeare 2002, 2013). At its height, the medical model dominated all discourse—medical, academic, political and mainstream—about disability. For example, in 1980, the World Health Organisation (WHO) essentially enshrined a medical model conception of disability in its International Classification of Impairments, Disabilities and Handicaps by defining disability as 'any restriction or lack (resulting from an impairment) of ability to perform an activity in the manner or within the range considered normal for a human being'. Worse still, the medical model was harnessed to justify numerous eugenic policies and laws: under the medical model, people with disabilities possessed defective genetic material, and by sterilizing, segregating or otherwise preventing people with disabilities from having children, you could ostensibly remove this genetic material from society (Arstein-Kerslake 2015).

While such eugenic policies thankfully became less common (though by no means absent), the medical model continued to shape academic perceptions of people with disabilities' fitness to parent even into the 1990s. For example, a spate of flawed psychological research from the 1980s and 1990s found that 'disability severely limits parenting ability and often leads to maladjustment in children' (Kirshbaum and Olkin 2002; Crawford 2003). Only in the 2000s was it uncovered that these findings, while presented as fact deduced from scientific experimentation and sociological research, were actually pathological assumptions based on the authors' own prejudices (Kirshbaum and Olkin 2002; Crawford 2003).

And while the medical model is now much more taboo in most academic circles, it is still insidiously prevalent in wider society. As recently as last year, the Office of the Public Advocate strongly castigated the widely held but 'mistaken belief that a diagnosis of disability, particularly cognitive disability or mental disorder, constitutes a static and irremediable barrier to effective parenting' (Carter 2016). One reason for the medical model's continued predominance in the social consciousness is that 'the voices and experience of women with disabilities are almost non-existent in the literature on reproduction and parenting' (Frohmader 2009). A second reason is that matters of family are seen to be distinctively private, and so are resistant to lobbying and advocacy efforts (Frohmader 2009). A third reason is that where parents with disabilities ask for help, this is used against them as 'proof' that they are inadequate parents, creating an environment in which people with disabilities are pressured to parent behind closed doors (Grue and Laerum 2002; Frohmader 2009).

When it comes to adoption legislation, the medical model is directly relevant in three ways to the parenting rights people with disabilities enjoy. First, Victoria's—and other countries'—adoption regimes were written and passed by Parliament long before the medical model became so taboo; therefore, in many instances, the old words of the legislation still mirror medical model ideas. Second, adoption regimes from around the world, including Victoria's, almost always involve the unfettered decision-making of caseworkers and relinquishing parents. As the medical model continues to pervade societal thinking about people with disabilities, many decision-makers will logically hold medical model views (Frohmader 2009). Third, it is important to remember that even successful adoptive parents will likely face stigma based on medical model thinking even if they are successful in adopting a child: 'community attitudes rather than their physical limitations caused the major problems for mothers with disabilities' (Westbrook and Chinnery 1995; Frohmader 2009). While this article focuses on change needed to allow people with disabilities to adopt in the first place, future research must explore how to support successful adoptive parents with disabilities to overcome that stigma.

5.2. The Social Model

The social model was the first paradigm shift to occur in thinking about disability since the medical model came to dominate medical and societal discourse. Specifically, the social model refers to the structural analysis of people with disabilities' exclusion that emerged from Britain in the 1970s (Malacredia 2009). Its central thesis is perhaps best expressed by the following statement from the Union of Physically Impaired Against Segregation (UPIAS) (1974), an advocacy network instrumental in the development and propagation of the social model:

> [I]t is society that disables physically impaired people. Disability is something imposed on top of our impairments, by the way we are unnecessarily isolated and excluded from full participation in society.

The social model is a structural model because it explains disability in relation to, and as a direct result of, 'contemporary social organisation' (UPIAS 1974). Under the social model, disability is a 'social creation' (Shakespeare 2013) resulting from the 'lack of fit between a body and its social environment' (Goering 2015). Essentially, disability is reimagined as a form of social oppression (Oliver 1996; Finkelstein 1980; Abberley 1987), analogous to the exclusion of other minority groups (Hahn 1988). Further, the social model reverses the causal chain suggested by the medical model: it is not people's impairments themselves but rather socially constructed barriers that cause disability (Barnes and Mercer 1996).

At the heart of the social model is a distinction between impairment and disability (Shakespeare 2013). Under the medical model, the concept of impairment is yoked to the concept of disability by virtue of the fact that disability is defined as the possession of an impairment (Sutherland 1981; Shakespeare 2002). In contrast, the social model severs these two terms: while the former is a 'private reality', the latter is a societal construct (Goering 2015). This idea is encapsulated in UPIAS' (1974) definition of disability as '[t]he disadvantage or restriction of activity caused by a contemporary social organisation which takes little or no account of people who have physical impairments'.

Applied in the context of parenting, the social model tells us that if people with disabilities face difficulties when parenting, it is only because of the way society is structured to make raising a child easiest for those without a disability (Frohmader 2009). Thomas and Curtis (1997) posit that these barriers infiltrate many layers of society: they are 'attitudinal, institutional and environmental'. Further, Frohmader (2009) explains that these barriers pervade every stage of parenthood, at least for women: 'when they think about having a child, become pregnant, come into contact with maternity and related services and when they become parents'.

Perhaps the best evidence of socially constructed barriers to parenting is the testimony of parents with disabilities who describe the creative and ingenious measures they take to overcome such barriers. For example, the Facebook group Wheelie Good Moms (2016) features mothers who are also wheelchair users. On the group's page, they share the ways they amend their daily routine to overcome barriers to parenting, such as modifications to change tables, cots and strollers so as to be wheelchair-friendly. Such modifications throw into harsh relief the minutiae of everyday life—down to the height of change tables—that stand to make parenting difficult for people with disabilities.

The social model is relevant to this article mainly because of its explicit endorsement in the CRPD, the legal instrument that guarantees the right of people with disabilities to adopt. As this article will discuss in Part III, the CRPD explicitly endorses the social model as the appropriate paradigm through which to interpret the legal obligations of signatories (see the preamble and art 1).

More broadly, it is also a normative benchmark for how adoption law and practice should operate in general. Within disability scholarship, it has significant 'currency' (Goodley 2011). Normatively speaking, Shakespeare (2013) argues that the social model is a better way of thinking about people with disabilities for three reasons: first, it is helpful instrumentally in allowing researchers to identify the barriers facing people with disabilities; second, it is effective politically because it is 'is easily explained and understood'; third, it is helpful psychologically because it places the onus for creating change on society, not the individual.

5.3. *Beyond the Social Model*

While for a significant time, the social model of disability was considered 'orthodoxy' in the disability community (Barnes 2003; Shakespeare 2013), this is no longer the case. Initial critiques focused on the separation between the theoretical social model and the daily bodily experiences of impairment felt by many people with disabilities (Shakespeare 2013). This critique was particularly pertinent in the context of parenting: Chapman et al. (2015) found that some parents 'placed illness and impairment at the very centre of their parenting'. They gave such examples as 'a parent feels sad at not being able to pick their child up to comfort them when they have hurt themselves, or to carry a child upstairs to put them in bed when they are asleep'. Despite these critiques, the social model still remained 'orthodoxy' from a theoretical perspective, at least in the early years after the turn of the millennium.

More recently, however, disability scholarship has questioned the social model, also from a theoretical perspective. One of the most well-known critiques is that offered by Shelley Tremain (the *deconstructionist* critique). At the heart of Tremain's critique is a deconstruction of the impairment/disability dichotomy set up by the social model of disability (Goodley 2011). As discussed, the social model of disability concedes that impairments are 'essential, biological characteristics of a 'real' body upon which recognizably disabling conditions are imposed' (Tremain 2002). Tremain (2002) deconstructs the impairment/disability dichotomy which underpins the social model of disability, by arguing that the concept of impairment is as constructed and illusionary as the concept of disability which it allegedly underlies. This is because impairments only exist in comparison of 'rather culturally specific regulatory norms and ideals about human function and structure, competence, intelligence, and ability'. While the social model posits that culture acts on impairments to create disability, Tremain argues that cultures creates both disability and impairments: 'impairment has been disability all along'.

In turn, and applying Michel Foucault's concept of *biopower*, she argues that conceptualising impairments as intrinsic biological attributes helps sustain oppressive power structures. She argues that the social model of disability is actually damaging for people with disabilities because it 'legitimise[s] the disciplinary regime that generated it in the first place'. It does this by perpetuating the myth of a healthy or normal body, in contrast to which people with disabilities remain categorized as *other* and therefore receive differentiated, and lesser, treatment. Goodley (2011), summarising Tremain's work, posits that 'Tremain has made the case that this conception of impairment as a naturalized phenomenon endangers the potentially critical work of disability studies'.

Tremain's critique has important consequences for adoption law. As it is a predominantly discursive theory, these consequences often have to do with language. For example, the social model might celebrate explicit legislative protections for adoptive parents with impairments, whereas Tremain's theory suggests that such affirmative protections still relegate people with disabilities to a category of *otherness* and therefore jeopardise their integration in society.

5.4. *Which Model Then?*

It is hardly surprising that not all disability writers agree on the theoretical basis of disability advocacy. Even outside of the approaches listed in this article, disability writers in different parts of the world each have their own way of articulating disability theory (e.g., the cultural model in the US and Canada and the relational model in Nordic countries) (Goodley 2011). In addition, critiques of old models such as Tremain's, as well as new models such as the human rights model (Blanck et al.), continue to emerge.

Yet, it has long been a guiding and fundamental principal of disability research that writing remain grounded in emancipation and prioritise progress over theoretical squabbles (Barnes 2003). To this end, this article posits that no one approach need be understood as the sole or guiding theoretical basis of change to adoption regimes. A better approach is perhaps one which finds the synchronicities between them and draws on their respective strengths. The social model and Tremain's critique are not mutually exclusive in all respects. Both models seek to illuminate the social barriers currently facing people with disabilities, and place the onus squarely on governments and other power structures (as opposed to people with disabilities themselves) to bring about the required change.

This said, one important difference between the social model and Tremain's critique is that only the former is explicitly referred to in the CRPD as the lens through which each article is to be read. As such, the social model of disability is legally binding on signatories: it is incumbent on signatory states to adopt the social model as a purposive approach when implementing their treaty obligations. For this reason, this article will rely most heavily on the social model in interpreting the articles of the CRPD. In doing so, this article acknowledges that arguments underpinned by the social model hold the most weight, legally speaking, and may therefore provide the quickest and most sure route to emancipation for people with disabilities. Nevertheless, this article will, where possible, also draw on Tremain's and other critiques and theories to develop a notion of best practice with regard to adoption regulation.

6. The Human Right to Adopt

As a benchmark against which to measure the Victorian adoption framework, this article refers to art 23 of the CRPD.

6.1. The Convention

Before the implementation of the CRPD in 2006, there were very few protections for people with disabilities to be found in international instruments. Despite a plethora of instruments explicitly naming other minority groups and granting them affirmative protections, such affirmative protections were virtually inexistent for people with disabilities[5] (art 25 of the Universal Declaration of Human Rights (1948) was an exception to this, yet even then it only guaranteed an 'adequate' standard of living for people with a 'disability'). While broad-brush instruments like the Universal Declaration of Human Rights and the International Covenant on Civil and Political Rights purported to prevent discrimination against any person (including people with disabilities)[6], these generic instruments ultimately failed to generate the kind of protections that people with disabilities were asking for and desperately needed (Freeman et al. 2015; Kayess and French 2008).

The CRPD was the first binding international human rights instrument to explicitly address disability. It goes beyond a mere anti-discrimination treaty: it creates new state obligations—both positive and negative—which were absent from any prior treaty. Further, the CRPD is binding on all signatories (as at the time of writing, there are 160, including Australia) and includes an international monitoring mechanism: the Committee on the Rights of Persons with Disabilities (the Committee) (Freeman et al. 2015). The CRPD represented the first real pan-national attempt to protect the rights of people with disabilities, and explicitly enshrined the social model of disability in its interpretive principles (see Part B) (Goodley 2011; Kayess and French 2008).

---

5 Art 25 of the Universal Declaration of Human Rights. GA Res 217A (III), UN GAOR, 3rd Sess, 183rd Plen Mtg, UN Doc A/810 (entered into force 10 December 1948).

6 International Covenant on Civil and Political Rights. Opened for signature 16 December 1966, 999 UNTS 171 (entered into force 23 March 1976).

The CRPD's legitimacy as a benchmark flows not just from its passage as a United Nations General Resolution, but also from the method of its construction and implementation. It entailed unprecedented 'centrality of persons with disability and their respective organisations in the CRPD negotiation process' (Kayess and French 2008). For example, disability rights non-governmental organisations (NGOs) were active members of the Ad Hoc Committee charged with drafting the CRPD (Kayess and French 2008). Further, people with disabilities continue to be involved in the implementation and monitoring of the CRPD, with a majority of the eighteen Committee members identifying as people with disabilities (Office of the High Commissioner on Human Rights 2016).

6.2. Article 23

Article 23 of the CRPD is titled 'Respect for Home and Family'. It purports to deal with 'all matters relating to marriage, family, parenthood and relationships', and speaks to many issues pertinent to parents or prospective parents with disabilities, from consenting to marriage to retention of fertility.

This article is concerned with art 23(2) which provides:

> States Parties shall ensure the rights and responsibilities of persons with disabilities, with regard to guardianship, wardship, trusteeship and adoption of children or similar institutions'; in all cases the best interests of the child shall be paramount. States Parties shall render appropriate assistance of persons with disabilities in the performance of their child-rearing responsibilities (emphasis added).

6.3. Interpretation of Article 23(2)

6.3.1. Words

By its plain words, art 23(2) gives a two-tier protection for people with disabilities with regard to adoption.

First, it purports to guarantee the 'rights and responsibilities' of persons with disabilities 'with regard to ... adoption of children or similar institutions'. This frames adoption as an inalienable right, and puts (at least) a negative obligation on states not to take that right away from people with disabilities. This section applies the general prohibitions against discrimination in arts 4 and 5 of the CRPD in the context of adoption.

Second, art 23(2) puts an obligation on signatory states to render 'appropriate assistance to persons with disabilities in the performance of child-rearing responsibilities'. This goes further than the obligation to guarantee their rights: it puts a positive obligation on Parties to assist people with disabilities to exercise their rights as parents. While the plain words of that section leave it open whether the obligation to provide 'appropriate assistance' extends to helping people with disabilities become adoptive parents in the first place, previous Committee jurisprudence and the purpose of the document strongly suggest that it does.[7]

6.3.2. Purpose

Paragraph (e) of the CRPD Preamble makes it clear that the CRPD and its articles are to be understood by reference to the social model:

> [Signatories are] [r]ecognizing that disability is an evolving concept and that disability results from the interaction between persons with impairments and attitudinal and environmental barriers that hinders their full and effective participation in society on an equal basis with others.

---

[7] UNCRPD (United Nations Committee on the Rights of Persons with Disability). Draft General Comment on Article 6: Women with Disabilities. CRPD/C/14/R.1. 2015.

While certain commentators point out that the CRPD perpetuates the medical model by using the term 'persons with disabilities' (Kayess and French 2008), jurisprudence from the Committee has reiterated the need for a purposive approach to interpretation of the CRPD in line with the social model (Kayess and French 2008).

Interpreting art 23 through the lens of the social model supports the idea that it carries both negative and positive obligations. Where difficulties carrying out parenting responsibilities are caused by societal barriers, it is logical that the state would need to provide 'additional assistance' to people with disabilities to help them overcome societal barriers to parenthood, including assistance to access the right to adopt.

In addition, art 3 lists the 'general principles' which are to guide the interpretation of all articles of the CRPD and include 'non-discrimination', 'full and effective participation and inclusion in society' and 'equality of opportunity'. These equally support the idea that the CRPD and art 23 puts a positive obligation on the state to provide additional assistance to people with disabilities to allow them to achieve the state of full integration suggested by these principles.

6.3.3. Other Articles

Of course, no article of the CRPD is designed to be stand-alone. Other articles also elaborate on what meaning should be given to art 23. Specifically, art 2 of the CRPD defines 'discrimination on the basis of disability' as follows:

> "Discrimination on the basis of disability" means any distinction, exclusion or restriction on the basis of disability which has the purpose or effect of impairing or nullifying the recognition, enjoyment or exercise, on an equal basis with others, of all human rights and fundamental freedoms in the political, economic, social, cultural, civil or any other field. It includes all forms of discrimination . . .

Importantly, this definition captures and prohibits both direct and indirect discrimination. The difference between them is as follows (Doyle 2007):

- Direct discrimination occurs where the legislative framework explicitly treats someone unfavorably because they are a person with a disability;
- Indirect discrimination occurs where the legislative framework does not mention disability but has the practical effect of disadvantaging people with disabilities.

In relation to art 23, this means both direct and indirect discrimination constitute a failure to ensure the 'rights and responsibilities' of people with disabilities with regard to adoption. That is, it is immaterial whether the rights of people with disabilities are curtailed explicitly or implicitly, because the obligation to uphold the right of people with disabilities to adopt remains unmet.

6.3.4. Best Interests of the Child

It is important to note the two-prong protection offered to people with disabilities is tempered by the assertion in art 23 that in all cases 'the best interests of the child shall be paramount'. These words come from the United Nations Convention on the Rights of the Child[8], and are equally present in the Victorian adoption legislation. Disability literature has shown how the words 'best interests' (whether used in relation to children or people with disabilities themselves) is a societal construct used by decision-makers to curtail the rights of people with disabilities (Arstein-Kerslake 2015). As such, these words seriously jeopardise the effectiveness of art 23 (and the related Victorian adoption legislation) in practice and their inclusion in art 23 is problematic.

---

[8] Convention on the Rights of the Child, opened for signature 20 November 1989, 1577 UNTS **3** (entered into force 2 September 1990).

'Best interests' is a term peppered throughout nearly all adoption legislation (be it international, national or state). While it is beyond the scope of this article to historicise the concept of 'best interests', it is sufficient to say that the term has been strongly criticized by disability and other writers for obscuring the interests and rights of parents with disabilities. Even more problematically, questions remain as to what term, if any, could fill its place and whether such a term could avoid creating the same problems (Steele 2016).

This said, a strict social model interpretation resolves some, if not all, of the tension created by the words 'best interests of the child'. That is, where the state provides adequate resources to people with disabilities to overcome the hurdles to parenting they face, their parenting will match that of any person without a disability and logically, the best interests of the child are not threatened (Frohmader 2009).

6.3.5. Committee Jurisprudence

In its State Reports, Concluding Observations and General Comments, the Committee provides concrete guidance on how the articles of the CRPD are to be read. Regrettably, there is little Committee jurisprudence that pertains to article 23; and in the instances the Committee has spoken to art 23, it has never specifically mentioned adoption.

Nevertheless, other Committee jurisprudence can still inform how art 23 is to be interpreted. For example, in its Draft General Comment on Women with Disabilities released May 2015, the Committee identified that in order to protect the rights of women under art 6 ('Women with disabilities'), 'it is necessary to ensure universal accessibility [and] design [of] product, objects, instruments and devices' related to motherhood.[9] The Comment gives the examples of 'babies' bottles with handles, prams designed to be clipped on to wheelchairs or pushed with one hand, wheelchair-accessible nappy changers'.[1] The Committee's long list of universally accessible parenting tools exemplifies the wide scope of services likely captured by the words 'additional support' under art 23. This could extend beyond assistive technology to include financial support and free or affordable healthcare.

The Committee went on to say that, for the purposes of art 12 ('Equal recognition before the law'), ' ... effective measures must be adopted to provide women with disabilities access to the support they may require in exercising their legal capacity'.[11] Significantly, the Committee required 'effective measures' despite art 12 making no direct reference to such measures or additional assistance. This strongly suggests that the reference to 'additional assistance' in art 23 extends to effective measures to help people with disabilities access the right to adopt in the first place (not just assistance once they have adopted). The Committee is clearly of the view that the rights enshrined in the CRPD are not worth stating unless they carry a positive obligation on signatories to help people with disabilities enjoy those rights, whether or not language alluding to such a positive obligation is present.

The CRPD is thus a complex and powerful instrument. While this article focuses on art 23, it draws on the whole text and history of the CRPD, as well as Committee jurisprudence, to extrapolate the obligations imposed on signatory states to do with adoption by people with disabilities.

7. The Victorian Adoption Framework

There are many different types of adoption and the adoption process is jurisdiction-specific, even between Australian states. This section will distinguish local adoption from other types of adoption, before describing how local adoption occurs in Victoria.

---

9 UNCRPD (United Nations Committee on the Rights of Persons with Disability) Draft General Comment on Article 6: Women with Disabilities. CRPD/C/14/R.1. 2015.

1 Convention of the Rights of Persons with Disabilities, opened for signature 13 December 2006, 2515 UNTS 3 (entered into force 3 May 2008).

11 UNCRPD (United Nations Committee on the Rights of Persons with Disability) Draft General Comment on Article 6: Women with Disabilities. CRPD/C/14/R.1. 2015.

7.1. The Instruments

In Australia, local adoption legislation is the responsibility of state rather than federal parliament (VLRC 2007). Nevertheless, Victoria's adoption framework is shaped by international, national and local instruments.

At an international level, Australia is a signatory to the United Nations Convention on the Rights of the Child. The treaty requires that the best interests of the child are the paramount consideration. This is enshrined directly in the Adoption Act 1984 (Vic) (the Act).

At the national level, the Commonwealth has endeavoured to standardise national adoption practices via the 1997 National Principles in Adoption (the Principles) (Department of Health and Human Services 1997) as well as the Standards in Adoption 1986 (the Standards) (Department of Health and Human Services 1986). Protocol in Victoria requires caseworkers to make reference to the Principles in assessing couples' suitability for an adoption order.

In Victoria, these international and national obligations are enshrined in the Act and the Regulations[12]. The Department of Health and Human Services (the Department), a branch of Victorian executive government, issues the Adoption and Permanent Care Procedures Manual (the Manual). The Manual interprets the Act and the Regulations, effectively setting out a two-stage process for the selection of adoptive parents.

7.2. The Decision-Makers

The Act vests decision-making power with regard to adoption processes in the County Court, the Secretary of the Department and the principal officer of an approved agency.

The Court's involvement is limited to the start and end of the adoption process: they affirm or dispense with the consent of the relinquishing parents and they make the final adoption order. Given that adoption hearings are only called once a successful couple has been chosen by a caseworker, the most input a judge could feasibly have on the process of selecting adoptive parents is the rejection of a proposed couple.

As a result, all substantive decision-making power with regard to the choice of successful adoptive parents rests with the Secretary of the Department (the Secretary) or the principal officer of an approved agency (essentially providing for adoption to be undertaken by both public and private adoption agencies). In practice, the decision-making power of the Secretary and the principal officer is delegated to adoption caseworkers, who are obliged to follow the Manual in carrying out their work. In referring to 'caseworkers', this article is referring to adoption workers in both the public and private sectors.

7.3. The Approval Stage

There are two stages to the adoption process and disability is considered—both explicitly and implicitly—during both stages. The first is approval for a 'section 13 order' from the Secretary or the principal officer (i.e., a caseworker) that a person is a 'fit and proper person to adopt a child'.

The only substantive requirement for a section 13 order coming from the Act is that an applicant must be married or in a de facto couple for two years (see s 11 of the Act). According to the relevant second reading speech, s 13's purpose is 'for a child to be adopted by persons who are able to provide a secure and lasting family relationship', however the Minister did not elaborate further[13]. In this way, the Act itself is largely silent with regard to the impact of a disability on 'a section 13 order.

As such, it falls to the Regulations to set out the substantive criteria for a section 13 order. The following criteria are relevant in the context of this article:

---

[12] Adoption Regulations 2008.

[13] Hansard (Victorian Legislative Council). 12 April 2000. Parliamentary Debates (H reg Thomson, Minister for Small Business).

> Reg 35(a) The health of the applicants, including emotional, physical and mental health, is suitable; and
>
> Reg 35(d) The applicants' financial circumstances are suitable.

To obtain a section 13 order, prospective couples must put their application in writing, supply evidence and attend information sessions and interviews with their allocated caseworker (Department of Health and Human Services 2001).

7.4. The Linking Stage

A section 13 order is no guarantee of an adoption order: approval for a section 13 order merely grants a couple the right to be considered during the linking stage. Linking refers to the process by which a decision is made to place a particular adoptive child with a couple who has obtained a section 13 order. The decision-making power with regard to linking is once again vested in the Secretary or the principal officer and delegated to caseworkers.

This phase of the selection process is much less transparent than the approval phase. First, the factors used to link a child with an adoptive family are less defined than those that govern the s 13 order. The Manual lists only these factors:

> The age of the respective parties, race, national, cultural and social background, religion, educational capacities, personalities, geographic location, availability of support services, expectations of contact and capacities in regard to any disability (emphasis added).

Second, it is unclear who makes the decision to link a child with an adoptive couple. The plain words of the Act and the Regulations suggest all decision-making power rests with the Secretary or the principal officer (see s 20(1) of the Act and reg 36 of the Regulations), notwithstanding that they are obliged to consider 'any wishes expressed by a parent of the child in relation to the religion, race or ethnic background of the proposed adoptive parents' under s 15(1)(b) of the Act. However, General Principle 23 of the National Principles says that 'birth parents have the right to ... be involved in the planning for the placement of the child'. Such involvement is also expressly provided for by the Manual, which requires that at the time of relinquishing a child, 'birth parents are asked if they wish to be actively involved in selecting an adoptive family'. If they so wish, the Manual provides for a two-step shortlisting process undertaken by the caseworkers and birthparents together (Department of Health and Human Services 2001):

(1) Caseworkers make an initial shortlist of 'two to three' profiles that 'have been assessed as suitable for the child';
(2) The relinquishing parent is then able 'to indicate the couple with whom they would prefer the child to be placed'.

The Manual states that 'it is unlikely that a link would be pursued where a birth parent was opposed to that link' (Department of Health and Human Services 2001). Therefore, in practice, both relinquishing parents and caseworkers hold a degree of decision-making power during the linking stage, against the plain words of the Act and the Regulations.

In Victoria, much like in other countries, adoption thus occurs through a multi-layered, multi-tiered system involving different decision-makers with different levels of power. These stages are dictated and governed by an eclectic mix of state and federal legislation and international instruments. In the next Part, this article will discuss how the decision-making process dictated by these instruments discriminates against people with disabilities and fails to meet the obligations imposed by the CRPD.

8. Analysis

Having established both the obligations of art 23 of the CRPD as well as the way that the Australian state of Victoria regulates local adoption, this article will now directly compare the two to see whether they align. What follows is a stage-by-stage analysis of Victoria's adoption regime, which fails in myriad ways to implement Australia's obligations under the CRPD.

8.1. *Direct Discrimination during the Approval Stage*

The first source of discrimination under Victoria's adoption framework occurs during the approval process for a section 13 ('fit and proper person') order. Under the Regulations, the caseworker is obliged to consider reg 35(a): the 'health of the applicants, including emotional, physical and mental health'. (While beyond the scope of this essay, reg 35(a) has important parallels to the criteria used to justify removal of children from parents with disabilities and their placement in OOHC.)

The Act's inclusion of questions of disability in the medicalised language of 'health' is problematic. This is because it focuses the analysis on the 'health of the applicants' (emphasis added), as opposed to the way society does not cater for their impairment. However, this is not a per se a breach of art 23—it all depends on what is done with the health information that a person discloses. If caseworkers use the health information disclosed by a person with a disability as a way of providing that person more tailored assistance, then reg 35(a) could well be argued to uphold art 23 of the CRPD.

Unfortunately, the Standards and the Manual provide an interpretation of reg 35(a) which offends the CRPD. According to the Standards and the Manual, being of 'physical and emotional health' means being 'able to provide for the needs of the child at least until the child achieves social and emotional independence' (Department of Health and Human Services 2001). In making such a determination, the caseworker is obliged to consider 'any health related issues raised by the applicant and its implications for parenting on a day-to-day and long term basis' (emphasis added). An example given is an impairment that 'affect[s] day-to-day coping such as limitations of mobility' (Department of Health and Human Services 2001).

In effect, the Manual requires that, for a person with a disability to be deemed 'healthy', they must be able to explain how their impairment will not affect their ability to 'provide for the needs of the child'. That is, 'fitness to parent' and disability are presumed to be negatively correlated, and the onus is on the person with a disability to disprove that assumption holds true in their personal case.

The Department's view that disability is a necessary hindrance to a section 13 order is further evidenced by the following explanation on a Department website. Under the heading 'What if I have a disability?' the response is that '[f]ull medical checks and histories are required to make sure you have the ability to care for a child now and into the future' (Department of Health and Human Services 2013).

The assumption that people with disabilities are less able to provide for the needs of a child, which the Manual forces caseworkers to adopt in assessing prospective parents, constitutes direct discrimination. This assumption prevents people with disabilities from obtaining section 13 orders, without which they cannot adopt. As such, it is a breach of the negative obligation contained in art 23 of the CRPD, not to curtail the rights of people with disabilities with respect to adoption.

8.2. *Indirect Discrimination during the Approval Stage*

8.2.1. Regulation 35(d): 'Suitable Financial Circumstances'

Under reg 35(d) the Secretary or authorised agency must consider the applicant's financial circumstances in determining suitability for a section 13 order.

Unfortunately, people with disabilities face significant day-to-day financial hurdles (Deane 2009). The higher cost of living faced by people with disabilities is well established (under the social model, this is because people with disabilities are forced to invest in overcoming social barriers such as ableist design) (Deane 2009). In addition, Attwood (2001) data has demonstrated that people with disabilities are less likely to be employed, thereby forcing people with disability to rely on the Disability Support Pension (DSP) to cover these costs. However, it is almost universally agreed within the disability community that the DSP is insufficient (Deane 2009). Paradoxically, it is a requirement of Australia's DSP that people with disabilities have below a certain amount in their bank accounts before becoming eligible for the income support (Deane 2009), even though the Regulations explicitly prioritise adoptive parents with high bank balances.

In light of these proven financial barriers faced by people with disabilities, reg 35(d) falls short of the negative obligation contained in art 23 of the CRPD not to curtail the rights of people with disabilities with regard to adoption. While disability does not form an explicit part of the criteria, people with disabilities will be less able than others to fulfill the requirement of 'suitable financial circumstances' on account of the financial barriers they disproportionately face.

Broadly, the inclusion of 'health' and 'financial circumstances' as two stand-alone criteria in the legislation, despite the obvious connections between these two criteria for people with disabilities, evidences at best a complete ignorance for the societal barriers faced by people with disabilities. At worst, the legislation can be accused of slipping into eugenics era notions of 'biologically fit' parents, with essentially no room in the legislation for people with disabilities to become parents through adoption.

8.2.2. Section 11(1): Married/De Facto Couple 'for Not Less Than Two Years'

A second potential source of discrimination is the requirement that adoptive parents be married or in a de facto relationship for two years. Putting to one side the queer critique of requiring someone to be in a couple to adopt which lies outside the scope of this article (Warner 2000), it is relevant to make two points.

First, people with disabilities are excluded from forming sexual and/or loving relationships more than people without a disability (Kempton and Kahn 1991; Fennell 1992; Arstein-Kerslake 2015; Young 2012). Given this, people with disabilities are less likely to be able to fulfill the requirement of coupledom in the Act and so are indirectly excluded from adoption. This is another failure to meet the negative obligation in art 23.

A second concern is that if a person with a disability engages in a relationship with another person with a disability, the direct and indirect discrimination that occurs under regs 35(a) and 35(d) could occur two-fold (i.e., in relation to both parents).

8.3. Direct Discrimination during the Linking Stage

As discussed, linking is, in practice, a two-stage joint decision by the caseworker and the relinquishing parent(s): the former makes a shortlist of suitable families, and the latter chooses the specific family to become the adoptive family.

The first risk of discrimination lies in the Manual's requirement that caseworkers consider adoptive parents' 'capacities in regard to any disability' (Department of Health and Human Services 2001). In a similar way to reg 35(a), this language alludes to the medical model idea that disability is a hurdle to good parenting, without being prima facie discriminatory.

The more insidious risk of discrimination, however, is the unclear vesting of decision-making capacity between caseworker and relinquishing parent, as well as the lack of other substantive criteria which these decision-makers must follow. This means both the short-listing and the final decision stand to be influenced not only by the personal prejudices of the caseworker, but also those of the relinquishing parent(s). As discussed above, the medical model of disability continues to shape societal views of parenting ability. As such, prejudice is a real and very likely risk. In light of this likely discrimination, this article argues that the Manual's abdication of decision-making power to relinquishing parents is a breach of the negative obligation art 23 not to curtail the adoption rights of people with disabilities. Committee jurisprudence suggests that art 23 contemplates that adoption processes would at least be governed by enumerated criteria and include the possibility of judicial review.[14]

At the very least, the abdication of decision-making power to relinquishing parents during the linking stage is a failure to meet the positive obligation contained in art 23. As discussed, the words 'additional assistance' in art 23 put a positive obligation on states to provide help to people with disabilities to overcome social barriers to adoption. Social barriers likely include prejudicial attitudes. This phase of the adoption framework thus falls short of the obligation to provide 'additional assistance' because it knowingly subjects people with disabilities to a decision-making process where they stand to be discriminated against.

Handing over this decision-making power is a complete abdication of power by the state and the courts to the broader population. It is akin to letting a population vote on the rights of a protected minority. Further, it completely undoes any other protections which may have been achieved by the legislation for people with disabilities. As the next Part will discuss, the CRPD does not dictate that relinquishing parents cannot be involved in the decision-making process; however, it does require that the state intervene—such as through education or by giving them criteria to follow—so that people with disabilities are not discriminated against.

8.4. Lack of Publicly Available Information

A widely identified problem with the provision of parenting information is that it fails to cater for people with disabilities (Frohmader 2009). Unsurprisingly, this same problem applies to information about adoption. In Victoria, the only targeted information for people with disabilities relating to local adoption is the uncomfortable reminder on a generic adoption site that '[f]ull medical checks and histories are required to make sure you have the ability to care for a child now and into the future' (Department of Health and Human Services 2013).

This lack of information is a breach of the positive obligation contained in art 23. By requiring that countries take 'additional steps' to help people with disabilities exercise their right to parenthood, art 23 clearly contemplates that signatories will provide information and services which educate the relevant group how to take advantage of that right.[15]

This lack of public information is all the more problematic in a context where people with disabilities believe that they are less, or not at all, eligible to become adoptive parents. As it happens, this conception exists widely within the disability community. Grace (2014) says: 'So I got this idea that people would notice me with the kids and take them away if they saw me alone with them as I would be so clearly Autistic and disabled as to be disallowed from adoption'. Booth et al. (2005) echoes this sentiment, explaining: 'I dread that I'll be presumed incompetent from the outset and my child will be unnecessarily removed'.

Given people with disabilities hold these views, the positive obligation contained in art 23 is more extensive: 'additional assistance' likely extends to addressing such views until people with disabilities feel empowered to adopt, such as through public education campaigns. The online information about adoption currently provided to people with disabilities in Victoria manifestly falls below this benchmark.

As discussed, people with disabilities stand to be discriminated against both directly and indirectly by the plain words of the Victorian legislation and its interpretation by the Department's Manual. In addition, the unfettered decision-making power of relinquishing parents and a lack of publicly available information for people with disabilities looking to adopt, ensure that at every stage of the

---

14 UNCRPD (United Nations Committee on the Rights of Persons with Disability) Draft General Comment on Article 6: Women with Disabilities. CRPD/C/14/R.1. 2015, para. 43.

15 UNCRPD (United Nations Committee on the Rights of Persons with Disability) Draft General Comment on Article 6: Women with Disabilities. CRPD/C/14/R.1. 2015, para. 38.

adoption process, people with disabilities stand to lose out. All these problems must be addressed for Victoria to bring its adoption regime in line with Australia's obligations under the CRPD.

9. Solutions

This article suggests the following changes to Victoria's local adoption framework. While these changes represent a significant overhaul of the current system, incorporating revision of legislation as well as cultural change within the Department and private adoption agencies, such an overhaul is necessary in order to bring Victoria's adoption framework in line with Australia's obligations under art 23. Such changes are explicitly required by art 4(b) of the CRPD, which mandates that signatories 'take all appropriate measures, including legislation, to modify or abolish existing laws, regulations, customs and practices that constitute discrimination against persons with disabilities'.

While these changes are discussed in relation to the Victorian adoption regime, many of them have broader application. The legislative changes suggested seek to enact art 23 obligations, and so can provide inspiration to lawmakers and advocates in any CRPD signatory state. Equally, the changes relating to education, information resources, and Committee and advocate action can be implemented anywhere in the world.

9.1. Action from the Victorian Parliament and the Department

9.1.1. Remove or Amend Criteria That Lead to Direct Discrimination during the Approval Stage

The direct discrimination which occurs during the approval process for a section 13 order has two sources, broadly speaking, both of which need to be addressed. First, it comes from the words of the Act and the Regulations: while these instruments do not compel caseworkers to look upon disability *disfavorably*, per se, they still compel those decision-makers to consider disability. Second, and more directly, discrimination during the approval stage derives from the Manual's interpretation of the statutory requirements. The Manual not only inversely correlates disability and fitness to parent, but it also requires that to be considered for a section 13 order, people with disabilities must explain their impairments by way of doctors' reports and medical documents (Department of Health and Human Services 2001). Such medical reports obviously encourage caseworkers to view an application from a person with a disability through the lens of the medical model, i.e., to consider that their impairment is a necessary burden on their capacity to parent.

As the Manual simply interprets the Act and the Regulations (and must be updated when the latter instruments are amended), the best option is to amend reg 35(a). However, the appropriate amendment may depend on whether a social model or deconstructionist approach is adopted. A pure proponent of the social model of disability might argue that the best option is to amend reg 35(a) by replacing the word 'health' with 'impairments', and to include a note to the effect of:

> In considering the impairments of the applicants, the Secretary or authorised agency should undertake a holistic assessment, considering both the challenges that a person's impairment might pose for their ability to parent and how they might overcome them.

Such an amendment would oblige the decision-maker to consider the ways that a person with a disability can offer a different but equally valid version of parenting.

In contrast, Tremain's deconstructionist critique of the social model revolves around the fact that the category of 'impairment' reinforces the segregation experienced by people with disabilities. Under this paradigm, the best option would be to remove reg 35(a) altogether so that there is no legislative basis on which to distinguish between people with and without disabilities. However, a risk of this approach is that it fails to account for, and combat, the conscious and unconscious bias likely exercised by caseworkers and relinquishing parents during their holistic analysis.

In this case, there are no easy answers and there is a need for consultation of the disability community on this question. Perhaps one option, which lies between the two theories, is to replace the word 'health' (in both the regulation and the accompanying note) with the word 'body' or 'person'. Such a holistic, neutral term avoids circumscribing to the notion that there is a normal 'healthy' body from which people with impairments deviate, but still leaves room for the decision- maker to consider how societal barriers might make it hard for people with certain bodily characteristics (be they related to physical, intellectual or mental health disabilities) to make it hard for someone to parent.

A more ambitious amendment of reg 35(a) might also include a statutorily enshrined mechanism for applicants to provide a personal statement outlining the social barriers they face and how they might overcome them. This would give the adoptive parents a way to frame any challenges they may face as deriving from society (as opposed to any bodily quality they possess themselves).

Notably, legislative change in this area is important not only because it enshrines the protection of people with disabilities in law, but also because it sends a powerful social message about the Victorian Parliament's commitment to people with disabilities. This can have the flow-on effect of destigmatising disability more broadly (Gelber and McNamara 2015). Obviously, the problem spoken about in this essay (that people with disabilities have difficulty adopting) connects to the systemic social problem of family formation for people with disabilities. Harnessing the signaling and symbolic power of law is but one of the useful mechanisms available to combat this broader social problem, particularly if it can get people speaking about the difficulties people with disabilities face—perhaps for the first time, in Australia.

9.1.2. Provide Financial Support to Compensate for Indirect Discrimination under reg 35(d)

Removing or amending criteria which lead to indirect discrimination would be counterproductive in this case. Not only is financial security considered by the Victorian government as necessary for successful parenting (going by reg 35(d)), but moreover, people with disabilities have consistently argued that they need greater financial support, including to raise children (Frohmader 2009; National Council on Disability 2012).

Instead, the appropriate solution is to provide people with disabilities additional support so they can meet those other criteria, including financial support. Currently, people with disabilities receive no special treatment or resources to help them become adoptive parents (Department of Health and Human Services 2013). Yet, financial and other support for people with disabilities looking to adopt would allow Victoria to discharge both its negative and positive obligations under art 23: it prevents people from disabilities from being discriminated against indirectly (by allowing them to satisfy the requirement of suitable financial circumstances), while also providing them with 'additional measures' to exercise their right to parenthood.

9.1.3. Legislate Caseworkers' Decision-Making Power during the Linking Stage

People with disabilities stand to face both conscious and unconscious discrimination from caseworkers during the short-listing phase of the linking stage. This can be mitigated by implementing criteria that caseworkers are obligated to follow during the short-listing process (similar to reg 35). Similar to the changes suggested for the s 13 order process, this would include a specific statement that a person will not be overlooked on account of an impairment.

9.1.4. Educate Relinquishing Parent(S), Caseworkers and Society More Broadly on the Parenting Ability of People with Disabilities

Discrimination from relinquishing parents during the linking process is a more complex obstacle. This is because the decision-making capacity of the relinquishing parent(s) is currently a protected aspect of the decision-making process, at international, national and state law. Notwithstanding that the protection of decision-making power of relinquishing parents is problematic, the government is powerless with regard to the attitudes and prejudices of relinquishing parents.

The unwillingness of relinquishing parents to consent to certain adoption orders on account of discriminatory attitudes was considered in the VLRC's report on Assistive Reproductive Technology and Adoption (VLRC 2007) albeit in relation to same-sex couple adoption and homophobia. In that report, the VLRC recommended that adoption be open to same-sex couples. In making that recommendation, the report contemplated that certain relinquishing parents would not want their child raised by same-sex parents on account of religious or other beliefs. This meant that same-sex couples stood to be discriminated against. To mitigate against this discrimination, the report recommended that caseworkers receive training to educate the relinquishing parents on the parenting ability of same-sex parents.

The same recommendation can be applied in this context. Without affecting a relinquishing parent's rights or autonomy, the Victorian Parliament can mandate that caseworkers educate relinquishing parents on the social model view of parenting with a disability: where people with disabilities are provided with support to overcome societal barriers, the inherent parenting ability of people with disabilities is no less than that of anyone else.

More broadly, these same educational campaigns need to be rolled out as grassroots programs for caseworkers as well as in Australian society more broadly. As discussed, the problem of adoption does not exist in a vacuum: it is intrinsically connected to the way the Australian state and society more broadly views the parenting capacities of people with disabilities. As such, the solution will require both a top-down and bottom-up approach which encompasses both immediate legal protections but also gradual re-education of the community from where a lot of ignorance and discrimination currently emanates.

9.1.5. Provide Tailored Information to People with Disabilities That Want to Adopt

As discussed, a lack of information catering for people with disabilities feeds an already pervasive societal perception that people with disabilities cannot or should not adopt. The Department needs to provide tailored, relevant information to people with disabilities about the adoption process as well as about parenting with an impairment. Even a devoted web page would be an improvement on the status quo, but other suitable services include special information sessions for people with disabilities and specialised caseworkers. This is not only required on account of the positive obligation in art 23, but is also explicitly required by art 4(h) which requires 'accessible information to persons with disabilities about . . . support services and facilities'.

9.1.6. Fund Universally Designed Technology and Programs

Even before people with disabilities investigate the possibility of adoption, many people with disabilities will be put off by the difficulties they will face being parents if they are successful in gaining an adoption order. While these difficulties are many and varied, and stem largely from societal ignorance, a specific difficulty which the government can directly combat is the lack of technology and facilities designed for people with disabilities. Not only are such technologies mandated by the positive obligation in art 23, but they are explicitly required by art 4(f) which requires that signatories 'undertake or promote research and development of universally designed goods, services, equipment and facilities'.

Such technologies and programs—from strollers to babies' bottles to parenting classes to easily intelligible parenting booklets—will have a bottom-up impact, encouraging more people with disabilities to seek to become parents (Llewellyn et al. 2010). This will increase the visibility of the current problem and further encourage change of the machinery which currently stops people with disabilities from adopting.

9.1.7. Give Support to Parents with a Disability Looking to Adopt a Child Who Also Has a Disability

In an interview with the author of this article, disability activist Booth et al. (2005) argued that parents with disabilities are sometimes uniquely placed to help a child with disabilities enjoy their full rights. She posits that children with disabilities have special needs that are better provided by parents with a similar or the same disability. This transcends knowing how to provide a child with the physical infrastructure to mitigate the effects of an impairment: it is also a mentoring role that a person without a disability is unable to offer. In her words, Booth et al. (2005) says: 'I think there are things that I, as a woman with a disability, can teach a child about living in a world that doesn't represent them'. From this point of view, not only are the best interests of children with disabilities compatible with the parenting of people with disabilities; their interests are sometimes better served with the involvement of parents with disabilities.

Under the current system, people with disabilities are paradoxically further removed from adopting children with disabilities. Such children are only linked with applicants who are considered exceptionally 'fit and proper' parents under the Manual's current (discriminatory) metric. Therefore, people with disabilities are less likely than a person without a disability to be linked with a child with a disability.

A similar scheme already exists for the adoption of Indigenous Australian children and/or children that have a particular religion (see reg 35(f) of the Regulations). A model such as this is particularly pertinent given children with disabilities are currently overrepresented in adoptive agencies (Australian Institute of Health and Welfare 2016; Department of Health and Human Services 2014). This scheme goes beyond just providing additional support to Indigenous parents or those of a particular religion; it actually prioritizes their application to be an adoptive parent.

Such a scheme could already be implemented under current legislation, by reading 'cultural identity' in reg 35(f) widely to include the disability community. However, this must go hand-in-hand with more funding for parents with disabilities looking to adopt, and re-training of caseworkers to enable them to see disability not as a burden, but as a benefit, for parenting.

Of course, a risk of such support is that it suggests that parents with disabilities only adopt children of their 'own kind', further segregating people with disabilities. For this reason, any such system must be thoroughly discussed with the disability community, and should probably opt toward simply giving support to parents who already want to adopt a child with a disability, instead of always pairing prospective parents with disabilities with children with disabilities.

9.2. Action from the Committee

In addition, the Committee must take action to provide Australia and other countries with more jurisprudence on art 23. Admittedly, the Committee must use its words wisely: its State Reports often address signatories whose human rights abuses against people with disabilities relate to other very pressing issues. Nevertheless, the current lack of clarity and substance to do with art 23 makes it difficult for disability advocates to lobby the Victorian government. A General Comment from the Committee on art 23 would be ideal. In the interim, the Committee should start mentioning art 23 in its State Reports.

9.3. Action from Disability Advocates and Allies

This article does not suggest that the onus is on those suffering human rights abuses to create the necessary change. For this reason, lobbying from disability allies remains a necessity. However, a key problem with lobbying efforts may be that the current framework operates behind closed doors—many people with disabilities do not speak publicly about the discrimination they face seeking to become parents (see Part V) (Frohmader 2009). As such, litigation could bring vital visibility to lobbying efforts.

Article 1 of the Optional Protocol to the CRPD allows for the making of individual complaints to the Committee about violations of the CRPD by signatories. While this article has identified a strong prima facie case for violation of art 23 by Victorian adoption law, art 2(d) of the CRPD requires that all domestic remedies have been exhausted before a complaint can be brought under the CRPD Optional protocol. Without offering a view on the merits of such claim, this article suggests that a useful direction for future research would be the viability of a claim brought by a person with a disability who has been denied a section 13 order under the Equal Opportunity Act 2010 (Vic) or the Charter of Human Rights and Responsibilities Act 2006 (Vic).

10. Hidden Impairments

While the overarching effect of Victoria's current scheme is to disenable people with disabilities from adopting, there is a potential exception to this rule: those with invisible or hidden impairments. Hidden impairments and impairments which are not outwardly visible (Montgomery 2001). There is significant academic literature on how people with hidden impairments are treated differentially on account of their impairment being less visible (Montgomery 2001; Samuels 2003; Ginsberg 1996). Where a person with a hidden impairment is treated as a person without a disability, this is referred to as passing (Ginsberg 1996).

Victoria's adoption framework is a prime example of a situation where passing is possible. While the Regulations require disclosure of all relevant 'health' information, they do not define the meaning or scope of the word 'health'. This means that people with certain disabilities might not be required to disclose, or might choose not to disclose, certain impairments. Such hidden impairments might include sensory impairment below a certain level, learning and cognitive differences and repetitive strain injuries (Samuels 2003).

There is dissensus within the disability community on the ethics of passing. Samuels (2003) defends the right of people with disabilities to 'pass' in order to gain a more beneficial position in society. This is because, under the social model, they are in no way responsible for the structural disadvantage which they are seeking to avoid (even if they may suffer feelings of 'misrecognition and internal dissonance' as consequences of passing) (Samuels 2003).

Other theorists propose that passing creates a splinter within the disability community. Where certain people with disabilities remain invisible, this makes the overall group look smaller and makes progress on disability human rights harder to achieve (Kleege 1999). Under this view, there is a positive obligation on people with disabilities to disclose their disability during the adoption process (Wendell 1996): '[p]assing is the sign of the sell out' (Walker 2001).

A third approach to passing is offered by Cal Montgomery: his approach is to reject the distinction between visible and non-visible identities that makes 'passing' possible in the first place (Montgomery 2001). Drawing on the social model, Montgomery (2001) argues that passing refers only to whether onlookers can see the barriers that a person with a disability faces, and not whether those barriers actually exist. Therefore, passing emerges from the gaze of society, and not the actions of an individual.

For the purposes of this article, it is sufficient to note that adoption legislation can facilitate passing; in the Victorian case, the adoption legislation provides a set of criteria which draw a line (albeit a blurry one) through the disability community, making it harder for some to adopt, but not others.

There is no provision of the CRPD that deals with this phenomenon. While it is beyond the scope of this article to offer a fully-fledged solution, it recommends that the Victorian Parliament—and other CRPD signatories—be cognisant of the visible/hidden impairment dynamic in creating solutions. Those solutions which carve out exceptions for certain types of disabilities (e.g., people with mobility impairments are entitled to a section 13 order) may reinforce the divide and make long-term change more unattainable for the entire disability community. This reinforces one of the recommendations above: that the Parliament should focus on change that allows caseworkers to make holistic assessments of parenting.

11. Conclusions

The difficulty faced by people with disabilities looking to adopt is an important issue in and of itself. The CRPD expressly names adoption as a right belonging to people with disabilities. In addition, given many adoption regimes, including Victoria's, hinge on a court or panel's assessment of whether a person could be a good parent, adoption systems have a lot to say about how the state views the family unit, and how people with disabilities fit into that conception. Given that law has the ability to shape societal views, adoption law also has important connections to how our society views the parenting capabilities of people with disabilities.

While research in the area of parenting rights (as well as Committee jurisprudence, for that matter) has tended to overlook significance of the right to adopt, this article has sought to restate its importance. Specifically, this article has shown that Victoria's adoption framework, both on article and in practice, violates Australia's obligations under art 23 of the CRPD. Paradoxically, the adoption framework that should implement Australia's obligations under art 23(2) has in fact become one of the societal barriers that Australia committed to eradicating by ratifying the CRPD.

Not only do the Act and the Regulations fail to contain any of the positive obligations envisaged by art 23(2), more worryingly, the Manual that implements Victoria's adoption law openly espouses a medical model conception of people with disabilities' ability to parent. In addition, the current framework hands over vast swathes of unfettered decision-making power to caseworkers and relinquishing parent(s), without providing affirmative protections for people with disabilities against discrimination by those decision-makers. The nuance between hidden and visible identities has the capacity to further complicate the effect of the adoption framework on the disability community.

More broadly, this article used Victoria as a case study to show that discrimination against people with disabilities does not just come from people's prejudices; it also hides insidiously within the words of adoption legislation. Any CRPD signatory with legislation which resembles Victoria's—which includes other Australian states, the UK and the many US states—must realise the discrimination emanating from their own legislative instruments and undertake meaningful reform to allow people with disabilities to adopt.

Future research must continue to explore the support which governments can offer people with disabilities once they succeed in becoming parents. Unfortunately, a more crucial first step toward adherence to art 23 for many CRPD signatories is the eradication of certain barriers to parenthood that people with disabilities face. This article has shown that one such barrier is often the adoption process.

References

Abberley, Paul. 1987. The Concept of Oppression and the Development of a Social Theory of Disability. *Disability, Handicap and Society* 2: 5–19. [CrossRef]

Anthony, Thalia, and Honni van Rijswijk. 2012. Parental 'consent' to child removal in Stolen Generations cases. In *Past Law, Present Histories*. Edited by Diane Kirkby. Canberra: ANU E-Press.

Arstein-Kerslake, Anna. 2015. Understanding sex: The right to legal capacity to consent to sex. *Disability & Society* 30: 1459–73.

Attwood, Bain. 2001. The Stolen Generations and genocide: Robert Manne's in Denial: The Stolen Generations and the Right. *Aboriginal History* 25: 163–72.

Australian Bureau of Statistics. 2012. Disability, Ageing and Carers, Australia: Summary of Findings. Available online: http://www.abs.gov.au/ausstats/abs@.nsf/lookup/A813E50F4C45A338CA257C21000E4F36?opendocument (accessed on 28 May 2017).

Australian Institute of Family Studies. 2016. Children in Care: CFCA Resource Sheet. Available online: https://aifs.gov.au/cfca/publications/children-care (accessed on 16 July 2017).

Australian Institute of Health and Welfare. 2016. Adoptions Australia 2015-16. Available online: http://www.aihw.gov.au/WorkArea/DownloadAsset.aspx?id=60129558075 (accessed on 17 July 2017).

Barnes, Colin. 2003. What a Difference a Decade Makes: Reflections on Doing 'Emancipatory' Disability Research. *Disability & Society* 18: 3–17.

Barnes, Colin, and Geoffrey Mercer. 1996. *Exploring the Divide: Illness and Disability*. Leeds: The Disability Press.

Barnes, Colin, and Geof Mercer. 1997. Breaking the Mould? An Introduction to Doing Disability Research. In *Doing Disability Research*. Edited by Colin Barnes and Geof Mercer. Leeds: The Disability Press.

Blanck, Peter, Eilionóir Flynn, and Gerard Quinn. Forthcoming; *A Research Companion to Disability Law*. Galway: Ashgate.

Booth, Tim, Wendy Booth, and David McConnell. 2005. The Prevalence and Outcomes of Care Proceedings Involving Parents with Learning Difficulties in the Family Courts. *Journal of Applied Research in Intellectual Disabilities* 18: 7–17. [CrossRef]

Brown, Jax Jacki. 2015. Australia's Coming Around on Same-Sex Adoption, But Will It Ever Happen For People With Disability? Available online: http://junkee.com/australia-is-on-board-with-same-sex-adoption-but-will-things-ever-change-for-those-with-disability/71088#mPzv7RO2kBhRUh7Q.99 (accessed on 4 April 2016).

Carter, Barbara. 2016. Rebuilding the Village: Supporting Families Where a Parent Has a Disability. Available online: http://www.publicadvocate.vic.gov.au/our-services/publications-forms/241-rebuilding-the-village-supporting-families-where-a-parent-has-a-disability-report-2-child-protection-2015?path= (accessed on 28 May 2017).

Chapman, Rohhss, Sue Ledger, Louise Townson, and Daniel Docherty. 2015. *Sexuality and Relationships in the Lives of People with Intellectual Disabilities: Standing in My Shoes*. London: Jessica Kingsley Publishers.

Clarke, Harriet, and Richard Olsen. 2003. *Parenting and Disability: Disabled Parents' Experiences of Raising Children*. Bristol: The Policy Press.

Collins, Carol. 1999. Reproductive Technologies for Women with Physical Disabilities. *Sexuality and Disability* 17: 299–307. [CrossRef]

Crawford, Nicole. 2003. Parenting with a Disability. *Monitor on Psychology* 34: 68.

Deane, Kirsten. 2009. SHUT OUT: The Experience of People With Disabilities and Their Families in Australia. Available online: https://www.dss.gov.au/our-responsibilities/disability-and-carers/publications-articles/policy-research/shut-out-the-experience-of-people-with-disabilities-and-their-families-in-australia (accessed on 6 April 2016).

Department for Child Protection and Family Support. 2016. Thinking about Adoption? Available online: https://www.dcp.wa.gov.au/FOSTERINGANDADOPTION/ADOPTIONANDHOMEFORLIFE/PAGES/ALLABOUTADOPTION.ASPX#1 (accessed on 28 May 2017).

Department for Education. 2014. Draft Statutory Guidance on Adoption. Available online: http://minimumstandards.org/adoption_statutory_guidance_2014.pdf (accessed on 28 May 2017).

Department of Health and Human Services. 1986. Adoption Standards. Available online: http://www.dhs.vic.gov.au/about-the-department/documents-and-resources/reports-publications/adoption-and-permanent-care-standards-1986 (accessed on 4 November 2016).

Department of Health and Human Services. 1997. National Principles in Adoption. Available online: http://www.dhs.vic.gov.au/about-the-department/documents-and-resources/reports-publications/national-principles-in-adoption-1997 (accessed on 4 November 2016).

Department of Health and Human Services. 2001. Adoption and Permanent Care Manual. Available online: http://www.dhs.vic.gov.au/__data/assets/pdf_file/0012/589593/apc_procedure_manual_2aug04.pdf (accessed on 4 November 2016).

Department of Health and Human Services. 2013. Adoption and Permanent Care—Frequently Asked Questions. Available online: http://www.dhs.vic.gov.au/for-individuals/children,-families-and-young-people/adoption-and-permanent-care/adoption-and-permanent-care-frequently-asked-questions#content-heading-14 (accessed on 4 April 2016).

Department of Health and Human Services. 2014. Adoption. Available online: https://www.betterhealth.vic.gov.au/health/healthyliving/adoption (accessed on 4 April 2016).

Doyle, Oran. 2007. Direct Discrimination, Indirect Discrimination and Autonomy. *Oxford Journal of Legal Studies* 27: 537–53. [CrossRef]

Fennell, Phil. 1992. Balancing Care and Control: Guardianship, Community Treatment Orders and Patient Safeguards. *International Journal of Law End Psychiatry* 15: 205–35. [CrossRef]

Finkelstein, Victor. 1980. *Attitudes and Disabled People: Issues for Discussion*. Leeds: World Rehabilitation Fund.

Fleming, Grace. 2015. Disability Discrimination of Prospective Adoptive and Foster Parents. Master's thesis, University of Minnesota, Minneapolis, MN, USA.

Freeman, Melvyn Colin, Kavitha Kolappa, Jose Miguel Caldas de Almeida, Arthur Kleinman, Nino Makhashvili, Sifiso Phakathi, Benedetto Saraceno, and Graham Thornicroft. 2015. Reversing hard won victories in the name of human rights: A critique of the General Comment on Article 12 of the UN Convention on the Rights of Persons with Disabilities. *The Lancet Psychiatry* 2: 844–50. [CrossRef]

Frohmader, Carolyn. 2009. Parenting issues for women with disabilities in Australia. Available online: http://wwda.org.au/wp-content/uploads/2013/12/parentingpolicyarticle09.pdf (accessed on 6 April 2016).

Gelber, Katherine, and Luke McNamara. 2015. The Effects of Civil Hate Speech Laws: Lessons from Australia. *Law and Society* 49: 631–64. [CrossRef]

Ginsberg, Elaine. 1996. *Passing and the Fictions of Identity*. Durham: Duke University Press.

Goering, Sara. 2015. Rethinking disability: The social model of disability and chronic disease. *Current Reviews in Musculoskeletal Medicine* 8: 134–38. [CrossRef] [PubMed]

Goodley, Dan. 2011. *Disability Studies: An Interdisciplinary Approach*. London: SAGE Publications.

Grace, Elizabeth. 2014. Your Mama Wears Drover Boots. In *Criptiques*. Edited by Caitlin Wood. San Bernardio: May Day Publishing.

Grue, Lars, and Kristin Laerum. 2002. 'Doing Motherhood': Some experiences of mothers with physical disabilities. *Disability and Society* 17: 671–83. [CrossRef]

Hahn, Harlan. 1988. The Politics of Physical Differences: Disability and Discrimination. *Journal of Social Issues* 44: 39–47. [CrossRef]

Hellman, Deborah, and Sophia Moreau. 2013. *Philosophical Foundations of Discrimination Law*. Oxford: Oxford University Press.

Horin, Adele. 2010. Refugee Children Removed. The Sydney Morning Herald: Available online: http://www.smh.com.au/nsw/refugee-children-removed-20100418-smn6.html (accessed on 16 July 2017).

Hunt, Paul. 1966. A Critical Condition. In *Stigma: The Experience of Disability*. Edited by Paul Hunt. London: Geoffrey Chapman.

IASSID (International Association for the Scientific Study of Intellectual Disabilities). 2008. Parents Labelled with Intellectual Disability: Position of the IASSID Special Interest Research Group on Parents and Parenting with Intellectual Disabilities. *Journal of Applied Research in Intellectual Disabilities* 21: 296–307.

Kayess, Rosemary, and Phillip French. 2008. Out of Darkness into Light? Introducing the Convention on the Rights of Persons with Disabilities. *Human Rights Law Review* 8: 1–34. [CrossRef]

Kempton, Winifred, and Emily Kahn. 1991. Sexuality and People with Intellectual Disabilities: A Historical Perspective. *Sexuality and Disability* 9: 93–111. [CrossRef]

Kirshbaum, Megan, and Rhoda Olkin. 2002. Parents with Physical, Systemic or Visual Disabilities. *Sexuality and Disability* 20: 65–80. [CrossRef]

Kleege, Georgina. 1999. *Sight Unseen*. New Haven: Yale University Press.

Llewellyn, Gwynnyth, David McConnell, and Luisa Ferronato. 2003. Prevalence and outcomes for parents with disabilities and their children in an Australian court sample. *Child Abuse and Neglect* 27: 235–51. [CrossRef]

Llewellyn, Gwynnyth, Rannveig Traustadottir, David McConnell, and Hanna Bjorg Sigurjonsdott. 2010. *Parents with Intellectual Disabilities: Past, Present and Futures*. Chichester: Wiley-Blackwell Publishing.

Malacredia, Claudia. 2009. Performing Motherhood in a Disablist World: Dilemmas of Motherhood, Femininity and Disability. *International Journal Qualitative Studies in Education* 22: 99–117. [CrossRef]

Montgomery, Cal. 2001. A Hard Look at Invisible Disability. Available online: http://www.ragged-edge-mag.com/0301/0301ft1.htm (accessed on 19 August 2017).

National Council on Disability. 2012. National Disability Policy: A Progress Report. Available online: https://ncd.gov/progress_reports/Aug202012 (accessed on 17 July 2017).

Office of the High Commissioner on Human Rights. 2016. Elected Members of the Committee on the Rights of Persons with Disabilities. Available online: http://www.ohchr.org/EN/HRBodies/CRPD/Pages/Membership.aspx (accessed on 17 July 2017).

Oliver, Michael. 1996. *Understanding Disability: From Theory to Practice*. New York: St. Martin's Press.

Radcliffe, Victoria. 2008. "Being Brave": Disabled Women and Motherhood. Master's dissertation, The University of Leeds, Leeds, UK.

Samuels, Ellen. 2003. My Body, My Closet: Invisible Disability and the Limits of Coming out. *Journal of Lesbian and Gay Studies* 9: 233–55. [CrossRef]

Senate Community Affairs References Committee. 2015. Out of Home Care. Available online: http://www.aph.gov.au/binaries/senate/committee/clac_ctte/completed_inquiries/2004-07/inst_care/report/report.pdf (accessed on 17 July 2017).

Shakespeare, Tom. 2002. The Social Model of Disability: An Outdated Ideology? *Research in Social Science and Disability* 2: 9–28.

Shakespeare, Tom. 2013. The Social Model of Disability. In *The Disability Studies Reader*. Edited by Lennard Davis. New York: Routledge.

Shakespeare, Tom, Kath Gillespie-Sells, and Dominic Davies. 1996. *The Sexual Politics of Disability: Untold Desires*. New York: Cassell.

Steele, Linda. 2016. Court authorised sterilisation and human rights: Inequality, discrimination and violence against women and girls with disability. *UNSW Law Journal* 39: 1002–37.

Sutherland, Allan. 1981. *Disabled We Stand*. London: Souvenir Press.

Thomas, Carol, and Penny Curtis. 1997. Having a Baby: Some Disabled Womens' Reproductive Experiences. *Midwifery* 13: 202–9. [CrossRef]

Tremain, Shelley. 2002. On the Subject of Impairment. In *Disability/Postmodernity: Embodying Disability Studies*. Edited by Marian Corker and Tom Shakespeare. London: Bloomsbury Publishing.

UPIAS (Union of the Physically Impaired Against Segregation). 1974. Policy Statement. Available online: http://disability-studies.leeds.ac.uk/files/library/UPIAS-fundamental-principles.pdf (accessed on 28 April 2016).

VLRC (Victorian Law Reform Commission). 2007. Assisted Reproductive Technology & Adoption. Available online: http://www.lawreform.vic.gov.au/all-projects/art-adoption (accessed on 6 April 2016).

Walker, Lisa. 2001. *Looking Like What You Are: Sexual Style, Race and Lesbian Identity*. New York: New York University Press.

Warner, Michael. 2000. *The Trouble with Normal: Sex, Politics, and the Ethics of Queer Life*. Cambridge: Harvard University Press.

Wates, Michele. 2002. Disability and Adoption: How Unexamined Attitudes Discriminate against Disabled People as Parents. *Adoption and Fostering Journal* 26: 49–56. [CrossRef]

Wendell, Susan. 1996. *The Rejected Body: Feminist Philosophical Reflections on Disability*. New York: Routledge.

Westbrook, Marry T., and Darien Chinnery. 1995. The Effect of Physical Disability on Women's Childbearing and Early Childrearing Experiences. *Australian Disability Review*, 3–17.

Young, Stella. 2012. Don't Look Past My Disabled Body. The Sydney Morning Herald. Available online: http://www.smh.com.au/lifestyle/life/citykat/dont-look-past-my-disabled-body--love-it-20120712-21ycy.html (accessed on 4 April 2016).

9

Living on the Global Peripheries of Law: Disability Human Rights Law in Principle and in Practice in the Global South

Vera Chouinard

School of Geography and Earth Sciences, McMaster University, Hamilton, ON L8S 4K1, Canada; chouinar@mcmaster.ca

Abstract: This article develops the notion that poorer nations of the Global South are particularly disadvantaged in terms of realizing disabled people's human rights in practice. This is because they are situated in what is termed the global peripheries of law. These are peripheries in which very limited human and financial resources are available to practically realize disability human rights (reflecting processes such as the outmigration of trained professionals, devaluation of currency as a condition of debt repayment, and dependence on agricultural exports and imports of expensive manufactured goods, including medicine, from the Global North). Being on the global peripheries of law also reflects legacies of colonial and neo-colonial violence and oppression in an unequal global capitalist order, such as ongoing and widespread violence against women and unsafe working conditions—both of which result in death and the geographically uneven production of impairment. This uneven production of impairment also needs to be considered as an important part of understanding disability human rights law in a global context. Following a brief overview of the U.N. convention on the human rights of disabled people and the U.N. Covenant on Economic, Social and Cultural Rights to provide a global legal context and of the Inter-American Human Rights System to provide a regional legal context, the article illustrates why it is so difficult to realize disabled people's human rights in practice in the Global South, through a case study of Guyana.

Keywords: global peripheries of law; disability; human rights; production of impairment; U.N. Convention on the Rights of Disabled People; Guyana case study

---

We live in extraordinary times and places. These are characterized, in part, by globalization, the concentration of wealth amongst an elite few, a deeply unequal neo-liberal global capitalist order, a rise in precarious employment particularly amongst younger persons, ageing populations in developed nations and ongoing struggles to assert the human rights of persons with impairments and illnesses, who are disabled by attitudinal and social barriers to inclusion in the Global North and South. In this article, I am particularly concerned with what it is like to be on the global peripheries of law in the poorer nations of the Global South and this is illustrated through a case study of disabled people's rights and lives in Guyana.

In this article, I conceptualize global peripheries of law as places in the world where it is particularly difficult to realize human rights in practice. Historically, these peripheries are the legacies of imperialism, and colonial and neo-colonial oppression. As such, they also reflect the deeply unequal and unjust neo-liberal capitalist global order in which we live today. I argue that this helps us to make sense of why some countries are particularly disadvantaged in terms of their capacity to improve disabled people's lives through disability human rights law. This conceptualization also builds on my earlier work on legal peripheries in disabled people's human rights in Canada (Chouinard 2001) and the notion that living the law in principle and in practice are often fundamentally at odds when we are located at the peripheries of law.

I develop these arguments as follows. First, I provide a conceptualization of what it means to be situated on the global peripheries of law. Then, in order to provide a global human rights context, I consider the development of the United Nations Convention on the Rights of Persons with Disabilities and the U.N. Covenant on Economic, Social and Cultural Rights and some of the human rights they enshrine and aspire to. Next, I provide a regional human rights context for the subsequent case study of disabled people's human rights and lives in Guyana. I do this by considering the development and limitations of the Inter-American Human Rights System. This is followed by a case study of how disability human rights law is being lived, in principle and in practice, in the developing nation of Guyana.

1. Conceptualizing Global Peripheries of Law

What does it mean to be situated at the peripheries of law? For some legal scholars, it refers to occupying especially disadvantaged places in law and society (see for e.g., The Griffith Law Review (2015) special issue focusing on the links between disability and criminal law). I concur with this general meaning but with a geographer's caveat that those at the peripheries of law are also spatially disadvantaged in important ways. Still, there is more to experiences of being on the peripheries of law than this.

As the following quote suggests, being situated at the peripheries of law is also about encountering tensions or contradictions between how law is lived in discourse and in principle and how it is lived in practice:

> ... the socio-spatial production of legal peripheries or places in which law as discursively represented and law as lived are fundamentally at odds. These are places of 'shadow citizenship and entitlement'—important to the cultural representation of neo-liberal democracies as inclusionary and tolerant of diversity, but lived as places of profound exclusion in which basic human rights are routinely denied. It is from such peripheral, disempowered locations that disabled Canadians are struggling to claim their places in society and space. (Chouinard 2001, p. 186)

Countries of the Global South are particularly disadvantaged in this regard as a result of centuries of colonial oppression and exploitation and their disempowered positions in the current neo-liberal global capitalist order. This means that they have especially limited human and financial resources to draw upon in realizing legal rights in practice. This is reflected in processes such as the outmigration of trained professionals, including lawyers, to the Global North, historically high national debt loads and devalued currency that makes it difficult or impossible to purchase commodities such as medicine or mobility and other aids for persons with illnesses or impairments, from countries of the Global North despite depending upon these countries for such goods. As the feminist philosopher and bioethicist Jaggar (2002) explains, countries of the Global North and elites in those countries (as well as elites in the South) continue to benefit from a post-colonial neo-liberal capitalist order in which developing nations' labour power is exploited, natural and agricultural resources are exported, and in which countries are forced to buy manufactured goods (such as medicine, fertilizer and agricultural machinery) from the Global North. Such imbalances in power fuel widespread poverty and poor health, particularly amongst more vulnerable groups such as women (Jaggar 2002).

Being on the global peripheries of law is also about experiencing especially severe disjunctures between what people aspire to achieve through law and what is actually achieved in practice. I discuss and illustrate this in the case study analysis of Guyana presented later in this paper—drawing on interviews I conducted with disability activists in the country.

Existing on the global peripheries of law also involves being in especially marginal places of 'shadow citizenship'. These are places in which the state and legal system may appear to recognize and assert the human rights of vulnerable citizens such as disabled people and in doing so help to create the illusion of an inclusive society. At the same time, however, shadow citizens lack the means (e.g., financial, insufficient access to legal expertise and to mobility and other aids) to claim those rights in practice.

This is not to deny that there are important legacies of colonial exploitation and oppression, and life on the global peripheries of law in countries of the Global North. This is the case with respect to indigenous people and especially women and girls in countries such as Canada, for instance, who have had to struggle for legal recognition of traditional rights to land, self-governance, for Indian status, and also for freedom from oppressive practices such as forced education in church-run residential schools aimed at 'killing the Indian in the child' and assimilation, and the disappearances and murders of indigenous women (for further discussion, see for example: Bell and Anderson 2017; Hanson 2008). Violence against indigenous women is higher than that experienced by other women in Canada (Kubik et al. 2009) and has prompted a National Inquiry into Missing and Murdered Indigenous Women and Girls that commenced in 2016. Aboriginal people in countries of the Global South, such as the Amerindian people of Guyana, are arguably in even more disempowered and disabling locations on the global peripheries of law—struggling to deal with human rights abuses arising through human trafficking, very limited access to health care and education in their relatively isolated hinterland communities, contamination of water supplies (through mining of bauxite and gold), and insufficient access to resources such as culturally appropriate teaching materials that would aid in the preservation of communities' cultural heritages. Here the gap between the human rights that Amerindian people aspire to (such as equality of opportunity and the preservation of culture) and what can be delivered in practice is especially severe (Cultural Survival 2015). As I argue later in this article this is also true with respect to non-indigenous disabled persons' rights in Guyana.

There is no doubt that disabled people also remain on the margins or peripheries of law in countries such as Canada. Indeed, the Canadian Human Rights Commission (CHRC), in its 2016 report to the Parliament of Canada, noted that 60% of all human rights complaints it receives concern discrimination on the basis of disability (and many of these are related to employment) (Canadian Human Rights Commission 2016). But these are arguably not global peripheries of law in the sense of directly arising from colonial exploitation and oppression except for disabled aboriginal people who experience poorer health and greater impairment than many non-aboriginal Canadians. However, this situation is especially dire and difficult to address in countries situated on the global peripheries of law, such as Guyana, owing to very limited financial and human resources.

One advantage of conceptualizing disabled people's human rights in terms of global peripheries of law is that this helps to frame the realization and denial of those rights as matters of global injustice. This in turn encourages recognition that impairment and disability issues are intrinsically linked to people's places in a profoundly unequal global capitalist order and lends a political urgency to addressing these issues in this wider context.

2. Getting Global and Regional: The U.N. Convention on the Rights of Persons with Disabilities and the Inter-American System of Human Rights

The United Nations Convention on the Rights of Persons with Disabilities (CRPD), after five years of consultation between U.N. officials and states in the Global North and South and disabled persons' organizations, was adopted in December 2006. Following initial ratification by a record number of states (81) as well as the European Union, the convention came into force in May 2008 (Harpur 2012; Kayess and French 2008). The international convention was the first to explicitly address disabled people's human rights although some rights were interpreted prior to this in relation to general human rights conventions. In addition, the U.N. Convention on the Rights of the Child (which came into force in September 1990) mentioned disabled children once. In this context, the CRPD is frequently seen as a milestone in international disability human rights law and in global disability activism. There is also an Optional Protocol to the Convention that established a U.N. Committee on the Rights of Persons with Disabilities. The Committee is responsible for assessing individual and group complaints of violations of the rights of persons with disabilities in states that are party to the Convention and recommending courses of action to remedy them. States are also obliged to regularly report on the implementation of disabled persons' human rights to enable the Committee to monitor implementation of the Convention over time and space (Office of the High Commissioner on Human Rights 2018a). All but one of the 18 experts serving on the committee are disabled persons.

Scholars and activists, however, do not always agree on the significance and promise of the CRPD. Harpur (2012) argues that it has facilitated a paradigm shift in disability human rights law whereby there is, as in the social model of disability, recognition that people with impairments are disabled by environmental and social barriers. However, and unlike early radical social models of disability pioneered in the U.K., there is also recognition of the need to address the experiences and ramifications of impairment in disabled people's lives (such as the need for government support for rehabilitation and other services and housing that accommodates living needs). He also points out that the CRPD has helped to reinforce the importance of involving disability organizations in the development and implementation of the Convention. Degener (2016) argues that with the CRPD we have moved from a social model of disability to a human rights approach. She sees a number of advantages to this, including recognition of disabled people's inalienable right to dignity, an understanding that human rights are to be respected despite differences in mental and bodily status, and scope to think about the affirmation and denial of rights in terms of the intersectionality of identities. Megret (2008) contends that the Convention contributes not just to the recognition of universal human rights as applying to persons with disabilities but also recognizes rights, such as the right to full and equal participation in society, that reflect the specific circumstances of disabled people. Others, such as Kayess and French (2008, p. 34), are more guarded and critical in their views of the CRPD and its potential. In the conclusion to their article they argue:

> If there is truly to be a shift to a coherent new disability rights paradigm in international law, it will be important that CRPD interpretation and implementation efforts penetrate beyond populist social model ideas to a more sophisticated understanding of impairment and disability in its social context. Additionally, it must be recognised that despite the CRPD's extensive exposition of disability rights, some crucial areas, including bioethics and compulsory treatment, are barely grazed by the CRPD text. The CRPD is therefore a crucial buttress and facilitator of a disability rights agenda, but it is not a proxy for that agenda. Some disability rights issues still remain untouched or undeveloped in international human rights law. Consequently, it will be important that disability human rights activists neither undervalue, nor overestimate, the role and scope of the CRPD and its potential contribution to securing the human rights of persons with disability into the future.

Others share such concerns. Freeman et al. (2015) argue that the U.N. committee attempting to oversee implementation of the CRPD, in its statement on article 12, went too far in asserting that all individuals at all times have the capacity to make decisions regarding matters such as treatment that would further other human rights goals such as receiving the best health care possible. They note that at least some disability organizations in countries such as South Africa and India have overwhelmingly supported the notion that people with mental and physical disabilities are sometimes unable to make informed decisions, for example when delusional or in a coma. In response to such criticisms, the Committee on the CRPD has insisted that in extenuating circumstances, such as when a person is in mental distress and a danger to themselves or others, that supported decision-making should take the place of decisions made by others such as health care professionals (Office of the High Commissioner of Human Rights 2018b).

Nonetheless, the legal principles of the CRPD are lofty and ambitious. As the World Health Organization (2011, p. 9) puts it:

> A range of international documents have highlighted that disability is a human rights issue, including the World Programme of Action Concerning Disabled People (1982), the Convention on the Rights of the Child (1989), and the Standard Rules on the Equalisation of Opportunities

> for People with Disabilities (1993). More than 40 nations adopted disability discrimination legislation during the 1990s. The CRPD—the most recent, and the most extensive recognition of the human rights of persons with disabilities—outlines the civil, cultural, political, social, and economic rights of persons with disabilities. Its purpose is to "promote, protect, and ensure the full and equal enjoyment of all human rights and fundamental freedoms by people with disabilities and to promote respect for their inherent dignity".

But, as indicated above, there are challenges and unresolved issues in terms of further articulating, and realizing in practice, the human rights of disabled persons. Outlining all of these is beyond the scope of the present paper (but for more detailed commentary on the Convention, see (Della et al. 2017). However, to help to put disability human rights law and disabled people's lives in Guyana in a global context, I now want to turn to a critique that is long overdue—namely, the efficacy of applying a disability human rights approach developed in relatively affluent nations of the Global North, such as the U.S. and Canada, to advancing the rights and well-being of disabled people in the Global South.

The dominance of Northern discourses that frame disability issues as matters of human rights at the global scale is, as authors such as Meekosha and Soldatic (2011) point out, a key legacy of a long historical trajectory of colonial and neo-colonial oppression. This oppression included taken-for-granted practices of valuing the ideas, social practices and societal organization of Northern nations (e.g., as modern and progressive) over those of poorer nations in the Global South (e.g., as more 'primitive' or traditional). This hegemony is illustrated, for example, by the fact that many Southern nations embraced this disability human rights campaign. This was undoubtedly important in forging international solidarity amongst disability activists and building networks for future action. What it arguably did not do, or did not do enough of, is pushing the boundaries of how disability issues are understood and addressed in nations of the Global South. Disability scholars point out that disability issues in the Global South need to be understood in terms of how nations and bodies are situated in an uneven global capitalist order that still bears the marks of colonial and neo-colonial oppression. So, for example, Meekosha and Soldatic (2011) note that one of the legacies of this oppression is the often especially deep poverty in which people in the Global South live. This poverty not only causes impairment (e.g., through malnutrition) but also causes especially severe barriers to inclusion such as lack of access to transportation, education and adequate health care.

To address such issues Meekosha and Soldatic (2011) suggest the need for a deeper, richer conception of disability issues as involving an uneven politics of impairment that is as important as disabling barriers to inclusion and well-being. In a similar vein, Chouinard (2012, 2014) insists on considering disability to be as much about the geographically uneven production of impairment (e.g., through war, violence against women, the organ trade, poverty and especially unsafe conditions of work in poorer nations) as it is about barriers and the violation of human rights.

There are two fundamental problems here. The first is that an exclusive focus on human rights can encourage exaggerated confidence in the power of law alone to improve disabled people's lives since it fails to explicitly critique the uneven geography of access to the resources needed to realize such rights. The second problem is that, in failing to recognize the links between the uneven production of impairment and disparities in capacities to enforce rights due to global inequality, scholars and activists miss important opportunities to explicitly frame disability issues as matters of global injustice. Some may argue that the problem is not so much the hegemony of Northern conceptions of disability as matters of human rights as it is an overly narrow conception of those rights, which fails to address issues such as violence and gender. While there is some merit to this view, it arguably remains important to look beyond human rights per se to adequately contextualize disabled people's lives and struggles for social change.

The U.N. Covenant on Economic, Social and Cultural Rights was adopted in December 1966 and opened for ratification and came into force in January 1976. Its articles outline general human rights principles and goals and as such, provide a general international framework for protecting and advancing the human rights of diverse groups such as disabled and indigenous people. Among the general human rights it enshrines are the rights to adequate food and freedom from hunger, to not be forcibly or otherwise removed from one's home, to enjoy the right to work and to have favourable conditions of work, to ensure the equal right of women and men to enjoy the economic, social and cultural rights set out in the Covenant, and the right to adequate health care. Article 2.2 of the Covenant commits signatory states to ensuring freedom from discrimination on various bases of human difference:

> The States Parties to the present Covenant undertake to guarantee that the rights enunciated in the present Covenant will be exercised without discrimination of any kind as to race, colour, sex, language, religion, political or other opinion, national or social origin, property, birth or other status. (U.N. General Assembly 1966, p. 2)

It is important to note that the concept of the progressive implementation of economic, social and cultural human rights, which arguably simplistically assumes that these rights will be realized over time as states, even poorer nations such as Guyana, gain economic resources and the government and legal infrastructure needed to enforce them, informs the Covenant. The only caveat is that states will only be expected to act 'within the means available to them'. Specifically, Article 2.1 states:

> Each State Party to the present Covenant undertakes to take steps, individually and through international assistance and co-operation, especially economic and technical, to the maximum of its available resources, with a view to achieving progressively the full realization of the rights recognized in the present Covenant by all appropriate means, including particularly the adoption of legislative measures. (U.N. General Assembly 1966, p. 2)

The Inter-American System of Human Rights pre-dates the International Convention on the Rights of Persons with Disabilities by many years. It began with the creation of the Inter-American Commission on Human Rights in 1959. This was followed in 1978 by the entry into force of the American Convention on Human Rights and establishment of the Inter-American Court of Human Rights. The articles of the American Convention cover a wide range of human rights including the right to life, security of the person, freedom, protection from inhumane treatment and the progressive implementation of economic, social and cultural rights. It also sets out the roles of the Inter-American Commission on Human Rights and the Inter-American Court, the former being responsible for investigating alleged human rights violations and determining which cases proceed to the Court (Organization of American States 2018)[1]. A key challenge in its early years, which coincided with the Cold War and fears about the potential spread of communism in Latin and Central America and the Caribbean, was dealing with authoritarian/military regimes responsible for murdering or 'disappearing' activists who opposed their regimes. Goldman (2009) contends that if the success of the Inter-American system is measured in terms of the reparations made for this flagrant violation of human rights in countries such as Argentina and Guatemala then it can be seen as remarkably successful. It has, however, also been plagued by on-going problems. It is seriously under-funded relative to the activities it undertakes. Despite growing needs to investigate alleged human rights abuses in the region and growing caseloads, the Commission and Court receive less than 10% of OAS funding. In the 2007 fiscal year the Commission's budget was $3,845,100.00 (U.S. dollars) and the Court's was $1,656,300.00 (U.S.). This compares to a budget of $72,171,000.00 (U.S.) for the European Court of Human Rights in the same fiscal year (Dulitzky 2011, p. 134).

---

1 The Organization of American States was founded in 1948 in part to bolster security amongst member states in the Western hemisphere and in response to perceived threats of the spread of communism. Headquartered in Washington, D.C., the OAS gradually took on other roles such as dispute resolution between member states (e.g., regarding borders, trade) and promoting better economic, political and cultural conditions in member states. Some leaders, such as Hugo Chavez of Venezuela, have denounced the OAS as a 'puppet' of the United States. Nonetheless with the entry into force of the American Convention on Human Rights and establishment of the Inter-American Court of Human Rights, both in 1978, the OAS signaled an intent to strengthen its role in monitoring and addressing human rights issues in the region (Editors 2018).

Under-funding has forced the Commission and Court to seek additional external funding for their activities (e.g., from Europe) but still funding falls far short of demands to investigate, document, process and litigate cases. This has resulted in insufficient personnel and a growing backlog of cases (Dulitzky 2011). It has also helped to limit the capacity of the Commission to make site visits to assess the human rights situations in some of its OAS member nations (there are 35). In the case of Guyana, it was only in 2016 that the Commission visited the country for the first time on a fact-finding mission on human rights (Rivero 2016). This is despite rampant human rights abuses such as police violence, domestic violence, violence against LGBTI youth, trafficking in women and the severe impoverishment of many vulnerable groups including disabled people. It was also six years after disability activists finally, after approximately a decade of struggle, succeeded in getting the Guyana Government to pass a Disability Act aimed at protecting disabled persons' human rights.

With these points in mind, I now illustrate why a deeper and more global conception of impairment and disability is needed in the context of understanding disabled people's rights, lives and struggles in the developing nation of Guyana.

3. From Principle to Practice? Impairment and Disabled People's Human Rights in Guyana

Guyana is a lower middle-income country (Gjaltema et al. 2016, p. 14) located on the northeastern coast of South America. Colonized first by the Dutch and later the British, the predominately Afro-Guyanese and Indo-Guyanese population, many descendants of slaves and indentured servants who labored on sugar plantations, is considered culturally part of the Caribbean. As of 2016, Guyana had a total population of 773,303 (World Bank 2016). Due to outmigration, there are now more Guyanese living abroad than in the country.

According to U.N. estimates 7–10% of the population of developing countries are disabled. This means that approximately 73,000 people in Guyana are disabled. In 2005, the National Commission on Disability, established in 1997 as an advisory body to the Government of Guyana, released the results of a survey of 1485 disabled people (Mitchell 2005). It noted that poverty was widespread and contributed to the production of impairment as well as financial barriers to accessing services such as health care and education (Mitchell 2005). Unemployment is widespread with 40% of the unemployed disabled people surveyed reporting that they had lost their jobs as a result of becoming impaired. Another 9% were trained and skilled but lacked opportunities to do paid work. Negative attitudes toward and treatment of disabled people were common (affecting 79% of respondents) and included people feeling ashamed of disabled family members and keeping them hidden from public view (Mitchell 2005). These problems and others persist today (e.g., Chouinard 2014).

Guyana signed the U.N. Convention on the Rights of Persons with Disabilities in 2010 and ratified the international treaty in 2014. The treaty is meant to encourage signatory nations to enact and enforce human rights laws for disabled people. It also has established an international committee to deal with complaints about violations of disabled people's human rights. Also in 2010, after many years of lobbying by disability activists and organizations, the Government of Guyana passed a Disability Act meant to protect the rights of disabled people to accessible environments, equal opportunity in education and employment, access to services such as health care and rehabilitation, and freedom from discrimination on the basis of disability. Unfortunately, however, disability organizations and other civil society groups report that the Act is not being enforced (Worth et al. 2017).

As argued above, one of the difficulties of addressing the oppression and exclusion of disabled people in terms of human rights is that this often does not take into account the geographically uneven production of impairment at the global scale. So, for example, people in Guyana experience severe and multiple forms of violence resulting in impairment or death. Police violence against civilians is endemic with the highest rate of police shootings of civilians in the world (Chouinard 2012). There is also violence in the illegal narcotics trade. Racialized violence remains an ongoing problem. Reflecting a violent colonial past and patriarchal oppression, there are also cutlass attacks (cutlasses being used to harvest sugar cane) resulting in impairment or death. Women are most often the victims and the perpetrators are usually men (Chouinard 2012). According to the Guyanese organization Help and Shelter (2011) as many as two out of every three women in the country are victims of domestic violence.

With the help of three female Guyanese interviewers (named in the acknowledgements to this article), from 2007–2015, 110 disabled women and men shared their life stories. At least four of those stories were about becoming impaired as a result of violence. Three different women reported being attacked with a cutlass by male partners or acquaintances. One lost her right arm in the attack, another lost both forearms and the third lost the use of one of her hands. A fourth interviewee reported losing his sight as a result of acid being thrown in his face by members of a drug cartel (Chouinard 2012). These are criminal acts producing impairment or death and are violations of basic human rights (e.g., to security of the person), and yet such acts remain very prevalent in Guyana. It is important to recognize, as well, that these acts are harrowing and traumatic and cause not only physical but also psychological impairment. A case in point is that of Cora (pseudonym) whose story is outlined below.

Cora arrived at her daughter's house one day and hearing her screams went upstairs to a bedroom. There she found her son-in-law chopping her daughter with a cutlass. She tried to intervene but was unsuccessful. Then moments later her son-in-law chopped her daughter in the head. Her daughter moaned, "Ah me dead" and dropped to the floor. Cora fled downstairs. Even though her daughter's body was lifeless Cora continued to hear her son-in-law chopping the body upstairs. In shock, she tried to flee the house but was accosted by the son-in-law who began chopping one of her hands. Bleeding profusely, she begged him to stop saying "look at all this blood—why do you want to do that?" To her surprise he stopped and she ran next door to a friend's house for help.

Cora's story illustrates just how terrifying these instances of domestic violence can be; resulting in this case, in one woman's death and in another woman's serious physical impairment.

Why, despite laws in place that in principle protect women's human rights do these kinds of attacks persist? Part of the explanation lies in the limitations of judicial and police services. A recent report by the U.S. State Department (2015, p. 10) on human rights in Guyana had the following to say about domestic violence:

> Domestic violence and violence against women, including spousal abuse, was widespread. The law prohibits domestic violence and allows victims to seek prompt protection, occupation, or tenancy orders from a magistrate. The police received 2170 reports of domestic violence cases, and 1131 persons were charged. Penalties for violation of protection orders include fines up to 10,000 Guyanese dollars (GYD) ($50) and 12 months' imprisonment. Survivors frequently were unwilling to press charges due to a lack of confidence in obtaining a remedy through the courts. Some preferred to reach a pecuniary settlement out of court. There were reports of police accepting bribes from perpetrators and other reports of magistrates applying inadequate sentences after conviction.

Marta, another woman who became impaired as a result of a cutlass attack by her male partner, lost both of her forearms. Her case illustrates the personal toll that lenient sentences take on women who are victims of chopping violence. Her partner was sentenced to seven years in jail even though Marta's impairments, impoverished conditions of life (e.g., lack of electricity and piped water in the home), and only very temporary access to extremely basic prosthetic devices meant that she would be disabled for the rest of her life. She was further disabled and excluded by attitudinal barriers that blamed her for the violent attack (e.g., gossip that she was promiscuous) and associated acts of 'shunning' and she said sadly that because of this she no longer felt a part of Guyanese society. With only one niece to assist her in her home she lived in terror that her male partner would return once he was released from jail and further injure or kill her. Such fears about vulnerability to violence were further accentuated by difficult living conditions. Dependence on her niece to assist with tasks such as turning on a generator for lighting meant that Marta had to wait alone in the dark in the evenings for her niece to return before she had light in her home.

Violence also in some cases worsened impairment and, along with barriers such as poverty and negative attitudes, worked to further marginalize and exclude disabled women in public and private spaces of life. Sarah, a woman who was mentally ill, was unable to communicate with her interviewer and so her mother was interviewed instead. Her mother related how Sarah was subjected to violence such as name-calling and having stones thrown at her if she ventured outside the home and into the local community because people recognized her as "not right in she head". Sarah also experienced violence in the home. It was not unusual for her children to beat her when they thought she had done something wrong in places such as the kitchen. Such experiences of abuse added to the trauma associated with being mentally ill. Sarah was also not receiving the medical treatment she needed—her home was located in a village a considerable distance away from the capital city of Georgetown and her family could not afford the transportation to either the National Psychiatric Hospital in Canje, Berbice or the Georgetown Public Hospital psychiatric ward where, at the time of the interview, only two psychiatrists were available. Guyana has a chronic shortage of psychiatrists and psychiatric support workers due to a combination of outmigration and limited resources for training. A 2013 newspaper report (Alleyne 2013), summarized the situation in the country in the following way:

> It has been twenty years since the PPP/C government took office against a backdrop of increasing numbers of mentally ill persons on the streets, but still there does not appear to be a comprehensive plan to address the problem. Mental health experts spoken to by this newspaper point out that the numbers of doctors and the facilities available remain woefully inadequate, in addition to which law reforms have not been made [there is a separate mental health act that dates from 1930]. At one point there was a mass rounding up of the mentally ill so that they would not be visible on the streets during a major event, but this was not followed up by any attempt to secure treatment for them.

Not surprisingly in such circumstances, the human rights of mentally ill people are repeatedly violated in practice as they face widespread stigma and discrimination in terms of employment and economic well-being, lack of cultural acceptance, and lack of access to services such as the judiciary, education and health care. In 2016, the Ministry of Health announced that it would open a new mental health unit in Georgetown with five psychiatrists as well as support staff (Disabled People's International, Department of Public Information 2016). It remains to be seen, however, how far this will go in diminishing mental impairment and securing human rights in practice for people with mental illness in Guyana. Concerns are already being raised that the five psychiatrists with the new unit have to service approximately 100,000 patients each and that social work and other staff are also scarce. This is in a country that has the highest rate of suicide in the world (Bhagirat 2017).

People with physical impairments also reported being abused in and/or outside the home. Mark, who was partially paralyzed on his left side as a result of a stroke, talked about the verbal abuse he was subjected to if he ventured outside his home and into the local community and how it made him feel hated and excluded. Another stroke survivor, Jim, noted how he was now shunned by and isolated from family members—with at least some believing that strokes were contagious. This meant he could not look to family for the assistance he needed with activities such as cooking and cleaning. Karen, who was missing a foot at birth, recounted how, as a young child, she overheard a nurse advising her mother to have her killed. It was a deeply traumatic experience that denied even her right to exist. As a young woman, she lived with her aunt and suffered psychological and physical abuse at the hands of the aunt's daughter and nephew. She was treated as a 'defective' outsider and mocked for not having a foot. She was told she did not have the right to make decisions in the home —even about her own belongings—and was beaten when she tried to assert this right. In desperation, she turned to the police for help but, despite physical evidence of the beatings, they did not assist. Finally, she took the only escape route open to her and moved out. Such acts of hate and devaluation, isolation and neglect, and violent oppression clearly violate disabled people's human rights to inclusion, respect, safe and secure environments, and in cases such as Karen's even the right to life itself.

Extreme economic disadvantage was a fact of life for many of the people with impairments and illnesses interviewed. Of the 81 interviewees for whom employment status is known, only four were in full-time employment: Bob was mobility impaired and used a wheelchair and worked at shoe repair in a market stall in Georgetown, Nigel, also mobility impaired and a wheelchair user, worked in an office staff position at Guyana Power and Light, Jody was visually impaired and worked as a local radio host in Georgetown, and Trisha, who was mobility impaired and a wheelchair user, also worked in an office job. Three interviewees reported sporadic employment (e.g., selling small items, tiling, making chair backs) with two of these (both wheelchair users and visibly impaired) noting that customers paid them less than their able counterparts because they were disabled. The remainder of the interviewees struggled to survive on meager government income assistance (the equivalent of one to two U.S. dollars per day). In three cases, this was augmented by periodic small remittances from family living abroad but this source of income was unreliable.

Poverty and discrimination act as barriers to mobility and accessing spaces such as those used for disability activism and the provision of health care. Representatives of disability organizations based in Georgetown interviewed by the author noted that their membership declined quickly due to the high costs of transportation to meetings. Guyana does not have public or paratransit systems and relies on private mini-buses or taxis for persons who cannot afford private vehicles or who are unable to drive. The mini-buses are highly profit-driven and focus on having as many passengers as possible as well as quickly arriving at destinations so that more passengers can embark and pay for transit. The former is a problem because mini-bus drivers frequently refuse to stop to pick up visibly impaired people such as those using wheelchairs or walkers. This is because their aids take up space that could otherwise be filled by paying passengers. The latter emphasis on arriving and departing quickly also contributes to impairment and death as a result of accidents. The problem of being refused mini-bus transit service was sufficiently severe to prompt disability organizations to launch a 'right to ride' campaign. Unfortunately, the campaign was unsuccessful for the most part and so disabled people continue to be denied rights to the mobility they need to be able to access spaces that could help to empower and enable them in their daily lives.

Widespread poverty amongst disabled people also acts as a barrier to accessing aids such as wheelchairs and walkers and the prostheses made in the single rehabilitation centre in Georgetown. Costs to import aids such as wheelchairs are high and this means that most are provided by charitable organizations such as Food for the Poor. Even so, these aids are not available to everyone who needs one. It is also expensive to import materials for prostheses, and with patients expected to cover the costs of materials (with the government and donors covering overhead and labour costs), lack of income acts as a barrier to accessing the prosthetic devices that people, such as Marta, need to mitigate impairment and lead more enabling lives. The Ptolemy Reid Centre in Georgetown, a rehabilitation centre, which now houses the only prosthetic unit in the country, estimates that since this service commenced in 1994 it has assisted 2000 people with prosthetic devices (Charles and Chigbo 2017). Still, access to prosthetic aids remains a problem for people such as Marta.

Cultural attitudes and practices also contribute to the violation of the human rights of persons with disabilities in Guyana. Rights to inclusion and equal opportunity are often compromised in practice when family members feel ashamed of a disabled family member, and as a result, hide them away in the home. It is not uncommon for disabled children to be kept hidden and out of the educational system for life. In some cases, disabled children are even chained to heavy furniture such as beds so they cannot leave the house. Such forced isolation also helps to explain why facilities such as the Open Doors Centre, a national job training centre for disabled people located in Georgetown, has had difficulties recruiting students for its programs—even though these are badly needed (Kaiteur News 2017). Disability activists interviewed as part of this study also point out that such practices contribute to low turnouts at public disability events, perceptions that there are not many disabled people in Guyana and politicians who have been slow to act on disability issues. Activists believe these are some of the reasons why it took almost a decade of lobbying to pressure the government into enacting a national Disability Rights Act in Guyana.

Whatever the challenges of realizing disabled people's human rights in practice in Guyana, the ten leaders of disability organizations who were interviewed as part of this study insisted that progress on disability issues would only be made once a national Disability Human Rights Act was in place (as noted above this happened in 2010). This in part reflects the global hegemony of a human rights framework for understanding disability issues. But it is also a significant 'leap of faith' that the Act will be enforced through the courts and government agencies. Also civil society organizations, as noted above, report that to date this has not been the case. This is perhaps not surprising in a context in which financial and human resources to address disability issues are very scarce, reflecting processes such as dependence on the importation of expensive manufactured goods from the Global North, the devaluation of currency as a term of debt repayment, and the outmigration of trained professionals from the country. This is not to say there is no progress on disability issues. The disability movement has developed over time in the country and leaders of such organizations as Young Voices of Disabled People contend that awareness of disabled people and their rights is on the rise (Admin 2013). Still, there is, arguably, a pressing need to consider the situation in Guyana in terms of the globally uneven geographic production of impairment. Legacies of a violent and patriarchal colonial past persist in pervasive violence, particularly against women—violence that results in impairment and even death. The high cost of importing aids such as wheelchairs or materials for prostheses mean that not all who need these aids to mitigate impairment receive them. This is also exacerbated by the outmigration of trained medical professionals in search of better wages and working conditions. Transportation costs, a chronic shortage of mental health professionals, and high costs of some medications, mean that people with mental illness also do not receive the treatment they need to diminish mental impairment. Many disabled people face poverty and discrimination in terms of access to transportation compounding their limited mobility and excluding them from potentially empowering and enabling spaces of life such as disability organization meetings.

4. Where Do We Go from Here? Towards Enabling Geographies of Impairment and Disability in the Global South

In this article, I have argued for a richer and deeper understanding of the geographically uneven production of impairment and disabling conditions of life at the global scale, and in countries of the Global South. Such an approach recognizes the legacies of a long and violent history of colonial and neo-colonial oppression manifest, for instance, in the chopping violence against women that still occurs in Guyana and results in impairment, death, the lack or loss of employment, deepening poverty and other disabling conditions of life. Patriarchal oppression is also at work here as manifest, for example, in tendencies to blame women for the violence they experience and related practices such as 'shunning' or avoidance. This too, has disabling consequences such as socio-spatial isolation. Marta, the woman who lost both forearms to chopping was, for instance, also deeply distressed to learn through the grapevine that one of her nephews was threatening his girlfriend with the same form of violence if she did not 'stay in line'. As the Guyana case study helps to show, cultures of disability are also geographically uneven and this is important to consider when assessing why human rights enjoyed in principle are not being realized in practice. While there are some cultural commonalities between Guyana and countries of the Global North, such as activists embracing a human rights perspective on disability issues, there are also divergences as well. The latter include the especially severe stigma and shame associated with mental and physical impairment and associated practices such as keeping disabled family members hidden away in the home. We also need to be cognizant of people's and nations' places in the uneven global political-economic order, as shown in Guyana's case by widespread and deep poverty that both causes impairment and exacerbates disabling conditions of life (e.g., through lack of access to prostheses, medicine). Disabled people in Guyana are also disadvantaged by the outmigration of trained professionals such as lawyers and doctors and the strain this puts on already very limited training resources. Nor is it surprising that rampant human rights abuses persist given the country's disadvantaged place in the international human rights system, as illustrated in this article with respect to the Inter-American system. There are, of course, internal factors at work here, such as corruption and bribery. The RefWorld (2016) report on human rights in

Guyana notes that it is not uncommon for magistrates to be bribed in exchange for imposing lighter sentences on violent offenders, or for women who are victims of violence not to report it to the police because they do not think justice will be served in court.

One advantage of thinking about disability human rights laws and issues in terms of global peripheries of law is that it also encourages us to understand that the production of impairment and disabling conditions of life are both global justice issues and need to be considered in that wider context. This approach also allows us to problematize both impairment and disability as about more than simply the violation of human rights. The Rana Plaza collapse in April 2013 in Bangladesh, for example, killed almost 1300 people and injured and impaired more than 2500 others (mostly as a result of the need for amputation of crushed limbs). This tragedy occurred because plant owners/managers valued profit over human safety and forced workers to continue to labour in a garment factory that they believed to be unsafe as a result of cracks in the walls that they had noticed the previous day (The Guardian 2015). The case drags on in the courts in Bangladesh but critics argue that too little is being done to make conditions in garment factories safer and prevent injury, impairment and death (Jazeera Media Network 2016). The case illustrates how the production of impairment in the Global South goes hand in hand with treating workers as cheap, exploitable and easily replaced. It also shows how the violation of human rights to a safe and secure workplace can have profoundly disabling consequences. Many of those injured in the collapse can no longer work due to psychological trauma as well as physical injuries—this in turn contributes to poverty and an inability to purchase necessities such as medicine, food and transportation.

Taking the uneven production of impairment and illness seriously also allows us to better appreciate the complex interconnections between violations of human rights, impairment, and disabling conditions of life across a wider range of phenomena. Women forced into the global sex trade, for example, often have documentation such as passports confiscated by traffickers and pimps to help ensure that they do not try to flee. In the country illegally, they are afraid to turn to the police for help because of the threat of deportation. Threats of violence are also sometimes made against family members back in the women's countries of origin as a way of 'keeping them in line'. The sex trafficking of women, as well as children, violates human rights to life, liberty and security of the person (UN Women 2017), but it also often results in psychological and physical impairment. It is worth noting that trafficking often occurs from poorer, less developed nations to more developed ones—this is because of disabling conditions of life such as widespread poverty that make women and children more desperate for income and jobs, and thus more vulnerable to traffickers.

Finally, if we consider the production of impairment and illness and disabling conditions of life such as poverty, global inequality and discriminatory acts that cause impairment and violate disabled people's human rights, to be matters of global injustice, then we can begin to imagine a more enabling and inclusive world. But building such a world in practice will take courage and the determination to do things differently by, for example, challenging ableist practices of evaluating job performance in terms of quantity rather than quality and failing to recognize the extra work that disabled people often do to be part of our workplaces in the first place. It will take a redistribution of wealth from the Global North to the South to sustain more enabling conditions of life (such as better working conditions, access to prostheses and other aids) in the long-term. It will also require a fairer distribution of wealth between the elite few and most people in countries of the Global South, such as Guyana, so that barriers to disabled people's inclusion and well-being, such as grinding poverty can be eliminated. Also, it will take ongoing efforts to 'think outside the box' of framing disability issues exclusively in terms of human rights as conceived of in countries of the Global North. Nations in the Global South have a critical role to play in encouraging a more expansive, encompassing view of the issues at stake in our highly unequal global capitalist order—an order which disproportionately impairs, sickens and disables people in the Global South. Scholars, political leaders and disability activists in these countries are well positioned to raise awareness about the human suffering and denial of rights that a globally unequal geography of impairment and disability entails. It is high time that we work toward the kinds of changes that will help to make being on the global peripheries of law a thing of the past.

Acknowledgments: I would like to thank the disabled women and men in Guyana who shared their life stories and the three Guyanese women who assisted with interviews with them: Cora Belle, Halima Khan, and Norma Adrian.

References

Admin. 2013. Advocate Calls for Implementation of Disability Act. *Guyana Times International*, January 4. Available online: http://www.guyanatimesinternational.com/?p=22998 (accessed on 1 December 2017).

Alleyne, Oluatoyin. 2013. Mental Health Care in Guyana. Lack of psychiatrists, facilities, support. *Staebroek News*, July 7.

Bell, Catherine, and William B. Anderson. 2017. Indigenous Rights in Canada. Revised by Gretchen Albers. Note Entry Originally Published in 2006. Available online: http://www.thecanadianencyclopedia.ca/en/article/aboriginal-rights/ (accessed on 2 November 2017).

Bhagirat, Lakhram. 2017. Mental Health Unit making strides in care delivery. *Guyana Times*, June 20. Available online: https://guyanatimesgy.com/mental-health-unit-making-strides-in-care-delivery/ (accessed on 7 December 2017).

Canadian Human Rights Commission. 2016. Annual Report to Parliament. Available online: http://www.chrc-ccdp.gc.ca/eng/content/publications (accessed on 4 June 2017).

Charles, Collin, and Samuel Chigbo. 2017. Reintegrating People with Disabilities. *Kaiteur News*, April 30. Available online: https://www.kaieteurnewsonline.com/2017/04/30/reintegrating-people-with-disabilities/ (accessed on 30 November 2017).

Chouinard, Vera. 2001. Legal Peripheries: Struggles over Disabled Canadians' Places in Law, Society and Space. *The Canadian Geographer* 45: 186–97. [CrossRef]

Chouinard, Vera. 2014. Precarious Lives in the Global South: On being disabled in Guyana. *Antipode* 46: 340–58. [CrossRef]

Chouinard, Vera. 2012. Pushing the Boundaries of Our Understanding of Disability and Violence: Voices from the Global South (Guyana). *Disability and Society* 27: 777–92. [CrossRef]

Cultural Survival. 2015. Convention on the Economic, Social and Cultural Rights Shadow Report Submission: Indigeneous Rights Violations in Guyana. Paper presented at the 56th Session, Geneva, Switzerland, September 21–October 9. Available online: http://tbinternet.ohchr.org/Treaties/CESCR/Shared%20Documents/GUY/INT_CESCR_CSS_GUY_21656_E.docx (accessed on 11 January 2018).

Degener, Thereisa. 2016. Disability in a Human Rights Context. *Laws* 5: 35. Available online: http://www.mdpi.com/2075-471X/5/3/35 (accessed on 13 February 2018). [CrossRef]

Della, Fina, Valentina, Rachele Cera, and Giuseppe Palmisano, eds. 2017. *The United Nations Convention on the Rights of Persons with Disabilities: A Commentary*. Berlin: Springer.

Disabled People's International, Department of Public Information. 2016. New Mental Health Unit to Open in Georgetown. Available online: http://www.dpi.com/ (accessed on 7 December 2017).

Dulitzky, Ariel. 2011. The Inter-American Human Rights System Fifty Years Later: Time for changes. *Quebec Journal of International Law (Special Edition)* 127: 127–64.

Editors. 2018. Organization of American States. *Encyclopedia Britannica*. Available online: https://www.britannica.com/topic/Organization-of-American-States (accessed on 14 February 2018).

Freeman, Melvin C., Kavitha Kolappa, Miguel Calas de Almeida, Arthur Kleinman, Niko Makhasvili, Sisifo Phakiahi, Benedetto Saraceno, and Graham Thornicroft. 2015. Reversing hard won victories in the name of human rights: a critique of the General Comment on Article 12 of the U.N. Convention on the Rights of Persons with Disabilities. *Lancet Psychiatry* 2: 844–50. [CrossRef]

Gjaltema, Taeke, Candice Gonzales, and Louise Ebbeson. 2016. An analysis of the status of implementation of the Convention on the Rights of Persons with Disabilities, ECLAC headquarters for the Caribbean, Studies and perspectives series. Available online: http://200.9.3.98/handle/11362/5043 (accessed on 14 February 2018).

Hanson, Stephen. 2008. The Residential School System in Canada. Available online: http://indigenousfoundations.arts.ubc.ca/the_residential_school_system/ (accessed on 2 November 2017).

Harpur, Paul. 2012. Embracing the new disability rights paradigm: The importance of the Convention on the Rights of Persons with Disabilities. *Disability & Society* 27: 1–14.

Help and Shelter. 2011. *Domestic Violence Pamphlet*. Georgetown: Help and Shelter.

Jaggar, Alison M. 2002. Vulnerable Women and Neoliberal Globalization: Debt Burdens Undermine Women's Health. *Theoretical Medicine and Bioethics* 23: 425–40. [CrossRef] [PubMed]

Jazeera Media Network. 2016. Rana Plaza Court Case Postponed in Bangladesh. *Bangladesh News: Al Jazeera*, August 14. Available online: http://www.aljazeera.com/news/2016/08/rana-plaza-tragedy-bangladesh-puts-18-trial-160823051641161.html (accessed on 6 December 2017).

Kaiteur News. 2017. Open Doors Centre Marks 15 Years, Strives for Inclusivity. *Kaiteur News*. Available online: https://www.kaieteurnewsonline.com/2016/05/14/open-doors-centre-marks-15-years-strives-for-inclusivity/ (accessed on 1 December 2017).

Kayess, Rosemary, and Phillip French. 2008. Out of Darkness into Light? Introducing the Convention on the Rights of Persons with Disabilities. *Human Rights Law Review* 8: 1–34. [CrossRef]

Kubik, Wendee, Carrie Bourassa, and Mary Hampton. 2009. Stolen Sisters, Second Class Citizens, Poor Health: The Legacy of Colonization in Canada. *Humanity and Society* 33: 18–34. [CrossRef]

Meekosha, Helen, and Karen Soldatic. 2011. Human Rights and the Global South: the case of disability. *Third World Quarterly* 32: 1383–98. [CrossRef]

Megret, Frederic. 2008. The Disabilities Convention: Human Rights of Persons with Disabilities or Disability Rights? *Human Rights Quarterly* 30: 494–516. [CrossRef]

Mitchell, Hannah. 2005. *Raising the Profile of Disability in Guyana: An Agenda for Action*. Georgetown: National Commission on Disability.

Office of the High Commissioner on Human Rights (OHCHR). 2018a. The Optional Protocol to the Convention on the Rights of Disabled Persons. Available online: http://www.ohchr.org/EN/pages/home.aspx (accessed on 1 February 2018).

Office of the High Commissioner of Human Rights (OHCHR). 2018b. Convention on the Rights of Persons with Disabilities: Article 12 Equal Recognition by the Law Subsection 3 on the Right to Supported Decision-Making. Available online: www.ohchr.org (accessed on 4 February 2018).

Organization of American States. 2018. The American Convention on Human Rights (ca. 1969). Available online: www.oas.org/dil/treaties_B-32_American_ConventiononHuman_Rights.pdf (accessed on 24 January 2018).

RefWorld. 2016. Country Reports on Human Rights Practices–Guyana. Available online: http://www.refworld.org/country,,,,GUY,,58ec8a2c13,0.html (accessed on 14 February 2018).

Rivero, María Isabel. 2016. IACHR Concludes Working Visit to Guyana. *OAS Press Release*. Available online: http://www.oas.org/en/iachr/media_center/preleases/2016/148.asp (accessed on 24 January 2018).

The Guardian. 2015. Rana Plaza Collapse: dozens charged with murder. Available online: https://www.theguardian.com/world/2015/jun/01/rana-plaza-collapse-dozens-charged-with-murder-bangladesh (accessed on 4 June 2017).

U.N. General Assembly. 1966. International Covenant on Economic, Social and Cultural Rights. December. Available online: http://www.ohchr.org/Documents/ProfessionalInterest/cescr.pdf (accessed on 25 January 2018).

UN Women. 2017. Sex Trafficking Is a Grave Violation of Human Rights and a Form of Violence against Women and Children, U.N. Entity to End Violence against Women and Children. Available online: http://www.endvawnow.org/en/articles/538-sex-trafficking-is-a-grave-violation-of-human-rights-and-a-form-of-violence-against-women-and-children.html (accessed on 6 December 2017).

U.S. State Department. 2015. *Country Reports on Human Rights Practices: Guyana*. Washington: United States State Department Bureau of Democracy, Human Rights and Labour.

World Bank. 2016. 2016 population Guyana. Available online: https.2016populationGuyana (accessed on 15 February 2018).

Worth, Nancy, Laurence Gagnon-Simard, and Vera Chouinard. 2017. Disabling Cities. In *Urbanization in Global Context: Canadian Perspectives*. Edited by Peake Linda and Alison L. Bain. Oxford: Oxford University Press, pp. 309–25.

10

Freedom of Opinion and Expression: From the Perspective of Psychosocial Disability and Madness

Fleur Beaupert

Independent Scholar, Sydney 2000, Australia; fbeaupert@outlook.com

Abstract: This article argues that civil mental health laws operate to constrict how people think, understand, and speak about psychosocial disability, madness, and mental distress. It does so with reference to views and experiences of mental health service users and psychiatric survivors (users and survivors) and their/our accounts of disability, madness, and distress, such as those articulated by the emerging field of Mad studies. The analysis considers the application of the rights to freedom of opinion and expression that are enshrined in the *International Covenant on Civil and Political Rights* and other international human rights instruments to the mental health context. The article explores the suppression of freedom of opinion and expression that is effected through the symbolic violence of psychiatry and the mental health paradigm. Focusing on Australian legal frameworks, the article discusses how the material violence and coercion characterising mental health laws compound this process. It is further argued that civil mental health laws, by codifying the tenets of psychiatry and the mental health paradigm so as to render them largely unassailable, validate the ontological nullification of users and survivors. The foregoing analysis exposes dangers of adopting a functional test of mental capacity as the pre-eminent legal standard for authorising involuntary mental health interventions. It is suggested that considering freedom of opinion and expression from the perspective of psychosocial disability and madness reinforces the Committee on the Rights of Persons with Disabilities' interpretation that such interventions are incompatible with international human rights standards.

Keywords: mental health law; Convention on the Rights of Persons with Disabilities; International Covenant on Civil and Political Rights; psychosocial disability; Mad studies; freedom of expression; freedom of opinion; coercion; symbolic violence; capacity

---

1. Introduction

This article examines the suppression of freedom of opinion and expression by mental health (law). The international human rights to freedom of opinion and expression are understood to act as 'enablers' for a range of civil and political rights and 'the good working of the entire human rights system' (O'Flaherty 2012, pp. 629–31). International human rights bodies have long acknowledged the importance of these rights for political participation and the democratic process, in addition to the enjoyment of the rights to freedom of assembly and association (Human Rights Committee 2011, p. 1). Further, the value of freedom of opinion and expression for the protection of social, economic, and cultural interests is increasingly recognised (O'Flaherty 2012, p. 631), including the development of societies (Sen 1999, pp. 152–54), education, and women's ability to make informed decisions of particular relevance to them (Commission on Human Rights 2000). Their application in the specific context of disabled people, including people with psychosocial disabilities, has not been a focus in international human rights discourse. The new era of disability rights heralded by the advent of the

Convention on the Rights of Persons with Disabilities (CRPD),[1] which embodies the indivisibility and interdependence of civil and political rights and economic, social, and cultural rights (Degener 2016, p. 5), provides an opportune moment in which to reconsider these foundational human rights.

Sections 2 and 3 explain key concepts and terms that are used throughout this article, including symbolic violence, madness, and psychosocial disability. In Section 4, I outline components of the international human rights to freedom of opinion and expression and the relevance of these rights to disability. In Section 5, I consider how the views and experiences of mental health service users, survivors of psychiatry, and other people with psychosocial disability (users and survivors) demonstrate that denial of freedom of opinion and expression is implicated in psychiatry and the mental health paradigm at multiple levels. This extends to forms of colonial and cultural oppression operating at the global level. I also discuss the growing body of knowledge of users and survivors about madness, distress and psychosocial disability. The discussion shows how the symbolic power of psychiatry and the mental health paradigm operates to constrain and silence ways of knowing, expressing, opining, and being that may be vital to a person's sense of self, a process of symbolic violence that cultivates the ontological nullification of users and survivors.[2]

Australian civil mental health laws[3] provide for an individual to be detained, or made subject to a community treatment order, in order to force mental health interventions upon them. As a federation, Australia is comprised of states and territories, each of which has its own mental health statute. Focusing on Australian legal frameworks, Section 6 provides an overview of mental health laws and reflects on debates about their compatibility with international human rights standards, paying particular attention to the concept of (in)capacity.

Section 7 describes the coercive project of mental health law and the interrelationship between the material violence and symbolic violence that are inherent in this body of law. It is argued that mental health laws solidify restrictions on the freedom of opinion and expression of users and survivors. It is further argued that, by codifying certain tenets of psychiatry and the mental health paradigm so as to render them largely unassailable, mental health laws validate the ontological nullification of users and survivors. It is suggested that these suppressive processes radically diminish opportunities for individual self-expression and for the epistemologies of users and survivors to exert influence on societal systems and structures.

2. Symbolic Violence

An analysis of freedom of opinion and expression from the perspective of psychosocial disability and madness illuminates the 'symbolic violence' that is perpetrated by psychiatry and the mental health paradigm and reified by mental health laws.

Symbolic violence is perpetrated where an actor, usually the State, dominates symbolic struggles in a particular social sphere—struggles over the making of meanings and construction of social realities—and thus monopolises associated symbolic power (Bourdieu 1990, pp. 135–37). The processes by which psychiatry and the mental health paradigm push aside, diminish and nullify other understandings of experiences and interactions that are labelled as 'mental illness', are increasingly recognised as involving symbolic violence (Crossley 2004, p. 172; Lee 2013). The symbolic power thereby exerted is founded on a dominant ideology, including 'fundamental precepts, such as the existence of mental 'illnesses', the pathologisation of certain behaviours/beliefs deemed socially

---

1 *Convention on the Rights of Persons with Disabilities*, opened for signature 30 March 2007, 2515 UNTS 3 (entered into force 3 May 2008) (CRPD).

2 'Ontological violence' or nullification occurs when a dominant ideology delivers an interpretation that 'determines the very being and social existence of the interpreted subjects' (Žižek 2008, p. 62).

3 Although similar issues are raised by forensic mental health and disability laws, my focus here is on civil mental health laws. The term 'mental health laws' is used throughout this article when referring to civil mental health laws, which are termed 'civil commitment laws' in some countries.

unacceptable and the location and the causes of mental distress' (Kinouani 2015). Flick Grey has spoken of how this ideology comprises a 'specific biomedical, diagnosis-driven universe of meaning' which silences and marginalises 'the lived truth of those in contact with the mental health system' (Coopes 2017).

In referring to the 'mental heath paradigm' and the 'medical model', I am referring to systems of meaning that derive substantially from the discipline of psychiatry as a subset of medicine.[4] These systems of meaning, which dominate mental health service delivery, presuppose and privilege psychiatric understandings of madness and distress as involving 'illness' and 'disorder', which must be cured, fixed, and managed. The Special Rapporteur on the Right to Health has recently made recommendations aimed at addressing 'the imbalance of the biomedical approach in mental health services' (Human Rights Council 2017, p. 20). Aspects of psychiatry and mental health services may temper the excesses of this approach. For example, psychiatrists may be sensitive to their patients' social relationships and circumstances in making diagnoses, providing advice, and recommending treatment, and may attend most closely to experiences that actually seem to bother their patients. Clinicians in mental health services will reach different views, informed by their various disciplinary backgrounds and a range of ideas, which will influence real world decisions and outcomes. Certain critical strains within psychiatry emphasise 'the dangers of simply suppressing' madness 'with drugs or other means' (Critical Psychiatry 2017). Yet these forces would be hard-pressed to alter the tenets forming the very roots of these systems of meaning.

3. On Terminology

The CRPD was formulated after extensive deliberations, and, uniquely, input from a number of disabled people's organisations, including the World Network of Users and Survivors of Psychiatry.[5] The application of the CRPD to psychosocial disability is made clear in Article 1, in which it is stated that persons with disabilities include 'those who have long-term physical, mental, intellectual or sensory impairments'. Although the term 'mental impairments' is used in the CRPD, the associated disability is recognised in Article 1 as involving the interaction of such actual or perceived 'impairments'[6] with 'various barriers' that may hinder a person's 'full and effective participation in society on an equal basis with others'. This part of the CRPD is understood to incorporate the 'social model' of disability (see Degener 2016, p. 2).[7] The term 'psychosocial disability' is now commonly used by activists, advocates, and scholars applying the CRPD framework and provisions to protect the rights of users and survivors.

Madness and mental distress are in the process of being re-imagined as distinct from, and part of, disability. The choice of particular words to name and categorise a person, experience, or encounter in this context is a political choice that may operate tacitly to either preserve or resist the dominant paradigm (Burstow 2013, p. 82) and be indicative of heated conceptual battles (Diamond 2013, p. 64). Whilst 'mental health service user' and 'consumer' are terms commonly employed in government and public discourse, people on the receiving end of mental health services frequently use a variety of different terms to describe themselves. The term 'consumer', implying an acceptance of psychiatry's medical model by someone who has real choices in the marketplace, may be considered misleading given the reality of involuntary mental health interventions, and is insulting to those who have suffered psychiatric abuse (see Weitz 2003, p. 71).

---

4 On the hegemonic nature of psychiatric discourse see Burstow (2013, pp. 80–81).

5 For the list of non-governmental organisations representing disabled people that participated in the CRPD negotiations, see United Nations Enable (2007).

6 The role of the concept of 'impairment' within the social model of disability has been subject to criticism by disability theorists (for example Hughes and Paterson 1997) and doubt has been cast on the applicability of this concept to psychosocial disability (Penson 2015).

7 The origins and development of the social model of disability are addressed in Barnes (2012).

Two terms that embody resistance to psychiatric discourse are 'Mad' and 'psychiatric survivor'. The term 'psychiatric survivor' has been embraced by many to show

> pride in our history of surviving discrimination and abuse inside and outside the psychiatric system, in advocating for our rights and in our personal and collective accomplishments—that psychiatric survivors are much more than a diagnostic label (Reaume 2008).

The term 'madness', which has in recent history been used in derogatory fashion, has been reclaimed since the emergence of the antipsychiatry movement and is used by some individuals and constituencies to affirm emotional, spiritual, and neuro-diversity (Menzies et al. 2013, pp. 10–11; Costa 2008). Rejecting the very categories of madness and sanity, Erick Fabris proposes the upper-case, proper noun 'Mad', to encompass people *considered* 'mentally ill', 'for political action and discussion' (Fabris 2013, p. 139).

'Madness' and its derivatives are controversial terms that may be considered offensive, including by many mental health service users. 'Disability', however, is far from achieving universal acceptance amongst users and survivors when it comes to self-identification (for example Beresford et al. 2010, pp 19–20). Jana Russo and Debra Shulkes, writing about the European user/survivor movement, have expressed concern about 'an implicit, and sometimes openly stated, demand that we all adopt the disability framework', particularly given that people's ability to self-define is often already diminished by the application of psychiatric labels and diagnoses (Russo and Shulkes 2015, p. 33).

'Mental illness' and 'mental disorder' are products of the diagnostic medical model, whereas 'psychosocial disability' aligns with the social model of disability and acknowledges the socially constructed nature of disability. 'Person with psychosocial disability' is a term that can be used to refer to people who may define themselves in various ways vis-à-vis their interaction with mental health services, including people 'who do not identify as persons with disability but have been treated as such, e.g., by being labeled as mentally ill or with any specific psychiatric diagnosis' (World Network of Users and Survivors of Psychiatry 2008). The political value of this term is captured by Tina Minkowitz who sees it 'as a bracketed space', allowing for individuals to identify needs for support and assert rights-claims when necessary (Minkowitz 2014, p. 461).

My choice to use the terms 'madness', 'mental distress' and 'psychosocial disability' in this article represents an attempt to heed the calls of Russo and Shulkes for 'an open-ended exploration of what different terms and concepts mean to different people' (Russo and Shulkes 2015, p. 34), and of Alice Hall that 'language is necessary in order to critique, challenge and re-write the stories and structures through which disabilities have been traditionally understood (Hall 2016, p. 8).'

4. The International Human Rights to Freedom of Opinion and Expression

The stifling of political dissent, workers' rights, media communications, artistic expression, and religious freedom are some of the areas that have been central to the development of domestic and international jurisprudence concerning the rights to freedom of opinion and expression. A number of international instruments have addressed threats posed to freedom of expression by expanded laws directed at combating terrorism and protecting national security and public order, such as offences of 'encouraging', 'praising' and 'justifying' terrorism, or engaging in 'extremist activity' (see Parmar 2015). A 2016 report of the Special Rapporteur on the promotion and protection of the right to freedom of opinion and expression stressed the potential for such measures to undermine the media, critical voices and activists (United Nations General Assembly 2016). Scholarship has taken up issues such as challenges that are associated with new information technologies, including internet governance (Benedek and Ketteman 2014), and the suppression of diverse gender identities (Nunan 2010).

The growing body of commentary about sharing and receiving ideas and information via digital technologies is particularly relevant when considering how to promote freedom of opinion and expression for people with disability (see Goggin 2017, p. 2). Yet, turning attention to disability in this sphere may yield valuable insights for theorising and implementing the rights to freedom of opinion and expression for all people, such as by destabilising assumptions about what constitutes 'normal' communications and expanding possibilities for activating communication rights (Goggin 2017). Confronting the meaning of the rights to freedom of opinion and expression specifically from the perspective of psychosocial disability and madness within disability human rights law may similarly enrich wider understandings of these rights. To date, there has been little consideration of the application of these rights to the mental health context, although concerns surrounding gross limitations on freedom of opinion and expression are implicit in much activism, advocacy, and research by users and survivors and their/our allies, as will be discussed in Section 5.

The first appearance of the rights to freedom of opinion and expression in an international human rights instrument was in Article 19 of the *Universal Declaration of Human Rights* (UDHR),[8] which states:

> Everyone has the right to freedom of opinion and expression; this right includes freedom to hold opinions without interference and to seek, receive and impart information and ideas through any media and regardless of frontiers.

Article 19 of the *International Covenant on Civil and Political Rights* (ICCPR)[9] encompasses the right to hold opinions without interference and the right to freedom of expression, with the right to freedom of expression further enfolding

> freedom to seek, receive and impart information and ideas of all kinds, regardless of frontiers, either orally, in writing or in print, in the form of art, or through any other media of [a person's] choice.[10]

A notable difference between the UDHR and ICCPR formulations is that the UDHR treats freedom of opinion and expression as belonging to a single right, whereas the ICCPR demarcates two distinct rights and groups the subsidiary right to 'freedom of information', together with the right to freedom of expression. Whilst the term 'freedom of expression' dominates international legal discourse, assuming the subsumption of freedom of information within its parent right, there is a complex relationship between what may be seen as two 'contiguous' rights—to freedom of expression and to freedom of (access to) information (McGonagle and Donders 2015, pp. 2–6). In this article, I refer to the 'rights to freedom of opinion and expression' to refer to the body of rights and obligations enshrined in Article 19 of the ICCPR, which contains the 'principal global expression of the right' (O'Flaherty 2012, p. 633).

The Human Rights Committee, which oversees the implementation of the ICCPR, published a new General Comment on Article 19 in 2011, *General Comment No. 34: Article 19: Freedoms of opinion and expression* (General Comment No. 34). This instrument notes the interdependence of the rights to freedom of opinion and expression, 'with freedom of expression providing the vehicle for the exchange and development of opinions' (Human Rights Committee 2011, p. 1). The only reference to disability is in the section on 'freedom of expression', which makes clear that 'all forms of expression and the means of their dissemination' are protected by Art 19(2), and mentions sign languages in the associated list (Human Rights Committee 2011, p. 3).

The re-articulation of the rights to freedom of opinion and expression in Article 21 of the CRPD displays a much-needed focus on freedom of information and communication rights. It supplements Article 19 of the ICCPR primarily by enumerating elements concerning seeking, receiving, and imparting information and ideas through diverse technologies, modes, and communication styles. Article 21 provides the following non-exhaustive list of actions States Parties must take to realise the rights to freedom of opinion and expression:

---

8 *Universal Declaration of Human Rights*, GA Res 217A, UN Doc A/810 91 (10 December 1948).

9 *International Covenant on Civil and Political Rights*, opened for signature 19 December 1966, 999 UNTS 172 (entered into force 23 March 1976) (ICCPR).

10 ICCPR, Art 19(2).

(a) Providing information intended for the general public to persons with disabilities in accessible formats and technologies appropriate to different kinds of disabilities in a timely manner and without additional cost;
(b) Accepting and facilitating the use of sign languages, Braille, augmentative and alternative communication, and all other accessible means, modes and formats of communication of their choice by persons with disabilities in official interactions;
(c) Urging private entities that provide services to the general public, including through the Internet, to provide information and services in accessible and usable formats for persons with disabilities;
(d) Encouraging the mass media, including providers of information through the Internet, to make their services accessible to persons with disabilities;
(e) Recognizing and promoting the use of sign languages.

Article 21, which includes a requirement for States Parties to take measures to ensure that people with disability can exchange information and ideas through all forms of communication of the person's choice, can thus be seen as vital to securing the participation of people with disability in all aspects of life. The emphasis seems to have been placed upon the technical and mechanical aspects of communication. This article is primarily concerned with the openness of the substance of communications and their epistemic underpinnings.

In the wake of the CRPD's entry into force, much of the debate about protecting the human rights of people with disability, including people with psychosocial disability, has focused on the right to equal recognition before the law contained in Article 12 and the requirements for States Parties:

- to recognise that people with disability 'enjoy legal capacity on an equal basis with others in all aspects of life';[11] and
- to take measures 'to provide access by persons with disabilities to the support they may require in exercising their legal capacity'.[12]

This debate has been substantially preoccupied with whether the CRPD permits substitute decision-making, such as guardianship and involuntary mental health interventions, and how States Parties can comply with the requirement to provide support in the exercise of legal capacity, as required by Article 12(3) (often termed 'supported decision-making'). The paradigm shift in the approach to legal capacity embodied in Article 12 of the CRPD (Beaupert and Steele 2015), as discussed in Section 6, has generated a vast body of commentary. A pivotal strand in the gradual broadening in scholarship to engage in more holistic fashion with the CRPD (for example, Arstein-Kerslake 2017; Beaupert et al. 2017) concerns the lawful material violence perpetrated against people with disability, violence that would not be tolerated in other contexts and against non-disabled bodies (Steele 2014; Steele and Dowse 2016; Spivakovsky, forthcoming).

Turning attention to the rights to freedom of opinion and expression offers promise for enhancing and complementing these enquiries in a number of respects. Applying these rights to mental health laws specifically may give additional insight into harms that are caused by the legal reification of the symbolic power of psychiatry and the mental health paradigm, including the lawful material violence constituted by involuntary mental health interventions. The Committee on the Rights of Persons with Disabilities (CRPD Committee), which is the body charged with monitoring the CRPD, has released a General Comment dealing with Article 12 of the CRPD, *General Comment No. 1: Article 12: Equal Recognition before the Law* (General Comment No. 1), concluding that substitute decision-making arrangements, including detention and other involuntary interventions pursuant to mental health laws, contravene Art 12 in addition to other provisions of the CRPD, and must therefore be abolished

11 CRPD, Art 12(2).
12 CRPD, Art 12(3).

(Committee on the Rights of Persons with Disabilities 2014). One question that follows is whether an additional consideration supporting the abolition of mental health laws lies in the need to protect the 'negative' aspects of the rights to freedom of opinion and expression (i.e., non-intervention by the State). Given the manner in which the 'lives, experiences and opinions' of people with disability are fundamentally devalued and invalidated (Spivakovsky, forthcoming), the scope of States' 'positive' obligations to establish legal, policy, and administrative machinery to support freedom of opinion and expression (Kenyon et al. 2017) is equally relevant.

Freedom of opinion and freedom of expression are valuable concepts because they are not limited to speech, and are therefore well-suited to encompassing the diverse modes of communication and expression that people with disability may use to interact with other people and the world. Crucially, the notion of rights to freedom of opinion and expression holds potential for disrupting the symbolic power and epistemic authority of psychiatry by validating opinions and expressions of users and survivors that conflict with the mental health paradigm. Further, an approach from this standpoint may assist in preventing the (further) pathologisation of both their/our resistance to this dominant paradigm (see Hamilton and Roper 2006, pp. 420–21; Spivakovsky, forthcoming) and their/our wider socio-political dissents (for example Metzl 2009). In fact, struggles over the creation of 'truths' across Mad and disability activism and scholarship share groundings in resistance against assignments of impairment and illness through dominant medical epistemologies (Lewis 2013, p. 117). Karen O'Connell has interrogated the ambivalent position that eccentricity occupies in (disability) law, and the increasing tendency to pathologise eccentric behaviour, with a view to destabilising the categories of disability and normalcy (O'Connell 2017). Similarly, asserting the importance of 'freeing' the opinions and expressions of people with disability about their/our actual or perceived 'impairments' or 'illness'—whether regarding idiosyncracies, spiritual beliefs, unusual experiences, altered states of consciousness, distress, pain, discomfort, social needs, oppression, health, or desire to be left alone—may work to dislodge, enrich, and connect apparently fixed social and legal categories.

Freedom of opinion, according to General Comment No. 34, covers 'all forms of opinion', 'including opinions of a political, scientific, historic, moral or religious nature' (Human Rights Committee 2011, p. 2). Article 19(2) of the ICCPR on the right to freedom of expression protects the exchange of 'information and ideas of all kinds, regardless of frontiers'. In emphasising the inexhaustible nature of the forms of protected information and ideas, General Comment No. 34 lists political discourse, commentary on personal and public affairs, canvassing, discussion of human rights, journalism, cultural and artistic expression, teaching and religious discourse as being included amongst the expressions protected by Article 19 (Human Rights Committee 2011, p. 3). There is nothing to suggest that a person's opinions and expressions about their experiences of psychosocial disability or interactions with mental health services would be excluded. In light of growing concern about the questionable evidence base for mental health interventions (see Human Rights Council 2017, pp. 7–8; Whitaker 2010) and serious physical harms and lower life expectancies that are associated with these interventions (The Royal Australian & New Zealand College of Psychiatrists 2016; Lawrence et al. 2013), the imperative to protect an individual's ability to form their own opinions about what is happening, and should happen, to their mind and body—and to act on those opinions—is heightened.

The right to freedom of expression is subject to the restrictions set out in Article 19(3) of the ICCPR, specifically 'restrictions as are provided by law and are necessary':

(a) For respect of the rights or reputations of others;
(b) For the protection of national security or of public order (ordre public), or of public health or morals.

The circumstances in which freedom of expression will be protected under international law are circumscribed. The above restrictions to do not apply to the right to freedom of opinion, which, according to General Comment No. 34, may not be infringed even during a state of emergency (Human Rights Committee 2011, pp. 1–2). I am primarily interested in exploring the nature and implications of denial of freedom of opinion and expression for users and survivors; this article does not undertake legal analysis of whether mental health laws contravene Article 19 of the ICCPR and/or Article 21 of the CRPD. In particular, I do not examine whether restrictions that are imposed by mental health laws on the freedom of expression of people falling within their jurisdiction would come under the legally permissible restrictions.

The following section addresses the suppression of freedom of expression and opinion in the mental health context with reference to the views, experiences, and epistemologies of users and survivors and the symbolic violence that operates to marginalise these perspectives.

5. Unravelling the Symbolic Violence of Psychiatry and the Mental Health Paradigm

The symbolic violence of psychiatry and the mental health paradigm perpetrates diverse, sometimes blatant, and sometimes very subtle harms, by categorising the distress that people experience and facilitating a range of mental health interventions across institutional and community settings (Lee 2013). The deeply stifling and suppressive effects of psychiatry and the mental health industry have long been theorised.[13] Erving Goffman's work on mental asylums tracked the career of inmates and suggested that the asylum's structures, regimes, and rules imposed a status beyond the patient's control, whilst discrediting their story (Goffman [1961] 2007). Goffman's observations led him to describe asylums as 'total institutions', which radically altered inmates' personal identity (Goffman [1961] 2007). The following accounts of users and survivors confirm the thesis that psychiatry and the mental health paradigm can set in motion processes that destroy a person's sense of self.

Cath Roper has described the outcome of being psychiatrised, and co-opted into medical ways of making meaning of one's madness, and distress as follows: 'Our sense of self crumbles, our way of being in the world, what we know, how we make meaning, is disparaged and wrong' (Roper, forthcoming). Patricia Deegan, sharing her experience of being diagnosed with 'mental illness' at a young age, has said:

> Our personhood and sense of self continued to atrophy as we were coached by professionals to learn to say, "I am a schizophrenic"; "I am a bi-polar"; "I am a multiple". And each time we repeated this dehumanizing litany our sense of being a person was diminished as "the disease" loomed as an all powerful "It", a wholly Other entity, an "in-itself" that we were taught we were powerless over (Deegan 1996).

The notion that an institution or worldview can radically alter someone's identity implies that there is a reprogramming of thoughts and opinions about one's self and one's place in the world. The symbolic violence of psychiatry and the mental health paradigm can stifle thoughts, foreclosing possibilities for understanding and conceptualising one's own experiences. This process can preclude the forming and expressing of other opinions and understandings about what is happening, understandings that may be vital for a person to make sense of, work through, or embrace their experiences. Instead, it can instil a complete lack of self-confidence and faith in oneself, as elucidated by Ji-Eun Lee relying on descriptions by users and survivors of how they internalised the reality offered by clinicians of their 'resistance to treatment' and 'incompetence' (Lee 2013, p. 116).

Jana Russo has encapsulated the causal connection between the symbolic violence of psychiatry and the denial of the freedom of opinion and expression of users and survivors in describing how 'finding the right words', and even thinking through one's experiences, are challenging processes when 'we constantly meet psychiatry as a point of reference' (Russo 2016, p. 76). Katie Aubrecht's description of coercion in mental health treatment demonstrates how this encounter can destroy one's sense of self to the point of being completely uncertain about one's thoughts and opinions, or feeling almost possessed by the text of 'illness':

[13] Scholarship in this tradition includes the following, among many others: (Szasz [1960] 1997; Goffman [1961] 2007; Foucault [1964] 2001; Chamberlin [1997] 2012); Fabris (2011); Rapley et al. (2011); Arrigo (2012); Newnes (2016).

> Under the watchful gaze of a physician, I was taught to read experiences, red cheeks, heavy hearts, and knots, as symptoms of mental illness and as tests of my character. I was constantly quizzed about how well I knew the experiences I had were actually true experiences. I couldn't be sure what I felt, liked, or wanted anymore. I did, however, become ever more familiar with what doctors felt, liked, and wanted, and that those would be the right things to feel, like, and want (Fabris and Aubrecht 2014, p. 191).

The impression that is created by such accounts is that when medical systems of meaning about madness and distress are imposed upon an individual this may actually suffocate thoughts and opinions that will enable them to express how they are feeling, what they are experiencing, and their views on what should happen and what supports—if any—they would find useful. Constructions of psychiatrised people[14] as 'disordered', 'incompetent' and 'dangerous' can entail epistemic disqualification of an individual as a legitimate 'knower' who can speak on their own behalf (Liegghio 2013). Further, supplanting an individual's thoughts and opinions with a system of meaning that destroys their very sense of self goes to the core of being and human dignity (see Liegghio 2013; Roper, forthcoming). This is a manifestation of 'ontological violence', described by Slavoj Žižek as occurring when a dominant ideology delivers an interpretation that 'determines the very being and social existence of the interpreted subjects' (Žižek 2008, p. 62).

Decades of resistance by ex-patients, psychiatric and mental health system survivors, consumers, mental health service users, advocates, practitioners, academics, and other allies have cultivated epistemologies grounded in experiential knowledge that challenge psy-based[15] understandings about 'mental illness' (Menzies et al. 2013, pp. 3–9). Whilst such dissents are often co-opted and manipulated to reinforce mental health industry agendas (Penney and Prescott 2016), different constituencies of users and survivors continue to work strategically to engage their/our own knowledge, histories and identities to build distinct visions and realities of healing, social justice, and political change (for example, Costa et al. 2012; Russo and Sweeney 2016). One spearhead of these initiatives is the emerging field of enquiry, Mad studies.

Mad studies operates as a praxis within which divergent perspectives and disciplines can connect as part of a collective project aiming to

> engage and transform oppressive languages, practices, ideals, laws and systems, along with their human practitioners, in the realms of mental 'health' and the psy sciences, as in the wider culture (Menzies et al. 2013, p. 13).

Mad studies is particularly relevant when considering freedom of opinion and expression from the perspective of psychosocial disability and madness because of its explicit focus on deploying the opinions and experiences of Mad constituencies, and celebrating their expression, in order to 'contest regimes of truth' (Menzies et al. 2013, pp. 14–15). In working to transform and transcend dominant medical approaches to madness, Mad studies does not deny that users and survivors may experience 'psychic, spiritual and material pains and privations' and want help in dealing with these experiences:

> To the contrary, it is to acknowledge and validate these experiences as being authentically human, while at the same time rejecting clinical labels that pathologize and degrade; challenging the reductionist assumptions and effects of the medical model; locating psychiatry and its human subjects within wider historical, institutional and cultural contexts; and advancing the position that mental health research, writing, and advocacy are primarily about opposing oppression and promoting human justice (Menzies et al. 2013, p. 10).

---

[14] The term 'psychiatrisation', which refers to processes that construct and produce people as 'mentally ill', subverts understandings of madness and mental distress as individualised pathologies (LeFrançois and Coppock 2017, p. 165).

[15] Rose (1998) contends that the psy sciences (psychology, psychiatry, and other disciplines that designate themselves with the prefix psy) constitute techniques for the disciplining of human difference.

In discussing possibilities for harnessing the individual and collective experiences and knowledge of users and survivors, Peter Beresford emphasises that users and survivors have different and diverse *knowledges* and that experiential knowledge takes many forms (Beresford 2016, p. 42). Some of these knowledges are comparatively well-established (see Mills 2014, p. 144), such as the hearing voices movement, which positions the experience of hearing voices, and other unusual beliefs and experiences, as something real and meaningful (Intervoice The International Hearing Voices Network), thereby subverting explanations of such experiences as symptoms of 'mental illness' or 'psychosis'. Others are emerging, such as the 'Mad approach to grief', which Jennifer Poole and Jennifer Ward offer up to 'start a conversation' about 'getting under', 'feeling', and 'claiming' grief, in part to challenge the increasing medicalisation of grief through the development of a broadening array of psychiatric diagnostic categories (Poole and Ward 2013). Research conducted on mental health service users' views about their experiences of mental health issues and interactions with mental health services revealed limitations the medical model places upon people's ability to truly make sense of the wider social context of madness and distress (Beresford et al. 2010).

Whilst such knowledges diverge in important ways, many of them share in common a dissatisfaction with the dominant medical model and the constraints that it imposes on their/our abilities and opportunities to name and make meaning of our experiences. Some users and survivors consider certain experiences labelled as symptoms of 'mental illness' to be meaningful processes that they wish to explore rather than numb through the use of medication (Spandler and Calton 2009, p. 245). Thus, Poole and Ward speak of 'grief liberation practices' run by people who have been constructed as disordered 'because of how they expressed and communicated the pain' and who 'know what it is to break open the bone of grief and story it from down deep' (Poole and Ward 2013, p. 103). These knowledges indicate that experiences that are frequently classified as symptoms of 'mental illness' are for some users and survivors forms of expression in and of themselves, which need to be felt, voiced, and lived through on one's own terms. Helen Spandler and Tim Calton posit the 'right to *experience* psychosis ... without *forced* treatment/medication ... but with maximum *support*' in response to this need (Spandler and Calton 2009, p. 246), throwing into sharp relief the denial of freedom of opinion and expression that can accompany an approach which predominantly seeks to eliminate or dull such 'symptoms'.

Article 21 of the CRPD does not explicitly direct itself to this outlook on expression and the interconnection between expression and the different epistemologies and ways of being of people with disability. On one level, the exploration in this article points to the potential limitations of the CRPD in addressing fundamental injustices connected to deference to medical epistemologies that enact 'mental illness' as a negative attribute residing in the mind and body in framing the social needs and political demands of people with psychosocial disability. On another level, I am using the concept of freedom of opinion and expression as a springboard to interrogate concerns which underlie and give further content to articulations and theories of rights under the banner of the CRPD. Degener writes that the CRPD provides for a new concept of 'transformative equality', which goes beyond combating discriminatory behaviour, structures, and systems to require positive measures that change the offending structures and address hierarchical power relations (Degener 2016, p. 24). Further engaging the substantive dimensions of the concept of freedom of opinion and expression for disabled people—in addition to procedural aspects relating to modes of, and technologies for, expression and communication—may enliven this project.

Whilst there are unifying threads in the experiences and histories of users and survivors, the potential for the Mad movement—particularly through (sometimes unwitting) attempts to universalise experiences of madness and mental distress—to itself subjugate the knowledges of marginalised individuals, communities, and identities (Gorman 2013) should be acknowledged as part of the complexity of denial of freedom of opinion and expression at work in this context. Within different constituencies of users and survivors, hierarchies that privilege and centre certain experiences can trivialise the process of meaning-making for people for whom there is no well-established knowledge base (Grey 2017). Every person's experience of seeking access to, using, or being abused by, mental health services, and how this experience interacts with their identities, relationships, and social positionings, is unique. Yet, allowing for the expression of unique experiences may require a conscious broadening in outlook to address certain commonalities within marginalised communities. Colin King, for example, explains how the invisibility of whiteness within European psychiatry serves to obscure the neo-colonial processes underpinning diagnoses of 'psychosis' and 'schizophrenia' assigned to African and black men (King 2016). In cautioning against 'the solidification of an 'essential' Mad identity', Rachel Gorman exposes a troubling lack of engagement by the Mad movement and disability studies with analyses of race, poverty, migration, and the global (Gorman 2013).

With the onset of the Movement for Global Mental Health (Movement for Global Mental Health 2017), and the World Health Organization's prioritisation of global mental health promotion (Wildeman 2013), considerations of freedom of opinion and expression expand beyond individual and collective expressions and experiences of user and survivor constituencies towards ethno-cultural expression and freedom. In her exploration of how global mental health policy can be read as a form of colonial discourse, China Mills uncovers how psychiatric practice can become an instrument of rights violations masked as benevolent health interventions in parts of the global South (Mills 2014, pp. 4–6). Mills concerns about Global Mental Health lead her to ask: 'as this knowledge is exported as a universal standard, a global norm, what other ways of knowing are lost, or forced to speak in whispers?' (Mills 2014, p. 7). The racism and colonialism that in many respects underpins psy discourses can threaten 'the cultural survival of Indigenous spirituality and healing', impacting ongoing struggles for Indigenous sovereignty (Tam 2013, p. 297). Users and survivors in India are utilising the framework of the CRPD to contest the colonial impositions of the asylum, mental health law, and practices of segregation and exclusion that have become 'inextricably mixed into the project of providing mental health services' (Davar 2005).[16] The next steps in reform of laws and policies relating to mental health and disability in the global North thus have pressing socio-political implications both within and beyond its borders.

The discussion in this section has hinted at the breadth of the denial of freedom of opinion and expression that is effected through the symbolic violence of psychiatry and the mental health paradigm. It has also been suggested that such suppression of different ways of knowing, expressing, and opining cuts to the essence of being and humanness, manifesting as a form of ontological violence against the inherent human dignity that forms the foundation of international human rights.[17] Before considering how these harmful suppressive effects are compounded by civil mental health laws in the final section, Section 6 provides an overview of these legal frameworks and debates surrounding their compliance with the CRPD.

6. Civil Mental Health Laws, the Convention on the Rights of Persons with Disabilities and (In)Capacity

The trajectory of law's relationship to madness when it comes to civil confinement and control of people with psychosocial disability is often characterised as involving a central tension between 'rights-based legalism' and paternalism or clinical discretion (McSherry and Weller 2010, pp. 4–5). Mental health law reform in the global North has tended to oscillate between allowing medical professionals substantial discretion over the treatment and detention of people with psychosocial disability and requiring more extensive legal oversight of these processes (Bean 1986, p. 14). A persistent assumption underlying these reforms has been that some level of formal involuntary psychiatric intervention in the lives of individuals with psychosocial disability is necessary in order to

---

16 The scope of this article precludes a fuller account of the relationship between freedom of opinion and expression and global mental health promotion and Western medical imperialism (see (Davar 2005; Jayawickrama and Rose 2017; Bayetti and Jain 2017; Mills 2014), for exploration of relevant intersections).

17 See ICCPR, Preamble: 'Recognizing that these rights derive from the inherent dignity of the human person'.

protect health and safety. The advent of the CRPD has eroded this assumption. At present, however, mental health laws in many jurisdictions typically make provision for two classes of compulsory intervention, which are effected through a legal 'involuntary order':[18] (a) inpatient commitment or detention in a mental health facility; and (b) outpatient commitment or a community treatment order (CTO), requiring submission to mental health interventions and compliance with other conditions whilst living in community settings. Another element of formal coercion pursuant to mental health laws is the administration of unwanted drugs and procedures to individuals subject to an involuntary order.

In Australia, the statutory criteria that must be satisfied for a person to be made subject to an involuntary order[19] include core prerequisites that: (a) the person has 'mental illness' or 'mental disorder' variously defined;[20] and (b) owing to that condition, 'treatment' is required in order to protect the person or other people from harm. The immediacy and level of seriousness of the requisite harm varies between jurisdictions and typically extends to a risk of deterioration in the person's condition or health. An additional requirement, often termed 'the least restrictive alternative principle', is that there must be no less restrictive means of providing the 'treatment'.[21] Secondary statutory criteria relating to the proposed intervention may also apply, such as the need for immediate or efficacious 'treatment' to be provided (see Carney et al. 2011, p. 58).

A more recent arrival in four Australian jurisdictions—Western Australia, Tasmania, South Australia, and Queensland—is a requirement that the person lacks 'decision-making ability' in relation to, or the capacity to consent to, the proposed intervention.[22] Although a lack of decision-making ability is not a prerequisite to making an involuntary order in the other jurisdictions, the relevant mental health statutes do now incorporate important provisions and requirements regarding obtaining consent and consideration of decision-making ability that limit the circumstances in which involuntary mental health interventions can occur.[23] The closely related concepts of mental capacity and decision-making ability discussed further below, which have become pivotal in disability human rights discourse, go to the heart of the rights to freedom of opinion and expression. This is because their formulation in and through mental health, disability, and capacity laws implies that the opinions and expressions of people considered to lack mental capacity or decision-making ability are so unworthy of being taken seriously that they can be overridden.

Decision-making about involuntary mental health interventions under Australian mental health laws is primarily shared between clinicians, in particular, psychiatrists and other doctors, and MHTs (or an equivalent body such as a generalist tribunal).[24] MHTs are multi-disciplinary quasi-judicial bodies that are established in each state and territory, sitting at the apex of the primary decision-making

---

18 I adopt this term to refer to the various orders that authorise involuntary mental health interventions pursuant to civil mental health or commitment laws throughout this article.

19 *Mental Health Act 2014* (Vic), s. 5; *Mental Health Act 2007* (NSW), ss. 12–15 (detention) and 53–54 (community treatment order); *Mental Health Act 2015* (ACT), ss. 58 (psychiatric treatment order) and 66 (community care order); *Mental Health and Related Services Act* (NT), ss. 14–15A (involuntary admission) and 16 (involuntary treatment in the community); *Mental Health Act 2016* (Qld), s. 12; *Mental Health Act 2009* (SA), ss. 10, 16 (community treatment orders), 21, 25, 29 (inpatient treatment orders); *Mental Health Act 2013* (Tas), ss. 39 and 40; *Mental Health Act 2014* (WA), s. 25.

20 Some Australian mental health statutes broaden the scope of involuntary intervention beyond people considered to have a 'mental illness' to cover other people with disability, such as people who are considered to be 'mentally disordered' or to have a 'mentally disturbance' or 'cognitive impairment' in certain circumstances: see, for example, *Mental Health and Related Services Act* (NT), ss. 15–15A; *Mental Health Act 2007* (NSW), s. 15.

21 This principle does not form part of the statutory criteria that must be satisfied in order for an involuntary order to be made by the MHT in Tasmania, although it should be factored into decision making under the *Mental Health Act 2013* (Tas) by virtue of ss. 12(d) and 62(a).

22 The terminology and formulations used for this criterion vary: see *Mental Health Act 2016* (Qld), ss. 12(1)(b), 14; *Mental Health Act 2009* (SA), ss. 5A, 10(1)(c), 16(1)(c), 21(ba), 25(ba), 29(ba); *Mental Health Act 2013* (Tas), ss. 7, 40(e); *Mental Health Act 2014* (WA), ss. 18, 25(1)(c).

23 See *Mental Health Act 2014* (Vic), ss. 68–76; *Mental Health Act 2007* (NSW), ss. 68(h1); *Mental Health Act 2015* (ACT), ss. 78, 56. In the Northern Territory and the Australian Capital Territory one of the prerequisites is that the person lacks decision-making ability, *or* has refused, treatment; in the Northern Territory the standard lifts to unreasonable refusal: *Mental Health and Related Services Act* (NT), s. 14(b)(iii); *Mental Health Act 2015* (ACT), ss. 58(2)(b), 66(2)(b).

24 The term mental health tribunal (MHT) will be used to refer to the MHT or equivalent body in each jurisdiction.

hierarchy (Carney et al. 2011). MHT decisions may be appealed to the courts, although appeals are not a frequent occurrence in most jurisdictions. Typically, an interim period of involuntary detention for assessment purposes can lead to a longer formal period of involuntary intervention. The MHT is in most cases responsible for making the initial involuntary order and conducting further hearings to determine if the person continues to satisfy the relevant statutory criteria on the order's expiry or the next review date. Similar criteria apply for authorising detention and making a CTO. Uniquely, in NSW, a separate lower threshold test is prescribed for making a CTO in some situations,[25] comparable to the standard applying to preventive outpatient commitment regimes in place in some United States jurisdictions (Player 2015, pp. 175–81).

One distinct trend in recent mental health law reform in the global North has been towards a stronger due process model, or increased procedural protections, such that laws provide for more stringent and frequent oversight by courts or quasi-judicial bodies (Carney et al. 2011, p. 5). However, recent reforms have expanded the situations in which involuntary psychiatric interventions may be authorised in several respects (Gooding 2017, p. 31). The introduction of CTOs, for example, has extended the locus of involuntary mental health interventions into the community. Whilst CTOs are now well-embedded in the Australian mental health law landscape, they have sparked controversy in other jurisdictions where they have been only relatively recently established, such as Scotland (Taylor 2016) and many parts of the United States (Player 2015, pp. 162–63). Outpatient commitment has far-reaching coercive implications, intruding into many aspects of a person's life (Fabris 2011, pp. 136–49), and the presumption that CTOs are a less restrictive alternative to detention has been called into question (Callaghan and Newton-Howes 2017, pp. 908–10). The situational context in which involuntary mental health interventions can be authorised has also broadened in some jurisdictions through changes to the relevant statutory criteria (Appelbaum 2006).

Given this trend towards *expansion*, it is imperative to continue grappling with questions surrounding the compatibility of mental health laws with human rights standards and the wider ethics of involuntary mental health interventions.

The Convention on the Rights of Persons with Disabilities and Involuntary Mental Health Interventions

Historically, mental health laws largely grounded the authority for their involuntary interventions in 'mental illness' and 'dangerousness' criteria. The shift towards 'incapacity' or 'lack of decision-making ability' as an additional or alternative rationale has commonly been viewed as a progressive development (Fistein et al. 2009). The entry into force of the CRPD has destabilised this perspective.

There is now a sharp divergence between mental health laws depending upon whether they incorporate a prerequisite that the person lacks the capacity to consent to the proposed intervention. Many commentators have pointed to the seemingly anomalous nature of mental health laws that do not include such a criterion. It has frequently been argued that this position discriminates unjustifiably against people with psychosocial disability, since informed consent is foundational to laws governing health care generally (Large et al. 2008, p. 878; Callaghan et al. 2013). Long before the entry into force of the CRPD, similar reasoning led commentators to propose the abandonment of separate mental health legislation in favour of generic health care or incapacity legislation applying to anyone lacking the capacity to consent to proposed medical treatment (Gordon 1993; Szmukler and Holloway 1998; Wand and Chiarella 2006). Thus the creep into mental health laws of incapacity-related prerequisites to involuntary interventions is often understood to be a delimiting, rights-respecting measure (Fistein et al. 2009).

The CRPD prescribes a regenerated outlook on (in)capacity, as epitomised in Article 12 (Equal recognition before the law). Article 12(1) states the underlying principle that 'persons with disabilities have the right to recognition everywhere as persons before the law'. The remaining provisions expose

[25] *Mental Health Act 2007* (NSW), s. 53(3), (5).

how domestic formulations of legal capacity have undermined this principle in its application to people with disability. Article 12(2) demands recognition of the 'legal capacity' of people with disability on an equal basis with others. Legal capacity is a constitutive concept in numerous legal systems, encompassing an individual's ability to hold rights and duties (legal standing); and their ability to exercise those rights and duties (legal agency) (Committee on the Rights of Persons with Disabilities 2014, p. 3). Article 12(3) provides that States Parties 'shall take appropriate measures to provide access by persons with disabilities to the support they may require in exercising their legal capacity'. The short-hand term 'supported decision-making' is often used to describe measures contemplated by Art 12(3), although this term does not appear in the CRPD's text. Different understandings of this term indicate that 'supported decision-making' 'refers to a collection of various demands ... [which] centre upon boosting the agency of persons with disabilities, offering them resources for making choices among good options about how to live' (Gooding 2017, p. 11).

Denial of the legal capacity of people with disability on the basis that they lack the mental capacity to make decisions about their/our own lives, or to participate in various private and public processes, has been endemic throughout history. People with disability who are considered to lack mental capacity have been legally prevented, for example, from getting married, voting, entering into contracts, and deciding what happens to their/our bodies and minds (Committee on the Rights of Persons with Disabilities 2014, p. 2). Laws in numerous countries continue to effect deprivations of liberty and denials of legal personhood on the basis of distinct approaches to mental capacity, known as the 'status approach', the 'outcome approach' and the 'functional approach' (Committee on the Rights of Persons with Disabilities 2014, p. 4). The status approach to mental capacity denies legal capacity purely on the basis of a person's status as a person with disability, or a medical diagnosis, whereas the 'outcome approach' attributes incompetence on the basis that a person has made a decision that is considered to have negative consequences (Committee on the Rights of Persons with Disabilities 2014, p. 4). A third, highly-contested approach, is the 'functional approach', which denies legal capacity where a person is considered to lack mental capacity on the basis of a specified assessment process, which often involves attempting to determine 'whether a person can understand the nature and consequences of a decision and/or ... can use or weigh the relevant information' (Committee on the Rights of Persons with Disabilities 2014, p. 4).

In General Comment No. 1 on the right to equal recognition before the law, the CRPD Committee interpreted Article 12 of the CRPD as requiring the abolition of substitute decision-making regimes, such as guardianship and mental health laws (Committee on the Rights of Persons with Disabilities 2014, p. 6). The Committee's view is that Article 12 is contravened when people with disability are denied legal capacity on the basis of mental capacity tests, including tests adopting a functional approach to mental capacity. This interpretation therefore inverts the long-standing view that various disability-specific regimes providing for substitute decision-making grounded in an incapacity rationale are protective, and instead casts them as discriminatory measures (Beaupert and Steele 2015, p. 162). Historically, as Linda Steele explains, 'through the division of human rights subjects on the basis of mental capacity and incapacity, human rights *accommodated*, and, in fact, were *premised upon* the differential and discriminatory treatment of people with mental incapacity' (Steele 2016, p. 1014). Further, General Comment No 1 ascribes multiple violations of the rights of people with psychosocial disability to mental health laws and other substitute decision-making regimes applying to people with disability, including contravention not only of Art 12 of the CRPD, but also Art 14 (Liberty and security of person), Art 15 (Freedom from torture or cruel, inhuman or degrading treatment or punishment), Art 16 (Freedom from exploitation, violence and abuse), Art 17 (Protecting the integrity of the person), and Art 25 (Health) (Committee on the Rights of Persons with Disabilities 2014).

The CRPD Committee's interpretation has precipitated candid debate about whether States Parties are under an obligation pursuant to international human rights law to absolutely prohibit involuntary mental health interventions and other substitute decision-making regimes that regulate the lives of disabled people. However, much academic and public policy discussion in the wake of General

Comment No 1 proceeds on the assumption (or reaches the conclusion) that substitute decision-making for people with disability is warranted in some circumstances, and rather considers the bases on which such arrangements are permissible in light of the CRPD's provisions. Indeed, a number of States Parties to the CRPD have entered interpretive declarations, indicating their understanding that substitute decision-making regimes do not breach the provisions of the CRPD.[26] A prominent interpretation of Article 12 is that a functional approach to mental capacity is the dividing line between laws that are consistent with, and those that infringe, the CRPD (for example Dawson 2015). This position corresponds in many respects with earlier analyses that general incapacity or health care laws, rather than mental health laws, should govern the situations when others can make decisions about the lives and bodies of people with psychosocial disability with a view to providing health care.

In 2014, the Australian Law Reform Commission (ALRC) completed a landmark review of equal recognition before the law and legal capacity for people with disability, which considered the implications of the CRPD for domestic law reform (Australian Law Reform Commission ALRC). The Commission noted the interchangeable nature of a functional approach to mental capacity and a test of 'decision-making ability' (see Australian Law Reform Commission ALRC, pp. 71–72), variations of which now form part of the prerequisites for making an involuntary order in the mental health statutes in four Australian jurisdictions, alongside various combinations of the core and secondary criteria, as noted above.[27] A test of 'decision-making ability' assesses a person's mental capacity based on factors such as their ability to understand, retain, and weigh information that is relevant to a specific decision and to communicate that decision (Australian Law Reform Commission ALRC, pp. 200–1). The ALRC considered that an assessment of 'decision-making ability' that delinks this concept from diagnosis or disability and focuses on assessing the support a person needs to exercise legal agency avoids the pitfalls of a status approach to mental capacity (Australian Law Reform Commission ALRC, pp. 70–73). According to the CRPD Committee, a functional approach to assessing mental capacity (or decision-making ability) is flawed, firstly, because it is discriminatorily applied to people with disability, and, secondly, because it 'presumes to be able to accurately assess the inner-workings of the human mind and, when the person does not pass the assessment . . . denies ... [them] a core human right' (Committee on the Rights of Persons with Disabilities 2014, p. 4).

Functional abilities in the mental health context are determined with reference to medical and psy-based epistemologies that defer to psychiatry, via a process turning in large measure on a person's 'mental illness' diagnosis and status as a person with a psychosocial disability that judges their views about interventions proposed by psychiatrists and other clinicians. For example, the first requirement of the Queensland incapacity criterion is that the person must be 'capable of understanding . . . that the person has an illness, or symptoms of an illness, that affects the person's mental health and wellbeing'.[28] This formulation demands that a person, to be considered as having mental capacity, must form and express opinions about their experiences that align substantially with medical conceptions of 'mental illness'. It is unlikely that delinking decision-making ability from diagnosis or disability in the wording of a mental health statute would disturb these mechanisms. Accordingly, Steele and I contend that a test of 'decision-making ability' to determine whether involuntary mental health interventions are warranted is a veiled status approach to mental capacity (Beaupert and Steele 2015, 2017).

As discussed in the following section, the gradual encroachment of an incapacity or 'lack of decision-making ability' prerequisite to involuntary mental health interventions carries with it significant risks associated with codifying the notion that there is in an intrinsic association between incompetence and psychosocial disability.

---

[26] For example, Australia, Ratification (with Declarations), registered with the Secretariat of the United Nations 17 July 2008, 2527 UNTS 289 (date of effect 16 August 2008).

[27] *Mental Health Act 2016* (Qld), ss. 12(1)(b), 14; *Mental Health Act 2009* (SA), ss. 5A, 10(1)(c), 16(1)(c), 21(ba), 25(ba), 29(ba); *Mental Health Act 2013* (Tas), ss. 7, 40(e); *Mental Health Act 2014* (WA), ss. 18, 25(1)(c).

[28] *Mental Health Act 2016* (Qld), s. 14(1)(a)(i).

7. Juridical Denial of Freedom of Opinion and Expression: Interlocking Material and Symbolic Violence

Whilst much of this article is concerned with symbolic violence, the denial of freedom of opinion and expression that occurs in the mental health context is deeply bound up in material violence. As Steele has written, non-consensual medical treatment, detention, and physical and chemical restraint are exceptionally legally permissible when applied to people with disability under particular legal frameworks, comprising forms of 'disability-specific lawful violence' (Steele 2014). Mental health laws form one such legal framework, which legalises acts that would amount to civil and/or criminal wrongs, such as the crimes of battery and assault, if perpetrated in other contexts and against nondisabled people (see Steele 2014). This section, firstly, considers how the (threat of) material violence produced by involuntary mental health interventions intensifies the denial of freedom of opinion and expression that is effected through the symbolic violence of psychiatry and the mental health paradigm. Secondly, it is argued that the medico-legal discourse of mental health laws, by consecrating this symbolic violence, operates to manipulate and nullify individual ways of knowing and being, and to radically diminish opportunities for the epistemologies of users and survivors to exert influence on societal systems and structures. Constructions of people with psychosocial disability as lacking capacity and 'insight' are central to these processes of dehumanisation.

7.1. The Suppressive Effects of Mental Health Law's (Threat of) Material Violence

The coercion, control, and force effected upon users and survivors through Australian mental health laws operate at multiple levels. A formal involuntary order provides the overarching mandate for the forced administration of specific drugs and procedures to an individual. On a day to day basis, clinicians are for the most part responsible for authorising the administration of drugs and other interventions.[29] MHT or other independent authorisation is typically only mandated for the performance of more exceptional procedures, such as electroshock and neurosurgery, in specified circumstances.[30] Even where clinicians are obliged to consult individuals who have involuntary status before providing or administering drugs or undertaking procedures, or to seek their informed consent in the first instance,[31] there is an expectation that 'treatment' will be provided. Drugs and procedures may be forced upon a person against their will, and even if they are considered to have the capacity to give informed consent, with the exception of electroshock and neurosurgery in some jurisdictions.

Many users and survivors characterise their interactions with mental health services and detention in mental health facilities as involving violent, torturous assaults on their bodies and minds (for example Lee 2013, p. 110). The experience of being in a psychiatric ward, which may include being placed in seclusion and administered with unwanted drugs, can be physically, psychically, and emotionally harmful and oppressive. Being forcibly administered with drugs or procedures has been described by users and survivors as a terrifying and degrading experience that 'breaks the spirit' (Lee 2013, p. 112). Forced administration of drugs also produces painful and damaging physical effects. Fabris uses the term 'chemical incarceration' to describe the prolonged imposition of drug treatment without a person's consent, regardless of whether the treatment is administered pursuant to mental health laws or in other contexts such as schools, prisons and hospitals (Fabris 2011, pp. 114–31). Drugging of individuals in nursing homes or of people with cognitive disability or intellectual disability in residential homes, for example, would equally be covered.

---

29 In the Northern Territory and Tasmania, the MHT is responsible for pre-approving treatment to be provided to a person subject to involuntary treatment, although clinicians can administer treatment outside this authority in specified circumstances: *Mental Health and Related Services Act* (NT), s. 55; *Mental Health Act 2013* (Tas), s. 41(2)(c).

30 *Mental Health Act 2014* (Vic), s. 96 (electroshock), s. 102 (neurosurgery); *Mental Health Act 2007* (NSW), s. 96 (electroshock); *Mental Health Act 2015* (ACT), s. 157 (electroshock); *Mental Health Act 2016* (Qld), s. 236 (electroshock), s. 239 (non-ablative neurosurgery); *Mental Health Act 2009* (SA), s. 42 (electroshock), s. 43; *Mental Health Act* (WA), Pt 21, Div 6 (ECT), Pt 21, Div 7 (neurosurgery).

31 For example, *Mental Health Act 2014* (Vic), s. 70.

The process of chemical incarceration, which is an embodied, visceral, physically violent process induces physical effects, such as numbing, fatigue, and cognitive restriction, which render an individual malleable and weaken their ability to resist; the chemical impact of the drug on the brain 'leads to pacification' (Fabris 2011, p. 115). It appears that the physical effects of drugging can reinforce the oppression involved in the 'textual' diagnostic and 'treatment' process, through suppressing abilities to form opinions and to 'seek, receive and impart information and ideas'.[32] Thus one's own body can become an alien place of interlocking material and symbolic imprisonment, as evidenced by Aubrecht's description of coercion in mental health treatment:

> What you describe as chemical incarceration, for me, meant being restrained in what felt like someone else's body. Pharmaceutical reason confined me within a glass bubble that separated me from my body and my body from the world. Voices were muffled, and responses were delayed and over determined. Within a biomedicalized world of one, I was encouraged to imagine the medication as a guide that would lead me to adjust to the timelines of respectable 'reality' (Fabris and Aubrecht 2014, p. 191).

Not everyone who is subject to involuntary mental health interventions is administered with drugs through the use of physical force. Some people 'consent' or 'acquiesce'. Yet, the coercive project of mental health law manifests in pernicious fashion at this point, where a person may be faced with a 'choice' of refusing proposed interventions and being detained or subject to a CTO for even longer, or 'agreeing' and being returned to a situation that more closely resembles their daily life.

Choice is limited in the mental health context, where medication is presumed necessary and service provision is predicated on the ability to use physical force to ensure compliance. Sjöström's work has shown how the 'coercion context' of the mental health paradigm can be leveraged so as to secure individuals' 'consent' to mental health interventions across both involuntary and voluntary settings, blurring the boundary 'between coercive measures and patients' voluntary acceptance of treatment' (Sjöström 2006, p. 37). A study of patient perceptions of 'leverage' in community mental health settings showed that the pressures experienced by users and survivors come not only from within mental health services, but also beyond, and extend beyond pressure to comply with 'treatment' as an end in itself, to pressures to maintain 'treatment' and 'stay well' in order to secure other 'gains' (Canvin et al. 2013); access to critical social services, such as housing support or social security, may effectively be contingent upon individuals' compliance with psychiatric interventions in some cases. Even where clinicians do not actively use informal coercion to secure their patients' compliance, knowledge that formal coercion is a possibility can lead people to 'internalise' the notion that drugs and medical procedures are necessary (Rogers 1998). The nature of 'informed consent' becomes particularly tenuous where formal coercion is legally permissible (Carney et al. 2007).

Mental health laws embed coercive forces throughout numerous aspects of the lives of users and survivors. These forces extend to lawful violence prior to the making of an involuntary order, such as where police are empowered to apprehend a person and transport them to a mental health facility. Social and relational pressures and informal coercion may be overlayed upon the numbing effects of medication, which are sometimes administered deliberately to induce compliance with other drugs (Minkowitz 2007, p. 424). Further, methods of inducing compliance can extend to coercing individuals to adopt particular behaviours to demonstrate their recovery, such as women being 'pressured to put on makeup and present a more feminine appearance as a sign of 'getting better' (Minkowitz 2007, p. 424). Guilaine Kinouani concisely captures the catch-22 situation users and survivors who seek to resist hegemonic forces within mental health services can find themselves in:

32 See ICCPR, Art 19(2) (enshrining the right to freedom of expression).

> I can choose to accept a diagnosis of psychosis and find it useful. However, the fact remains that not doing so may well mean that I cannot access services, that I am deemed to lack insight and thus subjected to more oppressive forms of 'treatment' (Kinouani 2015).

The domination of lawful violence in the mental health context can thus wear down an individual's will to resist, constraining the ability to express one's opinions and potentially 'changing the personality' by destroying 'identity, self-concept, relationship to the world, and inner subjective experience' (see Minkowitz 2007, p. 421) through an elaborate interplay of formal and informal coercion.[33]

7.2. Medico-Legal Incapacitation of the Expressions, Opinions and Epistemologies of Users and Survivors

Fiona Campbell's work on the relationship between law and disability explains how law partners with medicine in rendering disability within 'official' realities that reinforce negative attitudes and stereotypes about disability, for example, through narratives of tragedy, suffering, and catastrophe (Campbell 2009, pp. 34–37). The dialectic relation between law and psychiatry similarly encodes medico-legal expressions which invalidate people 'for their articulated and lived difference' (Arrigo 2012, p. xxii); for people with psychosocial disability oppressive medico-legal narratives frequently revolve around 'risk' and 'incompetence' (Liegghio 2013). Legal rendering of disability can impose official definitions and categories of 'deficiency' based on medical categorisations which deny the private realities, opinions and expressions of people with disability (Campbell 2009, p. 37). Mental health laws providing for involuntary mental health interventions operate to embed psychiatry's configurations of madness and mental distress, to the exclusion of other understandings.

MHTs have been observed to 'mould' the information presented to them by the parties to their proceedings into a form that satisfies the prerequisites for involuntary intervention, frequently deferring to clinical opinion. Jill Peay's study of MHTs operating under the *Mental Health Act 1983* (Eng and Wales), concentrating primarily on 'restricted' or forensic patients, found that the tribunals routinely endorsed clinical recommendations, 'almost irrespective of the content of the recommendation' (Peay 1989, p. 209). The study observed the misapplication of the relevant statutory criteria via a 'back-to-front' process, whereby some MHT panels reasoned backwards to a pre-determined outcome, heavily influenced by pragmatic considerations, such as subjective assessments of risk (even very low level risk) and available support options (Peay 1989). According to a later study conducted in the same jurisdiction by Elizabeth Perkins, clinical judgments about a person's 'insight' into their alleged condition and compliance with proposed interventions tended to be uncritically accepted by MHT panels operating under civil mental health laws, and witnesses and narratives were placed on a 'credibility' spectrum, which positioned patients' narratives as least credible when weighing up the evidence (Perkins 2003).

Turning to Australian MHTs applying civil mental health laws, research on the use of the concept of 'insight' by Victorian MHT panels found that this concept allowed panels to 'medicalize arguments put forth by persons subjected to mental health review board hearings, thereby framing the person's self-perceptions and choices as evidence of pathology' (Diesfeld and Sjöström 2007, p. 98). Observations of MHT hearings conducted by Carney et al.'s comparative study of Australian MHT operations found that even where the opinions of the person at the centre of proceedings were sought by panels, they were 'sometimes ... treated as an exhibit, in that their performance and behaviour at the hearing [was] judged as evidence pertaining to their mental illness' (Carney et al. 2011, p. 215). In these situations, the person's opinions and expressions were largely used as a means of establishing evidence of mental illness, lack of insight, and non-compliance with clinical advice. Constructions of people with psychosocial disability as 'incompetent' are a primary mechanism by which they/we are marginalised, silenced, and, ultimately, 'disqualified as legitimate knowers' (Liegghio 2013, p. 126). Maria Liegghio has described how such 'epistemic disqualification' effectively

33 On law's violence, and the violence and coercion that inhere in judicial interpretive acts, see Cover (1986).

renders individuals out of existence (Liegghio 2013, p. 124). Further embedding a functional approach to mental capacity in mental health laws as a pivotal prerequisite to involuntary mental health interventions, by codifying the association between psychosocial disability and incompetence that is already implicit in these laws, risks exacerbating this invalidation of the ways of knowing and being of people with psychosocial disability.

General Comment No 34 states that the rights to freedom of opinion and expression in the ICCPR prohibit 'any form of effort to coerce the holding or not holding of any opinion', and that 'freedom to express one's opinion necessarily includes freedom not to express one's opinion' (Human Rights Committee 2011, p. 3). In maintaining that involuntary mental health interventions contravene the universal prohibition of torture, Minkowitz has comprehensively described the abusive nature of the process of obtaining information and a 'confession' from people who resist psychiatric diagnosis and treatment (Minkowitz 2007, pp. 421–25). MHT processes can entail a further element of coercion of individuals into particular admissions and understandings of their situation, and the consolidation of these admissions and understandings as the official version of events that justifies making an involuntary order. For example, a process of intense questioning in pursuit of a certain response was observed by Perkins' study where MHT panels felt that clients were hiding something. Perkins termed this approach a "catching out' technique': leading questions were asked to lure patients into revealing the presumed truth regarding their condition and their understanding of their condition (Perkins 2003, p. 72). Some MHT panels go to great lengths to establish whether a person *accepts* that they have a mental illness and need medication to alleviate their condition. If a person does not succumb completely to the medico-legal understanding of the compliant, 'insightful' patient, mental health law may re-invent them as 'incompetent', and therefore eligible for involuntary mental health interventions.

Historically, users and survivors who seek to resist the medical model and the mental health paradigm have frequently been denied the symbolic capital that is necessary to make their/our own meanings about psychosocial disability, experiences of madness and mental distress, and encounters with mental health services.[34] Mental health laws reinforce this process of epistemic invalidation, which is so deeply embedded within laws and cultural practices that it is largely invisible. This legal interpretive process causes a kind of 'overlock', that strengthens and prevents fraying of the symbolic power of psychiatry. Official discourses can stabilise and compound the appearance of 'lawful violence' in the disability sector as therapeutic and necessary at the structural level (Spivakovsky, forthcoming). I suggest that one consequence of the denial of freedom of opinion and expression that is effected through mental health laws is to systematically wrest symbolic power from people with psychosocial disability by conferring an 'absolute, universal value' on the symbolic capital that is possessed by psychiatry (see Bourdieu 1990, p. 136).

Dinesh Wadiwel has analysed how systems of violence against people with disability both 'materially produce disability' and constitute an 'epistemic problem', where regularised violence and torture are simultaneously concealed and reconstructed as benevolent and necessary (Wadiwel 2017; see Steele 2014). Wadiwel suggests a connection between the failure to name material acts of violence against people with disability and the epistemological construction of people with disability as 'not having a dignity to violate' (Wadiwel 2017, p. 389). The epistemological struggle that is demarcated in this article similarly implicates a denial not only of legal personhood, but also an ontological nullification of humanness—the designation of a border between who is and is not considered a human to be treated with dignity and whose experiences, opinions, thoughts and feelings should be respected and acted on (see Roper, forthcoming). Further, the legal codification of people with psychosocial disability as lacking capacity, through mental health laws, may materially construct

---

34 See Bourdieu regarding the situations in which people are denied the ability to imprint meaning upon the structure of social space through the operation of symbolic violence (Bourdieu 1990, pp. 134–35).

individuals as not having a dignity to violate, weaving these negative constructions into both a person's sense of self and the official records that will influence future legal and administrative decision-making about that person.

In affirming that people with disability are rights-holders who enjoy legal capacity on an equal basis with others in all aspects of life, the CRPD arguably strives towards contestation of the symbolic violence that has pervaded society's relationship with disability and madness. This is evident from the statement of the Committee on the Rights of Persons with Disabilities in General Comment No. 1 on Article 12 of the CRPD that mental capacity is 'contingent on social and political contexts, as are the disciplines, professions, and practices, which play a dominant role in assessing mental capacity' rather than being 'as is commonly presented, an objective scientific and naturally occurring phenomenon' (Committee on the Rights of Persons with Disabilities 2014, p. 4). Acknowledging the contingent nature of 'mental capacity' not only exposes as discriminatory the historical denial of the legal capacity of people with disability, but also disrupts the very categories of mental capacity and incapacity and any attempts to define legal capacity with reference to these categories.

It is unsurprising that reflection on denial of freedom of opinion and expression in this context animates the debate about the right to equal recognition before the law enshrined in Article 12 of the CRPD. The demand of Article 12 targets the coercion underpinning and effected through mental health (law) at the points of convergence between the material violence and symbolic violence of this body of law. The analysis in this article suggests that allowing the State to inflict material violence upon its citizens, and other people within its territory, in the form of involuntary mental health interventions systematically stifles attempts to think, feel, opine, express, and imagine outside of psychiatry's schema. This may hinder recognition and further development of the epistemologies of users and survivors, as well as stifling individual self-expression. Ending involuntary mental health interventions may significantly expand possibilities for the lived truths of users and survivors to shape the responses and support options that are available to people with psychosocial disability at individual and structural levels. These considerations add weight to the interpretation of the Committee on the Rights of Persons with Disabilities that substitute decision-making pursuant to mental health laws contravenes Article 12, and other provisions, of the CRPD.

8. Conclusions

This article has examined aspects of the relationship between the rights to freedom of opinion and expression and madness and psychosocial disability. I explored how the symbolic violence of psychiatry and the mental health paradigm operates to suppress the opinions and expressions of people with psychosocial disability. This enquiry was in part guided by experiences and epistemologies of mental health service users and survivors of psychiatry. I discussed how the denial of freedom of opinion and expression that is effected through the symbolic violence of psychiatry and the mental health paradigm is compounded and consecrated when wielded as part of the coercive project of mental health law. I argued that codifying 'incapacity' as a prerequisite to involuntary mental health interventions may further amplify this process. I also argued that mental health (law) may produce a form of ontological violence, fundamentally altering the opinions, expressions, and ways of being of people with psychosocial disability. Finally, I suggested that these combined considerations reinforce the interpretation of the Committee on the Rights of Persons with Disabilities that Article 12 and other provisions of the CRPD require the absolute prohibition of involuntary mental health interventions.

My exploration of the rights to freedom of opinion and expression from the perspective of psychosocial disability and madness ultimately folded back into mental health law's problematic of coercion. This problematic entails a mutually reinforcing relationship between the material violence that is immanent in denial of legal personhood under civil mental health laws and the symbolic violence of psychiatry and the mental health paradigm. It also connects to scholarship and debates about the deployment of medico-legal and psychiatric epistemologies in ways that silence the political resistance and claims of marginalised groups at the intersections of different coercive legal frameworks, such as people in immigration detention (Joseph 2016) and incarcerated people labelled as 'mad Muslim terrorists' (Patel 2014).

Probing the contours of the denial of freedom of opinion and expression that permeates involuntary mental health interventions holds value, for people with psychosocial disability and beyond, because it demands, in the first instance, a 'stripping bare' to the immediate wishes, feelings, concerns, and communications (or attempts to communicate) of individuals and constituencies. This may assist in delineating physical, psychical, social and political aspects of these opinions and expressions and their connections to different political and historical struggles. Giving effect to the requirement in Article 4(3) of the CRPD to 'closely consult with and actively involve persons with disabilities, including children with disabilities, through their representative organizations' in developing and implementing laws and policies to implement the CRPD calls for direct and genuine engagement with the opinions and expressions of disabled people.

Acknowledgments: I want to thank Linda Steele for her comments on earlier versions of this article, in particular regarding the relationships between different forms of violence operating in the disability and mental health contexts. I am also grateful to the three anonymous referees for their helpful comments.

References

Australian Law Reform Commission (ALRC). 2014. *Equality, Capacity and Disability in Commonwealth Laws*; Sydney: ALRC. ISBN 978-0-9924069-3-6.

Appelbaum, Paul. 2006. Law and Psychiatry: Twenty-Five Years of Law and Psychiatry. *Psychiatric Services* 57: 18–20. [CrossRef] [PubMed]

Arrigo, Bruce. 2012. *Punishing the Mentally Ill: A Critical Analysis of Law and Psychiatry*. Albany: State University of New York Press. ISBN 0-7914-5404-5.

Arstein-Kerslake, Anna. 2017. Special Issue: Disability Human Rights Law. *Laws*. Available online: http://www.mdpi.com/journal/laws/special_issues/Disability_Human_Rights_Law (accessed on 29 December 2017).

Barnes, Colin. 2012. Understanding the Social Model of Disability: Past, Present and Future. In *Routledge Handbook of Disability Studies*. Edited by Nick Watson, Alan Roulstone and Carol Thomas. London: Routledge, pp. 12–29. ISBN 978 0 203 14411 4.

Bayetti, Clement, and Sumeet Jain. 2017. Problematising Global Mental Health. In *Routledge International Handbook of Critical Mental Health*. Edited by Bruce Cohen. London: Routledge, pp. 364–75. ISBN 978-1-315-39958-4.

Bean, Philip. 1986. *Mental Disorder and Legal Control*. Cambridge: Cambridge University Press. ISBN 0-521-30209-9.

Beaupert, Fleur, and Linda Steele. 2015. Questioning Law's Capacity. *Alternative Law Journal* 40: 161–65. [CrossRef]

Beaupert, Fleur, and Linda Steele. 2017. Legal Capacity and Australian Law Reform: Missed Opportunities? Paper presented at the 2nd Session of the Working Group on Model Bill on CRPD Implementation and Inclusion of the Persons with Psychosocial Disabilities in Asian Countries, Organized by KAMI, Institute for Legal Studies, Yonsei University Law School & Asian Law Centre with support of Share Sarangat, Center for the Human Rights of Users and Survivors of Psychiatry, Seong-San Bioethics Institute, Seoul, Korea, September 12–13.

Beaupert, Fleur, Linda Steele, and Piers Gooding. 2017. Special Issue: Disability, Rights and Law Reform. In *Law in Context*. Sydney: The Federation Press. ISBN 9781760021603.

Benedek, Wolfgang, and Matthias C. Ketteman. 2014. *Freedom of Expression and the Internet*. Strasbourg: Council of Europe Publishing. ISBN 978-92-871-7702-5.

Beresford, Peter. 2016. The role of survivor knowledge in creating alternatives to psychiatry. In *Searching For a Rose Garden*. Edited by Jasna Russo and Angela Sweeney. Monmouth: PCCS Books, pp. 40–48. ISBN 978-1-910919-30-9.

Beresford, Peter, Mary Nettle, and Rebecca Perring. 2010. Towards a Social Model of Madness and Distress. Joseph Rowntree Foundation. Available online: https://www.jrf.org.uk/report/towards-social-model-madness-and-distress-exploring-what-service-users-say (accessed on 1 October 2017).

Bourdieu, Pierre. 1990. *In Other Words: Essays towards a Reflexive Sociology*. Cambridge: Polity Press. ISBN 0-7456-0659-8.

Burstow, Bonnie. 2013. A Rose by Any Other Name: Naming and the Battle against Psychiatry. In *Mad Matters: A Critical Reader in Canadian Mad Studies*. Edited by Brenda A. Le François, Robert Menzies and Geoffrey Reaume. Toronto: Canadian Scholars' Press Inc., pp. 79–90. ISBN 978-1-55130-534-9.

Callaghan, Sascha, and Giles Newton-Howes. 2017. Coercive Community Treatment in Mental Health: An Idea Whose Time Has Passed? *Journal of Law and Medicine* 24: 900–14.

Callaghan, Sascha, Christopher Ryan, and Ian Kerridge. 2013. Risk of suicide is insufficient warrant for coercive treatment for mental illness. *International Journal of Law and Psychiatry* 36: 374–85. [CrossRef] [PubMed]

Campbell, Fiona Kumari. 2009. *Contours of Ableism: The Production of Disability and Abledness*. Basingstoke: Palgrave Macmillan. ISBN 978-0-230-57928-6.

Canvin, Krysia, Jorun Rugkåsa, Julia Sinclair, and Tom Burns. 2013. Leverage and other informal pressures in community psychiatry in England. *International Journal of Law and Psychiatry* 36: 100–6. [CrossRef] [PubMed]

Carney, Terry, David Tait, and Stephen Touyz. 2007. Coercion is Coercion?: Reflections on clinical trends in use of compulsion in treatment of anorexia nervosa. *Australasian Psychiatry* 15: 390–95. [CrossRef] [PubMed]

Carney, Terry, David Tait, Julia Perry, Alikki Vernon, and Fleur Beaupert. 2011. *Australian Mental Health Tribunals: Space for Fairness, Freedom, Protection & Treatment?* Sydney: Themis Press. ISBN 978-1-92111-305-5.

Chamberlin, Judi. 2012. *On Our Own: Patient-Controlled Alternatives to the Mental Health System*. Lawrence: National Empowerment Centre, First published 1977. ISBN 0 900 577 83 4.

Commission on Human Rights. 2000. *Resolution 2000/38: The Right to Freedom of Opinion and Expression*. Resolution 2000/38, UN Doc E/CN.4/RES/2000/38; Quezon City: Commission on Human Rights. Available online: http://ap.ohchr.org/Documents/gmainec.aspx (accessed on 10 October 2017).

Coopes, Amy. 2017. Standing Ovation for Powerful Calls to Democratise Mental Health Services. *Croakey*. Available online: https://croakey.org/standing-ovation-for-calls-to-democratise-mental-health-services/ (accessed on 5 November 2017).

Costa, Lucy. 2008. Mad Pride in our Mad Culture. *Bulletin* 374: 4. Available online: http://www.csinfo.ca/bulletin/Bulletin_374.pdf (accessed on 1 November 2017).

Costa, Lucy, Jijian Voronka, Danielle Landry, Jenna Reid, Becky McFarlane, David Reville, and Kathryn Church. 2012. Recovering our Stories: A Small Act of Resistance. *Studies in Social Justice* 6: 85–101. [CrossRef]

Cover, Robert. 1986. Violence and the Word. *Yale Law Journal* 95: 1601–29. [CrossRef]

Critical Psychiatry. 2017. Psychiatry in Transition—Critical Psychiatry Network 2017 Conference Report. Available online: http://www.criticalpsychiatry.co.uk/index.php/news/445-psychiatry-in-transition-critical-psychiatry-network-2017-conference-report (accessed on 5 December 2017).

Crossley, Nick. 2004. Not being mentally ill: Social movements, system survivors and the oppositional habitus. *Anthropology & Medicine* 11: 161–80.

Committee on the Rights of Persons with Disabilities. 2014. *General Comment No. 1: Article 12: Equal Recognition before the Law*. 11th sess, UN Doc CRPD/C/GC/1; Geneva: Committee on the Rights of Persons with Disabilities, Available online: http://tbinternet.ohchr.org/_layouts/treatybodyexternal/Download.aspx?symbolno=CRPD/C/GC/1&Lang=en (accessed on 10 October 2017).

Davar, Bhargavi. 2005. Disabilities, colonisation and globalisation: How the very possibility of a disability identity was compromised for the 'insane' in India. In *Madness, Distress and the Politics of Disablement*. Edited by Helen Spandler, Jill Anderson and Bob Sapey. Bristol: Policy Press, pp. 215–28. ISBN 978-1-4473-2809-4.

Dawson, John. 2015. A realistic approach to assessing mental health laws' compliance with the UNCRPD. *International Journal of Law and Psychiatry* 40: 70–79. [CrossRef] [PubMed]

Deegan, Patricia E. 1996. There's a Person in Here. Paper presented at the Sixth Annual Mental Health Services Conference of Australia and New Zealand, Brisbane, Australia, September 16. Available online: https://www.patdeegan.com/pat-deegan/lectures/conspiracy-of-hope (accessed on 1 October 2017).

Degener, Theresia. 2016. Disability in a Human Rights Context. *Laws* 5: 35. [CrossRef]

Diamond, Shaindl. 2013. What Makes Us a Community? Reflections on building Solidarity in Anti-sanist Praxis. In *Mad Matters: A Critical Reader in Canadian Mad Studies*. Edited by Brenda A. Le François, Robert Menzies and Geoffrey Reaume. Toronto: Canadian Scholars' Press Inc., pp. 64–78. ISBN 978-1-55130-534-9.

Diesfeld, Kate, and Stefan Sjöström. 2007. Interpretive Flexibility: Why Doesn't Insight Incite Controversy in Mental Health Law. *Behavioral Sciences and the Law* 25: 85–101. [CrossRef] [PubMed]

Fabris, Erick. 2011. *Tranquil Prisons: Chemical Incarceration under Community Treatment Orders*. Toronto: University of Toronto Press. ISBN 978 1 4426 4376 5.

Fabris, Erick. 2013. Mad Success: What Could Go Wrong When Psychiatry Employs Us as "Peers"? In *Mad Matters: A Critical Reader in Canadian Mad Studies*. Edited by Brenda A. Le François, Robert Menzies and Geoffrey Reaume. Toronto: Canadian Scholars' Press Inc., pp. 130–39. ISBN 978-1-55130-534-9.

Fabris, Erick, and Katie Aubrecht. 2014. Chemical Constraint: Experiences of Psychiatric Coercion, Restraint, and Detention as Carceratory Techniques. In *Disability Incarcerated: Imprisonment and Disability in the United States and Canada*. Edited by Liat Ben-Moshe, Chris Chapman and Allison C. Carey. New York: Palgrave Macmillan, pp. 185–200. ISBN 978-1-137-388476.

Fistein, E. C., A. J. Holland, I. C. H. Clare, and M. J. Gunn. 2009. A comparison of mental health legislation from diverse Commonwealth jurisdictions. *International Journal of Law and Psychiatry* 32: 147–55. [CrossRef] [PubMed]

Foucault, Michel. 2001. *Madness and Civilization: A History of Insanity in the Age of Reason*. London: Routledge, First published 1964. ISBN 0-415-25385-3.

Goffman, Erving. 2007. *Asylums: Essays on the Social Situation of Mental Patients and Other Inmates*. New Jersey: Transaction Publishers, First published 1961. ISBN 978-0-202-30971-2.

Goggin, Gerard. 2017. Communication, Rights, Disability, and Law: The Convention on the Rights of Persons with Disabilities in National Perspective. *Law in Context* 35(2): 129–49.

Gooding, Piers. 2017. *A New Era for Mental Health Law and Policy: Supported Decision-Making and the UN Convention on the Rights of Persons with Disabilities*. Cambridge: Cambridge University Press. ISBN 978-1-107-1407-4-5.

Gordon, Robert M. 1993. Out to pasture: A case for the retirement of Canadian mental health legislation. *Canadian Journal of Community Mental Health* 12: 37–55. [CrossRef] [PubMed]

Gorman, Rachel. 2013. Mad Nation? Thinking through Race, Class, and Mad Identity Politics. In *Mad Matters: A Critical Reader in Canadian Mad Studies*. Edited by Brenda A. Le François, Robert Menzies and Geoffrey Reaume. Toronto: Canadian Scholars' Press Inc., pp. 269–80. ISBN 978-1-55130-534-9.

Grey, Flick. 2017. Just Borderline Mad. *Asylum*. Available online: http://asylummagazine.org/just-borderline-mad-by-flick-grey/ (accessed on 1 October 2017).

Hall, Alice. 2016. *Literature and Disability*. London: Routledge, ISBN 978-0-415-63221-8.

Hamilton, Brenda, and Cath Roper. 2006. Troubling 'insight': Power and possibilities in mental health care. *Journal of Psychiatric and Mental Health Nursing* 13: 416–22. [CrossRef] [PubMed]

Hughes, Bill, and Kevin Paterson. 1997. The social model of disability and the disappearing body: Towards a sociology of impairment. *Disability & Society* 12: 325–40.

Human Rights Committee. 2011. *General Comment No. 34: Article 19: Freedoms of Opinion and Expression*. 102nd sess, UN Doc CCPR/C/GC.34; Geneva: Human Rights Committee. Available online: http://tbinternet.ohchr.org/_layouts/treatybodyexternal/Download.aspx?symbolno=CCPR%2fC%2fGC%2f34&Lang=en (accessed on 30 December 2017).

Human Rights Council. 2017. *Report of the Special Rapporteur on the Right of Everyone to the Enjoyment of the Highest Attainable Standards of Physical and Mental Health*. 35th sess, UN Doc A/HRC/35/21, March 28; Geneva: Human Rights Council. Available online: http://ap.ohchr.org/documents/dpage_e.aspx?m=100 (accessed on 30 December 2017).

Intervoice (The International Hearing Voices Network). 2017. Home. Available online: http://www.intervoiceonline.org/ (accessed on 1 October 2017).

Jayawickrama, Janaka, and Jo Rose. 2017. *Routledge International Handbook of Critical Mental Health*. Edited by Bruce Bohen. London: Routledge, pp. 348–61. ISBN 978-1-315-39958-4.

Joseph, Ameil J. 2016. *Deportation and the Confluence of Violence within Forensic Mental Health and Immigration Systems*. Basingstoke: Palgrave Macmillan. ISBN 978-1-349-55826-1.

Kenyon, Andrew, Eva-Maria Svensson, and Maria Edström. 2017. Building and Sustaining Freedom of Expression. Considering Sweden. *Nordicom Review* 38: 31–45. [CrossRef]

King, Colin. 2016. Whiteness in psychiatry: The madness of European misdiagnoses. In *Searching for a Rose Garden*. Edited by Jasna Russo and Angela Sweeney. Monmouth: PCCS Books, pp. 85–92. ISBN 978-1-910919-30-9.

Kinouani, Guilaine. 2015. Neutrality, Power and Psychiatry: Shifting Paradigm through Praxis. *Race Reflections*. Available online: https://racereflections.co.uk/2015/12/13/neutrality-power-and-psychiatry-shifting-paragdim-through-praxis/ (accessed on 1 October 2017).

Large, Matthew M., Christopher J. Ryan, Olav B. Nielssen, and R. A. Hayes. 2008. The danger of dangerousness: Why we must remove the dangerousness criterion from our mental health acts. *Journal of Medical Ethics* 34: 877–81. [CrossRef] [PubMed]

Lawrence, David, Kirsten J. Hancock, and Stephen Kisely. 2013. The gap in life expectancy from preventable physical illness in psychiatric patients in Western Australia: Retrospective analysis of population based registers. *British Medical Journal* 346: f2539. Available online: http://www.bmj.com/content/346/bmj.f2539 (accessed on 28 December 2017). [CrossRef] [PubMed]

Lee, Ji-Eun. 2013. Mad as Hell: The Objectifying Experience of Symbolic Violence. In *Mad Matters: A Critical Reader in Canadian Mad Studies*. Edited by Brenda A. Le François, Robert Menzies and Geoffrey Reaume. Toronto: Canadian Scholars' Press Inc., pp. 105–21. ISBN 978-1-55130-534-9.

LeFrançois, Brenda, and Vicki Coppock. 2017. Psychiatrised Children and their Rights: Starting the Conversation. *Children & Society* 28: 165–71.

Lewis, Bradley. 2013. A Mad Fight: Psychiatry and Disability Activism. In *The Disability Studies Reader*, 4th ed. Edited by Lennard J. Davis. London: Routledge, ISBN 978-0415630511.

Liegghio, Maria. 2013. A Denial of Being: Psychiatrization as Epistemic Violence. In *Mad Matters: A Critical Reader in Canadian Mad Studies*. Edited by Brenda A. Le François, Robert Menzies and Geoffrey Reaume. Toronto: Canadian Scholars' Press Inc., pp. 122–29. ISBN 978-1-55130-534-9.

Tarlach McGonagle, and Yvonne Donders, eds. 2015. *The United Nations and Freedom of Expression and Information: Critical Perspectives*. Cambridge: Cambridge University Press. ISBN 978-1-107-08-386-8.

McSherry, Bernadette, and Penelope Weller. 2010. Rethinking Rights-Based Mental Health Laws. In *Rethinking Rights-Based Mental Health Laws*. Edited by Bernadette McSherry and Penny Weller. Oxford: Hart Publishing, pp. 3–10. ISBN 978-1-84946-083-5.

Menzies, Robert, Brenda A. LeFrançois, and Geoffrey Reaume. 2013. Introducing Mad Studies. In *Mad Matters: A Critical Reader in Canadian Mad Studies*. Edited by Brenda A. Le François, Robert Menzies and Geoffrey Reaume. Toronto: Canadian Scholars' Press Inc., pp. 1–26. ISBN 978-1-55130-534-9.

Metzl, Jonathan. 2009. *The Protest Psychosis: How Schizophrenia Became a Black Disease*. Boston: Beacon Press. ISBN 978-0-8070-0127-1.

Movement for Global Mental Health. 2017. About. Available online: http://www.globalmentalhealth.org/about (accessed on 15 October 2017).

Mills, China. 2014. *Decolonizing Global Mental Health: The Psychiatrization of the Majority World*. London: Routledge. ISBN 978-1-84872-160-9.

Minkowitz, Tina. 2007. The United Nations Convention on the Rights of Persons with Disabilities and the Right to Be Free from Nonconsensual Psychiatric Interventions. *Syracuse Journal of International Law and Commerce* 34: 405–28.

Minkowitz, Tina. 2014. Rethinking criminal responsibility from a critical disability perspective: The abolition of insanity/incapacity acquittals and unfitness to plead, and beyond. *Griffith Law Review* 23: 434–66. [CrossRef]

Newnes, Craig. 2016. *Inscription, Diagnosis, Deception and the Mental Health Industry: How Psy Governs Us All*. Basingstoke: Palgrave MacMillan, ISBN 978-1-137-3-31296-9.

Nunan, Richard. 2010. Social Institutions, Transgendered Lives, and the Scope of Free Expression. In *Freedom of Expression in a Diverse World*. Edited by Deirdre Golash. Dordrecht: Springer, pp. 189–211. ISBN 978-90-481-8998-4.

O'Connell, Karen. 2017. Eccentricity: The case for undermining legal categories of disability and normalcy. *Journal of Media & Cultural Studies* 31: 352–64.

O'Flaherty, Michael. 2012. Freedom of Expression: Article 19 of the International Covenant on Civil and Political Rights and the Human Rights Committee's General Comment No 32. *Human Rights Law Review* 12: 628–54. [CrossRef]

Parmar, Sejal. 2015. Limits to freedom of expression: Lessons from counter-terrorism. In *The United Nations and Freedom of Expression and Information: Critical Perspectives*. Edited by Tarlach McGonagle and Yvonne Donders. Cambridge: Cambridge University Press, pp. 428–42. ISBN 978-1-107-08386-8.

Patel, Shaista. 2014. Racing Madness: The Terrorizing Madness of the Post-9-11 Terrorist Body. In *Disability Incarcerated: Imprisonment and Disability in the United States and Canada*. Edited by Liat Ben-Moshe, Chris Chapman and Allison C. Carey. New York: Palgrave Macmillan, pp. 201–16. ISBN 978-1-137-388476.

Peay, Jill. 1989. *Tribunals on Trial: A Study of Decision-Making under the Mental Health Act 1983*. Oxford: Clarendon. ISBN 9780198252498.

Penney, Darby, and Laura Prescott. 2016. The co-optation of survivor knowledge: The danger of substituted values and voice. In *Searching For a Rose Garden*. Edited by Jasna Russo and Angela Sweeney. Monmouth: PCCS Books, pp. 50–61. ISBN 978-1-910919-30-9.

Penson, William. 2015. Unsettling impairment: Mental health and the social model of disability. In *Madness, Distress and the Politics of Disablement*. Edited by Helen Spandler, Jill Anderson and Bob Sapey. Bristol: Policy Press, pp. 57–66. ISBN 978-1-4473-2809-4.

Perkins, Elizabeth. 2003. *Decision-Making in Mental Health Review Tribunals*. London: Policy Studies Institute. ISBN 853747911.

Player, Candice. 2015. Involuntary Outpatient Commitment: The Limits of Prevention. *Stanford Law and Policy Review* 26: 159–238. [CrossRef]

Poole, Jennifer M., and Jennifer Ward. 2013. "Breaking Open the Bone": Storying, Sanism, and Mad Grief. In *Mad Matters: A Critical Reader in Canadian Mad Studies*. Edited by Brenda A. Le François, Robert Menzies and Geoffrey Reaume. Toronto: Canadian Scholars' Press Inc., pp. 94–104. ISBN 978-1-55130-534-9.

Mark Rapley, Joanna Moncrieff, and Jacqui Dillon, eds. 2011. *De-Medicalizing Misery: Psychiatry, Psychology and the Human Condition*. Basingstoke: Palgrave Macmillian. ISBN 978-0-230-34250-7.

Reaume, Geoffrey. 2008. A History of Psychiatric Survivor Pride Day during the 1990s. *Bulletin* 374: 2–3. Available online: http://www.csinfo.ca/bulletin/Bulletin_374.pdf (accessed on 1 November 2017).

Rogers, Anne. 1998. The meaning and management of neuroleptic medication: A study of patients with a diagnosis of schizophrenia. *Social Science and Medicine* 47: 1313–23. [CrossRef]

Roper, Cath. Forthcoming; Capacity does not reside in me. In *Critical Perspectives on Coercive Interventions: Law, Medicine and Society*. Edited by Claire Spivakovsky, Kate Seear and Adrian Carter. London: Routledge.

Rose, Nicholas. 1998. *Inventing Our Selves: Psychology, Power, and Personhood*. Cambridge: Cambridge University Press. ISBN 0-521-64607-3.

Russo, Jasna. 2016. Towards our own framework, or reclaiming madness part two. In *Searching For a Rose Garden*. Edited by Jasna Russo and Angela Sweeney. Monmouth: PCCS Books, pp. 73–84. ISBN 978-1-910919-30-9.

Russo, Jasna, and Debra Shulkes. 2015. What we talk about when we talk about disability: making sense of debates in the European user/survivor movement. In *Madness, Distress and the Politics of Disablement*. Edited by Helen Spandler, Jill Anderson and Bob Sapey. Bristol: Policy Press, pp. 27–42. ISBN 978-1-4473-2809-4.

Jasna Russo, and Angela Sweeney, eds. 2016. *Searching For a Rose Garden*. Monmouth: PCCS Books. ISBN 978-1-910919-30-9.

Sen, Amartya. 1999. *Development as Freedom*. Oxford: Oxford University Press. ISBN 978-0-19-829-758-1.

Sjöström, Stefan. 2006. Invocation of coercion context in compliance communication—Power dynamics in psychiatric care. *International Journal of Law and Psychiatry* 29: 36–47. [CrossRef] [PubMed]

Spandler, Helen, and Tim Calton. 2009. Psychosis and Human Rights: Conflicts in Mental Health Policy and Practice. *Social Policy & Society* 8: 245–56.

Spivakovsky. Forthcoming; The impossibilities of 'bearing witness' to the violence of coercive interventions in the disability sector. In *Critical Perspectives on Coercive Interventions: Law, Medicine and Society*. Edited by Claire Spivakovsky, Kate Seear and Adrian Carter. London: Routledge.

Steele, Linda. 2014. Disability, abnormality and criminal law: Sterilisation as lawful and 'good' violence. *Griffith Law Review* 23: 467–97. [CrossRef]

Steele, Linda. 2016. Court Authorised Sterilisation and Human Rights: Inequality, Discrimination and Violence against Women and Girls with Disability. *University of New South Wales Law Journal* 39: 1011–15.

Steele, Linda, and Leanne Dowse. 2016. Gender, Disability Rights and Violence against Medical Bodies. *Australian Feminist Studies* 31: 187–202. [CrossRef]

Szasz, Thomas. 1997. *The Manufacture of Madness: A Comparative Study of the Inquisition and the Mental Health Movement*. Syracuse: Syracuse University Press, First published 1960. ISBN 978 0 8156 0461 7.

Szmukler, George, and Frank Holloway. 1998. Mental health legislation is now a harmful anachronism. *Psychiatric Bulletin* 22: 662–65. [CrossRef]

Tam, Louise. 2013. Whither Indigenizing the Mad Movement? Theorizing the Social Relations of Race and Madness through Conviviality. In *Mad Matters: A Critical Reader in Canadian Mad Studies*. Edited by Brenda A. Le François, Robert Menzies and Geoffrey Reaume. Toronto: Canadian Scholars' Press Inc., pp. 281–97. ISBN 978-1-55130-534-9.

Taylor, Mark. 2016. Community treatment orders and reduced time in hospital: A nationwide study, 2007–2012. *BJPsych Bulletin* 40: 124–26. [CrossRef] [PubMed]

The Royal Australian & New Zealand College of Psychiatrists. 2016. The Economic Cost of Serious Mental Illness and Comorbidities in Australia and New Zealand. Available online: https://www.ranzcp.org/Files/Publications/RANZCP-Serious-Mental-Illness.aspx (accessed on 5 November 2017).

United Nations Enable. 2007. Working Group on a Convention. Available online: http://www.un.org/esa/socdev/enable/rights/ahcwg.htm#membership (accessed on 3 January 2018).

United Nations General Assembly. 2016. *Report of the Special Rapporteur on the Promotion and Protection of the Right to Freedom of Expression*. 71st sess, UN Doc A/71/373, September 6; New York: United Nations General Assembly. Available online: http://www.ohchr.org/EN/Issues/FreedomOpinion/Pages/Annual.aspx (accessed on 31 December 2017).

Wadiwel, Dinesh. 2017. Disability and torture: Exception, epistemology and 'black sites'. *Continuum* 31: 388–99. [CrossRef]

Wand, Tim, and Maria Chiarella. 2006. A conversation: Challenging the relevance and wisdom of separate mental health legislation. *International Journal of Mental Health Nursing* 15: 119–27. [CrossRef] [PubMed]

Weitz, Don. 2003. Call Me Antipsychiatry Activist—Not "Consumer". *Ethical Human Sciences and Services* 5: 71–72. [PubMed]

Whitaker, Robert. 2010. *Anatomy of an Epidemic: Magic Bullets, Psychiatric Drugs, and the Astonishing Rise in Mental Illness in America*. New York: Crown Publishers. ISBN 978-0-307-45242-9.

Wildeman, Sheila. 2013. Protecting Rights and Building Capacities: Challenges to Global Mental Health Policy in Light of the Convention on the Rights of Persons with Disabilities. *The Journal of Law, Medicine & Ethics* 41: 48–73.

World Network of Users and Survivors of Psychiatry. 2008. Psychosocial Disability. Available online: http://www.wnusp.net/index.php/crpd.html (accessed on 1 November 2017).

Žižek, Slavoj. 2008. *Violence*. London: Profile Books.

11

Drawing the Line: Disability, Genetic Intervention and Bioethics

Adam Conti

Graduate student, Melbourne Law School, University of Melbourne, 185 Pelham St., Carlton, VIC 3053, Australia; aconti@student.unimelb.edu.au

Abstract: Meteoric scientific advances in genetic technologies with the potential for human gene editing intervention pose tremendous legal, medical, social, ethical and moral issues for society as a whole. Persons with disabilities in particular have a significant stake in determining how these technologies are governed at the international, domestic and individual levels in the future. However, the law cannot easily keep up with the rate of scientific progression. This paper aims to posit a methodology of reform, based on a core value of human dignity, as the optimal course of action to ensure that the interests of persons with disabilities, other possibly marginalised groups, and the scientific community, are balanced fairly. The paper critically analyses the current law and varying bioethical perspectives to ultimately conclude that a clear principled approach toward open discussion and consensus is of paramount importance to have any chance of devising an effective regulatory regime over human gene editing technology.

Keywords: disability; human rights; genetics; gene editing; bioethics; governance; human dignity; eugenics; germline; Convention on the Rights of Persons with Disabilities

---

The true good is in the different, not the same (Menand 2004).

1. Introduction

Popular, professional and scholarly interest in genetics and their influence on human variability, behaviour and development has grown exponentially in recent years. In no small part has this interest been bolstered by mainstream media coverage of large-scale collaborative scientific initiatives like the Human Genome Project, which endeavoured to identify and map the human genome and determine the sequence of nucleotide base pairs that make up our DNA. Even over a decade ago, the President's Council on Bioethics asserted that:

> [W]e have entered upon a golden age for biology, medicine, and biotechnology. With the completion of (the DNA sequencing phase of) the Human Genome Project and the emergence of stem cell research, we can look forward to major insights into human development, normal and abnormal, as well as novel and more precisely selected treatments for human disease ... In myriad ways, the discoveries of biologists and the inventions of biotechnologists are steadily increasing our power ever more precisely to intervene into the workings of our bodies and minds and to alter them by rational design (President's Council on Bioethics 2003, pp. 4–5).

Our knowledge and expertise in the realm of genetic engineering and methods through which to alter our genetic makeup have expanded exponentially since that statement. Science continually pushes the contemporary boundaries of what can be done just as much as it does for what we think should or should not be done. In 2017, we now have access to ground-breaking technologies that are becoming more accurate and inexpensive, and therefore more widespread. Human genome editing is one such practice that is rapidly advancing with the potential to outpace legal regulation at the national, international and institutional levels.

Atypical biotechnological advancement and (lack of) regulation poses a vast array of ethical, social, legal and human rights issues for the disability human rights movement. From one perspective, misuse of these technologies could quite quickly develop into a new eugenics movement akin to humanity's sordid and abominable forays into such immoral practices throughout history. From another, it beckons new horizons for the human race and promises of a 'better' human or a 'better' life for those already living with disabilities. This debate touches on notions of normality, discrimination and fundamental values of human dignity, and prompts a number of unsettling questions. Will society's attitudes towards and treatment of persons with disabilities become determinant purely on their genetic makeup? Will such people be further ostracised as a result of potentially not having 'desirable' genetic traits? Will there be active eugenic practices to 'eradicate' genetic disability? Most importantly, will there be a way to stop that from happening?

This paper aims to search for an answer to the last question so as to negate the need to ask the former ones. It contends that genomic technology, its use and development, should be appropriately regulated in the future so as to balance the interests of science with those of people with disabilities. Section 2 briefly elucidates humanity's abhorrent past of eugenic practices in the 20th Century. By tracking technological advancement in the human genetic modification sphere, it draws analogies between the two eras to shed light on the well-founded concern of some disability rights advocates that it risks delving into the realm of a 'neo-eugenics' movement. Section 3 canvasses the opposing bioethical theories that underpin various legal, medical, social, ethical and moral perspectives in this area. Section 4 explores and critically analyses the way in which the international community and individual nation states (particularly Australia) have attempted to effectively protect the interests of those with disabilities in light of these technological advances. Finally, Section 5 will propose a human rights model of reform to remedy flaws and omissions in the current regulatory system, such that disability rights advocates have a powerful and influential voice in shaping a genetic tool that has the capacity to shape how they live their lives.

Ultimately, the greatest obstacle for effective regulation is the undeniable fact that the rapid development of these technologies is unstoppable. However, the way in which they are used can be changed and controlled. With the implementation of appropriate international and domestic regulatory regimes that not only consider the past and present, but also comprise an element of foresight, persons with disabilities are less likely to be adversely affected. That is the rationale for this paper. Developing genetic technologies pose a crucial and eventually universal issue as they become more accessible and less expensive; undoubtedly the quickest way to their abuse.

2. Classical and Neo-Eugenics

Prevailing attitudes towards the 'other' are often influenced by the contemporary and prevailing social, political, cultural and technological developments at any point in human history. This section aims to track eugenics, as one such attitude, from its oldest form through to the current day in order to exemplify the issues that genetic technologies pose for people with disabilities.

2.1. Classical Eugenics: How Far Have We Gone?

Eugenics is not a new concept. The term's classical meaning was originally articulated by Francis Galton as:

> the science of improving stock, which is by no means confined to questions of judicious mating, but [includes] all influences that tend in however remote a degree to give to the more suitable races or strains of blood a better chance of prevailing speedily over the less suitable than they otherwise would have had (Galton 1883, p. 17).

Essentially, it constitutes a set of beliefs and practices that advocate for 'improvement' of the human race by the application of genetic laws based on Darwin's theory of evolution and Mendelian laws of inheritance (Somsen 2009). Galton's theories were influential, rapidly spreading to the United States and beyond (Black 2008). They eventually birthed government-sponsored eugenics movements across the world, which aimed to both encourage those considered to have 'good' heritable traits to have more children and discourage or expressly prohibit those thought to be 'unfit' from doing the same (Baruch et al. 2005, p. 34).

Disability rights advocates are troubled by historical eugenics because such policies were almost always directed towards groups that had, or were perceived to have, physical or mental impairments (Amundson and Tresky 2008, p. 113). The starkest and most barbarian example of these practices was the Nazi 'racial hygiene' policy, which actively sought to prevent Germans from reproducing with people considered to be 'biologic threats' given their 'inferior' genes (Bachruch 2004, p. 419). A further offshoot of this policy was the Aktion T4 program. Pursuant to guidelines from the government, the program required German doctors to administer an involuntary 'mercy death' by euthanasia to patients deigned to be 'incurably sick, by critical medical examination' (Proctor 1988, p. 177). People with disabilities, confined to a mental health institution or otherwise impaired were quickly categorised as such (Amundson and Tresky 2008, p. 113), aligning with the program's underlying policy of negative eugenic 'cleansing' (Breggin 1993). Ultimately, historians estimate that between 200,000–250,000 people with physical and intellectual disabilities were murdered under the Aktion T4 program between 1939 and 1945 (Herberer 2002, p. 62; Burleigh 1994).

Francis Fukuyama, a previous member of the President's Council of Bioethics, consequently condemned this chapter of history as 'the last important political movement to explicitly deny the premise of universal human dignity' (Fukuyama 2002, p. 156). The harsh impact of these practices can still be felt today, particularly in communities of those with disabilities. The past highlights the great importance of discouraging the use of genetics, or any other trait or characteristic, as a rationale for discriminating against any person or group (Bachruch 2004, p. 420). If nothing else, the Nazi era should serve as a bleak reminder that there is a slippery slope between a eugenic ideology and a human atrocity. The only thing needed to bridge the gap between them is a 'tool'. What is worrying is that this next tool might be here sooner than expected.

2.2. *Genomic Technology as Neo-Eugenics: How Far Have We Come?*

An impressive number of ground-breaking technological and scientific developments over the last 40 years have drastically developed the scientific community's ability to manipulate genetic material. Baldi believes that these developments signify 'the end of our evolutionary odyssey' (Baldi 2001, p. 163). We can now test embryos for genetic defects, gender and disease even before implantation through in vitro fertilisation procedures, investigate gene function in a plethora of organisms (Dzau and Cicerone 2015, p. 411) and, as emphasised in this paper, may soon have the ability to alter our fundamental genetic makeup, which may in turn be inherited by our offspring (Hoge and Appelbaum 2012, p. 1549). Genome editing is a type of genetic engineering that allows for flexible insertion, deletion or replacement of deoxyribonucleic acid ('DNA') in cellular organisms through the use of engineered nucleases (Ishii 2015, p. 1).

The most recently developed, highly exalted and technologically disruptive gene editing tool is the CRISPR-Cas 9 ('CRISPR') system. Essentially, CRISPR is a family of engineered nucleases based on segments of a bacterial defence mechanism that both identifies and removes foreign viruses from the bacterial genome as an adaptive immune response (Hsu et al. 2014, p. 1264). Small parts of the viral DNA sequences are left scattered between repeated bacteria DNA sequences, known as 'clustered regularly interspaced short palindromic repeats' (or CRISPR), so that the bacteria can more easily protect itself against the same virus in the future.

A key aspect of the adaptive immune response is the protein Cas9, which can seek out, cut and eventually degrade viral DNA (Doudna 2015). Put simply, scientists have determined how to harness Cas9's capabilities into a tool that enables an organism's genome to be 'cut' or spliced at any targeted location specified by 'guide' ribonucleic acid ('RNA') molecules (Dzau and Cicerone 2015, p. 411), whether they be 'as large as an entire gene [or] as small as a single nucleotide' (Altman et al. 2015, p. 25).

What makes CRISPR such an incredible development in genetics is that it allows edits to become significantly more efficient, accurate and cost-effective, whilst being less technically problematic than ever before (Esvelt and Wang 2013, p. 1; Ledford 2015, p. 21). Its usage in the scientific community is growing rapidly as a result. In April 2015, Chinese scientists reported results of an attempt to alter the DNA of non-viable human embryos using CRISPR to correct a heritable blood mutation that causes beta thalassemia (Liang et al. 2015). The experiments resulted in changing only some of the genes, and had off-target effects on other genes. The scientists who conducted the research stated that CRISPR is not yet ready for clinical application in reproductive medicine. Even so, a point was made: if those embryos had been viable, then implanted in a woman and been brought to term, we would have created genetically modified humans (Center for Genetics and Society and Friends of the Earth 2015, p. 22).

Nevertheless, as with any disruptive technology, this unprecedented advance in genetic engineering holds great promise for generational therapeutics, but has sparked a large social and ethical debate. That debate will be further explored through the lens of bioethics and disability human rights in Section 3. Suffice it to say for now that what is especially concerning is that edits can be made not only in adult somatic cells, but also in germline cells, such as those in embryos and gametes. The crucial difference between somatic and germline cells is that the former is idiosyncratic and any effects of an edit are limited to a single individual, whilst genome changes to the latter can be inherited by offspring, thus impacting future individuals' bodies and minds (Ishii 2015, p. 19). To that end, the National Academies of Sciences and Medicine released a consensus statement of the Committee for the International Summit of Gene Editing, which emphasises that the alteration of germline cells is irresponsible and could have far-reaching, unintended, or adverse consequences for human evolution; genetically, culturally and, in terms of disability human rights, socially as well (National Academies of Sciences and Medicine 2015). Furthermore, many scientists, including Jennifer Doudna, one of the inventors of CRISPR, have urged a worldwide moratorium on clinical application of CRISPR to human germline modification until the full implications of the technology 'are discussed among scientific and governmental organisations ... and interest groups' (Baltimore et al. 2015; Lanphier et al. 2015).

To take a step back and examine what such developments might mean for persons with disabilities is a difficult and controversial task. In October 2015, the UN International Bioethics Committee stated that the ethical problems of human genetic engineering should not be confused with the ethical problems of 20th Century eugenics movements; however, it is still problematic because it challenges the idea of human equality and opens up new forms of discrimination and stigmatisation for those with disabilities. It is true that the ethos of the current technological phenomenon contrasts with that of classical eugenics, given that to some extent it has been accepted that 'it makes no evolutionary sense to drive our species through a man-made bottleneck of genetic uniformity' (Brosius and Kreitman 2000, p. 253).

Nevertheless, there are strong parallels to be drawn between the eugenics era and the growing role of human genetic modification following the Human Genome Project. As already noted, classical eugenics was concerned with selecting certain *people* through forced sterilisation, restrictive reproduction laws and secret killings (Fischer 2012, p. 1097). The growing concern is that a neo-eugenics movement may be instead focused on the selection of certain *genes* (King 2001, pp. 171–72). There are fears that the allure of the doctrine of social advancement that the Council for Responsible Genetics has termed 'biological perfectibility' will result in organised neo-eugenics programs that slowly but surely aim to eradicate genes that cause disability, whilst inserting inheritable 'better' genes (Council for Responsible Genetics 2005). Though, at least in Australia, the idea of such government-sanctioned programs appears too remote a possibility, in the past legitimate concerns have been expressed by the President of the American Association of People with Disabilities:

> One would hope that reactions to the Holocaust and the advent of the disability rights and independent living movements in the U.S. and around the world would have put an end to the eugenic efforts to eliminate disabled people ... Unfortunately, if we examine the rhetoric of some influential modern scientists and ethicists, we can see the emergence of a new eugenics tied to the rapid advances in scientific understanding of the human genome (Imparato 2004).

Similar statements have been echoed by Disabled Peoples International (DPI), which highlights that:

> Human genetics poses a threat to us because while cures and palliatives are promised, what is actually being offered are genetic tests for characteristics perceived as undesirable ... These technologies are, therefore, opening the door to a new eugenics which directly threatens our human rights ((Disabled Peoples International DPI, p. 3)).

These techniques may be aimed to eliminate disabling traits that are deemed 'abnormal', 'defective' or even 'cruel'. If disabling features in a foetus were to be seen as features that would render its life not worth living, then the same view would likely be taken for existing people already living with those same conditions (Jones 2011b, p. 103). Misapplication of genetic practice under such a pretence could quite clearly amount to eugenics. Notwithstanding that genetic disability does not account for all types of disability, such as those that are acquired through accident, injury and armed conflict, initiatives like the Human Genome Project could contribute to the creation of the notion of disability as deviance and people with disabilities, whether living or embryonic, as a different species whose lives are intrinsically less valuable than others (Turmusani 2004). If so, neo-eugenics would not be a retrospective regulation of living people, but rather a pre-emptive strike on unborn future generations (Witzany 2016, p. 281).

Furthermore, there are fears that human germline genetic modification will adversely affect human dignity and wider societal attitudes towards those living with disabilities, casting people as 'problems' that could have been avoided, and putting pressure on families to have genetically 'perfect' children (Baruch et al. 2005, p. 7). It is argued by Pollack that the negative end game of human germline modification is that those who have not had their genes modified, or who acquire disabilities or otherwise inherit them, will be born into a world 'with a complexity of genome different from what ... technology will be able to define as "normal' (Pollack 2015, p. 871). Neo-eugenics may therefore reduce persons with disabilities merely to their genetic makeup or origins, rather than as people of equal standing (Jones 2011b, p. 103; Iles 1996, p. 47). In a world where people with disabilities may already be considered by some as 'lesser', such a development would only serve to widen the gap that disability rights advocates must bridge. That sentiment is echoed by Baruch et al., who assert that the normalisation of genetic enhancement might 'decrease society's tolerance for and willingness to support and treat those living with disabilities'(Baruch et al. 2005, pp. 7, 27). Lander similarly highlighted the 'moral grayness' and eugenic practices that are inherent in genetic modification of human life (Lander 2015, p. 7). Ultimately, they conclude that CRISPR practice on human germlines can only proceed if there is a strong ethical argument to do so, or if necessity dictates it so. Otherwise, clinical practice should be banned.

In any case, the potential implications of human germline genetic modification for those with disabilities ultimately turn on the way in which tools such as CRISPR are utilised in the future. Will society be coerced (whether overtly or impliedly) into its widespread use, or will there be sufficiently effective and adaptable regulation that considers and protects disability human rights?

3. Disability, Bioethics and Human Rights: Clash or Cooperate?

How we conceptualise disability human rights and genetic technologies like human germline engineering and CRISPR tools frames the regulatory measures we believe are appropriate. To properly appreciate the current relevant law, and to ultimately point toward an appropriate model that balances human and scientific interests, we must first understand the human rights and bioethical principles that underpin various sides of this controversial debate. The discipline of bioethics is centred on the critical assessment of ethical and legal controversies that arise from emerging situations and possibilities brought about by advances in biological medicine (Smith 2012, p. 2). Therefore, it is pertinent to examine the three competing schools of thought on disability through an overarching bioethical lens:

(1) The traditional utilitarian medical model of disability;
(2) The pro-disability rights perspective of the social model;
(3) The human rights model of disability, a more recently emerging trend amongst disability rights scholarship.

As will become apparent in the following passages, one's bioethical perspectives and corresponding views on disability rights may affect their fundamental normative position on the issue of how technologies like CRISPR should or should not be used and regulated, and for what purpose. Generally, proponents of the medical model would be more open to the use of a less regulated CRISPR for curative purposes. In the same way, those who propound the social and dignitarian models may be more inclined to its opposition and greater regulation, in the former case on grounds of possible further systemic disadvantage to persons with disabilities, and in the latter case due to the threat of harm to their human dignity.

This paper asserts that it is a regulatory framework founded on the human rights model, or at the very least, a combination of the social model and human rights model, that best protects the rights and interests of people with disabilities in the face of rapid genetic technology advancement.

3.1. The Medical Model and Beneficence

Throughout history, people with disabilities have unfortunately been treated by some as tragic burdens and objects of pity by society (Kayess and French 2008, p. 5). This perspective stems from the medical model of disability, which focuses on an individual's limitations by viewing disability as a deficiency or deviation from the norm that requires cure, treatment, care and protection to alter the person so as to conform them to the existing social structures, processes and environments in which they live. This is an attempt to allow them to live a 'normal' life. Little emphasis is placed on the role the world and environment play in disabling people with impairments, thus well and truly earning the moniker 'the politics of disablement' (Oliver 1990). The medical model has existed at least since the advent of the Industrial Revolution (Oliver 1996) and sadly 'has guided and dominated clinical practice with the resulting assumption that both problems and solutions lie within disabled people rather than within society' (French 1994). As such, over the years the model has served to perpetuate negative and unhelpful attitudes and discriminatory practices that further oppress, ostracise and disable people with impairments (Finkelstein and Stuart 1996, pp. 175–76).

In a similar vein to 'curing' or 'eliminating' the harm of disability from the world are bioethical perspectives that strongly align with the medical model. A central tenet of bioethical study is the principle of beneficence, which comprises aims to achieve the two distinct, but related, goals of preventing harm and producing good (Smith 2012, p. 22). Of course, any application of this principle requires an advance assessment of three ethical dilemmas (Walters 1978, p. 50):

(1) what constitutes 'harm';
(2) what constitutes 'good';
(3) what are the possible negative social consequences that might come from new biomedical technologies in order to protect groups of individuals from that harm.

To the lay person, these propositions might appear to have subjective answers. The lay person would be right. However, utilitarian advocates of the medical model would hold that the best moral action in such a case is the one that maximises overall utility or benefit for the greatest number of people. To that end, Savulescu takes this basic bioethical creed a step further into the realm of disability and reproductive rights in claiming that a moral utilitarian principle of procreative beneficence exists (Savulescu et al. 2015). In summary, the principle requires that:

> couples (or single reproducers) should select the child, of the possible children they could have, who is expected to have the best life, or at least as good a life as the others, based on the relevant, available information (Savulescu et al. 2015, p. 415).

The position is that through available technologies like CRISPR, parents should aim to remove 'disease genes', which cause a genetic disorder or predispose the person to the development of a disease. This perspective, essentially a form of eugenic practice disguised as mere biological reductionism, argues that it is irrational to choose an embryo that will not have the 'best life'. It further cloaks itself as a morally persuasive, rather than coercive, principle. Its final and most chilling formation is seen in the views of philosophers like Peter Singer, who believe that 'the killing of a disabled infant is not morally equivalent to killing a person. Very often it is not wrong at all' (Singer 1993, p. 191).

As this paper will soon show, in reality disabilities are generally not experienced as 'pain and suffering', nor are persons with disabilities 'harmed' by their impairment (Jones 2011b, p. 102). In actual fact, most of the suffering occurs as a 'result of not enough human caring, acceptance and respect' as a human being like others without a disability (Saxton 1988, p. 222). Even so, this crucial misconception underpinning the medical model and principle of procreative beneficence grounds a utilitarian argument that, in the same way it is morally wrong to harm another human, it is morally wrong to bring a person with a disability into the world on the basis of the pain and suffering it would bring onto the newborn (Harris 1990). The conclusion reached by Harris is that it is kinder to prevent the birth of a person with a disability (Harris 1998, p. 118; Marzano-Parisoli 2001). Any argument that such a world is morally preferable must rest on the assumption that 'a life with even moderate disabilities or impairments is a life with less moral value than other lives' (Bennett 2009, p. 271). Therefore, utilitarian individualism perceives people with disabilities as:

> commodities to be 'serviced' and . . . as an economic burden on society; their defects are emphasised and their worth is judged by their contribution to society. Being objects of charity, they are patronised and, at worst, they are perceived as dehumanised 'others' (Parmenter 2005, p. 53).

This paper disagrees with the proposition that whether a person will live a 'good' or 'best life' is wholly dictated merely by a genetic sequence or trait that forms part of who they are (Asch 2000; Shakespeare 1995). In that respect, there can be no effective regulation of genetic technology to safeguard human rights under these principles because, at a fundamental level, they do not conceive of a person with a disability as a 'full-value human'.

3.2. The Social Model

Whereas the medical model locates the problem in the impairment of the individual, the contrasting social model views disability as a social construct of discrimination and oppression that denies or limits personhood, beyond the individual's condition (Kayess and French 2008, p. 5; Degener 2014, p. 4). At the heart of the social model is the notion of 'systemic disadvantage', which is highlighted in the structural, social and exclusory barriers purposely or inadvertently erected by society (Oliver 1990, p. 47). Furthermore, the social model is based on a series of dichotomies, between impairment and disability, social and medical models, and persons with and without disabilities (Shakespeare 2013, p. 216). In relation to the distinction between the terms 'impairment' and 'disability, the former relates to the individual on a private level, whilst the latter relates to society on a structural level. Impairment refers to 'a characteristic, feature or attribute within an individual which is long term and may . . . be the result of disease, genetics or injury' (Thomas et al. 1997, p. 2), and may affect appearance, function of mind or body and/or cause pain and fatigue. These physical, sensory, intellectual or psychological variations do not have to lead to disability unless society fails to accommodate and include people with those differences. Article 1 of the Convention on the Rights of Persons with Disabilities ('CRPD') provides an open definition of disability, such that it includes, but is not limited to 'those who have long-term physical, mental, intellectual or sensory impairments which in interaction with various barriers may hinder their full and effective participation in society on an equal basis with others' (United Nations 2007). In other words, disability is imposed over impairment by excluding individuals from being able to fully participate in society (Oliver 1996, p. 22). It is with these definitions in mind that we assess the relative merits and shortcomings of each conception of disability.

However, the social model has been criticised almost as much as the medical model (Shakespeare 2002). Whilst it has been instrumental in launching the disability movement, promulgating positive disability identity and encouraging barrier removal and rights legislation, it is ultimately a 'blunt instrument for explaining and combating the social exclusion that disabled people face, and the complexity of [their] needs' (Shakespeare 2013, p. 220). Its simplicity is its major flaw. In the context of human genetic engineering (or, in reality, any disruptive technology that affects the barriers people with disabilities might face) and CRISPR, utilisation of the social model, which lacks nuance, to underwrite any policy or regulatory rights protection regime is more difficult than it at first appears. Though the social model is indeed a useful tool for identifying systemic causes of disadvantage, it falls short in determining what action should be taken in response (Samaha 2007, p. 27). There is a disconnect between causation of the disability and policy, which produces an issue where the social model's account of causation forms the sole reason for social change (Samaha 2007, p. 37). The consequent issue then is that the resulting policy to remedy the issue is reactive. In a rapidly evolving technological landscape, to adequately protect the rights of persons with disabilities and other interest groups is not to retrospectively attempt to fix problems caused by scientific advancement, but rather to proactively create a global system of substantive and normative human rights.

Therefore, whilst a competent heuristic approach, the social model is imperfect (Degener 2014, p. 5). In light of the swift scientific advances made each week, if not each day, its utility is limited. Disability is an already complex issue made even more complex by the ethical and legal debate of genetic engineering. As such, we might be best served by a governance model underpinned by an alternative that more effectively allows for differing levels of analysis and policy.

3.3. Human Rights and Dignitarianism: A Way Forward

The third and final tenet of the bioethical and disability rights triad in the human genetic engineering debate is that of the emerging human rights model of disability and the complementary dignitarian ideology (Brownsword 2009, p. 25). This model builds upon the foundations of the social model and small aspects of the medical model, but goes further to enforce and protect the human rights of people with disabilities (Degener 2014, p. 29). First, it is contended that the anchor at the heart of modern human rights is the concept of human dignity (Degener and Quinn 2002, p. 30): a moral value attributable to each person by virtue of his or her humanity (Grant 2007) and independent of social status, gender, genetic makeup, physical or mental ability or any other characteristic (Basser 2011, pp. 19–20; Fukuyama 2002, pp. 14, 149). Human dignity is valuable especially for those who have traditionally been denied an equal place in society, because it reinforces the idea that all people are equal rights-bearers (Basser 2011, p. 21). Essentially, 'valuing human dignity means acknowledging the inherent worth of human beings; therefore violating dignity involves conveying the message that some are of less worth than others' (Reaume 2002–2003, p. 672).

In saying that, human dignity is a complex principle. It also involves a positive interpretation of 'humaneness' (Jones 2011a, p. 36). Basser elucidates four elements necessary for a person to be treated with dignity:

> First is the absolutely crucial requirement that a person's physical integrity is respected ... Secondly, human dignity means that every person has the inherent right to be treated as an individual with a personality ... Thirdly, human dignity means that a person must be

> given voice about any issues which affect their lives and must have the ability wherever possible to exercise choice. Finally, inherent dignity of any individual requires that he or she has access to a fair share of the goods of society (Basser 2011, p. 19).

The human rights model centres on these principles of inherent human dignity by focusing on a person's medical characteristics only if absolutely necessary. It states that the 'problem' is extrinsic to the person and grants autonomy to the individual in relation to decisions or circumstances affecting him or her (Quinn and Degener 2002, p. 14). The human rights model differs from the social model in many respects, but most importantly, it explains why enforceable and inalienable human rights do not require an absence of impairment (Degener 2014, p. 6), includes a broader set of rights available to persons with disabilities, and values impairment as part of human diversity and variation.

As opposed to the views of Savulescu and Harris, the human rights model's fundamental critique of human genomic technologies is that their eventual widespread availability, use and probable misuse ultimately undermines, devalues and disempowers persons with disabilities unless rights safeguards are developed (Jones 2011b, p. 41). These threats have not gone unnoticed by the disability community. Such techniques are often seen to have the capacity to both threaten and to safeguard human dignity (McLean and Williamson 2007, p. 41). On the one hand, they may be viewed as supporting dignity of human life by improving health and alleviating suffering, such as by minimising the number of infants born with impairments and genetic disease or by respecting the reproductive liberty of those already born. On the other hand, eliminating or seeking to minimise the existence of people with genetic impairment may be perceived as offending human dignity, and thus human rights. From the latter perspective, DPI has posited the ethical and moral problems of more widely available genetic technology rather poignantly:

> How can we live with dignity in societies that spend millions on genetic research to eradicate disease and impairment, but refuse to meet our needs to live dignified and independent lives? We cannot. We will not. The genetic threat to us is a threat to everyone. The value of life must not be reduced to a matter of genetic inheritance ((Disabled Peoples International DPI, p. 4)).

That being said, this paper does not posit that parents with children diagnosed with genetic disabilities and cognisant of their carrier status of the relevant genes are, in making reproductive decisions about the possibility of future offspring also being diagnosed with a genetic disability (such as prenatal diagnosis followed by pregnancy termination, or preimplantation genetic diagnosis), making judgments about the human dignity of their children already affected by the genetic condition. It is clear that any application of principles of human dignity to assess decisions made in relation to persons with genetic disabilities and their treatment must be more nuanced to avoid any such misconceptions.

This begs the question as to what role human dignity and the human rights model should play in ethically governing genetic development whilst protecting the rights and interests of persons with disabilities. Two conceptions of human dignity are relevant. The first conception is as a form of 'empowerment' by supporting individual autonomy (Brownsword 2009, p. 26). This is best exemplified in both the Universal Declaration of Human Rights ('UDHR'), which provides that 'all human beings are born free and equal in dignity and rights', and the CRPD, which aims to 'promote respect for [persons with disabilities'] inherent dignity' under Articles 1 and 3. The second conception is as a form of 'constraint' on the autonomy of scientists acting in ways that might infringe human rights (Brownsword 2009, p. 28). As will be discussed in Section 4, human dignity as constraint is axiomatic in the three UNESCO Declarations on bioethics and genetics, as well as the Council of Europe's Oviedo Convention. The centrality and prevalence of these concepts is the strongest support for the human rights model of disability and is therefore the best place to begin an analysis of the current legal system.

4. How Do We Regulate?

The legal and ethical implications of manipulating the human genome depict a nebulous future. The globalisation of technological advances like CRISPR has exposed the absolute inadequacy of the development of nation-based bioethics for effectively addressing the threats raised by genomic technology (Lenzerini 2006, p. 292). Vast cross-jurisdictional inconsistency of legal genetic regulation may permit practices of uncertain morality and legality, such as human germline engineering, to develop in countries unwilling to enact such regulations. Ultimately, this paper emphasises the fact that, at present, the existing framework of human rights is likely systemically inadequate to address all threats to human dignity caused by rapid developments in biogenetics (Lenzerini 2006, p. 447; Iles 1996, p. 41).

4.1. International Law

As already noted, international law instruments such as the UDHR and UNESCO Declarations provide for human dignity both as an operational principle and moral precept (McCrudden 2008, pp. 668–71). For the purposes of genetics, this section will focus on two international law schemes: the CRPD and the UNESCO Declarations.

4.1.1. CRPD

The first point of reference for any discussion of disability human rights instruments in the common day must be the CRPD. The CRPD was the first UN human rights treaty adopted in the 21st Century and was reportedly the most rapidly negotiated ever (UN Secretary General 2006). It has been touted as a 'great landmark in the struggle to reframe the needs and concerns of persons with disabilities in terms of human rights' (Kayess and French 2008, p. 2). In regards to many issues that face persons with disabilities, it succeeds in protecting their rights. Articles 1 and 3(a) both emphasise the CRPD's agenda to codify the inalienable human rights of persons with disabilities by virtue of their human dignity, equal in scope and force with people without disabilities (Degener 2014, p. 7). A plethora of other articles comprehensively elucidate the many rights that others take for granted. On this, it should be commended.

However, from the particular perspective of human genome modification, the CRPD falls far short of effectively limiting potential abuses of CRISPR tools in the future. According to Wolbring and Diep (2016, p. 10) the CRPD could apply to gene editing in two ways:

(1) regulating the actual use of gene editing technologies like CRISPR; and
(2) in the aftermath of gene editing becoming more readily used, minimising the negative social consequences for persons with disabilities.

For a number of reasons, the potential application and substantive effectiveness of the CRPD in governing actual use of gene editing technologies is unclear.

First, the CRPD does not conceive of the potential impact of genetic technologies. Terms such as 'genetics', 'bioethics' or 'eugenics' do not feature once in the document. These glaring omissions highlight a fundamental lack of foresight as to the future threat genetic technologies and their misuse may pose to the disability human rights cause.

Second, though it is arguable that the anti-discrimination protections provided under Article 5 could validly critique pre or post-birth gene editing interventions aimed at 'fixing' impairment, the CRPD would be of little utility if gene editing interventions of any and all genes were permitted (Wolbring and Diep 2016, p. 12). This is again an example of how the purposes for which CRISPR and other gene editing technologies are used is crucial to their effective governance.

Third, a person's inherent right to life and its enjoyment on an equal basis with others under Article 10 remains starkly silent on 'genetic science aimed at the elimination of impairment-related human diversity and pre-birth negative selection of foeti with identified or imputed impairment' (Kayess and French 2008, p. 29). The further omission of such eugenic practices is a significant flaw.

Fourth, Article 17, which states that 'every person with disabilities has a right to respect for his or her physical and mental integrity on an equal basis with others', is the most limited of the substantive rights. 'Physical integrity' clearly points towards internal physicalities of DNA makeup. A more robust right might have been useful in the context of human somatic and germline modification, but the statement is essentially confined to a principle with no specific application towards the human rights violations it purports to address. Therefore, the potential use of 'coercive State power for the purpose of 'treatment' remains without any specific regulation' (Kayess and French 2008, p. 30). It should be further noted that although Article 17 could draw attention to the involuntary treatments of a 'competent' adult. Even so, the right to physical and mental integrity is unlikely to apply if parents have genetic interventions performed on their children or embryos, or where adults with disabilities agree to genetic intervention (Wolbring and Diep 2016, p. 12).

Fifth, the general principle of 'respect for difference and acceptance of persons with disabilities as part of human diversity and humanity' articulated in Article 3 similarly expresses a principle with no application to particular situations. In this case, noting the role of eugenics or biological reductionism as grounds for failure to respect that difference would greatly improve the persuasive and moral force of the instrument.

Sixth, even if the above protections were more substantial, the definition of 'disabled people' under Article 1, whilst inclusive, appears to imply that embryos that have their somatic or germline cells modified and are adversely affected as a result (so as then to have a disability), would not have had any rights infringed as at the time of the modification because they did not have any human dignity upon which to infringe. This paper notes that whilst this regulatory 'gap' appears to exist, human dignity is arguably less effective in regulating the application of technologies like CRISPR to embryos. The conceptualisation of the moral and legal status of the embryo 'as a human' is an issue subject to a plethora of ethical, legal and religious complications that differ widely across and within countries. As such, this paper merely notes the wording of the CRPD to highlight that it might be less problematic for nation states to legislate with regard to these embryos instead, as will be discussed below in Section 4.2.

In contrast, the CPRD's role in preventing the deterioration of the lived experience of persons with disabilities following the rise of gene editing is slightly more promising. CRISPR may one day be used in genetic enhancement. 'Disability' under the CRPD is arguably a changing concept that includes future disability. Wolbring and Diep assert that the CRPD may be applicable to people who are currently considered non-disabled, but will be classified as disabled as ability expectations rise due to the prevalence of genetic and technological enhancement of human (Wolbring and Diep 2016, p. 14). Only time will tell whether, in mitigating these negative consequences, the CRPD will be used to demand access to particular genetic products and procedures or to restrict their use and, further, how robust such approaches will be.

Even so, the CRPD falls short, on balance, to adequately protect the rights of current and future persons with disabilities in respect of human genome engineering.

4.1.2. UNESCO Declarations: Is Soft Law Tough Enough?

Whilst not as recently endorsed as the CPRD, the UNESCO Declarations exist as a framework of non-binding international soft law that has specifically aimed to regulate bioethics at a universal level. The scheme comprises:

(1) The Universal Declaration on the Human Genome and Human Rights ('UDHGHR');
(2) The Universal Declaration on Bioethics and Human Rights ('UDBHR'); and
(3) The International Declaration on Human Genetic Data ('IDHGD').

Of the trio, the UDHGHR and UDBHR are the most relevant for present purposes. As such, the IDHGD will not be further discussed in this paper. The norms articulated in the UDHGHR and UDBHR, including the central tenets of human dignity and human rights, enjoy a wide consensus at the international level (El-Zein 2008, p. 318). In fact, they have become a legal and ethical reference point in the drafting of national laws and regulations around the world (Ida 2003, p. 368); a 'slow burn' influence. Nevertheless, it should be kept in mind that these Declarations are general in scope, and avoid dealing in specific detail with particular issues in biotechnology or bioethics. This was a deliberate choice by the UNESCO General Conference to proceed gradually and prudently (El-Zein 2008, p. 319). Even so, the provisions show a level of prescience as to the dangers the human race and persons with disabilities might face as human gene editing technology develops.

The UDHGHR aims to delineate and promulgate a universal ethical standard-setting framework that member States can and should utilise in determining and implementing their own bioethical policies. The Preamble takes as its starting point a cognisance of the potential advantages and dangers of human genomic research and applications, emphasising that 'such research should fully respect human dignity, freedom and human rights, as well as the prohibition of all forms of discrimination based on genetic characteristics'. It goes on to state a fundamental ethical principle of human rights and dignitarianism in Article 1:

> The human genome underlies the fundamental unity of all members of the human family, as well as the recognition of their inherent dignity and diversity. In a symbolic sense, it is the heritage of humanity.

The reference to the genome as 'the heritage of humanity' is of particular relevance to the utility and moral viability of human germline gene modification. 'Heritage' has strong connotations with heritability. It therefore appears that, given the genome underpins our inherent human dignity and inclusive diversity, Article 1 attempts to discourage the artificial alteration of inheritable human germline cells. Following this definition, it is also recognised that there is a global responsibility on the international community as a whole to protect the disadvantaged, beyond single States and governments (International Bioethics Committee 2015, p. 27).

Clearly, the UDHGHR does not specifically denounce eugenic ideals. However, Lenzerini (2006, p. 318) asserts that Article 6 does provide a general prohibition against a range of conduct that would encompass discriminatory neo-eugenic practices through genetic experimentation in stating that:

> No one shall be subjected to discrimination based on genetic characteristics that is intended to infringe or has the effect of infringing human rights, fundamental freedoms and human dignity.

Article 2 entrenches an individual's right to respect for their human dignity and diversity, rather than their value being reduced to a sum of their genetic characteristics. Article 3 further emphasises that the human genome is not static: it evolves over time. As such, the countless variations and mutations in our DNA and their potentialities are expressed and viewed differently depending on the individual's natural and social environment. When Articles 2, 3 and 6 are read in conjunction, the UDHGHR conveys a persuasive narrative of the importance of values like dignity, respect, uniqueness and diversity.

In turn, a cumulative reading of Articles 1, 2 and 6 highlights the overarching need to balance the possible positive and negative consequences associated with the growing prevalence of genetic technology. Most important for the purposes of safeguarding disability human rights are Articles 10 and 11. The former establishes the paramountcy of respect of human rights, freedoms and dignity of individuals of groups over research or research applications relating to the human genome. The latter forbids practices that are contrary to human dignity outright. This suggests that whilst knowledge is important for the advancement of the human race, it is the way in which that knowledge is utilised that determines whether human rights are violated by a subversion of human dignity (McLean and Williamson 2007, pp. 41–42).

Finally, Article 24 explicitly notes germline interventions as potentially contrary to human dignity. Though Article 24 is not a substantive protective right in itself, it does direct the International Bioethics Committee to make recommendations in relation to the identification, and arguably regulation, of such practices. By way of comparison, though Article 13 of the Oviedo Convention permits genome intervention for 'preventive, diagnostic or therapeutic purposes' (a point on which the UDHGHR is non-specific), it is pointedly made clear that this is so 'only if its aim is *not to introduce any modification in the genome of any descendants*' (emphasis added).

The relatively more modern UDBHR sheds further light on the proposed balance between individual rights and science referenced in the UDHGHR. Article 3 provides that human dignity, rights and fundamental freedoms are to be fully respected and, most importantly, 'the interests and welfare of the individual should have priority over the sole interest of science or society'. The content of such a provision is clear: the sanctity of human dignity and equality prevails over both the general interest to research and scientific progress and any other societal interest as a whole (Lenzerini 2006, p. 336).

These underlying principles militate against scholars like Savulescu, Singer and Harris interpreting provisions of the UDBHR in a manner consistent with utilitarian ideals of procreative beneficence, which arguably infringe human dignity. Article 4, for example, provides that:

> In applying and advancing scientific knowledge, medical practice and associated technologies, direct and indirect benefits to patients, research participants and other affected individuals should be maximised and any possible harm to such individuals should be minimised.

Whilst proponents of procreative beneficence would argue that the direct and indirect benefits to persons with disabilities lie in their 'release' from or 'cure' of impairment, with little actual 'harm', it cannot be properly considered to be the object to which the UDBHR is put.

Moreover, Article 8 provides a marked improvement over Article 17 of the CRPD in that it provides a more specific application of the principle of personal integrity:

> In applying and advancing scientific knowledge, medical practice and associated technologies, human vulnerability should be taken into account. Individuals and groups of special vulnerability should be protected and the personal integrity of such individuals respected.

The provision undoubtedly recognises that particular groups, like persons with disabilities, are especially susceptible to the adverse effects of misused genetic technologies. Researchers too must recognise, evaluate and re-evaluate the potentially far-reaching effects of their work at every stage, as required by Article 20. This continual cycle of risk assessment and management is imperative as a form of both self and peer-based regulation.

Finally, the UDBHR must necessarily defend the potential victims of discrimination. To that end, Article 11 mirrors Article 6 of the UDHGHR in that 'no individual or group should be discriminated against or stigmatised on any grounds, in violation of human dignity, human rights and fundamental freedoms.' Further, Article 14(2)(d) aims to direct the objectives of science and technology to the elimination of the marginalisation and the exclusion of persons on any grounds. Whether the whole of the scientific community will adhere to such broad dignity-based statements is unclear.

Despite its breadth, the applicability of the UDBHR may be restricted by the concession in Article 27 that these principles may be limited by state law in the interests of, among others, the protection of public health and the protection of the rights and freedoms of others. Again, it is unclear how a disability rights approach would contend with possibly competing notions of an 'obligation to let oneself be fixed' in the interests of public health frameworks, or the protection of the rights and freedoms of caregivers and others present in the lives of persons with disabilities (Wolbring and Diep 2016, p. 15). Further, a recurrent and seemingly endemic issue in instruments like the UNESCO Declarations in relation to human genetic engineering, is that an embryo cannot be seen to have human dignity so as to invoke the corresponding human rights (El-Zein 2008, p. 322).

In any case, the UNESCO universal soft law regime constitutes arguably the most comprehensive and solid foundation for the future international regulation of human genetic technology for both the interests of persons with disabilities and the broader human race. However, they are but a first step in such a difficult pursuit (El-Zein 2008, p. 318).

4.2. State Domestic Law

Despite the broad persuasive scope of such international instruments, they do not have any real binding force within each signatory nation state until domestic legislation to that effect is enacted. However, national policy frameworks governing human genome editing, both somatic and germline:

> extend across a continuum that distinguishes between degrees of permissiveness, that is, between legally binding legislation and regulatory and/or professional guidance or research versus clinical applications (Isasi et al. 2016, p. 337).

As such, many of these national regimes aim to imitate international law's emphasis on human dignity and diversity by leaning towards taking a more prohibitive stance, at least in relation to human germline gene modification (Basser 2011, p. 36). Many countries ban human germline engineering (Araki and Ishii 2014, p. 116). However, the regulatory landscape suggests that it is not totally prohibited worldwide. The arrival of CRISPR has, and will continue to, disrupt medical, legal and ethical consensus even further.

Where legislation imposes a prohibition or restriction on germline interventions, it is generally paired with severe criminal sanctions that range from long imprisonment terms to significant fines (Isasi et al. 2016, p. 337; Center for Genetics and Society 2015). For example, the Australian position is quite severely prohibitive. Section 15(1) of the relevant Commonwealth law (Prohibition of Human Cloning for Reproduction and the Regulation of Human Embryo Research Amendment Act 2006) and Section 11(1) of the identical Victorian law (Prohibition of Human Cloning for Reproduction Act 2008) provides that a person commits an offence and may be imprisoned for up to 15 years if:

(1) the person alters the genome of a human cell in such a way that the alteration is heritable by descendants of the human whose cell was altered; and
(2) in altering the genome, the person intended the alteration to be heritable by descendants of the human whose cell was altered (emphasis added).

Furthermore, Sections 20(3) and 16(3) of each respective statute also criminalise the intentional placement of such an altered cell into the body of a woman. Both provisions require an element of mens rea, which gives rise to some uncertainty as to their potential enforceability. Nevertheless, the dual rationale for such provisions in preventing alteration of the 'heritage of humanity' is clear. First, there is an evolutionary imperative to refrain from making germline changes, the implications of which are currently unknown. Second, doing so fundamentally violates the principle of human dignity entrenched in the UNESCO Declarations. Relevantly, if either practice were to become widespread or commodified, that violation would be even more greatly focused on the dignity and value of persons with disabilities (Isasi et al. 2016, p. 337).

At the opposite end of the spectrum are countries with permissive approaches that aim to promote scientific progress because of its perceived benefit to humanity. Under policies adopted in China and the United Kingdom, research conducted for reproductive purposes is permitted under strict regulation and clinical applications are not expressly criminalised (Isasi et al. 2016, p. 337). Of the plethora of approaches worldwide, not one is necessarily completely right or wrong. However, global inconsistency may be eroded over time as one country's procedure eventually becomes the scientific and ethical standard (International Bioethics Committee 2015, p. 27). Given the rate that science is progressing and technologies like CRISPR are becoming more accurate, it is likely that the permissive approach will gain traction. Therefore, in the case of that eventuality, it is necessary to assess a regulatory model that will protect persons with disabilities in a pro-genetic era.

5. How Should We Regulate?

In light of these shortfalls at both the international and national levels, this paper will attempt to posit a solution to the seemingly intractable issue of human gene editing research that has the greatest chance of a beneficial outcome for the disability and science communities alike. Two 'disclaimers' must be made at this juncture. First, this paper does not purport to propose a complete regulatory model per se, but rather a methodology to balance the interests of both the scientific and disability communities. Second, there is a general problem of inefficacy in legally regulating fast moving technologies like CRISPR. This paper contends that the most practical and ideal genetic research governance model is one grounded in human rights and dignity. It should involve a global discussion and consensus (insofar as is possible) including all relevant interest groups, especially those most likely to be disadvantaged by the use of gene editing technologies.

5.1. Why a Human-Rights Based Regulatory Framework?

There exist four potential oversight approaches to human germline editing technologies:

(1) a complete international ban;
(2) a temporary moratorium on research until ethical and scientific issues have been resolved;
(3) principled international and domestic regulation; or
(4) a laissez-faire approach (Bosley et al. 2015, pp. 383–85).

Given the heterogeneity of national ethical and legislative codes and the accessible cost of CRISPR, a complete ban or temporary moratorium will be virtually impossible to enforce worldwide (Altman et al. 2015, p. 26). Furthermore, a laissez-faire approach arguably creates the inevitable risk, especially in less stringently restricted countries, that research will be conducted before ethical due diligence. This could also lead to a patenting war, with all the likely unethical shortcuts that may entail, the winner of which will be granted enormous control over the development, scope and uses of CRISPR technology (Parthasarathy 2016). This leaves one option: regulation. Luckily, the institutional framework for regulation already exists in the UNESCO framework, national law and research guidelines. Nevertheless, an integrated and universal regulatory model must be actualised.

It is unclear exactly which form the regulatory model should take in order to remain effective and flexible whilst also instilling confidence in the people whose interests are to be protected. The broad literature on regulation yields many viable avenues. Whilst theories of decentralised or polycentric regulation (Black 2002, p. 4) often appear more applicable to the transnational context, they have had their legitimacy and accountability heavily criticised at that level. One promising framework that may be of great assistance in framing further debate on an appropriate and applicable model is Jonathan Kolieb's 'regulatory diamond' (Kolieb 2015), which builds on the seminal work of Ian Ayers and John Braithwaite in 'responsive regulation' theory (Ayres and Braithwaite 1992). The crux of responsive regulation is that regulatory instruments must adapt to the actions of the people or entities they aim to regulate. This determines the level of intervention required, and whether escalations or de-escalations are necessary over time.

However, a key shortcoming of the original Braithwaitian model was its sole focus on compliance with certain standards (Kolieb 2015, p. 143) and its corresponding omission in seeking improvement on the behaviour of those being regulated. The Koliebian model goes further in not only incorporating 'compliance regulation' (the regulatory mechanisms that encourage adherence to particular behavioural standards) but also 'aspirational regulation' (the regulatory mechanisms that encourage those regulated to improve their behaviour beyond minimal adherence to the minimum standards). The regulatory diamond points out that achieving compliance with legal requirements is only half of the solution to the problem being addressed. In this case, that problem is the growing viability and impact of genetic technologies. There is a powerful aspirational regulatory potential that has been untouched at this point. As Kolieb notes, from the perspective of a regulator:

> Their view of the regulated entity is no longer dominated by negative conceptions of an entity that needs to be curtailed and compelled to comply with minimum legal standards. With the diamond, the conception that pervaded responsive regulation theory is moderated by the understanding that regulated entities can also exceed such standards, and positively contribute to addressing the societal problem in question (Kolieb 2015, p. 161).

As CRISPR and other similarly disruptive technologies become more widespread, the inherent limitations of the law as a regulatory instrument mean that it should also be paired with other aspirational regulation instruments to drive researchers and private companies providing these services to act beyond the baseline legal requirements to secure the interests of persons with disabilities and other minorities as members of our society who might be adversely affected by the technologies. What such aspirational instruments might include will first depend on the minimum standard expected.

Then, putting aside aspirational regulation, why a model based on adherence to standards of human rights and dignity? There are multiple reasons for submitting CRISPR and other genetic technologies to regulation under the meta-norms of human rights and dignity:

(1) As highlighted in Section 4 of this article, the entirety of the UNESCO bioethical and human genome soft law framework is based on those foundational concepts. By mirroring those principles in a regulatory framework, it connects the legitimacy of UNESCO policy to the evolving international scientific and ethical practice (Somsen 2009, p. 114). Whilst there is no univocal ethic espoused in the Declarations, by and large the prevailing values are dignitarian and well suited to the current issue.
(2) An underlying ethic that focuses on the concept of human dignity as a constraint on autonomy is 'not only the most suitable for a liberal deliberative democracy' as in today's globalised society (Somsen 2009, p. 114), but is also the only possible answer to the reality of the disability community's disadvantaged position vis-à-vis continuous and rapid scientific advances like CRISPR (Fukuyama 1992; Brownsword 2004). The human rights model of disability is strongly complemented by, and shares largely the same objectives as, the idea of inherent human dignity. If the two ideas work in tandem, persons with disabilities will have the best chance at enacting beneficial reform at both international and national levels.
(3) A system of human rights and dignity has the potential to be flexible and adaptive to future technological change through the articulation of new international human rights principles specific to gene editing. The common acceptance of its underlying principles would also assist in its quick adoption by national regulatory agencies and parliaments (Mathews et al. 2015, p. 160). Whilst there is a considerable challenge in ensuring that such a regime is articulated clearly enough to be meaningful whilst not so broadly as to be arbitrary (Somsen 2009, p. 115), it is arguably the best theoretical framework at this point in time.

With these points in mind, we may conceptualise how best to formulate such a regime.

5.2. The Way There

Science is a global endeavour. As such, it is vital that nation-states and governments accept the principle of a shared global responsibility in relation to the editing of the human genome (International Bioethics Committee 2015, p. 27). An effective governance approach must be simple in operation, anticipatory and adaptive, and, most importantly in cases of disruptive technology, grounded in social acceptability after considering the views of all stakeholders (Reiss, p. 2). On social, ethical and evolutionary questions of this magnitude and nature, arguably the only way to achieve each of those objectives is through genuine collective discussion (Wolbring 2015, p. 446; Baker 2016, p. 273; Sarewitz 2015, p. 414; Araki and Ishii 2014, p. 18).

There are countless issues with universal governance of ethically polarising technologies, not the least of which are broad spectrum of secular, cultural and religious views of individuals, the public and government. Public policies on human gene editing range from prohibitionist, to regulated, to permissive. As such, it is likely unwise to set out, at least at this early stage, a comprehensive set of governance rules protecting human interests in the vain hope that they will be communicated, understood, implemented, obeyed and enforced overnight. Such thoughts are fanciful and of little assistance in resolving the ethical dilemma. On this point, Susan Peschin, the President and CEO of the Alliance for Ageing Research, stated that:

> Principles generally serve to motivate people to do the things that seem good and right, but without the constraints and external pressure of specific rules. Introduce specific regulations on the safety and efficacy of gene editing and that starts to infringe on people's ethical limits, which traditional medical product regulation is not designed to address (Peschin 2017).

This paper agrees. We must first reach a normative consensus to effectively frame the broad international law, regulations and customs to eventually, and ideally, 'trickle down' into entrenched and more easily enforceable national laws. Though they will likely differ to various extents, the overarching principles will guide legislative bodies to an ethical governance model predicated on the protection of human dignity for all, including people with disabilities (Reiss, p. 5).

The 'Res-AGo-rA'[1] research project, released in April 2016, offers a comprehensive governance framework for responsible research and innovation that ties in with the overarching human rights and dignity model. Essentially, it states that the first step in attaining some form of 'consensus' is for national ethical bodies and interest groups to come together to take responsibility for innovative advances and their societal consequences and draft agreed upon guidelines for research into gene editing (Lindner et al. 2016, p. 10). Richard Hayes, former Executive Director of the Centre for Genetics and Society, has expressed similar sentiments:

> A productive next step might be to have a high-level task force representing the full range of constituencies with major stakes in these issues undertake a comprehensive review and assessment of options for global oversight and regulation (Hayes, p. 8).

Therefore, regulators and scientists must listen to public, community and civil society organisations and many others, who in turn must each listen to each other (Center for Genetics and Society and Friends of the Earth 2015, p. 39). Of course, numerous scholars have highlighted the importance of the disability justice refrain, 'Nothing About Us, Without Us', in having any legitimate discussion about the regulation of gene editing technologies (Shakespeare 2015, p. 446; Wolbring 2015; Benjamin 2016, p. 51; Thompson, p. 46; Knoppers 2016, p. 272). The voices of those from the disability community must be heard. Ultimately, any discussion and eventual consensus relating to human germline modification research and clinical use must adhere to the principles of human dignity outlined above and exemplified in the UNESCO Declarations.

Recently, a Committee composed of members of the National Academy of Science ('NAS') and the National Academy of Medicine ('NAM') embarked on the gargantuan task of addressing how we should regulate gene editing technologies like CRISPR. The Committee ultimately advocated a strong public participation model in developing any governance frameworks. In its deliberations, it focused in particular on:

(1) safeguarding and promoting individual health and wellbeing;
(2) cautiously approaching novel technologies in response to consistently changing information;
(3) respecting individual rights;
(4) warding against undesirable social consequences; and

[1] Responsible Research and Innovation in a Distributed Anticipatory Governance Frame. A Constructive Socionormative Approach.

(5) equally and equitably distributing information, burdens and benefits (National Academies of Sciences and Medicine 2017, p. 23).

Crucially, it established seven key principles foundational to the governance of human gene editing, even across national and cultural borders (National Academies of Sciences and Medicine 2017, p. 24):

(1) Promoting wellbeing: this principle aims to prevent harm by applying genome editing technologies to increase health and wellbeing whilst ensuring a reasonable balance of risk and benefit for any such application;
(2) Transparency: this principle encourages the free flow of information between stakeholders, including full, frank and timely disclosure and meaningful public input and debate in all aspects of policymaking for CRISPR and related technologies;
(3) Due care: this principle requires careful and deliberate conduct by researchers in relation to their patients, including appropriate supervision and consistent reassessment of risks, advances in technology and medicine, and cultural opinions;
(4) Responsible science: this principle serves to set and maintain high research standards in compliance with the norms of international society and the profession. This includes quality research design, review and evaluation, transparency, and the correction of false or misleading data or analysis;
(5) Respect for persons: this principle necessitates cognisance of the inherent human dignity of all people and the freedom of and respect for personal choice. Genetic characteristics are not indicative of any greater or lesser moral value. Further, respect for persons embodies active commitments to prevent neo-eugenics movements akin to the past, and to destigmatise disability;
(6) Fairness: this principle obliges us to treat all equally, including in distributing risks and benefits of research and enabling the equitable access to resulting clinical applications of human gene editing;
(7) Transnational cooperation: this principle highlights the immense need for collaboration in both research and regulation, whilst accommodating for different cultural perspectives. Adherence requires, where possible, coordination of international regulatory standards and processes, and data sharing between scientific communities and regulatory authorities.

This paper cannot find evident faults with these principles. They are neither too broad and meaningless, nor narrow and overly restrictive, in that they allow space for nations to comply in their own ways, but with common and consistent objectives. There appears to be no set hierarchy or priority to any one value over the other, though this paper notes that the principles relating to respect to persons and fairness are obviously vital for the preservation of the interests of persons with disabilities.

As to what the content of any policy instruments that arise out of discussions, this paper cannot say in any great detail. A number of such instruments have been proposed in the past, including:

- A 2002 proposal, which called for a 'Convention on the Preservation of the Human Species', aimed to prohibit human reproductive cloning and human germline genetic modification, and establish national oversight systems that ensured that use of gametes or embryos met consent, safety and ethical standards (Annas et al. 2002).
- A 2007 proposal, which asserted that the concept of a complete ban on human reproductive cloning had essentially attained the status of customary international law, to codify this into an international instrument under the UNESCO framework (Kuppuswamy et al. 2007).
- A 2008 proposal, which posited a 'Genetic Heritage Safeguard Treaty' based on the 1970 Nuclear Nonproliferation Treaty, to serve the dual function of both encouraging responsible applications of human genetic research as well as delineating limits on those applications deemed 'undesirable' (Metzl 2008).

Whatever the future may hold, this paper hopes for a respectful and coherent debate and an influential international instrument (or at the very least, a series of regionalised instruments) that prioritises respect for and protection of human dignity of people with disabilities and other possibly marginalised groups over more scientific and neo-eugenic agendas in human genome editing.

6. Conclusions

The unprecedented speed of technological development in human genome editing in recent years is testament to the globalised scientific community's unyielding passion for knowledge. Yet, even with such a (hopefully) noble motivation, innovations such as CRISPR have the potential to be utilised as tools of neo-eugenics. If they were so used, especially in germline intervention, the potential ramifications on the rights and ways of life of members of the disability community are numerous and far-reaching. Through an analysis of bioethical principles and traditional and modern conceptions of disability, this paper suggests that human dignity is the core moral precept and value on which modern international and domestic law frameworks operate in this ethically problematic sphere. Furthermore, there are significant flaws, gaps and uncertainties in the existing regulatory system. This is not the place to suggest a new set of international bioethical guidelines to govern human genome editing whilst preserving the human rights of persons with disabilities; that is an issue for wide deliberation and consensus. Instead, this paper proposes a mechanism by which a new human-rights-based regulatory instrument may be conceived to benefit both the disability and science communities. A set of clearly articulated principles will set the necessary debate and discussion on the right course. Nevertheless, the time for action is now. As increasingly accurate genome editing technology proliferates across national borders, a coherent and cohesive international stance on the issue is more urgently needed than ever. Time waits for no human right.

References

Altman, Russ B., Shamik Mascharak, and Niklaus Evitt. 2015. Human Germline Crispr-Cas Modification: Toward a Regulatory Framework. *American Journal of Bioethics* 15: 25–29.

Amundson, Ron, and Shari Tresky. 2008. Bioethics and Disability Rights: Conflicting Values and Perspectives. *Bioethical Inquiry* 5: 111–23. [CrossRef]

Annas, George J., Lori B. Andrews, and Rosario M. Isasi. 2002. Protecting the Endangered Human: Toward an International Treaty Prohibiting Cloning and Inheritable Alterations. *American Journal of Law & Medicine* 28: 151–78.

Araki, Motoko, and Tetsuya Ishii. 2014. International Regulatory Landscape and Integration of Corrective Genome Editing into in Vitro Fertilization. *Reproductive Biology and Endocrinology* 12: 108. [CrossRef] [PubMed]

Asch, Adrienne. 2000. *Why I Haven't Changed My Mind about Prenatal Diagnosis: Reflections and Refinements*. Prenatal Testing and Disability Rights. Edited by Erik Parens and Adrienne Asch. Washington: Georgetown University Press.

Ayres, Ian, and John Braithwaite. 1992. *Responsive Regulation: Transcending the Deregulation Debate*. Oxford: Oxford University Press.

Bachruch, Susan. 2004. In the Name of Public Health—Nazi Racial Hygeine. *New England Journal of Medicine* 351: 417–20. [CrossRef] [PubMed]

Baker, Beth. 2016. The Ethics of Changing the Human Genome. *BioScience* 66: 267–73. [CrossRef]

Baldi, Pierre. 2001. *The Shattered Self: The End of Natural Evolution*. Cambridge: MIT Press.

Baltimore, David, Paul Berg, Michael Botchan, Dana Carroll, R. Alta Charo, George Church, Jacob E. Corn, George Q. Daley, Jennifer A. Doudna, Marsha Fenner, and et al. 2015. A Prudent Path Forward for Genomic Engineering and Germline Gene Modification. *Science* 348: 36–38. [CrossRef] [PubMed]

Baruch, Susannah, Audrey Huang, Daryl Pritchard, Andrea Kalfoglou, Gail Javitt, Rick Borchelt, Joan Scott, and Kathy Hudson. 2005. *Human Germline Genetic Modification: Issues and Options for Policymakers*. Baltimore: Genetics and Public Policy Center, Johns Hopkins University Berman Institute of Bioethics.

Basser, Lee Ann. 2011. Human Dignity. In *Critical Perspectives on Human Rights and Disability Law*. Edited by Marcia H. Rioux, Lee Ann Basser and Melinda Jones. Leiden: Martinus Nijhoff Publishers, pp. 17–36.

Benjamin, Ruha. 2016. Interrogating Equity: A Disability Justice Approach to Genetic Engineering. *Issues in Science & Technology* 32: 50–54.

Bennett, Rebecca. 2009. The Fallacy of the Principle of Procreative Beneficence. *Bioethics* 23: 265–73. [CrossRef] [PubMed]

Black, Edwin. 2008. *War against the Weak: Eugenics and America's Campaign to Create a Master Race*. New York: Dialog Press.

Black, Julia. 2002. Critical Reflections on Regulation. *Australian Journal of Legal Philosophy* 27: 1–46.

Bosley, Katrine S., Michael Botchan, Annelien L. Bredenoord, Dana Carroll, R. Alta Charo, Emmanuelle Charpentier, Ron Cohen, Jacob Corn, Jennifer Doudna, Guoping Feng, and et al. 2015. Crispr Germline Engineering—The Community Speaks. *Nature Biotechnology* 33: 478–86. [CrossRef] [PubMed]

Breggin, Peter. 1993. Psychiatry's Role in the Holocaust. *International Journal of Risk & Safety in Medicine* 4: 133–48.

Brosius, Jurgen, and Martin Kreitman. 2000. Eugenics—Evolutionary Nonsense? *Nature Genetics* 25: 253. [CrossRef] [PubMed]

Brownsword, Roger. 2004. What the World Needs Now: Techno-Regulation, Human Rights and Human Dignity. In *Global Governance and the Quest for Justice*. Edited by Roger Brownsword. Oxford: Hart Publishing, p. 203.

Brownsword, Roger. 2009. Human Dignity, Ethical Pluralism, and the Regulation of Modern Biotechnologies. In *New Technologies and Human Rights*. Edited by Thérèse Murphy. New York: Oxford University Press, pp. 19–84.

Burleigh, Michael. 1994. *Death and Deliverance: 'Euthanasia' in Germany, C.1900 to 1945*. Cambridge: Cambridge University Press.

Center for Genetics and Society. 2015. *Human Germline Modification: Summary of National and International Policies*. Berkeley: Centre for Genetics and Society.

Center for Genetics and Society and Friends of the Earth. 2015. *Extreme Genetic Engineering and the Human Future: Reclaiming Emerging Biotechnologies for the Common Good*. Berkeley: Center for Genetics and Society.

Council for Responsible Genetics. 2005. *Position Paper on Human Germline Manipulation*. Cambridge: Council for Responsible Genetics.

Degener, Theresia. 2014. A Human Rights Model of Disability. Available online: http://www.academia.edu/18181994/A_human_rights_model_of_disability (accessed on 10 June 2016).

Degener, Theresia, and Gerard Quinn. 2002. Survey of International, Comparative and Regional Disability Law Reform. In *Disability Rights Law and Policy: International and National Perspectives*. Edited by Silvia Yee and Mary Lou Breslin. Leiden: Martinus Nijhoff.

Disabled Peoples International (DPI). 2000. *Disabled People Speak on the New Genetics: DPI Europe Position Statement on Bioethics and Human Rights*. London: DPI Europe.

Doudna, Jennifer A. 2015. *How Crispr Lets Us Edit Our DNA*. London: TEDGlobal, Transcript.

Dzau, Victor J., and Ralph J. Cicerone. 2015. Responsible Use of Human Gene-Editing Technologies. *Human Gene Therapy* 26: 411–12. [CrossRef] [PubMed]

El-Zein, Souheil. 2008. International Regulation of Human Genetics. In *Genetic Engineering and the World Trade System*. Edited by Daniel Wuger and Thomas Cottier. New York: Cambridge University Press, p. 315.

Esvelt, Kevin M., and Harris H. Wang. 2013. Genome-Scale Engineering for Systems and Synthetic Biology. *Molecular Systems Biology* 9: 641. [CrossRef] [PubMed]

Finkelstein, Vic, and Ossie Stuart. 1996. Developing New Services. In *Beyond Disability: Towards an Enabling Society*. Edited by Gerard Hales. London: SAGE Publications.

Fischer, Bernard A. 2012. Maltreatment of People with Serious Mental Illness in the Early 20th Century: A Focus on Nazi Germany and Eugenics in America. *Journal of Nervous and Mental Disease* 200: 1096–100. [CrossRef] [PubMed]

French, Phillip. 1994. What Is Disability? In *On Equal Terms—Working with Disabled People*. Edited by Phillip French. Oxford: Butterworth-Heinemann.

Fukuyama, Francis. 1992. *The End of History and the Last Man*. New York: Free Press.

Fukuyama, Francis. 2002. *Our Posthuman Future: Consequences of the Biotechnology Revolution*. New York: Farrar, Strauss and Giroux.

Galton, Francis. 1883. *Inquiries into Human Faculty and Development*. London: Macmillan.

Grant, Evadné. 2007. Dignity and Equality. *Human Rights Law Review* 7: 299–329. [CrossRef]

Harris, John. 1990. The Wrong of Wrongful Life. *Journal of Law & Society* 17: 90–105.

Harris, John. 1998. *Clones, Genes and Immortality: Ethics and the Genetic Revolution*. Oxford: Oxford University Press.

Hayes, Richard. 2008. Is There an Emerging International Consensus on the Proper Uses of the New Human Genetic Technologies? Paper presented at the US House of Representatives Foreign Affairs Committee Subcommittee on Terrorism, Nonproliferation and Trade Hearing on Genetics and Other Human Modification Technologies: Sensible International Regulations or a New Kind of Arms Race? Los Angeles, CA, USA, June 19.

Herberer, Patricia. 2002. Targeting the "Unfit" and Radical Public Health Strategies in Nazi Germany. In *Deaf People in Hitler's Europe*. Edited by Donna F. Ryan and John S. Schuchmann. Washinton: Gallaudet University Press.

Hoge, Stephen K., and Paul S. Appelbaum. 2012. Ethics and Neuropsychiatric Genetics: A Review of Major Issues. *International Journal of Neuropsychopharmacology* 15: 1547–57. [CrossRef] [PubMed]

Hsu, Patrick D., Eric S. Lander, and Fenc Zhang. 2014. Development and Applications of Crispr-Cas9 for Genome Engineering. *Cell* 157: 1262–78. [CrossRef] [PubMed]

Ida, Ryuichi. 2003. Bioethics and International Law. In *Ordine Internazionale E Valori Etici*. Edited by Nerina Boschiero. Verona: Societa Italiana di Diritto Internazionale, p. 365.

Iles, Alastair T. 1996. The Human Genome Project: A Challenge to the Human Rights Framework. *Harvard Human Rights Journal* 9: 27–60. [PubMed]

Imparato, Andrew J. 2004. *Testimony: Senate Hearing on Prenatal Genetic Testing Technology*. Washington: United States Congress, Committee on Commerce, Science, and Transportation, Subcommittee on Science, Technology, and Space.

International Bioethics Committee. 2015. *Report of the Ibc on Updating Its Reflection on the Human Genome and Human Rights*. Paris: UNESCO.

Isasi, Rosario, Erika Kleiderman, and Bartha Maria Knoppers. 2016. Editing Policy to Fit the Genome? *Science* 351: 337–39. [CrossRef] [PubMed]

Ishii, Tetsuya. 2015. Germ Line Genome Editing in Clinics: The Approaches, Objectives and Global Society. *Briefings in Functional Genomics*. Available online: http://bfg.oxfordjournals.org/content/early/2015/11/27/bfgp.elv053.full (accessed on 14 June 2016).

Jones, Melinda. 2011a. Introduction: Dignity. In *Critical Perspectives on Human Rights and Disability Law*. Edited by Marcia H. Rioux, Lee Ann Basser and Melinda Jones. Leiden: Martinus Nijhoff Publishers, pp. 85–86.

Jones, Melinda. 2011b. Valuing All Lives—Even "Wrongful" Ones. In *Critical Perspectives on Human Rights and Disability Law*. Edited by Marcia H. Rioux, Lee Ann Basser and Melinda Jones. Leiden: Martinus Nijhoff Publishers, pp. 87–116.

Kayess, Rosemary, and Phillip French. 2008. Out of Darkness into Light? Introducing the Convention on the Rights of Persons with Disabilities. *Human Rights Law Review* 8: 1–34. [CrossRef]

King, David. 2001. Eugenic Tendencies in Modern Genetics. In *Redesigning Life? The Worldwide Challenge to Genetic Engineering*. Edited by Brian Tokar. London: Zed Books, pp. 171–81.

Knoppers, Bartha Maria. 2016. Human Gene Editing: Principles & Precedents. Available online: http://nationalacademies.org/cs/groups/genesite/documents/webpage/gene_172445.pdf (accessed on 3 May 2017).

Kolieb, Jonathan. 2015. When to Punish, When to Persuade and When to Reward: Strengthening Responsive Regulation with the Regulatory Diamond. *Monash University Law Review* 41: 136–63.

Kuppuswamy, Chamundeeswari, Darryl Macer, Mihaela Serbulea, and Brendan Tobin. 2007. *Is Human Reproductive Cloning Inevitable: Future Options for UN Governance*. Tokyo: United Nations University Press.

Lander, Eric S. 2015. Brave New Genome. *New England Journal of Medicine* 373: 5–8. [CrossRef] [PubMed]

Lanphier, Edward, Fyodor Urnov, Sarah Ehlen Haecker, and Michael Werner. 2015. Don't Edit the Human Germ Line. *Nature* 519: 410–11. [CrossRef] [PubMed]

Ledford, Heidi. 2015. Crispr, the Disruptor. *Nature* 522: 20–24. [CrossRef] [PubMed]

Lenzerini, Federico. 2006. Biotechnology, Human Dignity and the Human Genome. In *Biotechnology and International Law*. Edited by Francesco Francioni and Tullio Scovazzi. Portland: Hart Publishing, pp. 285–340.

Liang, Puping, Yanwen Xu, Xiya Zhang, Chenhui Ding, Rui Huang, Zhen Zhang, Jie Lv, Xiaowei Xie, Yuxi Chen, Yujing Li, and et al. 2015. Crispr/Cas9-Mediated Gene Editing in Human Tripronuclear Zygotes. *Protein & Cell* 6: 363–72.

Lindner, Ralf, Stefan Kuhlmann, Sally Randles, and Bjørn Bedsted. 2016. *Navigating towards Shared Responsibility*. Brussels: ResAGora.

Marzano-Parisoli, Maria Michela. 2001. Disability, Wrongful-Life Lawsuits, and the Human Difference: An Exercise in Ethical Perplexity. *Social Theory and Practice* 27: 637–59. [CrossRef]

Mathews, Debra J. H., Sarah Chan, Peter J. Donovan, Thomas Douglas, Christopher Gyngell, John Harris, Alan Regenberg, and Robin Lovell-Badge. 2015. Crispr: A Path through the Thicket. *Nature* 527: 159–61. [CrossRef] [PubMed]

McCrudden, Christopher. 2008. Human Dignity and Judicial Interpretation of Human Rights. *European Journal of International Law* 19: 655–724. [CrossRef]

McLean, Sheila, and Laura Williamson. 2007. *Impairment and Disability: Law and Ethics at the Beginning and End of Life.* London: Routledge.

Menand, Louis. 2004. The Science of Human Nature and the Human Nature of Science. In *Genetics, Disability, and Deafness*. Edited by John Vickrey Van Cleve. Washington: Gallaudet University Press, pp. 5–22.

Metzl, Jamie. 2008. Brave New World War. Center for Genetics and Society. Available online: http://www.geneticsandsociety.org/article.php?id=3985 (accessed on 1 June 2016).

National Academies of Sciences and Medicine. 2015. *On Human Gene Editing: International Summit Statement.* Washington: National Academies of Sciences and Medicine.

National Academies of Sciences and Medicine. 2017. *Human Genome Editing: Science, Ethics, and Governance.* Washington: National Academies Press.

Oliver, Michael. 1990. *The Politics of Disablement*. Basingstoke: Palgrave Macmillan.

Oliver, Michael. 1996. *Understanding Disability: From Theory to Practice.* New York: St. Martin's Press.

Parmenter, Trevor R. 2005. Are We Engineering Ourselves out of Existence? *Journal of Intellectual and Developmental Disability* 30: 53–56. [CrossRef]

Parthasarathy, Shobita. 2016. Crispr Dispute Raises Bigger Patent Issues That We're Not Talking about. *The Conversation.* April 4. Available online: https://theconversation.com/crispr-dispute-raises-bigger-patent-issues-that-were-not-talking-about-56715 (accessed on 13 June 2016).

Peschin, Susan. 2017. How Should We Regulate Genome Editing? *World Economic Forum.* Available online: https://www.weforum.org/agenda/2017/05/how-should-we-regulate-genome-editing/ (accessed on 2 June 2017).

Pollack, Robert. 2015. Eugenics Lurk in the Shadow of CRISPR. *Science* 348: 871. [CrossRef] [PubMed]

President's Council on Bioethics. 2003. *Beyond Therapy: Biotechnology and the Pursuit of Happiness.* Washington: President's Council on Bioethics.

Proctor, Robert N. 1988. *Racial Hygeine: Medicine under the Nazis.* Cambridge: Harvard University Press.

Quinn, Gerard, and Theresia Degener. 2002. *The Current Use and Future Potential Use of United Nations Human Rights Instruments in the Context of Disability.* New York and Geneva: Office of the United Nations High Commissioner for Human Rights.

Reaume, Denise G. 2002–2003. Discrimination and Dignity. *Louisiana Law Review* 63: 645–96.

Reiss, Thomas. 2015. Governance Approaches for Human Gene Editing Based on Responsible Research and Innovation. Paper presented at the National Academies of Sciences and Medicine's International Summit on Human Gene Editing, Washington, DC, USA, December 1–3.

Samaha, Adam. 2007. What Good Is the Social Model of Disability? *The University of Chicago Law Review* 74: 166. [CrossRef]

Sarewitz, Daniel. 2015. Crispr. Science Can't Solve It. *Nature* 522: 413–14. [CrossRef] [PubMed]

Savulescu, Julian, Jonathan Pugh, Thomas Douglas, and Christopher Gyngell. 2015. The Moral Imperative to Continue Gene Editing Research on Human Embryos. *Protein & Cell* 6: 476–79.

Saxton, Marsha. 1988. Prenatal Screening and Discriminatory Attitudes About Disability. *Women and Health* 13: 217–24. [CrossRef]

Shakespeare, Tom. 1995. Back to the Future? New Genetics and Disabled People. *Critical Social Policy* 44: 22–35. [CrossRef]

Shakespeare, Tom. 2002. The Social Model of Disability: An Outdated Ideology? *Research in Social Science and Disability* 2: 9–28.

Shakespeare, Tom. 2013. The Social Model of Disability. In *The Disability Studies Reader*. Edited by Lennard J. Davis. Abingdon: Routledge.

Shakespeare, Tom. 2015. Gene Editing: Heed Disability Views. *Nature* 527: 446. [CrossRef] [PubMed]

Singer, Peter. 1993. *Practical Ethics*, 2nd ed. Cambridge: Cambridge University Press.

Smith, George P., II. 2012. *Law and Bioethics: Intersections Along the Mortal Coil.* Abingdon: Routledge.

Somsen, Han. 2009. Regulating Human Genetics in a Neo-Genetic Era. In *New Technologies and Human Rights*. Edited by Thérèse Murphy. New York: Oxford University Press, pp. 85–127.

Thomas, Pam, Lorraine Gradwell, and Natalie Markham. 1997. Defining Impairment within the Social Model of Disability. *Greater Manchester Coalition of Disabled People*. Available online: http://disability-studies.leeds.ac.uk/files/library/thomas-pam-Defining-Impairment-within-the-Social-Model-of-Disability.pdf (accessed on 29 May 2016).

Thompson, Charis. 2015. Governance, Regulation, and Control: Of Which People, by Which People, for Which People? Paper presented at the National Academies of Sciences and Medicine's International Summit on Human Gene Editing, Washington, DC, USA, December 1–3.

Turmusani, Majid. 2004. Genetic Technology and the UN Disability Convention. *Disability World*. Available online: http://www.disabilityworld.org/12-02_05/news/genetictech.shtml (accessed on 3 June 2016).

UN Secretary General. 2006. Secretary-General Hails Adoption of Landmark Convention on Rights of People with Disabilities. SG/SM/10797-HR/4911-L/T/4400. December 3. Available online: http://www.un.org/press/en/2006/sgsm10797.doc.htm (accessed on 8 June 2016).

United Nations. 2007. UN Convention on the Rights of Persons with Disabilities, opened for signature 30 March 2007, 999 UNTS 3 (entered into force 3 May 2008).

Walters, LeRoy. 1978. Bioethics as Field of Ethics. In *Contemporary Issues in Bioethics*. Edited by Tom L. Beauchamp and LeRoy Walters. Los Angeles: Calif Dickenson, p. 49.

Witzany, Guenther. 2016. No Time to Waste on the Road to a Liberal Eugenics? *EMBO Reports* 17: 281. [CrossRef] [PubMed]

Wolbring, Gregor. 2015. Gene Editing: Govern Ability Expectations. *Nature* 527: 446. [CrossRef] [PubMed]

Wolbring, Gregor, and Lucy Diep. 2016. The Discussions around Precision Genetic Engineering: Role of and Impact on Disabled People. *Laws* 5: 37. [CrossRef]

Reconsidering Sheltered Workshops in Light of the United Nations Convention on the Rights of Persons with Disabilities (2006)

Charlotte May-Simera

Centre for Disability Law and Policy, National University of Ireland, H91 TK33 Galway, Ireland; c.may-simera1@nuigalway.ie

Abstract: Sheltered work and related practices remain a prevalent service for people with intellectual disabilities. However, as a result of being placed in these, participants overwhelmingly remain segregated and excluded from their wider communities. This paper explores whether, with the advent of the United Nations Convention on the Rights of Persons with Disabilities, we can at least begin to assess the equality implications of such placements and argue that the experience of segregation itself represents numerous rights violations and discrimination. Having considered traditional equality mechanisms and their bearing on people with intellectual disabilities, this discussion explores how far the Convention's re-envisioning of the basic principles of equality can perhaps provide a more promising outlook and ideological stance. Indeed, during the Convention's inception, the negotiations circled around the conflicting opinions as to the purpose, usefulness, and future of sheltered work, revealing the existing tensions between protection and autonomy, shrouding all disability policy discussions. As a result, the question of sheltered work is not explicitly addressed in the treaty and the Committee on the Rights of Persons with Disabilities have been unable to definitively declare that the practice of sheltered work constitutes an act of discrimination. However, the Committee does as times demand that sheltered workshops be phased out where it is obvious that the practice of sheltered work is directly linked to the exploitation of workers. Moreover, certain provisions in the Convention might help in determining wrongful discrimination in some, if limited, instances.

Keywords: intellectual disability; sheltered workshops; United Nations Convention on the Rights of Persons with Disabilities; equality; dignity; discrimination

---

1. Introduction

People with intellectual disabilities face considerable barriers in accessing employment in mainstream settings. These are largely attitudinal as well as systematic. Often a robust system of disability services and disability benefit payments, operate to deter people from becoming emancipated and independent from the rigid structures of traditional, all encompassing institutions. As a result, people with intellectual disabilities remain segregated from mainstream society. This paper aims to question this segregation and consider how the practice of placing people with intellectual disabilities in sheltered work settings contributes to their segregation and exclusion.

Specifically, this discussion will address how the widespread segregation of people with intellectual disabilities has persisted in light of evolved conceptions of equality. Arguably this segregation is founded in inequality as the result of unequal treatment. Despite the evolving nature of equality then, its development has not seen an equal regard of all members of society. This failure to encompass some groups of society can perhaps be rectified when we revisit the core purpose of existing human rights frameworks. This involves identifying the main purpose of equality which lies in bestowing upon each individual an equal concern for their inherent dignity. A renewed global commitment to equality as presented by the latest international human rights convention adopted in 2006, the United Nations Convention on the Rights of Persons with Disabilities (CRPD; Convention), will be assessed according to its potential to strengthen arguments against segregated policies such as sheltered work.

As the latest human rights treaty and the first to deal with disability specifically, the CRPD was eagerly awaited. The global disability community anticipated that it would bring about a sea change for all persons with disabilities based on its innovative approach to disability equality. Indeed, the treaty did deliver on this front and has prompted a widespread process of disability reform (Quinn 2009). However, some argue that it does not positively impact the lives of all persons with disabilities evenly (Dimopoulos 2010). Others consider that, even though they are equally entitled to benefit from the provisions of the Convention, people with intellectual disabilities have faced marginalization to such an extent that they are often not well placed to gain from its changes (ILO 2011). This paper therefore attempts to test how the Convention will fare in light of the on-going controversy over sheltered workshops and explore how far the treaty may instigate policy changes for people with intellectual disabilities.

The Problem with Sheltered Work

Before we begin our discussion we should perhaps explore the concept of sheltered work and adopt a working definition of practices included thereunder. This will not only highlight the existing concerns related to the practices but simultaneously also clarify why sheltered work is a suitable example to use in contemplating the reach and strength of the Convention. The act of placing persons in sheltered workshops was predominantly chosen because of its tangible effects experienced overwhelmingly only by persons labeled as having an intellectual disability. Thus, they provide a unique angle from which to address the debate over segregation and its justification. Moreover, the example of sheltered work was chosen based on the prevalence of segregated work and employment policies across the globe. Besides quota systems, sheltered employment, in its varied formats is one of the most widely used employment measures for people with disabilities across Europe (Mallender et al. 2015). Germany and Spain even reported a growth in sheltered workshop placements (Shima et al. 2008; Flores et al. 2011) and Dague (2012) finds that 75% of adults with intellectual disabilities in the US remained in sheltered work settings despite claims of exploitation (Kennedy 2007; Diament 2011; Cohen 2014). Even international bodies such as the Organization for Economic Co-operation and Development report of the on-going significance and widespread use of segregated employment settings in the wake of controversy (OECD 2003).

Despite their global popularity, there are perhaps as many common markers that denote a similar practice, as there are national, regional and context specific characteristics of the sheltered workshop. Based on the divergent and context-specific approaches, arriving at a distinct definition of sheltered work is therefore almost impossible. In light of these considerable difficulties, the International Labour Organization consider that, for the purposes of general discussions of these, sheltered workshops might best be understood as a conceptual idea rather than a definite employment policy (2003). It is therefore important to note that the term sheltered work, as it is used herein, denotes that act of placing predominantly people with intellectual disabilities in sheltered employment or work facilities where they are subject to atypical working conditions, for an extended period of time.

These defining markers are chosen based on their prevalence across welfare and employment systems globally, but other common indicators exist. For example, as is evident from their name, sheltered workshops are facilities that are 'sheltered' from general or regular work settings, often even geographically located in insulated and isolated places. These work settings are usually run by non-governmental organizations, for-profit or charitable organizations, either privately or on behalf of the State (Samoy and Waterplas 1992). Commonly, these protected environments almost exclusively provide work for people with disabilities, alongside other disabled people (Mallender et al. 2015). The tasks are usually carried out under the instruction of supervisors or trainers, involving the employment of persons without disabilities to support production and regulate the working environment. Comparative studies have discerned that with a few exceptions, sheltered work implies a manufacturing industry, often on a sub-contract basis (OECD 1992, 2003). The simple work activities undertaken can range from clerical activities to, assembling, packing, woodwork, manufacturing, servicing, sewing, or sheet metal work (Miglioire 2010). Other reports however point to the meaningless nature of the work conducted in the sheltered workshop (Holmqvist 2009).

The differences in approaches, on the other hand, prove to be perhaps one of the most discernable problems when discussing the phenomenon of sheltered work. These are also significant and arise from the varied approaches and opposing views as to the purposes and objectives of the sheltered workshop. Tracing the history of these institutions reveals that largely sheltered work settings have evolved from religious or medical institutions and were therefore run according to an ethos of charity and medical treatment. As a result, sheltered workshops, besides their employment and work objectives, can often continue to be regarded as therapeutic, rehabilitative, or specialist training provisions and are intertwined with States' health and social policy measures. This hybrid of treatment, training, and work interventions gives sheltered work settings a broad mandate and makes comparisons difficult and at times confusing.

Accordingly, such settings can also operate according to varied ideologies and headings, which can range from 'Work Centre' in the US to 'Occupational Activity Centre' in Portugal. Such irregularity can lead to unclear or confusing legal statuses, rendering participants in these systems as eternal clients or patients, as opposed to fully fledged workers (Visier 1998; Mallender et al. 2015). Particularly in Eastern European States, this has had alarming effects, where people remain isolated and exploited in sheltered workshops that are run as large institutions (Faničević 2008). Elsewhere, these uncertainties concerning sheltered workshop attendees has resulted in court cases taken by individuals challenging their non-worker status in Germany, Austria, and France with varied success (Court of Justice of the European Union 2013).

These cases and claims of exploitation are also often linked to debates over pay and wages in sheltered workshops. Despite national minimum wage regulations, these are often exempt from such regulations, as they are usually not regarded to be a typical work environments. This is the direct consequence of denying workers in sheltered workshops the formal recognition of their employment status (OECD 1992). Advocacy organizations, however, arguing for equal rights contend that some participants in sheltered workshops are entitled to receive a minimum wage because their working conditions are comparable to that of an employee (Inclusion Ireland 2007). The issue of pay is therefore a particularly controversial one, which has been fuelled by recent media reports revealing that the CEOs of sheltered industries and charities receive six-figure salaries, yet continue to exploit their workers in the US and in Ireland by paying sub-minimum wages (Holland 2007; Schecter 2013; Deegan 2015).

A review of the quantitative data available showed that across 24 American states on average sheltered workers earned $101 per month for approximately 74 h of work per month (Migliore et al. 2007). Low wages are a characteristic of sheltered workshops beyond the U.S. and a persistent feature of sheltered workshops on a global scale. In fact, most comparative research studies on sheltered work address the issue of low remuneration received by participants (Samoy and Waterplas 1992; Visier 1998; Mallender et al. 2015). The issue of payment has also been bought to the attention of international bodies such as the International Labour Organization, which heard a complaint against Japans 'welfare factories' alleging that their workers' low wages violated the relevant ILO Conventions (ILO 2009).

There are, however, opponents to the idea of paying sheltered workshop workers a minimum wage, as well as staunch advocates of the segregated system in general (Price 2016; Moore 2017). These represent more protectionist views of disability policy generally. This camp argues that, without such facilities, people would be left stranded with nothing to do. Moreover, without legislative exemptions, these would not be sustainable as a business, as sheltered workshops are generally not profit-making businesses. In fact, some run at a loss and are heavily reliant on state subsidies and grants. Others argue that the discussions over low wages in sheltered workshops are moot, as the payments received are not comparable to a wage, rather they are top up payments, received in addition to benefit payments (O'Reilly 2007). Others contend that sheltered workshops must continue as some individuals with disabilities will never receive a proper wage due to their inability to be economically productive and perform work of economic value (Corley 2014). Sheltered workshops then at least offer protection from the open labour market and a place for people with disabilities to meet.

Disability scholars have, however, pushed back on these views, arguing that they merely support archaic assumptions that people with intellectual disabilities are unable to work and therefore contribute meaningfully to their societies. This has led Visier (1998) and Taylor (2003) to denounce the sheltered workshop system because it fails to serve people with disabilities but rather contributes to their stigmatization as unproductive, worthless citizens. Even where the sheltered workshop is primarily intended to rehabilitate and treat its participants, disability is largely perceived as an 'incapacity', a label which, as Bach (2016) notes, the sheltered workshop only serves to foster, rather than remedy. Additionally, contrary to the aims of reducing obstacles to employment, the result of sheltered work placements and the effect of segregation often lowers expectations and enhances negative public attitudes making it more difficult for individuals to transition into meaningful employment (Kregel and Dean 2002). As a result of these low transition rates (in Germany, the rate is lower than 1%), persons with disabilities remain in sheltered employment, isolated from their communities (Gottlieb et al. 2010).

Bach (2016) remarks that workplace research shows that intellectually disabled individuals are often more loyal, reliable, and have lower rates of absenteeism compared to other workers. It is then not only the inappropriate wages or low transition rates that are a major factor in the sheltered workshop controversy, but the very reasoning behind the concept of sheltered and segregated workspaces. Unsurprisingly disability activists identify that it is often the negative perceptions and the persistent, underlying perception that people with intellectual disabilities are best segregated, as the toughest barriers to overcome (National Center for Learning Disabilities 2014). This is because, to many, a sheltered workshop placement represents an act of being 'sorted out' and separated from mainstream settings and communities. Instead, a system of 'specialized', disability-specific interventions and 'care' applies, which denies many the opportunities and experiences available to non-disabled peers. This can then be the root of ensuing, consequential symptoms that lead to poverty and an overall inferior legal status. The sheltered workshop system on a whole has thus come to represent a practice that fails to respect people with intellectual disabilities and moreover one that is premised on the denial of rights and opportunities.

As a discrete and insular minority within society, people with intellectual disabilities have been subject to purposeful unequal treatment, institutionalized and segregated to a disproportionally greater extent than individuals without intellectual disabilities. Disability rights campaigners argue that the long-standing practice of placing people in separate, specialist facilities has caused their exclusion, which has been broad in its scope and purposeful (Campbell and Oliver 1996). Often this is a result of systematic policy approaches which are, arguably, fundamentally discriminatory. First, because the very act of placing only persons with disabilities in segregated institutions amounts to unequal treatment compared to those without disabilities who are not placed in these. Second, referring to the common markers and negative outcomes of the placements noted above, in effect those placed in sheltered work settings are often materially poorer and are often denied the same rights as other workers. Overall, attaining substantively equal outcomes for workers in sheltered workshops compared to workers in open and competitive employment is almost impossible. A factor which is aggravated by the length of the placement.

This paper will proceed to argue that this experience of exclusion is largely based on the unchallenged notion that segregation is an inevitable consequence of living with a disability. This exclusion, however, interferes with the equal enjoyment of human rights generally and constitutes a violation of people's dignity. In this way, traditional equality models that consider how to achieve equality for other minority groups have been unable to include the characteristic of intellectual disability in their scope. In response to this shortcoming, this paper argues that we need to revert to the basic promises of equality and human rights law in our attempt to conceptualize an approach to equality that includes people with intellectual disabilities, using the Convention as a framework. This approach will rely on determining that every individual possesses an equal right to have their inherent dignity respected and to lead a dignified life. Using this as the litmus test of equality, this paper will attempt to question whether, considering that the experience of segregation that is so endemic to the practice, sheltered work infringes upon individuals right to lead a dignified life and otherwise interfere with the enjoyment and protection of their rights.

2. Equality

Indeed the practice of sheltered work throws up important debates. This includes considering whether or not such practices are inherently discriminatory, considering the endemic concerns and negative consequences of such placements that largely result from segregation, an integral part of the sheltered work experience. However, discussing whether it is fair or not requires a more contextual debate that reflects on disability equality generally, as well as one that considers the case of intellectual disability specifically. This is undoubtedly necessary considering that, throughout the evolution of equality, the conceptual shifts between formal, procedural, and substantive equality approaches have often failed to reflect on the intricacies of intellectual disability. This is largely due to the limited platforms on which people with intellectual disabilities have been able to advocate for their equal rights and thrash out the meaning of equality from their perspectives. As a result, people with 'severe' disabilities have been excluded from seminal discussions of justice and traditional equality. The field of disability discrimination has thus remained under-theorized and left wanting (Clifford 2014).

Perhaps this is because, in considering the application and limits of existing equality theories in terms of their sensitivity to the case of intellectual disability, we realize that it is still largely expected and accepted that this group will inhabit segregated spaces. Not only does the blanket segregation of this entire group go largely unchallenged, but it is often widely justified based on the group's (perceived) innate inability to attain the merit-worthy attributes to be considered as an 'equal' in the first place (Rioux 1994). These operational (mis-)conceptions as to their ability and therefore their eligibility are perhaps the biggest challenge to equality claims that people with intellectual disabilities face. Undeniably then, any discussion over whether segregation is still an acceptable form of discrimination must build upon practicable, if differentiated notions of equality and its overarching purpose. This will help us in our debate intended to reconsider the practice of sheltered work.

2.1. Is Segregation a Form of Discrimination?

Where academic attention has been paid to discussing how equality and disability intersect, Colker (2009) notes that 'separate' has often been considered as 'unequal' by disability campaigners. Increasingly this has also led to claims that to segregate persons with disabilities from their communities is a violation of their human dignity. Undeniably, these claims have supported arguments to close large, residential institutions and end the horrific practices therein (Brignell 2010). This has particularly gained footing in the US with the help of the landmark *Olmstead* (United States Supreme Court 1999) decision, which determined that people had the (human) right to receive services in the most integrated setting available (Flores 2017). This case was argued on the basis that the unnecessary segregation of persons with disabilities was a violation of their dignity and constituted a form of discrimination contrary to the Americans with Disability Act [1990]. While such a definitive statement of discrimination may not be as easily made in other jurisdictions lacking a similarly powerful civil rights bill, what we can learn from this American example is how central the idea of dignity to disability rights considerations is (Wohl 2016). The concept of dignity and its necessity for a good life featured heavily in finding that the unnecessary segregation wrongly denied individuals their right to access the community and their right to receive services in the least restricted setting (Caley 2010).

Disability scholar Degener (2016b), like Bach, notes that there are some underlying notions intrinsic to the sheltered workshops system that reveal a particularly harmful misconception about 'disability' that consequentially interfere with the respect for an individual's inherent dignity. These create a significant prejudice and serve to continuously justify the segregation of people with disabilities. Degener traces the use of segregated facilities such as sheltered workshops and their legitimacy back to a reliance on particularly two assumptions associated with the notoriously problematic medical model view of disability. This model describes an approach to disability that still determines the disability policy landscape today and continues to have a detrimental impact on the human rights claims of persons with intellectual disabilities under the cloak of protectionism. The first is that disabled persons, above all else, require medical interventions, shelter, and welfare services; a need that can override any consideration for the inherent dignity and autonomy of individuals; and the second is that impairment can preclude legal capacity and interfere with the eligibility for rights claims. In combination, these assumptions distract from the idea that people with intellectual disabilities can make rights claims and that their segregation is inherently discriminatory.

Unsurprisingly then, not everyone is convinced that segregating people into sheltered workshops is the result of discrimination that is harmful and therefore objectionable. Colker (2009) and Brennan-Krohn (2016) for example believe in the need to retain a reliance on disability-specific institutions regardless of whether these interfere with a person's right to choose, lead a dignified life, or effectively segregate certain groups from the rest of society. These equality theorists identify a need for practical approaches to disability policy that acknowledge and reflect upon the 'real differences that sometimes accompany disability' (Brennan-Krohn 2016). Similarly, bioethicists Asch, Blustein, and Wasserman contend (Asch et al. 2008) that the way in which Western society is currently organized, it is inevitable that some people will continue to have their needs singularly met by institutional arrangements.

Explaining why this will particularly continue to apply to people with intellectual disabilities, Brennan-Krohn (2016) elaborates that, while a fully accessible world in which all persons are included and where the difference of disability is fully nullified might be 'relatively easy to imagine for a person who uses a wheelchair', for a person with profound impairments, affecting their ability to interact and communicate, this will be much more difficult to achieve. According to this reasoning, it is then unlikely that the differential treatment of persons with complex disabilities will ever be challenged holistically. In other words, their segregation in a sheltered workshop is not regarded as discriminatory, primarily because they will never be able to take up any other form of employment and therefore be eligible for any other legal status than that of a passive participant, regardless of the substantial disadvantages of the sheltered work placement. The difference of their disability is simply deemed to be too profound to ever warrant any other form of service provision or full entitlement to the range of rights claims that others enjoy. Segregation is then not regarded as a form of discrimination but and inevitable consequence of disability and goes largely unchallenged.

2.2. Equality and Intellectual Disability—An Unhappy Liaison

The pursuit of equality through time has largely focused on ensuring equal rights to all citizens. As a result of this pursuit an interdependent relationship between two modes of rights has developed. This sees an intermingling and interdependence of equality of treatment, i.e., negative, legal rights, and positive, social rights to pursue substantive equality which may indeed require special treatment on a discriminatory basis. Disability scholars agree however that beyond the remit of the formal-substantive dimensions of equality, making rights tangible for people with intellectual disabilities requires additional attention (Silvers 1995; Reicher 2011). In fact, the traditional framework of rights has been notoriously weak in enforcing or protecting the rights of persons with intellectual disabilities. Undoubtedly, this is in part influenced by the preoccupation with solutions and remedies that comprise measurable entities that quantify what an equal outcome entails. These are premised on somewhat subjective opinions of justice and injustice and of what is fair and unfair. As noted above, 'intellectual disability' has then simply not been able to satisfactorily adhere to these binary understandings.

Young and Quibell (2000) consider that this difficultly largely stems from the fact that equality law in the Western, liberal tradition has focused too much on its subjects as autonomous individuals and on the protection of this autonomy from state interference. The individualistic nature of rights according to the liberal design presupposes that all rights holders are self-determining, independent agents. To the detriment of those who may require supports to act and make decisions, this requirement has systematically excluded some persons from the benefits of rights enjoyment and protection. As a result, certain groups who are deemed incapable of rational thought or autonomous agents quickly become ineligible; persons with intellectual disabilities especially have therefore been cast off as non-rights holders.

Although for some groups this illegitimate status may have been rectified over time (Winter 2003), persons with intellectual disabilities are still categorically deemed unqualified to be respected legal actors and rights holders because they are considered to lack autonomy or the ability for independent thought (Goodley and Katherine 2016). This is largely because, as Silvers (2005) acknowledges, these concepts are built on normative ideals and ideologies of normalcy that foster an apparition of a 'species typicality' upon which an eligibility standard is determined. Carlson (2001) similarly identifies that this standard is the product of 'cognitive ableism', a term coined by Carlson to describe the prejudice and the oppression of people with intellectual disabilities resulting from the bias towards individuals that seemingly demonstrate a normative cognitive ability.

The experience of exclusion then largely manifests itself owing to the perception that the intellectual disability characteristic entails an inherent, insurmountable difference—insurmountable in so far that no existing equality mechanism has been able to account and negate the challenges posed by the difference it represents. These are also considered too great to be accommodated by any legal or regulatory mechanism. Minow (1990) considers how in law the difference posed by intellectual disability is treated as intrinsic and solely regarded in terms of its bearing on the individual in question. All too readily then the exclusion experienced is regarded as an inevitable and natural consequence of living with impairment. The differential treatment in the form of segregation based on intellectual disability thus features as a part of legitimate employment and rehabilitation policies (Sheppard 2017).

The unchallenged nature of these dominant and rigid legal frameworks and policies compounds the unequal and unfair treatment of people with intellectual disabilities, harboring their stigmatization and the notion that their exclusion is inevitable. The effects of such systemic inequality can quickly become cumulative with particularly negative consequences for those most marginalized and silenced. Segregation and exclusion therefore pose a deeper challenge to equality than perhaps conventional acts of discrimination. This is particularly the case if we consider that institutional placements so impedes the exercise of rights afforded to everyone else outside the institution, that the placement therein alone, as opposed to a community-based setting or in the 'least restrictive settings possible', has been considered an act of discrimination, as in the *Olmstead* case (Bliss and Wells 2012). In the absence of such strong case law outside of the U.S., it will be useful to consider how the Convention will bear upon the arguments of how sheltered work intersects with the rights of persons with intellectual disabilities.

2.3. Equality and Dignity in the CRPD

The principle of equality is firmly rooted in international human rights law and is also central in the Convention.[1] As the leading norm therein, the principle of equality pursued in the treaty bestows

---

1 Article 1 of the CRPD establishes that the purpose of the Convention is to 'promote, protect and ensure the full and equal enjoyment of all human rights and fundamental freedoms by all persons with disabilities, and to promote respect for their inherent dignity'.

upon all persons an equal recognition and protection, securing all human rights to all persons on an equal basis. This follows the dogma of human rights law generally which understands that all rights are owed equally to all human beings by virtue of their common humanity. Theoretically then, there was perhaps no need for a new Convention, as existing treaty law incorporated people with disabilities in its protection. In their practical implementation, however, existing instruments were so broad and generic that certain 'grey areas' left particular groups effectively unprotected (MacKay 2006). In fact, similar to national equality frameworks, the 'universal' human rights regime had not proved to be all that effective in the context of disability, primarily because the conception of equality applied was not 'disability sensitive' enough to incorporate all individuals, and significant violations of individuals' dignity remained commonplace (Arnardóttir 2009). The Convention's main purpose was then to rectify this shortcoming by firmly placing a more substantive conception of equality at the centre of its provisions and clearly articulating a legal right to equality on behalf of persons with disabilities. Undeniably, it has been successful in achieving this and demonstrates a thorough re-interpretation of equality, based on the express adaptation of universal human rights to the unique situation of disability.

The Convention primarily re-envisions equality by emphasizing the basic principles of human rights law generally. In doing so, it reiterates the principles of equal concern and respect for each human being based on their shared and common humanity. This recognition is extended to decisively include all persons with disabilities, identifying that human rights are rights inherent to each human being and that all individual must be equally recognized as rights bearers and agents under the law. Moreover, the overall tenor and the rationale of the CRPD draws heavily on the core principles of integrity, dignity and the respect for difference which acknowledges that 'disability' is an integral part of humanity and contributes to human diversity (Bickenbach 1999).

Closer consideration of the Convention's general principles, as laid out in Article 3, thus reveals how the Convention embraces perhaps the most novel and dynamic conception of equality available at treaty level.[2] This article is pivotal as it is intended to guide the interpretation of the Convention as a whole, but also clarify how its individual articles are to be transposed into national legislation. The Convention anticipates that this will require multiple equality tools, demonstrating a thorough understanding of existing approaches and incorporating broad, philosophical notions of autonomy, independence, and respect for difference. Further evidence of how the Convention embraces its equality mandate is found in nearly every article that reiterates the importance of inclusion and the requirement that the rights therein can be enjoyed on an equal basis with others, focusing on accessibility and participation as supporting mechanisms. Moreover, the Convention presupposes procedural equality, expressly refers to equality of opportunity, and at times anticipates equality of results. The Convention also explicitly refers to practical policy tools to assist in achieving equality such as reasonable accommodation, affirmative action, 'specific measures', and its prescriptive Article 5 on equality and non-discrimination. Overall, the Convention embodies a multi-layered approach devoted to the ideal of universal equality for all, whilst simultaneously aware that equality is a dynamic concept that must be 'tailored to the specific realities and experiences of those whom it is supposed to serve' (Arnardóttir 2009).

Besides its unique application of equality concepts and tools, the Convention signifies an awareness of the social construction of disability. Essentially, the treaty effectively highlights particularly the structural disadvantages that contribute to the experience of disability which it aims to dismantle. This central objective is outlined in the Convention's preamble (y), where it declares that it 'will make a significant contribution to redressing the profound social disadvantage of persons

---

2 The concepts addressed in Article 3 signify that all rights, duties and freedoms are to be granted and implemented according to the principles of: '(a) the respect for inherent dignity, individual autonomy including the freedom to make one's own choices, and independence of persons; (b) non-discrimination; (c) full and effective participation and inclusion in society; (d) respect for difference and acceptance of persons with disabilities as part of human diversity and humanity; (e) Equality of opportunity; (f) Accessibility' (. . .).

with disabilities'. This is reflective of the social model of disability in which, as is widely known, the CRPD is rooted (Degener 2016a).

Perhaps the most transformative effect of this recognition of the need to challenge existing approaches and the resulting social disadvantages is, as Arstein-Kerslake (2014) aptly describes, that individuals with disabilities are no longer seen as passive recipients of 'special', 'protectionist', and largely segregated care. Central to the success of this Convention is the recognition that people with disabilities are rights holders in their own right, regardless of ability. Instead, the acknowledgement and protection of rights is unconditional and based on the sole premise of our shared humanity; eligibility is thus inconversant with merit. The Convention thus embodies a new conception that views individuals with disabilities not as ineligible and unqualified but 'as an equal who has been systematically marginalized and excluded from society and for whom State Parties must work for and with to achieve substantive equality' (Arstein-Kerslake 2014).

The Convention has then not only promoted global reform in disability policy towards the creation of more equal societies, but it also indicates how the concept of equality itself has evolved. Quite decidedly, it presents an approach to disability equality that bears upon the fundamental construct of human rights, requiring a restoration of the principles of equal respect for dignity and the identification of our collective, societal responsibility in achieving purposeful and meaningful lives. The Convention thus finally makes the 'dignity paradigm' a fundament of equality (Kalb 2011) by making a purposeful theoretical distinction between treating people equally (or decidedly unequally) in the distribution of resources and treating them *as equals*. It simultaneously also reiterates the universality, indivisibility, and inter-relatedness of all human rights according to the principle of universal, inherent dignity. Grant (2007) understands that the fundament of new human rights law owes to a reinterpretation of the 'equality of dignity paradigm', which acknowledges that equal respect and equal worth are the foundation for equal rights. Inevitably, considering sheltered work in a post-Convention era then requires discussing whether sheltered work and segregating practices are compatible with this focus now placed on the equal respect for inherent dignity, before anything else.

3. The CRPD and Its Take on Sheltered Workshops

Sheltered workshops and related practices were discussed during the drafting stages of the Convention. In fact, provided how frequently these were referred to in the contributions by each delegation, it is surprising then that sheltered work, often referred to as 'alternative work settings', were not mentioned in the final text. Besides the frequency, the transcripts of the discussions also reveal the discrepancies in approaches and attitudes towards disability held by delegations. These reflected the diverging approaches to disability policy that also manifest themselves in sheltered work practices with different, context-specific consequences for persons with intellectual disabilities. Accordingly, depending on the welfare and employment systems of the relevant delegations represented, these approaches ranged from paternalistic to inclusionist, from protectionist to rights-based interventions.

It is then particularly the discussions on sheltered work that reveal how these diverging attitudes and approaches came to head. In fact, the opinions differed to such an extent that the issue of sheltered workshops, and how, if at all, to deal with these in the treaty, were divided up until the very last minute of the drafting process. This reveals not only the political tightrope the Committee Chair, tasked with amending the draft text, had to walk, but also how widespread sheltered work practices are, as well as the views as to their purpose.

Overall, the transcripts reveal a general understanding amongst the negotiating community that people with intellectual disabilities experienced significantly higher levels of harmful discrimination and an extent of exclusion that remained largely unchallenged (United Nations Enable 2004a). However, only few delegations identified that the segregation resulting from placements in sheltered work settings where to be labeled as a wrongful from of discrimination and should thus be considered unacceptable. These opinions, largely voiced by (Disabled Persons Organizations (DPOs)), argued that sheltered work represented a form of unnecessary segregation, effectively leading to the exclusion of persons with disabilities. The practice was therefore an act of discrimination and was inconsistent with the very purpose of the Convention. Advocates regarded the drafting of an international disability rights convention as an ideal opportunity to categorically denounce these.

Many DPOs spoke out in opposition of sheltered workshops generally, arguing that these keep people excluded and foster notions that people with intellectual disabilities cannot be meaningfully employed. These argued that sheltered workshops were an outdated concept that signified a form of institutionalization, representing an ongoing barrier to inclusion as evidenced by the low transition rates from these to open employment. The International Disability Caucus, a coalition of DPOs set up for the purposes of negotiating the Convention, called for the elimination of all forms of institutionalization even those intended to fulfill the right to work. Challenging the notion that sheltered work created work opportunities, they contended that such measures represent limitations and fail to protect the right to work and to gain a living by work which is freely chosen (International Disability Caucus 2004). People with Disability Australia (PWDA) clarified that the Convention must not be construed as creating rights to segregated employment because this merely contributed to the permanent 'warehousing' of persons with disabilities. Rather, the Convention must affirm the right to full participation in the mainstream labour market.

Dignity also featured as a crucial concept during the discussions on the right to work. Broadly referring to work and training in sheltered workshops or in other confined environments, Palestine noted that the CRPD must protect the right to work and must include a reference to work that is freely chosen or accepted and 'preserves dignity'(United Nations Enable 2004b). The World Network of Users and Survivors of Psychiatry also commented that the issue of free choice was integral to the right to work (United Nations Enable 2004a). Cameroon emphasized the importance of strengthening the promotion of paid employment and suggested changes that emphasized independent, as well as remunerative work. Canada suggested including stronger wording that ensured career opportunities for all people with disabilities on the open labour market (United Nations Enable 2004b).

Despite these State interventions commenting on the right to choice of work and access to work on the open labour market, New Zealand was one of the only State delegations that specifically called for the closure of alternative work settings. It held that the Convention must clearly signal that sheltered work and other forms of segregation were no longer acceptable. Referring to the historic segregation of persons with disabilities, New Zealand emphasized that protecting people from unnecessary segregation was a pivotal issue (United Nations Enable 2005). The Convention needed to be unambiguous in its position on sheltered work so as to avoid presenting State Parties with a choice between providing either inclusive *or* segregated services. DPOs agreed that anything that can be construed as justifying and institutions and arguments that maintained sheltered workshops only served to reduce the responsibility of State Parties to support people with disabilities into open employment (United Nations Enable 2006).

Other delegations held opposing views. Accordingly, sheltered workshops should continue to exist, as these were a means employed by States to fulfill the right to work. A coalition of National Human Rights Institutions spoke out in support of sheltered work. The coalition argued that, from a legal perspective, the concept of sheltered work could be viewed as fulfilling the requirement on both State Parties and employers to reasonably accommodate workers with disabilities in the labour market. The practice of sheltered work should be revered as a form of reasonable accommodation and endorsed as a valid equality tool. Others agreed that because sheltered workshops would continue to exist based on the continued demand, the priority of the present Convention should then be on regulating rather than denouncing these (United Nations Enable 2004b). As the standard setting body in the area of work and employment, the ILO heavily weighed in on these debates. It explained that the Convention must reflect the 'reality' that some people are unable to work on the open labour market and that many people with disabilities worked in 'protected workshops'. Provisions for these alternative forms of work must be made (United Nations Enable 2004a). A failure to mention alternative workplaces would only harm those most marginalized and run the risk of aggravating the precariousness of the work situations that persons with disabilities were engaged in. Namibia agreed that the Convention should urge States to regulate the sector effectively by standardizing the rules and governance of these, harmonizing them with those of typical work.

Seemingly aware of the arguments both for and against sheltered work, as well as the Convention's overall purpose, the World Network of Users and Survivors of Psychiatry issued some pragmatic solutions. It considered that, based on their prevalence, sheltered work is likely to continue; however, the economic exploitation that is rampant and endemic in the sector must be curbed through regulation. The group recommended that the role of health care and rehabilitation services in sheltered work must not be overlooked. It urged the Committee to take note that, all too often then, what is called 'rehabilitation' is often 'busy-work' imposed on people instead of real opportunities promoting full social participation (United Nations Enable 2005).

Evidently, there were mixed opinions on the role of sheltered workshops and what these represented. These ranged from seeing these as genuine places of work, which required the application of rights-based employment regulations, to regarding such places as the embodiment of historical disadvantages, the harmful segregation and exploitation faced by people with disabilities using protectionist interventions. These divergent opinions culminated in a disagreement on whether the Convention should generally support or denounce these.

The Chair of the drafting committee ultimately chose not to include any reference to sheltered work practices in the final text of the Convention. This decision was based on the concerns raised by the disability community that these ultimately constituted unnecessary segregation and required careful review. Given how feverishly this issue was debated, it is nevertheless surprising that any reference to sheltered work was entirely omitted. Weller (2011) notes that this is a rare occasion that exemplifies the use of a purposeful silence in the Convention. As a tool for negotiation, silence was occasionally used in this manner for political reasons. This helped avoid an impasse over certain, contentious issues that could jeopardize the success of the whole Convention. If a specific aspect or decision was hotly debated and no agreement could be reached, silence over the matter was then a means to circumvent the problem and maintain a consensus securing the success of the negotiations.

As a result, the Convention is silent on sheltered workshops, which does little to help us in our attempt to consider sheltered work through the Convention's new equality prism and question its discriminatory implications. In fact, this has indeed, quite detrimentally, even had the opposite effect. Its silence has left a wide margin for potential misinterpretations or misuse thereof. The failure to reach an agreement on sheltered work has meant that State Parties have enacted the Convention inconsistently. Exploiting its silence on the matter, some have interpreted the Convention as justifying the continuation of sheltered work practices or used to argue for more segregated work provisions. The right to work as one that is fulfilled by sheltered settings or as a form of reasonable accommodation then effectively overrides the Convention's overall objective of inclusion. The Convention's overall stance on sheltered work has thus been subject to conflicting interpretations. For example, Mallender et al. (2015; IGOS 2011), taking a similar view to the Coalition of National Human Rights Institutions during the negotiations, consider that sheltered workshops are a form of reasonable accommodation. Reporting to the European Parliament then, these researchers suggest that the Convention even sets a legal obligation on States to provide sheltered workshops. A look to the how the Convention's treaty body, the Committee on the Rights of Persons with Disabilities, has embraced this silence and what it has interpreted it to mean for sheltered work practices may be more useful.

3.1. Concluding Observations, Sheltered Work Since the Adoption of the Convention

The Convention's silence on the topic of sheltered work has also impacted the interpretations thereof by the treaty body itself. This has become evident over the years through the accumulation of international jurisprudence and growing high-level commentary based on the Convention. The CRPD publishes their opinions on State implementation reports in the form of Concluding Observations.

These provide a suite of information on the state of disability reform since the adoption of the Convention in a given State and provide a unique insight into how the treaty has been interpreted both nationally and internationally, assessing its impact. On a broader scale, an analysis of the existing collection of Concluding Observations gives us perhaps the widest and most current impression of the sheltered work debate available. A review of these Committee reports clearly signals that sheltered work continues to dominate the field of employment services for specific groups and, as a result, their continued segregation and exclusion.

Commenting on the situation in Canada, the Committee noted that particularly women and young persons with disabilities remained in sheltered workshops (CRPD/C/CAN/CO/1) (Committee on the Rights of Persons with Disabilities 2017a). The prevalence of sheltered workshops in Slovakia and Serbia, including a significant rise in numbers of these in Bosnia Herzegovina, also caught the Committee's attention ((CRPD/C/SVK/CO/1) (Committee on the Rights of Persons with Disabilities 2016c); (CRPD/C/SRB/CO/1) (Committee on the Rights of Persons with Disabilities 2016d); (CRPD/C/BIH/CO/1) (Committee on the Rights of Persons Disabilities 2017b). It also remarked upon the increasing manifestation of a segregated labour market in Austria and Germany (CRPD/C/AUT/CO/1) (Committee on the Rights of Persons with Disabilities 2013) and that many other States used sheltered workshops and similar 'specialized' and segregated employment models to employ persons with disabilities (CRPD/C/BOL/CO/1) (Committee on the Rights of Persons with Disabilities 2016b).

Besides expressing concern over States' continued reliance on segregated systems to employ persons with disabilities, the Committee has also regularly expressed concern over the practices within such States. It often cited that minimal wages or other forms of payment received by workers were problematic (CRPD/C/AUT/CO/1) (Committee on the Rights of Persons with Disabilities 2013). The Committee, based on its observations, even considered that Hong Kong's sheltered workshops operated in a manner that violated Article 16 of the Convention that enumerated the right to freedom from exploitation, violence, and abuse. The Committee reached this conclusion based on the 'daily allowance' received by persons with disabilities working in sheltered workshops, which it found to be 'too low' and 'bordering exploitation' (CRPD/C/CHN/CO/1) (Committee on the Rights of Persons with Disabilities 2012). The Committee also expressed concern in relation to the practices in Occupational Activity Centres in Portugal, noting in particular the working conditions and the average wage received by workers with disabilities (CRPD/C/PRT/CO/1) (Committee on the Rights of Persons with Disabilities 2016a). The Committee also urged Korea and Germany to eliminate its sheltered workshops through 'immediately enforceable exit strategies'. (CRPD/C/DEU/CO/1) (Committee on the Rights of Persons with Disabilities 2015); (CRPD/C/KOR/CO/1) (Committee on the Rights of Persons with Disabilities 2014).

The collection of Concluding Observations reveal that the Committee has provided substantial and definitive commentary on sheltered or segregated employment structures. The Committee has overwhelmingly found that sheltered work and conditions thereof to be inconsistent with the Convention and contrary to human rights provisions therein. As a result, the Committee has consistently encouraged State Parties, many of which still heavily rely on sheltered work structures, to review such practices and related legislation and bring them in line with the Convention. At times, the Committee was even explicitly referred to the rights violations occurring in sheltered workshops. In light of its observations of Serbia, for example, the Committee required that the State dismantle its sheltered workshop system and ensure the respect of all rights at work, of all workers, 'in accordance with the Convention' (CRPD/C/SRB/CO/1) (Committee on the Rights of Persons with Disabilities 2016d). Similarly, the Committee encourages Portugal to review its practices and legislation concerning the operation of its Occupational Activity Centres, 'from a human rights perspective to bring them into line with the Convention' (CRPD/C/PRT/CO/1) (Committee on the Rights of Persons with Disabilities 2016a).

Despite the fact that, on these occasions, the Committee has expressed clear criticisms addressing the fact that some sheltered work practices were contrary to the provisions within the CRPD, it has not identified that the resulting experience of segregation itself was problematic. The Committee has therefore failed to address the experience of exclusion from an equality perspective. In relation to such a finding, in fact, the CRPD Committee has to date been quite conservative in its interpretations of the Convention. This is evident in its failure to explicitly call out the segregation experienced as part of the sheltered workshops placements as a form of discrimination itself. Arguably, this is a missed opportunity on behalf of the Committee to categorically denounce sheltered work practices and addressing how the ideologies therefore conflict with the aims of the Convention. While the Committee does refer to some problematic practices that may be the result of a sheltered work placement, such as differentiated wage payments and reduced working standards, it does not refer to the practice, nor the resulting segregation, as a form of discrimination itself.

3.2. Exclusion as a Form of Discrimination in the CRPD

While the Convention, and by implication the Committee, leave the vital question of sheltered work susceptible to (mis-)interpretations; the treaty elsewhere does specify that exclusion is an equality issue and potentially represents a form of discrimination. Under the Convention, State Parties are bound to ban discrimination on the basis of disability and must guarantee 'equal and effective legal protection against discrimination on all grounds' (Article 5(2), CRPD). Helpfully, Article 2 of the Convention clarifies that, specifically, some types of exclusion on the basis of disability shall be considered as a form of discrimination, specifically where it interferes with or has the 'effect of impairing or nullifying the recognition, enjoyment or exercise, on an equal basis with others, of all human rights and fundamental freedoms in the political, economic, social, cultural, civil or any other field' (Article 2, CRPD).

While Article 2 does not consider that *all* forms of exclusion are to be considered as discriminatory, it does suggest that it be tested for its implications. If these are so great as to impact upon the enjoyment of equal rights of persons with disabilities, then a finding of discrimination is present. Article 2 does not necessarily encourage an exploration of exclusion, which is rooted in any attention to dignity, or lend itself to a blanket statement that renders all segregation experienced in sheltered workshops as discrimination. Instead, it requires an assessment of the nuances and effect of each individual experience of segregation, in accordance with the Convention's overall commitment to a more substantive, tailored approach to equality. Representing a form of conditionality then, this has the potential of stifling the Convention's lofty aims of achieving greater, (unconditional) inclusion and increasing the social participation of all person with disabilities. Although the Convention employs an exciting combination of equality tools, it is ultimately still confined to their traditional functioning. This sees processes of equality subject to tried and tested mechanisms and existing anti-discrimination frameworks that are subject to the reservations thereof. Determining the equality implications of sheltered work is therefore not straightforward. Instead, a decision of whether the segregation experienced constitutes a form of discrimination will require an individual assessment of each claim and only elicit individual redress. The definition of discrimination as provided in Article 2 of the Convention is therefore only of limited significance in considering the practice of sheltered work as a whole.

4. Conclusions

This discussion takes the example of sheltered workshops to test the effectiveness of the Convention in challenging the segregation of people with intellectual disabilities. Sheltered workshops are chosen based on their notoriety as places of exploitation. Their controversial nature is long documented and has flared up debates addressing all aspects of equality. Linking the experience of segregation with the exclusion and social disadvantages experienced by people with intellectual disabilities, this paper questions the legitimacy of sheltered work in light of the Convention on the Rights of Persons with Disabilities. This required a discussion over how to better define equality for people with intellectual disabilities. It was argued that, because of the segregation experienced as a result of the placement in confined services with limited opportunities, sheltered work impedes upon participants' right to lead a life of equal worth and importance and their right to dignity.

The Convention then is committed to protecting the inherent dignity of all persons and employs innovative approaches to achieving disability equality. The Convention, however, does not grant us the satisfaction of a sweeping and explicit denouncing of sheltered work practices. As a result of complex negotiations, the CRPD has remained silent on the sheltered workshop debate. Without a clear position expressed therein, different interpretations of the Convention's bearing on these have been effected. As a result, the CRPD Committee are still addressing the same, known concerns of exploitation in regard to sheltered work that were identified during the negotiations. The Committee has at least used the Concluding Observations to point out, in certain instances, that sheltered workshops should be closed in favour of more open options.

Primarily, the difficulty in declaring that sheltered workshop placements are discriminatory lies in the varied and divergent definitions and purposes of these, which is in turn determined by dichotomous policy dimensions which can lie somewhere between rights-based and protectionist. As a result, the often conflicting interests representing protectionism on the one hand and autonomy on the other, which dominated the drafting of the Convention, continues to define the disability policy landscape today.

The Article 2 definition that includes exclusion as a potential form of discrimination is indeed a unique and exciting innovation of the Convention. However, as an interpretive provision, it is one that still exists within the confinement of traditional legal systems and requires individual tests for a finding of discrimination through the experience of exclusion. Each incident of segregation would then be tested for the harmful effect of that placement and its impact upon an individual's right to dignity and to lead a dignified life. This innovative definition cannot be used to challenge whole policies or argue for the closure of entire segregated systems.

Overall, the most prevalent employment services for persons with intellectual disabilities are still principally offered in segregated, institutional settings. Despite its novel and broad equality perspectives, the Convention has only had a limited bearing on the dichotomous power dynamics of the disability policy landscape. The non-discrimination and equality paradigms of the treaty, however noble and dignity-focused, has not effectively carried over to holistically address and the widespread exclusion of persons with intellectual disabilities who still largely inhibit separate spaces and lead segregated lives. One redeeming aspect originating from the Convention's framework is perhaps its potential in determining that exclusion and segregation in some circumstances is to be considered as discriminatory albeit only in individual cases. Therefore, while it cannot provide us with arguments for the blanket protection from segregation, the Convention may be used to provide individual rights protections and remedies.

References

Arnardóttir, Oddney Mjoll. 2009. A Future for Multidimensional Disadvantage Equality? In *The UN Convention on the Rights of Persons with Disabilities: European and Scandinavian Perspectives*. Edited by Oddny Mjoll Arnardóttir and Gerard Quinn. Leiden: Martinus Nijhoff, p. 41.

Arstein-Kerslake, Anna. 2014. *Restoring Voice to People: Realizing the Right to Equal Recognition before the Law of People with Cognitive Disabilities*. Galway: National University of Ireland.

Asch, Adrienne, Jeffrey Blustein, and David Wasserman. 2008. Criticizing and Reforming Segregated Facilities for Persons with Disabilities. *Journal of Bioethical Inquiry* 5: 157–67. [CrossRef]

Bach, Michael. 2016. Cited in Fuatai, Teuila. From Exploitation to Employment: Undoing Canada's Sheltered Workshop System. *Rabble News*, April 12.

Bickenbach, Jerome. 1999. Minority Rights or Universal Participation: The Politics of Disablement. In *Disability, Divers-Ability and Change*. Edited by Martha Jones and Lee Ann Basser. Leiden: Martinus Nijhoff.

Bliss, Charles, and Talley Wells. 2012. Applying Lessons from the Evolution of Brown v. Board of Education to Olmstead: Moving from Gradualism to Immediate, Effective, and Comprehensive Integration. *Georigia State Univeristy Law Review* 26: 705–39.

Brennan-Krohn, Zoe. 2016. Employment for People with Disabilities: A Role for Anti-Subordination. *Harvard Civil Rights-Civil Liberties Law Review* 51: 239–72.

Brignell, Victoria. 2010. When the Disabled Where Segregated. *The New Statesman*. December 15. Available online: http://www.newstatesman.com/society/2010/12/disabled-children-british (accessed on 13 January 2017).

Caley, Sylvia. 2010. The Olmsetad Decision: The Road to Dignity and Freedom. *Georigia State Univeristy Law Review* 26: 651–62.

Campbell, Jane, and Michael Oliver. 1996. *Disability Politics: Understanding Our Past, Changing Our Future*. Abingdon: Routledge.

Carlson, Licia. 2001. Cognitive Ableism and Disability Studies: Feminist Reflections on the History of Mental Retardation. *Hypatia* 16: 124–46. [CrossRef]

Clifford, Stacy. 2014. The Capacity Contract: Locke, Disability, and the Political Exclusion of "Idiots". *Politics, Groups, and Identities* 2: 90–103. [CrossRef]

Cohen, Rick. 2014. Are People with Disabilities Exploited in Sheltered Workshops? *Nonprofit Quarterly*, April 14.

Colker, Ruth. 2009. *When is Separate Unequal? A Disability Perspective*. New York: Cambridge University Press.

Committee on the Rights of Persons with Disabilities. 2012. *Concluding Observations on the Initial Report of China, Adopted by the Committee at Its Eighth Session (17–28 September 2012)*. CRPD/C/CHN/CO/1; Geneva: Committee on the Rights of Persons with Disabilities, para. 67.

Committee on the Rights of Persons with Disabilities. 2013. *Concluding Observations on the Initial Report of Austria*. CRPD/C/AUT/CO/1; Geneva: Committee on the Rights of Persons with Disabilities.

Committee on the Rights of Persons with Disabilities. 2014. *Concluding Observations on the Initial Report of the Republic of Korea**. CRPD/C/KOR/CO/1; Geneva: Committee on the Rights of Persons with Disabilities.

Committee on the Rights of Persons with Disabilities. 2015. *Concluding Observations on the Initial Report of Germany**. CRPD/C/DEU/CO/1; Geneva: Committee on the Rights of Persons with Disabilities.

Committee on the Rights of Persons with Disabilities. 2016a. *Concluding Observations on the Initial Report of Portugal**. CRPD/C/PRT/CO/1; Geneva: Committee on the Rights of Persons with Disabilities.

Committee on the Rights of Persons with Disabilities. 2016b. *Concluding Observations on the Initial Report of the Plurinational State of Bolivia**. CRPD/C/BOL/CO/1; Geneva: Committee on the Rights of Persons with Disabilities.

Committee on the Rights of Persons with Disabilities. 2016c. *Concluding Observations on the Initial Report of Slovakia**. CRPD/C/SVK/CO/1; Geneva: Committee on the Rights of Persons with Disabilities.

Committee on the Rights of Persons with Disabilities. 2016d. *Concluding Observations on the Initial Report of Serbia**. CRPD/C/SRB/CO/1; Geneva: Committee on the Rights of Persons with Disabilities.

Committee on the Rights of Persons with Disabilities. 2017a. *Concluding Observations on the Initial Report of Canada**. CRPD/C/CAN/CO/1; Geneva: Committee on the Rights of Persons with Disabilities.

Committee on the Rights of Persons Disabilities. 2017b. *Concluding Observations on the Initial Report of Bosnia and Herzegovina**. CRPD/C/BIH/CO/1; Geneva: Committee on the Rights of Persons with Disabilities.

Corley, Cheryl. 2014. Subminimum Wages for the Disabled: Godsend or Exploitation? *National Public Radio, Morning Edition*, April 23.

Court of Justice of the European Union. 2013. *Case-316/13. Gérard Fenoll v Centre D'aide par le Travail 'La Jouvene', Association de Parents et D'amis de Personnes Handicapées Mentales (APEI) D'avignon*. ECLI:EU:C:2015:200; Luxembourg: Court of Justice of the European Union.

Dague, Bryan. 2012. Sheltered Employment, Sheltered Lives: Family Perspectives of Conversion to Community-based Employment. *Journal of Vocational Rehabilitation* 37: 1–11.

Deegan, Gordon. 2015. Departing Rehab Staff got €3.2m in redundancy. *The Irish Independent*, November 4.

Degener, Theresia. 2016a. A Human Rights Model of Disability. In *Routledge Handbook of Disability Law and Human Rights*. Edited by Peter Blanck and Eilionoir Flynn. Abingdon: Routledge.

Degener, Theresia. 2016b. Disability in a Human Rights Context. *Laws* 5: 35. [CrossRef]

Diament, Michelle. 2011. Sheltered Workshops No Better than Institutions Report Finds. *Disability Scoop*, January 19. Available online: https://www.disabilityscoop.com/2011/01/19/sheltered-workshops-report/11974/ (accessed on 23 January 2018).

Dimopoulos, Andreas. 2010. *Issues in the Human Rights Protection of Intellectually Disabled Persons*. Abingdon: Routledge, p. 67.

Flores, Roseanne L. 2017. State Reform and Respect for the Rights of the Disabled People: A Reflection on the Olmstead Decision the Case of New York State. *Cogent Medicine* 4: 1–9. [CrossRef]

Flores, Noelia, Christina Jenaro, M. Begona Orgaz, and M. Victoria Martín. 2011. Understanding Quality of Life of Workers with Intellectual Disabilities. *Journal of Applied Research in Intellectual Disabilities* 24: 133–44. [CrossRef]

Franičević, Vojmir. 2008. *Decent Work Country Report- Croatia*. Geneva: ILO.

Goodley, Daniel, and Runswick-Cole Katherine. 2016. Becoming Dishuman: Thinking about the Human through Dis/Ability. *Discourse: Studies in the Cultural Politics of Education* 37: 1–15. [CrossRef]

Gottlieb, Aaron, William Myhill, and Peter Blanck. 2010. Employment of People with Disabilities. In *International Encyclopedia of Rehabilitation*. Buffalo: Center for International Rehabilitation Research Information and Exchange (CIRRIE).

Grant, Evadne. 2007. Dignity and Equality. *Human Rights Law Review* 7: 299–329. [CrossRef]

Holland, Kitty. 2007. Sheltered Workshops at the Centre for Exploitation Claims. *The Irish Times*, August 27.

Holmqvist, Mikael. 2009. Disabled People and Dirty Work. *Disability & Society* 24: 869–82.

Interest Group on Occupational Services (IGOS). 2011. *Partnership Project: "Quality Work Settings for All"*. Brussles: Interest Group on Occupational Services (IGOS), p. 34.

International Labour Organization (ILO). 2009. *Report of the Committee Set up to Examine the Representation Alleging Non-Observance by Japan of the Vocational Rehabilitation and Employment (Disabled Persons) Convention, 1983 (No. 159), Made under Article 24 of the ILO Constitution by the National Union of Welfare and Childcare Workers*. GB304/14/6, Mar. 2009. Geneva: ILO.

International Labour Organisation (ILO). 2011. *Promoting Training and Employment Opportunities for People with Intellectual Disabilities: International Experience*. Geneva: ILO, p. iii.

Inclusion Ireland. 2007. *A Chance to Work: A Discussion Paper on Work and Employment Services and Supports Available to people with an Intellectual Disability*. Dublin: Inclusion Ireland.

International Disability Caucus. 2004. Article 22 Right to Work, Prepared by the International Disability Caucus. Available online: http://www.un.org/esa/socdev/enable/rights/documents/ahc6idcda22infosheet_000.doc (accessed on 17 May 2017).

Kalb, Johanna. 2011. Litigating Dignity: A Human Rights Framework'. *Albany Law Review* 74: 1725–38.

Kennedy, E. B. 2007. Govt 'failing exploited Disabled Workers. *The Irish Times*, November 12.

Kregel, John, and David H. Dean. 2002. Sheltered vs. Supported Employment: A Direct Comparison of Long-Term Earnings Outcomes for Individuals with Cognitive Disabilities'. Available online: http://www.worksupport.com/main/downloads/dean/shelteredchap3.pdf (accessed on 12 October 2017).

MacKay, Don. 2006. Statement on Behalf of New Zealand at the Adoption of the Convention on the Rights of Persons with Disabilities by the United Nations General Assembly on 13 December 2006. Available online: http://www.un.org/esa/socdev/enable/convstatementgov.htm#nz (accessed on 20 January 2017).

Mallender, Jacqueline, Quentin Liger, Rory Tierney, Daniel Beresford, James Eager, Stefan Speckesser, and Vahé Nafilyan. 2015. *Directorate General for Internal Policies of the European Parliament, Policy Department A. Economic and Scientific Policy, Employment and Social Affairs. 'Reasonable Accommodation and Sheltered Workshops for People with Disabilities: Costs and Returns of Investments—Study for the EMPL Committee*. Brussels: European Parliament.

Miglioire, Alberto. 2010. Sheltered Workshops. In *International Encyclopedia of Rehabilitation*. Edited by John H. Stone and Maria Blouin. Buffalo: Centre of international Rehabilitation Research Information and Exchange, Available online: http://cirrie.buffalo.edu/encyclopedia/en/article/136/ (accessed on 15 February 2016).

Migliore, Alberto, Davi Mank, Tara Grossi, and Patricia Rogan. 2007. Integrated Employment or Sheltered Workshops: Preference of Adults with Intellectual Disabilities, their Families and Staff. *Journal of Vocational Rehabilitation* 26: 5–19.

Minow, Martha. 1990. *Making All the Difference: Inclusion, Exclusion and American Law*. Ithaca: Cornell University Press.

Moore, James. 2017. Rosa Monckton, It Will Never Be Morally Right to Pay Those with Learning Disabilities below the Minimum Wage. *The Independent*, March 3.

National Center for Learning Disabilities. 2014. *The State of Learning Disabilities*. New York: National Center for Learning Disabilities.

O'Reilly, Arthur. 2007. *The Right to Decent Work of Persons with Disabilities*. Geneva: International Labour Office.

Organization for Economic Co-operation and Development (OECD). 1992. *Employment Policy for People with Disabilities*. Labour Market and Social Policy Occasional Papers No. 8; Paris: OECD Publishing.

Organization for Economic Co-Operation and Development (OECD). 2003. *Transforming Disability into Ability: Policies to Promote Work and Income Security for Disabled People*. Paris: OECD Publishing.

Price, Rita. 2016. Families Fight to Keep Institutions, Sheltered Workshops Open. *The Coloumbus Dispatch*, April 15.

Quinn, Gerard. 2009. A Short Guide to the United Nations Convention on the Rights of Persons with Disabilities. In *European Yearbook of Disability Law: Volume 1*. Edited by Gerard Quinn and Lisa Waddington. Cambridge: Intersentia.

Reicher, Stella. 2011. Human Diversity and Asymmetries: A Reinterpretation of the Social Contract under the Capabilities Approach. *International Journal on Human Rights* 8: 167–79.

Rioux, Marcia. 1994. Towards a Concept of Equality of Well-Being: Overcoming the Social and Legal Construction of Inequality. In *Disability Is Not Measles: New Research Paradigms*. Edited by Marcia Rioux and Michael Bach. Toronto: L'Institute Roeher.

Samoy, Erik, and Lina Waterplas. 1992. *Sheltered Employment in the European Community*. Leuven: Katholieke Universtieit Leuven & Hoger Instituut voor de Arbeid.

Schecter, Anna. 2013. Disabled Workers Paid just Pennies an Hour- and its Legal. *NBC News*, June 25.

Sheppard, Colleen. 2017. *Contesting Systematic Discrimination: Law and Organizational Change*. Galway: Centre for Disabliity Law and Poliy, National Univeristy of Ireland, March 22.

Shima, Isilda, Eszter Zólyomi, and Asgar Zaidi. 2008. *The Labour Market Situation of People with Disabilities in EU25*. European Centre, Policy Brief (1). Vienna: European Center for Social Welfare Policy and Research.

Silvers, Anita. 1995. Reconciling Equality to Difference: Caring (f)or Justice for People with Disabilities. *Hypatia* 10: 30–55. [CrossRef]

Silvers, Anita. 2005. People with Disabilities. In *The Oxford Handbook of Practical Ethics*. Edited by Hugh LaFollette. Oxford: Oxford University Press.

Taylor, Steven. 2003. Workers with Disabilities Deserve Real Choices, Real Jobs. Available online: http://www.accessiblesociety.org/topics/economics-employment/shelteredwksps.html (accessed on 14 March 2016).

United Nations Enable. 2004a. *Daily Summary of Discussions Related to Article 22 Right to Work*. New York: United Nations Enable, vol. 3, #6.

United Nations Enable. 2004b. *UN Convention on the Rights of People with Disabilities Ad Hoc Committee Daily Summary: A Service Made Possible by Landmine Survivors Network*. New York: United Nations Enable, vol. 4, #7.

United Nations Enable. 2005. *Daily Summary of Discussion at the Fifth Session 3 February 2005, UN Convention on the Human Rights of People with Disabilities Ad Hoc Committee—Daily Summaries a Service Brought to You by RI (Rehabilitation International)*. New York: United Nations Enable, vol. 6, #9.

United Nations Enable. 2006. *Daily Summary of Discussion at the Seventh Session 25 January 2006, UN Convention on the Human Rights of People with Disabilities Ad Hoc Committee—Daily Summaries, a Service Brought to You by Rehabilitation International (RI)*. New York: United Nations Enable, vol. 8, #8.

United States Supreme Court. 1999. *Olmstead v. L.C., 527 U.S., 581, (1999)*. Washington: United States Supreme Court.

Visier, Laurent. 1998. Sheltered Employment for Persons with Disabilities. *International Labour Review* 137: 347–65.

Weller, Penelope. 2011. The Convention on the Rights of Persons with Disabilities and the Social Model of Health: New Perspectives. *Journal of Mental Health Law* 74–84. [CrossRef]

Winter, Jerry Alan. 2003. The Development of the Disability Rights Movement as a Social Problem Solver. *Disability Studies Quarterly* 23: 33–61. [CrossRef]

Wohl, Alison. 2016. Competitive Integrated Employment as a Civil Right for People with Disabilities. Paper present at the LEAD Center Webinar, Washington, DC, USA, November 8.

Young, Damon, and Ruth Quibell. 2000. Why Rights Are Never Enough: Rights, Intellectual Disability and Understanding. *Disability & Society* 15: 747–64.

13

Unveiling the Challenges in the Implementation of Article 24 CRPD on the Right to Inclusive Education

Delia Ferri

Department of Law, Maynooth University, Maynooth, Co. Kildare, Ireland; delia.ferri@mu.ie

Abstract: Since the 1970s, Italy has undertaken a process of inclusion of children with disabilities in mainstream schools, has implemented an anti-discriminatory educational policy, and abandoned segregated educational practices. In September 2014, the Italian Government initiated a process of "modernization" of the whole educational system, and attempted to fully align domestic legislation with the wide-ranging obligations enshrined in Article 24 CRPD. Law No. 107/2015 on the reform of the educational system empowered the Government to adopt legislative decrees to promote *inter alia* an effective and inclusive education for persons with disabilities. After a long and somewhat troubled process, a legislative decree on inclusive education was finally adopted in April 2017. This article, building upon previous research, critically discusses the innovations brought by this recent reform, situating them in the broader Italian legislative framework on the rights of people with disabilities. By focusing on Italy as a case-study, this article aims to reflect on the challenges surrounding the creation of an inclusionary educational system that goes beyond a mere integration in mainstream schools and ensures full and effective participation of all learners, meeting the standards imposed by Article 24 CRPD.

Keywords: UN Convention on the Rights of Persons with Disabilities; inclusive education; support teacher; Law No 104/1992; Law No 107/2015; legislative decree No 66/2017

---

1. Introduction

Italy has long implemented an anti-discriminatory educational policy, and abandoned segregated practices in education, by advancing a policy known as "school integration" (*integrazione scolastica*) since the 1970s (Caldin 2013). As noted elsewhere (Ferri 2017), even before the ratification of the UN Convention on the Rights of Persons with Disabilities (CRPD), in 2009,[1] the Italian legislative and policy framework was characterised by a relatively high standard of protection of the right to education of pupils with disabilities (Rossi et al. 2016; Addis 2015; Troilo 2012, 2016; Busatta 2016; Penasa 2014). Despite a progressive legal framework, however, numerous shortfalls have slowly emerged in the Italian school system. In the last few years, several complaints have been brought to court by parents of pupils with disabilities seeking to enforce the right to education, to combat alleged discrimination of disabled pupils at school, and ultimately to challenge the lack of implementation or the incorrect implementation of the legislation in place. The UN Committee on the Rights of Persons with Disabilities (CRPD Committee), in its Concluding Observations (COs) to the Italian Initial Report on the implementation of the Convention (CRPD Committee 2016a), while commending Italy for

---

1 Law of 3 March 2009 No 18 *'Ratifica ed esecuzione della Convenzione delle Nazioni Unite sui diritti delle persone con disabilità, con Protocollo opzionale, fatta a New York il 13 dicembre 2006 e istituzione dell'Osservatorio nazionale sulla condizione delle persone con disabilità'* in *Gazzetta Ufficiale* (OJ) of 14 March 2009 No 6.

the long-standing commitment in realizing inclusive education for persons with disabilities, has also identified legislative gaps and practical challenges to be addressed in order to fully implement Article 24 CRPD.

In 2014, a new2 reorganisation of the Italian educational system was triggered under the government led by Prime Minister Matteo Renzi. The Law No. 107/2015,[3] so called "*LaBuonaScuola*" (TheGoodSchool) has commenced a process of reform of various aspects of the educational provision in order to improve its efficiency, to enhance autonomy of schools (Cocconi 2015a, 2015b), and to boost the overall quality of education. It has set forth the criteria and principles that the Government must follow when adopting legislative decrees that regulate specific aspects of the educational system. Law No. 107/2015 also has *inter alia* engaged with many aspects related to the education of students with disabilities, empowering the Government to adopt a legislative decree on inclusive education. This Decree (No 66/2017)[4] on inclusive education was finally adopted in April 2017, after a relatively long and somewhat troubled process. Against this background, this article, building upon previous research (Ferri 2017, 2018a), aims to discuss the innovations brought by the Law No 107/2015 and its implementing Legislative Decree No. 66/2017, situating them in the broader Italian legislative framework. By focusing on Italy as a case-study, it endevours to provide a timely reflection on the challenges surrounding the creation of an inclusionary educational system that goes beyond a mere integration in mainstream schools and ensures full and effective participation of all learners as envisaged by Article 24 CRPD. After this introduction, the remainder of this article is divided into five sections. Building on the broad array of literature on the topic (Arnardóttir 2011; Broderick 2014; De Beco 2014; Shaw 2014; Cera 2015; Della Fina 2017), Section 2 begins with a short account of the obligations laid down in Article 24 CRPD, and examines the normative meaning of the concept of "inclusive education" purported by this provision. Section 3 briefly presents the Italian legal framework on the right to education of persons with disabilities. Section 4 discusses the most salient features of educational policy for persons with disabilities, and critically analyses its practical implementation in light of domestic case law. Section 5 examines the most recent developments: the new Law No. 107/2015 and the Legislative Decree No. 66/2017. This section does not discuss the new reform in its entirety. Rather it focuses on those provisions that purport innovations in respect to the inclusion of pupils with disabilities in schools. Taking into account the extreme complexity and intricacy of the Italian system, the section does not delve into the technicalities of the Decree, but aims to highlight in a general fashion some of the most notable provisions, assessing them vis a vis Article 24 CRPD. Section 6 concludes by reflecting on the challenges in the implementation of an inclusive and rights-based educational system encountered in Italy and by highlighting the extent to which the new Italian legislation might provide an example of good practice to other States Parties.

2. The Right to Inclusive Education in the UN Convention on the Rights of Persons with Disabilities

2.1. Inclusive Education in Article 24 CRPD

The CRPD recasts disability as a social construction and "brings a human rights dimension to disability issues" (De Beco 2014, p. 269). It embraces the view that disability stems primarily from the failure of the social environment to meet the needs and aspirations of people with disabilities, and is underpinned by the principles of non-discrimination and equality, which encompass the right to reasonable accommodation (Seatzu 2008; Kayess and French 2008). Its innovative character arises from its elaboration of existing human rights within the disability context. The CRPD does not simply

2 The Renzi reform is the latest (and probably the most ambitious) of a series of reforms of the educational system that have been launched since the late '1990s. An account of these reforms until 2011 has been traced by Grimaldi and Serpieri (2012).

3 In OJ of 15 July 2015 No 162.

4 In OJ of 16 May 2017 No. 122.

prohibit discrimination on the grounds of disability, but covers the whole spectrum of civil, political, economic, cultural and social rights. The CRPD specifically proclaims the right of persons with disabilities to education in Article 24. This provision is very wide and must not be interpreted in isolation. Rather, it must be read in conjunction with other rights provided in the text and in light of the general principles of the Convention, enunciated in Article 3.[5] The overall obligation Article 24 purports is the realization of an inclusive education system at all levels.

Article 24 CRPD, which is the first international legally binding instrument to contain a reference to the concept of quality inclusive education (Broderick 2014), builds on established soft law, such as the Jomtien World Declaration on Education for All (1990), the United Nations Standard Rules on Equalization of Opportunities for Persons with Disabilities (1993), and the Salamanca Declaration and Framework for Action (1994). However, Article 24 CRPD does not give a normative definition of inclusive education. The CRPD Committee has tried to fill this *lacuna*. It seems to have embraced the view of inclusion as "a dynamic approach of responding positively to pupil diversity and of seeing individual differences not as problems, but as opportunities for enriching learning", already advanced by the UNESCO (UNESCO 2005, p. 12), and has conceptualised inclusive education (CRPD Committee 2016b, para. 10) as

(a) A fundamental human right of all learners. Notably, education is the right of the individual learner and not, in the case of children, the right of a parent or caregiver. Parental responsibilities in this regard are subordinate to the rights of the child;
(b) A principle that values the well-being of all students, respects their inherent dignity and autonomy, and acknowledges individuals' requirements and their ability to effectively be included in and contribute to society;
(c) A means of realizing other human rights. It is the primary means by which persons with disabilities can lift themselves out of poverty, obtain the means to participate fully in their communities and be safeguarded from exploitation. It is also the primary means of achieving inclusive societies;
(d) The result of a process of continuing and proactive commitment to eliminating barriers impeding the right to education, together with changes to culture, policy and practice of regular schools to accommodate and effectively include all students.

In its General Comment No 4, the CRPD Committee has also sought to trace the boundaries among the concepts of exclusion, segregation, integration and inclusion in education, and clarified which actions are needed to ensure that children with disabilities participate within the mainstream education system and to fully fulfil the obligation included in Article 24 (CRPD Committee 2016b, para. 11). According to the Committee, exclusion "occurs when students are directly or indirectly prevented from or denied access to education in any form", while segregated education is "provided in separate environments designed or used to respond to a particular or various impairments, in isolation from students without disabilities". The Committee also contrasted integration as a "process of placing persons with disabilities in existing mainstream educational institutions, as long as the former can adjust to the standardized requirements of such institutions", with inclusion. The latter "involves a process of systemic reform embodying changes and modifications in content, teaching methods, approaches, structures and strategies in education to overcome barriers with a vision serving to provide all students of the relevant age range with an equitable and participatory learning experience and environment that best corresponds to their requirements and preferences". The Committee also made it clear that placing students with disabilities within mainstream schools, without accompanying support

[5] Article 3 enunciates the Convention's general principles, which include: respect for individual dignity, autonomy, and independence; respect for difference and acceptance of disability as human diversity; non-discrimination; equal opportunity; complete and meaningful participation; accessibility; gender equality; and respect for children's rights and support for their evolving capabilities.

and structural changes to the curriculum and teaching and learning strategies, does not accomplish the obligations laid down in Article 24 CRPD.

As highlighted by De Beco (2014, p. 287) Article 24 CRPD closely follows the social model of disability, since it requires Parties to achieve a truly inclusive non-discriminatory educational system by removing all the barriers to participation. In other words, in order to achieve an inclusive educational system States Parties must ensure that persons with disabilities can access an inclusive, quality and free primary and secondary education on an equal basis with others.

2.2. Overview of the Obligations of States Parties under Article 24 CRPD

Article 24(1) CRPD requires States Parties to guarantee inclusive education for all persons with disabilities at all levels and to ensure inclusive lifelong learning opportunities. Article 24(2) lists a series of measures that States Parties are required to adopt to create an inclusive educational system. As noted in a study of the Office of the High Commissioner for Human Rights (OHCHR 2013), these measures are not to be read separately one another, rather must be interpreted jointly, and in light of other provisions of the Convention. Without providing a detailed discussion (for further details see: (Della Fina 2017; Broderick 2014)), we limit ourselves to highlight that Article 24(2)(b) CRPD, read in conjunction with the general principle of accessibility, prescribes that the entire education system is accessible, "including buildings, information and communication, comprising ambient or frequency modulation assistive systems, curriculum, education materials, teaching methods, assessment and language and support services". An inclusive system should reflect "Universal Design", which is recognised by the CRPD, and should be accessible to all students, to the greatest extent possible, without the need for specific adaptation. However, reasonable accommodation must be provided to students with disabilities when needed (Article 24(2)(c) CRPD), together with "effective individualized support measures ... in environments that maximize academic and social development, consistent with the goal of full inclusion" (Article 24(2)(e) CRPD). Reasonable accommodation is designed to meet the specific needs of a person with a disability in a particular case, and concerned with the removal of the specific disadvantage to which a disabled student would otherwise be subjected by standard educational practices or systems. The CRPD Committee has clarified that accommodations include "changing the location of a class, providing different forms of in-class communication, enlarging print, materials and/or subjects in sign, or providing all handouts in an alternative format, providing students with a note-taker, or a language interpreter or allowing students to use assistive technology in learning and assessment situations" or "allowing a student more time, reducing levels of background noise" (CRPD Committee 2016b, para. 30). Support measures appear to be methods that "supplement the reasonable accommodations and add a human rights dimension to the right to education of persons with disabilities" (De Beco 2014). Examples of the latter according to the Committee are "the provision of sufficient trained and supported teaching staff, school counsellors, psychologists, and other relevant health and social service professionals, as well as access to scholarships and financial resources" (CRPD Committee 2016b, para. 32).

Article 24(3) CRPD requires State Parties to "enable persons with disabilities to learn life and social development skills to facilitate their full and equal participation in education", including Braille and sign-language, and to "train professionals and staff who work at all levels of education". Notably, this provision places a specific emphasis on the promotion of the linguistic identity of Deaf people, which is also mentioned in Article 30(4) CRPD[6]. According to Della Fina (2017, p. 455), the purpose of Article 24(3) is to guarantee that people with sensory impairments are not excluded from the

---

6 Article 30 CRPD, which provides the right of persons with disabilities to participate in cultural life, requires Parties to the Convention to take all appropriate measures to ensure that persons with disabilities have access to cultural materials, television programmes, films, theatre and other cultural activities, but also to places for cultural performances or services, monuments and sites. This Article provides for recognition and support of specific cultural and linguistic identity of persons with disabilities, including sign languages and deaf culture (for further discussion see (Ferri 2014)).

mainstream education system and receive instruction in the appropriate languages, modes, and means of communication in environments that maximize their development. This provision sets forth the only exception to inclusive education, allowing the education of blind, deaf, and deafblind children in special schools (Della Fina 2017; De Beco 2014; Broderick 2014). As discussed by Arnardóttir (2011), Article 24 CRPD confers the right to *choose* an inclusive education, thus attempting to strike a balance between the goal of full inclusion and the need, in very limited cases, of special education to meet specific needs of learners with disabilities.

Article 24(4) CRPD requires States Parties to take appropriate measures to employ qualified teachers having skills to teach in an inclusive environment. The CRPD Committee has stated that to fully implement this particular obligation, "States parties must ensure that all teachers are trained in inclusive education and that that training is based on the human rights model of disability" (CRPD Committee 2016b, para. 36). It has also affirmed that

> States parties must invest in and support the recruitment and continuous education of teachers with disabilities. This includes removing any legislative or policy barriers requiring candidates to fulfil specific medical eligibility criteria and the provision of reasonable accommodations for their participation as teachers. Their presence will serve to promote equal rights for persons with disabilities to enter the teaching profession, bring unique expertise and skills into learning environments, contribute to breaking down barriers and serve as important role models. (CRPD Committee 2016b, para. 37)

Lastly, Article 24(5) CRPD reaffirms the right of persons with disabilities to access to general tertiary education, vocational training, adult education and lifelong learning, on an equal basis with others.

All in all, Article 24 CRPD adopts a holistic approach (Palmer 2013). It places on State Parties various obligations, which require them to value the diversity of students with disabilities and to support different abilities in mainstream schools. While being subject to progressive realization within the maximum available resources, as stated by Article 4(2) CRPD, the implementation of the right to education must in fact be assured through the effective allocation of adequate financial and human resources, and the establishment of monitoring mechanisms (Broderick 2014).

3. The Right to Education of Persons with Disabilities in Italy: Overview of the Legal Framework

3.1. The Constitutional Framework

The general principle of protection and promotion of the rights of persons with disabilities, and in particular of their right to education, is anchored to Article 2 of the Italian Constitution (IC), which recognizes and guarantees "the inviolable rights of the person, both as an individual and in the social groups where human personality is expressed".[7] It is also informed by Article 3(1) IC, that provides for the principle of non-discrimination on the grounds of sex, race, language, religion, political opinion, and personal and social conditions, and by Article 3(2) IC, which establishes the principle of substantive equality. According to the latter provision, the State is called to remove the social and economic obstacles that limit the freedom and equality of the citizens and prevent the full development of the human being.

The right to education of persons with disabilities stems from different constitutional provisions, which must be read in combination, in light of the constitutional principles laid out in Articles 2 and 3 IC. Article 33 IC obliges the State to provide a State-school system accessible to all children and affirms the freedom for organisations and individuals to set up private schools with no cost for the

---

7 The English translation of the Italian Constitution is published by the Parliamentary Information, Archives and Publications Office of the Senate Service for Official Reports and Communication and can be found at http://www.senato.it/documenti/repository/istituzione/costituzione_inglese.pdf (accessed on 1 September 2017).

State. Article 34 IC establishes in general terms that "[s]chools are open to everyone", and that primary education, offered for at least eight years, is compulsory and free of tuition fees. Article 38(3) IC affirms that "disabled and handicapped persons are entitled to receive education and vocational training". A wide interpretation of the latter provision in combination with Articles 2 and 3 IC, has led the Italian Constitutional Court to shift from a paternalistic-charitable model of care to a social model oriented view of disability around the mid-eighties, and to spell out a wide-ranging right to inclusive education for people with disabilities (Colapietro 2011).

Since Italy is a regional State, besides the abovementioned provisions concerning the right to education, the IC sets forth the division of competence over educational matters between the State and the Regions. Art 117(1)(n) IC confers on the State the exclusive power to lay down "general provisions on education".[8] The Constitutional Court has established that these "general provisions on education" are concerned with the "basic characteristics" of the educational system,[9] and comprise: the general organisation of the system, the protection and promotion of the autonomy of each educational institution (Cocconi 2015b), the freedom to open private schools and parity between public and private (non-governmental) schools, minimum numbers of school hours per year, the teacher/student ratio, State financial resources, and also the inclusion of people with disabilities (Troilo 2012). When legislating on the basic characteristics of the school system, the State also addresses (and manages through the Ministry of Education, University and Research), two core components: teachers' qualifications and recruitment, as well as salaries.[10]

3.2. The Right to Education of Students with Disabilities in National Legislation

Within this constitutional framework, and long before the approval of the CRPD, when the global scene was still dominated by segregation policies, Italy represented an exceptional example of non-discriminatory educational legislation. The first provisions laying down the conditions and instruments necessary to ensure school integration of pupils with disabilities date back to the 70s. In particular Art. 28 of Law No. 118/71,[11] as interpreted by the Italian Constitutional Court in its decision No. 215/1987, and Law No. 517/77[12] (Addis 2015). The latter piece of legislation has been deemed to purport a change in society by stimulating acceptance of disability as part of human diversity (OECD 2007).

Law No. 104/1992 ("Framework Law for Care, Social Integration and Rights of Persons with Disabilities"),[13] which aims to remove obstacles, improve access and make it possible for disabled people to enjoy mainstream services and facilities (Siclari 2015), re-affirms the right to education and pursues "*integrazione scolastica*" in order to develop the abilities of person with disabilities. This piece of legislation also requires individualized plans for students with disabilities (*Piano educativo individualizzato—PEI*)[14] and the supply of didactic tools and assistive technology to schools, as well as

---

8 This Article must be read in conjunction with Article 33(3) IC that affirms that '[t]he Republic lays down general rules for education'.

9 Italian Constitutional Court, Judgment No 200/2009.

10 In addition, Art 117(1)(m) IC empowers the State to determine 'the basic level of benefits relating to civil and social entitlements to be guaranteed throughout the national territory'. The latter competence is aimed at ensuring equality of treatment among users who benefit from the educational services (and more generally social services) across the national territory. Such a cross-cutting national competence implies that whenever a regional law provides for benefits related to social rights (including the right to education), it must be subordinated to the national law that establishes the minimum standards with regard to those rights.

11 Law of 30 March 1971 No. 118, 'Conversione in legge del D.L. 30 gennaio 1971 n. 5 e nuove norme in favore dei mutilati ed invalidi civili' in OJ 2 April 1971 No 82.

12 Law of 4 August 1977 No 517 '*Norme sulla valutazione degli alunni e sull'abolizione degli esami di riparazione nonché altre norme di modifica dell'ordinamento scolastico*' in OJ 18 August 1977 No 224.

13 Law of 5 February 1992 No 104, '*Legge-quadro per l'assistenza, l'integrazione sociale e i diritti delle persone handicappate*' in OJ 17 February 1992 No 39.

14 This article will use the Italian acronym *PEI* in subsequent sections, as the acronym is commonly used in Italian scholarship on the topic.

other forms of technical assistance, when needed. Inclusion is, in practice, ensured by support teachers who provide additional individual instruction and educational support in order to meet the needs of each student with a disability.[15] As national courts have affirmed in different occasions, the support teacher's role is complementary to that of the classroom teacher (Manca 2010, pp. 337–38). Law No. 104/1992 also recognizes homeschooling for those who are temporarily unable to attend school.

In 2010, Law No. 170/2010[16] was passed in order to ensure the right to education to children with "specific learning difficulties" (*Difficoltà Specifiche di Apprendimento*—DSA), i.e., children with difficulties in reading (Dyslexia), writing (Graphic Dyslogia and Dysorthography), or in computing (Discalculia or numeracy problems). The general objective of this act is to give these children equal educational opportunities to successful and efficient education in accordance with their needs and abilities in mainstream schools, implementing teachers' preparation, ensuring a collaboration among teachers, parents and experts of the health services, envisaging targeted flexible educational plans. This law affirms the need for specialized training for teachers in supporting learners with these disabilities, recognizing that it is one of the major challenges to the full and effective inclusion of persons with disabilities in the education system.

Since its inception, no major changes to this framework have been introduced. The main previous reform of the education system (Law No 53/2003[17]) did not include any specific provision on the education of people with disabilities, and limited itself to making explicit reference to Law No 104/1992. In 2008, the Budget Law 2008,[18] as part of general austerity measures and budget cuts, fixed a maximum number of support teachers for children with disabilities who attend classes in public schools, and abolished the possibility (provided for in Article 40(l) of Law No 104/1992) of hiring additional support teachers under fixed-term contracts, who would provide specific educational assistance to children with severe disabilities. However, these provisos were referred to the Italian Constitutional Court (ICC) upon the request of the Sicilian Administrative Council. In its judgment, No 80/2010, the ICC declared them unconstitutional and affirmed that they infringed the fundamental right of education of children with disabilities, set forth in Art 38(3)(4) IC, and violated the principle of equality. Interestingly, the ICC in defining the 'content' of the fundamental right to education for persons with disabilities referred to Article 24 CRPD, in support of its reasoning. Overall, the Court argued that the core minimum guarantees to make the right to education of students with disabilities effective cannot be subject to financial conditions. The ICC pointed out that it is for the legislature to provide appropriate tools to implement the right to education, but underlined that legislative provisions cannot undermine the realisation of a fundamental right by making it conditional on the availability of financial resources (Ferri 2014, 2018b; Ferrari 2012). A recent case, which was decided by the ICC, reaffirmed that the right to education of people with disabilities must be effectively ensured, and that financial constraints cannot undermine the enjoyment of this fundamental right for people with disabilities.[19] In essence, the ICC reiterated that a formal recognition of the right by the legislation is not sufficient if the right is not guaranteed in practice (Blando 2017). The case concerned the transport of students with disabilities to school and their assistance. The Abruzzo regional law provided for a grant to be given to local authorities so that they could ensure transport and assistance to students with disabilities only "within the limits of available funds determined by the annual budget law". In doing so, the law made the regional contribution aimed at implementing the right of students with disabilities to transport services conditional and subject to budget constraints. The ICC, in line with its decision No. 80/2010, held

---

15 Support teachers are qualified teachers who must also obtain further specialized postgraduate training, the requirements of which are established in various bylaws, mainly ministerial decrees.

16 Law of 8 October 2010 No 170 '*Nuove norme in materia di disturbi specifici di apprendimento in ambito scolastico*' in OJ 18 October 2010 No 244.

17 Law of 28 March 2003 No 53 '*Delega al Governo per la definizione delle norme generali sull'istruzione e dei livelli essenziali delle prestazioni in materia di istruzione e di formazione professionale*' in OJ 2 April 2003 No 77.

18 Namely Art 2 paras 413 and 414 of the Law 24 December 2007 No 244 in OJ 28 December 2007 No 285.

19 Italian Constitutional Court, Judgment No 275/2016.

the regional provision to be unconstitutional. In particular, the Court believed that transportation services for students with disabilities are necessary to guarantee the right to inclusion for persons with disabilities and are an essential element in ensuring the participation of these pupils within the educational process.

4. Italian Educational Policies in a Nutshell and Their (Challenging) Implementation

In spite of the progressive legislative framework, highlighted above, and despite the role played by the ICC in safeguarding the full enjoyment of the right to education for students with disabilities, territorial divides (ISTAT 2016) and flaws have emerged in educational provision and in the actual implementation of Law No. 104/1992.

Territorial differences and mixed practices are partially due to the fact that Italian educational policy system is highly decentralised, and informed by the principle of subsidiarity and the principle of autonomy of schools and educational institutions.[20] The Ministry of Education, University and Research (*MIUR*) is generally responsible for educational policy at a national level. Regional School Offices—RSOs, local authorities and schools play a substantive role in the actual provision of educational services. Schools, in particular, are ultimately responsible for the practical implementation of inclusive education. They define curricula and educational offerings, organise teaching, assign support teachers, allocate hours of support and lay down the individualized education plan (*PEI*). Empirical research has shown that the autonomy of schools has *de facto* led to inclusive practices to be extremely heterogeneous across the territory (Anastasiou et al. 2015). In 2009, after the ratification of the CRPD, the Ministry adopted new "Guidelines on School Inclusion of Pupils with disabilities",[21] which collate a set of recommendations to improve the inclusion of children with disabilities (inspired by the CRPD), and to orient the action of both RSOs, and schools. Despite these guidelines and the MIUR's attempt to centrally orient the action of schools, Dovigo (2016) affirms that inclusion too often depends on the single educational setting, on "local customs". This author also claims that inclusive education is essentially "shaped" by individual school managers and teachers, and the interpretation of what constitutes an inclusive setting "differs widely among schools, and sometimes even among classes in the same school".

Statistic data have shown that there are gaps in educational provision and a lack of continuity in the support provided by teachers in schools (ISTAT 2016; Ferri 2018a). Lack of continuity in the support offered by support teachers is also due to the fact roughly 30% of support teachers ask for redeployment as main classroom teachers five years after obtaining their qualification (Devecchi et al. 2012). The reasons behind requests of redeployment are various, but educational research highlights that working conditions of support teachers are often draining and relationship with children, families, other teachers, and other professionals is, in several cases, problematic (Devecchi et al. 2012; Ianes et al. 2014).

Limited gaps in the legislation have emerged mainly in regards to accessibility of information and communication and accessibility of educational content, and in respect to the lack of legal recognition of alternatives modes of communication (CSS 2016), and Italian Sign language (*Lingua Italiana dei Segni—LIS*). The CRPD Committee, in its COs to the Italian Initial Report on the implementation of the Convention (CRPD Committee 2016a), also highlighted the lack of availability with regard to accessible learning materials and the lack of assistive technology. In addition, the Committee acknowledged that deaf children are not provided with *LIS* interpreters in school, and recommended Italy "desist from recommending general communication assistants as an exclusive alternative".

The most serious flaws concern the lack of provision of adequate support to students and are due to the failure to properly implement the legislation in place. This has been highlighted by the shadow

---

[20] These principles are established in the Italian Constitution. The principle of autonomy of schools is implemented by means of the Decree of the President of the Republic No 275 of 8 March 1999 in OJ 10 August 1999 No 186 providing schools with didactic, organisational and research autonomy.

[21] *Ministero dell'Istruzione*, Prot.n 4274.

report on the implementation of the CRPD of the Italian Disability Forum to the CRPD Committee (IDF 2016a, 2016b). The Italian National Observatory on the Situation of Persons with Disabilities[22] also underlined need to improve the operation of the existing system, and to make sure that the right to inclusive education is fully enjoyed by people with disabilities in practice in their everyday life.[23] Gaps have emerged through a series of court cases, mostly initiated by parents of children with learning or intellectual disabilities, in which the parents challenged the appropriateness of existing provision for their children. The National Statistic Office (ISTAT) detected that approximately 8% of families of primary school pupils and 5% of those in the secondary school level have appealed to the District Court or the Regional Administrative Court to obtain an increase in support hours. In almost all the cases that ended up in Italian administrative courts, the applicants asked for the annulment of the individual educational plan (*PEI*) adopted by the public educational institution limiting the number of support teacher hours available to the relevant student (Lottini 2011). Usually, the applicants claimed their right to benefit from the support teacher either for a greater amount of time or for the entire time of school attendance. In some cases, the applicant alleged *inter alia* the violation of the CRPD as ratified by Law No 18/2009.[24] In the majority of cases, administrative courts have annulled the contested measures and held that the *'quantum'* of the teaching support essential to enjoying that right has to be determined exclusively in relation to the need of the student with disabilities, and no other interests can be taken into consideration, not even in case of understaffed administrations.[25] In general, the ordinary district courts were asked to decide cases in which the applicants had filed a complaint outlining discrimination on the grounds of disability. Primarily, the applicants challenged decisions made by public schools to reduce the employment contract of a support teacher to a limited number of hours due to budgetary concerns, and maintained that these constituted an unlawful discrimination and infringements of the fundamental right to education. So far, Italian courts have held that the constitutional and legislative framework in place, read in conjunction or in light of the CRPD, effectively guarantees disabled students the support measures necessary to substantially enjoy the right to education, but make evident a failure to properly implement the legislation in force (Ferri 2017, 2018a, 2018b).

5. The Reform of the Educational System and Inclusive Education: A Step Change?

5.1. Law No. 107/2015 and Inclusive Education

As mentioned above in the Introduction, in September 2014, the Italian Government initiated a process of modernization of the whole Italian educational system and put on the table an additional funding of €3 billion to recruit school teachers and additional staff, but also to innovate facilities and introduce high-speed internet and Wi-Fi in all schools. Law No. 107/2015 (*Riforma del sistema nazionale di istruzione e formazione e delega per il riordino delle disposizioni legislative vigenti)*, so called

---

22 The Italian National Observatory on the Situation of Persons with Disabilities (*Osservatorio Nazionale sulla condizione delle persone con disabilità*) was created in order to implement Article 33(2) CRPD. It was meant to constitute the independent mechanism, but is organisationally placed within the Ministry of Labour and Social Policies, which finances it, and is chaired by the Ministry. It includes representatives of various ministries, including the MIUR, local authorities, Social Security Institutions, the National Statistics Institute, social partners (trade unions and industry organisations), as well as independent experts and DPOs. While it has monitoring tasks, the National Observatory is also a consultative body in charge of technical support for the elaboration and supervision of national disability policies. It promotes the implementation of the Convention, and prepares cross-cutting biannual action plans for promoting the rights of persons with disabilities across the whole range of policies, with a view to achieving the objectives established by the CRPD and by the European Disability Strategy. The First Bi-annual Action Plan on Disability was adopted by the National Observatory in 2013 (Decree of the President of the Republic of 4 October 2013 *'Programma di azione biennale per la promozione dei diritti e l'integrazione delle persone con disabilita'* OJ 28 December 2013 No 303).

23 Decree of the President of the Republic of 4 October 2013 *'Programma di azione biennale per la promozione dei diritti e l'integrazione delle persone con disabilita'* OJ 28 December 2013 No 303.

24 E.g., TAR Lombardia, Sez. 3, No 1895/2014.

25 E.g., TAR Calabria, Sez. 3, No 831/2011.

"LaBuonaScuola" (TheGoodSchool) has started an overall reform of Italian schools touching upon different aspects of the educational provision, including that of inclusive education (Cocconi 2015a). Being a delegation law,[26] Law No. 107/2015 provides for general principles and benchmarks that the Government must respect and follow when adopting legislative decrees (which have the same rank as ordinary laws) laying down detailed provisions.

Law No. 107/2015, along the lines traced by Law No. 104/1992, and similarly to its predecessors, aims to ensure that persons with disabilities are not excluded from the mainstream education system on the basis of disability, but included into regular schools and provided with adequate support for their inclusion. It is evident that this reform Law situates itself in continuity with precedent legislation on education and must be read in light and in combination with Law No. 104/1992.[27] Under Law No. 107/2015, schools remains responsible for defining educational offerings, organising teaching, assigning support teachers, allocating hours of support and laying down the *PEI* for each student with a disability. Article 1(14) of Law No 107/2015 requires schools to take into account the number of students with disabilities when indicating the overall number of support teachers needed and when organizing teaching activities. School directors have the power to reduce the number of students per class "in order to improve the teaching quality, also in relation to the needs of pupils with disabilities" (Art. 1(84)). These provisions are clearly aimed to ensure an effective education for students with disabilities. They seem, as envisaged by the CRPD Committee,[28] to require schools to fully respect the well-being of all students and to adequately assess the individuals' requirements and needs.

Article 1(24) of the Law explicitly states that teaching provided to students with disabilities will be ensured through the recognition of different modes of communication. Law No 104/1992 refers, in Article 13(1)(a), to assistive and technical devices to ensure the right to education, and, in Article 13(3) includes a generic reference to the duty of schools to provide "assistance for the autonomy and personal communication of pupils with physical or sensory handicaps". However, it does not mention augmentative and alternative forms of communication. Hence, Article 1(24) seems to fill a legal vacuum and appears to be innovative. It seems also to implement (at least partially) the obligation included in Article 24(3) CRPD. This provision could also be seen as a gateway to ensure *LIS* interpreters in schools, which had been so far neglected, as noted by the CRPD Committee (CRPD Committee 2016a).[29] This provision will soon be complemented by the law on the formal recognition of LIS and of Deaf people as a linguistic community, currently under discussion in the Italian parliament.[30] Once approved, this law will further guarantee the teaching of the sign language in primary and secondary primary schools, as well as the use of the *LIS* interpreters in high schools and universities. Regrettably, Article 1(24) makes it clear that the implementation of different communication modes must occur "without new or increased burdens on public finance". Interestingly, this formulation is very similar to the one adopted in respect to reasonable accommodations in public employment contexts. It is worth recalling that reasonable accommodation duties were included in anti-discrimination legislation only in 2013 (Ferri and Lawson 2016),[31] following the ruling of the CJEU in *Commission v Italy*.[32] The new provision

---

26 Article 76 of the Italian Constitution allows the Government to exercise legislative functions only when delegated by Parliament for a limited time and for specified purposes. The Parliament delegates to the Government the exercise of legislative functions through a delegation law that establishes the principles and criteria that the Government must follow and comply with when exercising the legislative function. The delegation law empowers the Government to adopt one or more legislative decrees, which are deliberated upon by the Council of Ministers.

27 It is important to note that the La 104/1992 remains the cornerstone of Italian disability law and policy, and the point of reference for any legislative reform which touches upon the rights of persons with disabilities.

28 See *supra* Section 2.

29 See above Section 4.

30 The bill was approved on the 3rd of October 2017 by the Italian Senate, is now under the examination of the Chamber of Deputies.

31 Law decree 28 June 2013 No. 76, OJ No 150 of 28 June 2013, then converted into Law 9 August 2013, No. 99, G.U. of 22 August 2013, No. 196, concerning 'Preliminary Urgent Measures for the promotion of employment, in particular of youngsters, of social cohesion and on and other Urgent financial measures'.

32 Commission v Italy, Case C-312/11, 4 July 2013, not yet published.

requires employers to adopt reasonable accommodations, however public employers must implement the duty "without new or increased burdens on public finance and human resources, financial and available under current legislation". This latter provision and Article 1(24) of Law No 107/2015 are clearly dictated by the very same need to contain public expenditures, in a time of harsh economic crisis. However, it is doubtful that such prescriptions comply with the CRPD.[33]

As mentioned above, Law No 107/2015 has empowered the Government to adopt a detailed legislative decree to promote the inclusion of students with disabilities in schools. Article 1(181) gives the mandate to the Government to adopt specific norms on inclusive education and reiterates the commitment towards the realization of a truly inclusive educational system within the legislative framework laid down in Law No 104/1992. It also restates the role of support teachers as the cornerstone of the Italian inclusive educational system. However, it calls the Government to redefine the role of the support teacher and of teaching staff to foster inclusion of students with disabilities, and to reform training and qualification systems for teachers. Article 1(181) also requires the Government to set forth specific provisions to ensure that curricular teachers, schools principals, and administrative staff undertake training on inclusion, thus recognizing that often one of the most obvious barriers to inclusive education are the lack of awareness and adequate training of school staff. Law No 107/2015 also takes stock the systemic flaws emerged in practice, such as the lack of continuity in the support offered by support teachers, and Article 1(181) requires the Government to make sure that pupils to enjoy the same support teacher across the course of their studies. Finally, Law No 107/2015 recognizes the dearth of data on inclusion and Article 1(181) calls the Government on elaborating specific indicators to evaluate the level of school inclusion. This latter aspect could help overcome the criticism expressed by the CRPD Committee in its COs (CRPD Committee 2016a) in relation to the lack of reliable data on the quality of education and the inclusion of students with disabilities. All in all, Article 1(181) of Law 107/2015 has given the Government a clear mandate to innovate the way in which the educational provision is administered, and to improve the way in which inclusive education is realized.

5.2. Legislative Decree No. 66/2017 on the Promotion of School Inclusion for Students with Disabilities: Lights and Shadows

Legislative Decree No. 66/2017 on school inclusion for students with disabilities (Norme per la promozione dell'inclusione scolastica degli studenti con disabilita', a norma dell'articolo 1, commi 180 e 181, lettera c), della legge 13 luglio 2015, n. 107) was approved on the 7th April 2017 and entered into force in May 2017. The process of approval was relatively short, but not smooth. The initial draft decree released by the Government on the 14th January 2017 was severely criticised by DPOs, which also questioned their lack of involvement in the process of elaboration of the text (Ferri 2018a), and encountered fierce opposition outside parliament from trade unions. In February 2017, the newly appointed Minster for Education declared that the text of the draft was to be modified in order to take into account the criticism raised, and claimed that inclusion remains a priority for the government (Ufficio Stampa MIUR 2017). On 16th March 2017, the Parliamentary Commissions in charge of the examination of the draft decree released a positive opinion on it, suggesting additional few modifications. The final text, composed by 20 articles preceded by a Preamble, along the lines traced by the Law No 107/2015, regulates the performance and quality of school inclusion indicators; certification procedures for school inclusion; school organisation, resource allocation; planning and design inclusion; and initial training of teachers for educational support. It attempts to implement the obligations laid down in the CRPD, which is mentioned in the Preamble, just after the relevant provisions of the Italian Constitution. Some provisions of the Decree have a limited innovative character, being more aimed to clarify and put order in what was already provided in various and scattered existing pieces

[33] It also doubtful that Article 1(24) could survive a constitutional review if a case is brought, as the ICC has so far been quite clear in stating that financial constraints cannot be used as an excuse to undermine the enjoyment of the fundamental right to education.

of legislation. This is for instance the case of Article 3, which better defines the role of local and regional entities in the provision of inclusive educational settings. The Decree however, presents undoubtedly, a number of positive innovative features, which nevertheless bring limited changes to the current system.

Article 1 of the Decree laying down the aims of the decree, attempts to define "inclusive education" and affirms that it "concerns all pupils and students, meets the different educational needs and is accomplished through educational and teaching strategies aimed at developing the potential of each individual" (Article 1(1)(a)). Significantly, the Decree uses only and quite consistently the term "inclusion", and defines it in manner that can be considered compliant to the CRPD. In this respect, the Decree makes a clear attempt, on the one hand, to avoid the use of the word "school integration" (*integrazione scolastica*) used in former legislation, and, on the other hand, to fully align the terminology used by Italian law with the wording of the CRPD. The CRPD Committee has contrasted integration, as a process of placing persons with disabilities in existing mainstream educational institutions without adjustments, with inclusion (CRPD Committee 2016b). Arguably, the Decree aims to put an end at the blurring and interchangeable use of those different terms in Italian laws and policies (*inter alia* D'Alessio 2011, 2013), and to place Italian educational policies in line with the CRPD, by recalling the role of accommodating different educational needs. The wording of Article 1 evokes Article 24(2)(e) CRPD, and the obligation to provide students with disability with access to "effective individualized support measures [...] in environments that maximize academic and social development, consistent with the goal of full inclusion". The Decree, in Article 1(1)(c), also affirms that inclusive education is a "fundamental commitment" for all those who participate in the educational settings. This alinea somewhat matches the words of the CRPD Committee that defined inclusive education as "the result of a process of continuing and proactive commitment to eliminating barriers impeding the right to education" (CRPD Committee 2016a).[34]

Article 2(2) states that inclusion is realised through the definition of the *PEI*. In this respect, unsurprisingly, Decree No 66/2017 locates itself in continuity with Law No. 104/1992, which already prescribed the adoption of the *PEI* as inclusion tool. The rationale behind the *PEI* is that of tailoring educational strategies and tools on the need of the student with disability, and to offer students an effective education, as prescribed by Article 24 CRPD. The Decree, however, clarifies that the number of hours of support enjoyed by the student will be decided by the school director only after the *PEI* is laid down and adopted in collaboration with the family. The number of hours, hence, will not anymore be included in the *PEI* itself, which will only highlight in general terms the support needed to adequately foster the potential of the student. This innovation seems clearly aimed to limit the complaints to courts and to put an end to the avalanche of judicial cases seeking the annulment of *PEI* in front of administrative courts because of the insufficient number of hours assigned to the student. This innovation leaves to the school greater autonomy, but also greater discretion in deciding the amount of hours of support after the *PEI* is adopted. This discretion is likely to escape the limit of judicial review of administrative courts.

In addition, by virtue of Article 7(2)(h) of the Decree, the *PEI* must be subject to "to periodic reviews during the year in order to ascertain the achievement of objectives and make any changes" which may prove necessary. The *PEI* has now become integral part of the broader "Individual Project" for the person with a disability, which is elaborated by the (territorially competent) local authority and is meant to tailor health and social services to the specific needs of the person. The Decree, hence, explicitly locates inclusive education within a broader individual strategy to ensure social inclusion and independent living for people with disabilities. The "Individual Project" was already prescribed by Article 14 of the Framework Law No 328/2000[35] concerning social services addressed to individuals

---

[34] See above Section 2.

[35] Law of 8 November 2000 No 328 *'Legge quadro per la realizzazione del sistema integrato di interventi e servizi sociali'* in G.U. of 13 November 2000 No 265.

and household, with a view to ensure " ... full integration of disabled people in family and social life, as well as in educational and vocational education and training". It is now mentioned Article 1(1)(b), which clarifies the important role of schools in the elaboration of the overall individual project, in collaboration with families, DPOs, and local authorities.[36]

Interestingly, Article 1(1) also mentions reasonable accommodation as an essential component of inclusive education. The wording of this provision is explicitly inspired by the CRPD, and highly innovative. In fact, although forms of reasonable accommodation were not unknown in the school system (Ferri 2018b), previous Italian legislation on education did not mention neither define this concept.

Another significant novelty is that the number of pupils with disabilities and their gender will be considered when establishing the number of non-teaching staff for each school (Article 3(2)(b) and (c)). According to Cocconi (2017), this means that the needs of students with disabilities must be seriously and effectively taken into account when allocating administrative and teaching staff to each school institution. The reference to gender seems quite notable as it is clearly meant to tackle intersectional disadvantage, in compliance with Article 6 CRPD.[37] In addition, this provision confirms that education provision cannot be governed just on the basis of efficiency and financial viability, but must respond to the needs of students, especially those with disabilities. It limits the discretion of State in identifying the necessary organizational, financial and personal resources.

Notably, school inclusion will now form integral part of the overall evaluation process of the quality of school institutions. In other words, the level of inclusiveness of the school will become one of the parameter to assess the overall quality of the same school. This is a positive development which must be welcomed as it might potentially nudge schools to pay more attention to the way in which, in practice, they realize inclusive settings.

The Decree, however, presents a few weaknesses. Although the Decree requires all the teachers (curricular teachers) to receive training on inclusive education, their role in enhancing inclusive education remains *de facto* marginal, being that mostly ensured by the support teacher. It is also unclear what training curricular teachers are in fact expected to undertake. Article 12 lays down rules for access to the teaching career for educational support in the kindergarten and primary school, and new requirements for support teachers in secondary schools. It requires support teachers to acquire a more solid grounding in social inclusion, after the achievement of the qualifying degree in education as a basic requirement for the teaching function. This should significantly contribute to improve the quality and inclusiveness of the educational system, but, in reality, the Decree has introduced a distinction between teaching qualifications for primary and secondary schools, whose rationale remains unclear. In addition, the Decree attempts to put an end to the turnover of support teachers that endangers the learning experience of students with disabilities and has long been criticised by parents of students with disabilities. However, Article 14 limits itself to provide a generic obligation to guarantee continuous and stable support to students with disabilities. The main novelty included in Article 14 is that fix-term contracts of fully qualified support teachers can be renewed by the school upon the request of the family of the disabled student. No systemic solutions have been adopted.[38]

---

36 In this respect, Decree No 66/2017 has also intervened to amend Article 14, which, in its revised formulation, establishes that the "Individual Project" includes the care and rehabilitation services provided by the National Health Service, the Individual Education Plan provided by the school institutions, the personal services provided by the local municipality, as well as the economic allowances designed to overcome situations poverty, marginalization and social exclusion. See also Article 6 of Decree No. 66/2017.

37 Article 6 "Women with disabilities" reads as follows: "1. States Parties recognize that women and girls with disabilities are subject to multiple discrimination, and in this regard shall take measures to ensure the full and equal enjoyment by them of all human rights and fundamental freedoms. 2. States Parties shall take all appropriate measures to ensure the full development, advancement and empowerment of women, for the purpose of guaranteeing them the exercise and enjoyment of the human rights and fundamental freedoms set out in the present Convention".

38 The draft text originally included an obligation on support teachers to remain within the role for ten years. The provision raised harsh criticism because, *ex littera lege,* the provision obliged teachers to stay in the support role, but not to remain in the same school or institution, thus being unuseful to ensure continuity of education and unduly forcing teachers to remain in a role. The final text removed this provision.

The most remarkable limit of the Decree (and probably of the whole reform) is, however, that the funding, which has been assigned to concretely implement the provisions included in the Decree, remains limited. The CRPD Committee has identified among the main barriers to the implementation of Article 24 CRPD "inappropriate and inadequate funding mechanisms to provide incentives and reasonable accommodations for the inclusion of students with disabilities" (CRPD Committee 2016b). In a country where education has been traditionally poorly funded, the lack of funding seems to be an obstacle to the full implementation of the CRPD. In this context, the ambitious definition of inclusive education laid down in Article 1 of the Decree runs the risk to remain a paper tiger, and the practical problems encountered so far are likely to remain unsolved.

6. Concluding Remarks

The CRPD Committee, in its General Comment No. 4 (CRPD Committee 2016b), acknowledged that, for many persons with disabilities around the world education is still available only in segregated settings, where they are isolated from their peers and where the education they receive is of an inferior quality. In this respect, it is undeniable that Italy has provided and still provides an important example of non-discriminatory educational system to be looked at (Kanter et al. 2014). Children with disabilities in Italy have the right to access free primary education and secondary education on an equal basis with others, in the communities in which they live. The legislation, as interpreted by the Constitutional Court, ensures to persons with disabilities the effective enjoyment of the right to education. Italian courts have so far acted as watchdogs, and have played a seminal role in unveiling the inefficiencies in the implementation of the legislation. They have provided an important example of the role judicial institutions can play in the realization of more equitable and accessible educational settings, and in ensuring that a progressive legislation is actually implemented.

Despite the important role of courts, as noted by Dovigo (2016), the evolution of the Italian school system shows that the abolition of special schools does not automatically lead to the full, meaningful inclusion of all pupils in mainstream education. The persistent gaps in actually providing an inclusive education emerged in the last few years have thus prompted a legislative reform of the education system. The ratification of the CRPD has also made evident the need to fully align Italian educational policies with Article 24 CRPD. Italy has shown a political commitment to ensure inclusive education, and this cannot go unnoticed. However, the new Law No. 107/2015 and the recent Legislative Decree No. 66/2017 merely attempt, without questioning the system itself, to improve its functionality. In compliance with the principles set forth in Law No 107/2015, Decree No. 66/2017 updates, reorganizes and rationalizes the legal framework in relation to the education of people with disabilities. It introduces some notable changes, but these appear mostly "cosmetic", even though they take into account Article 24 CRPD. The Decree undoubtedly endeavours to meet (some of) the recommendations of the CRPD Committee, and to solve some of the problems that emerged in case law and that were highlighted by DPOs, especially in relation to the practical support ensured to students with disabilities by support teachers. The text presents also weaknesses, especially when it comes to ensuring training for all teachers. Overall, it remains to be seen whether the changes will be sufficient to meet overall goal of creating a truly inclusive system, and how effective the changes introduced will be. In August 2017, the Ministry has clarified that the most innovative provisions (such as those on the *PEI*) will enter into force in 2019. This delay will allow schools to become familiar with the renewed system, and to put in place all the necessary procedural changes. However, it will, once again, postpone the full realization of a truly inclusive system.

All in all, the Italian case-study shows that inclusive education requires continuous efforts. Law No. 107/2015 and its correlated legislative decree will not (most likely) conclude a process of reform of inclusive education, rather offer additional impetus to continue on the reform and ultimately achieve the objectives of the CRPD. It also highlights that progressive legislation is never sufficient alone, but must be followed by the concrete development of inclusive educational practices.

References

Addis, Paolo. 2015. Il diritto all'istruzione delle persone con disabilità: Profili sostanziali e giurisprudenziali. In *I Diritti Sociali Nella Pluralità Degli Ordinamenti*. Edited by Elisabetta Catelani and Rolando Tarchi. Napoli: Editoriale Scientifica, pp. 150–76.

Anastasiou, Dimitris, James M. Kauffman, and Santo Di Nuovo. 2015. Inclusive education in Italy: Description and reflections on full inclusion. *European Journal of Special Needs Education* 30: 429–43. [CrossRef]

Arnardóttir, Oddný Mjöll. 2011. The Right to Inclusive Education for Children with Disabilities—Innovations in the CRPD. In *Making Peoples Heard: Essays on Human Rights in Honour of Gudmundur Alfredsson*. Edited by Eide Asbjørn, Jakob Th Möller and Ineta Ziemele. Leiden-Boston: Martinus Nijhoff, pp. 197–228.

Blando, Felice. 2017. Soggetti Disabilie Istruzione: La Lotta per il Diritto. Federalismi.it, 10/2017. Available online: http://www.federalismi.it/ApplOpenFilePDF.cfm?artid=34010&dpath=document&dfile=15052017132236.pdf&content=Soggetti+disabili+e+istruzione+-+stato+-+dottrina+-+ (accessed on 30 September 2017).

Broderick, Andrea. 2014. The Right to Inclusive Education: Article 24 of the UN Convention on the Rights of Persons with Disabilities and the Irish Experience. In *The Irish Yearbook of International Law*. London: Bloomsbury Publishing, pp. 25–60.

Busatta, Lucia. 2016. L'universo delle disabilità: Per una definizione unitaria di un diritto diseguale. In *Le Definizioni nel Diritto. Atti Delle Giornate di Studio 30–31 Ottobre 2015*. Edited by Fulvio Cortese and Marta Tomasi. Napoli: Editoriale Scientifica, pp. 335–64.

Caldin, Roberta. 2013. Current Pedagogic Issues in Inclusive Education for the Disabled. *Pedagogia Oggi* 2: 11–25.

Cera, Rachele. 2015. National Legislations on Inclusive Education and Special Educational Needs of People with Autism in the Perspective of Article 24 of the CRPD. In *Protecting the Rights of People with Autism in the Fields of Education and Employment: International, European and National Perspectives*. Edited by Della Fina Valentina and Rachele Cera. Cham, Heidelberg, New York, Dordrecht and London: Springer, pp. 79–108.

Cocconi, Monica. 2015a. La sfida decisiva dell'autonomia scolastica. *Giornale di Diritto Amministrativo* 4: 661.

Cocconi, Monica. 2015b. Gli ingredienti necessari per la ricetta di una «buona» autonomia scolastica. *Istituzioni del Federalismo* 3: 647.

Cocconi, Monica. 2017. Il Compimento del Cantiere Della C.D. Buona Scuola—Il Commento. *Giornale di Diritto Amministrativo* 4: 461.

Colapietro, Carlo. 2011. *Diritti dei Disabili e Costituzione*. Napoli: Editorile Scientifica.

CRPD Committee. 2016a. Concluding Observations on the Initial Report of Italy. Available online: http://www.ohchr.org/EN/HRBodies/CRPD/Pages/CRPDIndex.aspx (accessed on 20 October 2017).

CRPD Committee. 2016b. General Comment No 4 Article 24: Right to Inclusive Education (Adopted 26 August 2016). Available online: http://www.ohchr.org/EN/HRBodies/CRPD/Pages/GC.aspx (accessed on 20 September 2017).

CSS. 2016. Coordinamento Nazionale Famiglie di Disabili Gravi e Gravissimi. Shadow Report on Italy. Available online: http://www.ohchr.org/EN/HRBodies/CRPD/Pages/CRPDIndex.aspx (accessed on 20 September 2017).

D'Alessio, Simona. 2011. *Inclusive Education in Italy*. Rotterdam: Sense.

D'Alessio, Simona. 2013. Inclusive education in Italy: A reply to Giangreco, Doyle and Suter 2012. *Life Span and Disability* 16: 95–120.

De Beco, Gauthier. 2014. The right to inclusive education according to article 24 of the un convention on the rights of persons with disabilities: Background, requirements and (remaining) questions. *Netherlands Quarterly of Human Rights* 32: 263–87. [CrossRef]

Della Fina, Valentin. 2017. Article 24. In *The United Nations Convention on Human Rights: A Commentary*. Edited by Della Fina Valentina, Cera Rachele and Palmisano Giuseppe. Cham: Springer.

Devecchi, Cristina, Filippo Dettori, Mary Doveston, Paul Sedgwick, and Johnston Jament. 2012. Inclusive Classrooms in Italy and England: The Role of Support Teachers and Teaching Assistants. *European Journal of Special Needs Education* 27: 171–84. [CrossRef]

Dovigo, Fabio. 2016. *None Excluded. Transforming Schools and Learning to Develop Inclusive Education, Conference Proceedings*. Bergamo: University of Bergamo, p. 18.

Ferrari, Giulia. 2012. Insegnanti di sostegno per gli alunni portatori di handicap. *Giornale di Diritto Amministrativo* 12: 1248.

Ferri, Delia. 2014. Legal Scholarship and Disability in Italy. Recent Developments and New Perspectives. In *European Yearbook of Disability Law*. Edited by Lisa Waddington, Eilionoir Flynn and Gerard Quinn. Cambridge: Intersentia.

Ferri, Delia. 2017. Inclusive Education in Italy: A Legal Appraisal 10 Year after the Signature of the UN Convention on the Rights of Persons with Disabilities. *Ricerche di Pedagogia e Didattica—Journal of Theories and Research in Education* 12: 1–22.

Ferri, Delia. 2018a. The Past, Present and Future of the Right to Inclusive Education in Italy. In *The Right to Education of People with Disabilities CUP*. Edited by Shivaun Quinlivan, Gauthier De Beco and Janet Lord. Cambridge: Cambridge University Press, Forthcoming.

Ferri, Delia. 2018b. *The UN Convention on the Rights of Persons with Disabilities in Practice: A Comparative Analysis of the Role of Courts, OUP*. Edited by Lisa Waddington and Anna Lawson. Oxford: Oxford University Press, Forthcoming.

Ferri, Delia, and Anna Lawson. 2016. Reasonable Accommodation for Disabled People in Employment Contexts. Available online: http://ec.europa.eu/justice/discrimination/files/reasonable_accommodation_in_employment_final2_en.pdf (accessed on 30 September 2017).

Grimaldi, Emiliano, and Roberto Serpieri. 2012. The transformation of the Education State in Italy: A critical policy historiography from 1944 to 2011. *Italian Journal of Sociology of Education* 4: 146–80.

Ianes, Dario, Heidrun Demo, and Francesco Zambotti. 2014. Integration in Italian schools: Teachers' perceptions regarding day-to-day practice and its effectiveness. *International Journal of Inclusive Education* 18: 626–53. [CrossRef]

IDF. 2016a. First Alternative Report to the UN Committee on the Rights of Persons with Disabilities. Available online: http://www.ohchr.org/EN/HRBodies/CRPD/Pages/CRPDIndex.aspx (accessed on 20 September 2017).

IDF. 2016b. Italian Disability Forum's submission for the list of issues on Italy's State Report to the UN Committee on the Rights of Persons with Disabilities. Available online: http://www.ohchr.org/EN/HRBodies/CRPD/Pages/CRPDIndex.aspx (accessed on 20 September 2017).

Istituto Nazionale di Statistica (ISTAT). 2016. L'integrazione Degli Alunni con Disabilità Nelle Scuole Primarie e Secondarie di Primo Grado: Anno Scolastico 2015–2016 (ISTAT, 21 December 2016). Available online: www.istat.it/it/archivio/194622 (accessed on 20 September 2017).

Kanter, Arlene S., Michelle L. Damiani, and Beth A. Ferri. 2014. The Right to Inclusive Education under International Law: Following Italy's Lead. *Journal of International Special Needs Education* 17: 21–32. [CrossRef]

Kayess, Rosemary, and Phillip French. 2008. Out of darkness into light? Introducing the convention on the rights of persons with disabilities. *Human Rights Law Review* 8: 1–34. [CrossRef]

Lottini, Micaela. 2011. Scuola e disabilità. I riflessi della sentenza 80 del 2010 della Corte costituzionale sulla giurisprudenza del giudice amministrativo. *Il Foro Amministrativo Tar* 10: 2403–9.

Manca, Luigi. 2010. Articolo 24. In *La Convenzione ONU sui Diritti Delle Persone con Disabilità*. Edited by Sergio Marchisio, Rachele Cera and Valentina Della Fina. Roma: Aracne, pp. 329–42.

OECD (Organisation for Economic Co-operation and Development). 2007. *Students with Disabilities, Learning Difficulties and Disadvantages: Policies, Statistics and Indicators*. Paris: OECD.

OHCHR. 2013. Thematic Study on the Right of Persons with Disabilities to Education. Available online: http://www.ohchr.org/EN/Issues/Disability/Pages/ThematicStudies.aspx (accessed on 20 September 2017).

Palmer, Jason. 2013. The Convention on the Rights of Persons with Disabilities: Will Ratification Lead to a Holistic Approach to Postsecondary Education for Persons with Disabilities? Available online: https://ssrn.com/abstract=2243137 (accessed on 20 September 2017).

Penasa, Simone. 2014. La persona e la funzione promozionale della scuola: La realizzazione del disegno costituzionale e il necessario ruolo dei poteri pubblici. I casi dell'istruzione delle persone disabili e degli alunni stranieri. In *Tra Amministrazione e Scuola. Snodi e Crocevia del Diritto Scolastico Italiano*. Edited by Fulvio Cortese. Napoli: Edizionio Scientifiche Italiane.

Rossi, Emanuele, Addis Paolo, and Biondi Dal Monte Francesca. 2016. La Libertà di Insegnamento e il Diritto All'istruzione nella Costituzione Italiana. Rivista AIC. April 18. Available online: http://www.osservatorioaic.it/la-libert-di-insegnamento-e-il-diritto-all-istruzione-nella-costituzione-italiana.html (accessed on 20 September 2017).

Seatzu, Francesco. 2008. La Convenzione delle Nazioni unite sui diritti delle persone disabili: I principi fondamentali. *Diritti Umani e Diritto Internazionale* 3: 535–59.

Shaw, Belinda. 2014. Inclusion or choice? Securing the right to inclusive education for all. In *Human Rights and Disability Advocacy*. Edited by Maia Sabatello and Marianne Schulze. Philadelphia: University of Pennsylvania Press, pp. 60–68.

Siclari, Domenico. 2015. Riflessioni sullo statuto giuridico della disabilità nell'ordinamento italiano. *Il Diritto Dell'economia* 28: 553–73.

Troilo, Silvio. 2012. Tutti per uno o uno contro tutti? Il diritto all'istruzione e all'integrazione scolastica della persona disabile di fronte alla molteplicità dei soggetti obbligati (ed alla scarsità delle risorse disponibili). In *Scritti in Memoria di Alessandra Concaro*. Edited by Giuseppe D'Elia, Giulia Tiberi and Maria Paola Viviani Schlein. Milano: Giuffrè, pp. 753–80.

Troilo, Silvio. 2016. I 'nuovi' diritti sociali: La parabola dell'integrazione scolastica dei disabili tra principi e realtà. In *La Democrazia Costituzionale tra Nuovi Diritti e Deriva Mediale*. Edited by Giampietro Ferri. Napoli: Edizioni Scientifiche Italiane, pp. 57–81.

Ufficio Stampa MIUR. 2017. Miglioreremo Decreto su Inclusione Scolastica. Studentesse e Studenti con Disabilità Devono Avere pari Opportunità Formative (Ministero dell'Istruzione, Dell'Università e Della Ricerca, 9 February 2017). Available online: http://hubmiur.pubblica.istruzione.it/web/ministero/cs090217quater (accessed on 20 October 2017).

UNESCO. 2005. Guidelines for Inclusion: Ensuring Access to Education for All. Available online: http://unesdoc.unesco.org/images/0014/001402/140224e.pdf (accessed on 20 October 2017).

Permissions

All chapters in this book were first published in MDPI; hereby published with permission under the Creative Commons Attribution License or equivalent. Every chapter published in this book has been scrutinized by our experts. Their significance has been extensively debated. The topics covered herein carry significant findings which will fuel the growth of the discipline. They may even be implemented as practical applications or may be referred to as a beginning point for another development.

The contributors of this book come from diverse backgrounds, making this book a truly international effort. This book will bring forth new frontiers with its revolutionizing research information and detailed analysis of the nascent developments around the world.

We would like to thank all the contributing authors for lending their expertise to make the book truly unique. They have played a crucial role in the development of this book. Without their invaluable contributions this book wouldn't have been possible. They have made vital efforts to compile up to date information on the varied aspects of this subject to make this book a valuable addition to the collection of many professionals and students.

This book was conceptualized with the vision of imparting up-to-date information and advanced data in this field. To ensure the same, a matchless editorial board was set up. Every individual on the board went through rigorous rounds of assessment to prove their worth. After which they invested a large part of their time researching and compiling the most relevant data for our readers.

The editorial board has been involved in producing this book since its inception. They have spent rigorous hours researching and exploring the diverse topics which have resulted in the successful publishing of this book. They have passed on their knowledge of decades through this book. To expedite this challenging task, the publisher supported the team at every step. A small team of assistant editors was also appointed to further simplify the editing procedure and attain best results for the readers.

Apart from the editorial board, the designing team has also invested a significant amount of their time in understanding the subject and creating the most relevant covers. They scrutinized every image to scout for the most suitable representation of the subject and create an appropriate cover for the book.

The publishing team has been an ardent support to the editorial, designing and production team. Their endless efforts to recruit the best for this project, has resulted in the accomplishment of this book. They are a veteran in the field of academics and their pool of knowledge is as vast as their experience in printing. Their expertise and guidance has proved useful at every step. Their uncompromising quality standards have made this book an exceptional effort. Their encouragement from time to time has been an inspiration for everyone.

The publisher and the editorial board hope that this book will prove to be a valuable piece of knowledge for researchers, students, practitioners and scholars across the globe.

List of Contributors

Harold Braswell
Albert Gnaegi Center for Health Care Ethics, Saint Louis University, St. Louis, MO 63104, USA

Kimberly Mutcherson
Rutgers Law School, 217 N. 5th Street, Camden, NJ 08102, USA

Mary Ann Jackson
School of Architecture and Built Environment, Deakin University, Geelong 3220, Australia
Visionary Design Development Pty Ltd., North Melbourne 3051, Australia

Terry Carney
School of Law, University of Sydney, Eastern Ave., Camperdown, NSW 2006, Australia
Faculty of Law, University of Technology Sydney, 15 Broadway, Ultimo, NSW 2007, Australia

Mark C. Weber
College of Law, DePaul University, Chicago, IL 60604, USA

Laufey Löve and Rannveig Traustadóttir
Centre for Disability Studies, Faculty of Social and Human Sciences, University of Iceland, 101 Reykjavik, Iceland

Gerard Quinn
Centre for Disability Law & Policy, National University of Ireland, H91 TK33 Galway, Ireland

James Rice
Centre for Disability Studies, Faculty of Social and Human Sciences, and Department of Anthropology, University of Iceland, 101 Reykjavik, Iceland

Laura Elliott
Graduate student, Melbourne Law School, University of Melbourne, 185 Pelham St, Carlton, VIC 3053, Australia

Blake Connell
Melbourne Law School, The University of Melbourne, Melbourne 3053, Australia

Vera Chouinard
School of Geography and Earth Sciences, McMaster University, Hamilton, ON L8S 4K1, Canada

Fleur Beaupert
Independent Scholar, Sydney 2000, Australia

Adam Conti
Graduate student, Melbourne Law School, University of Melbourne, 185 Pelham St., Carlton, VIC 3053, Australia

Charlotte May-Simerav
Centre for Disability Law and Policy, National University of Ireland, H91 TK33 Galway, Ireland

Delia Ferri
Department of Law, Maynooth University, Maynooth, Co. Kildare, Ireland

Index